GW01465904

‎‎...ı ıaces

Maori Times, Maori Places

Prophetic Histories

Karen Sinclair

ROWMAN & LITTLEFIELD PUBLISHERS, INC.
Lanham • Boulder • New York • Oxford

ROWMAN & LITTLEFIELD PUBLISHERS, INC.

Published in the United States of America
by Rowman & Littlefield Publishers, Inc.
A Member of the Rowman & Littlefield Publishing Group
4720 Boston Way, Lanham, Maryland 20706
www.rowmanlittlefield.com

PO Box 317
Oxford
OX2 9RU, UK

Published in New Zealand in 2002 by Bridget Williams Books Limited
PO Box 5482, Wellington

Publication was assisted by the History Group of the Ministry for Culture and
Heritage, New Zealand

National Library of New Zealand Cataloguing-in-Publication Information Available
British Library Cataloguing in Publication Information Available

Library of Congress Cataloging-in-Publication Data

Sinclair, Karen, 1947–.
    Maori times, Maori places : prophetic histories / Karen Sinclair.
        p. cm.
    Includes bibliographical references and index.
    ISBN 0-7425-1638-5 (cloth : alk. paper)—ISBN 0-7425-1639-3 (pbk. : alk. paper)
    1. Maori (New Zealand people)—Religion. I. Title.

    BL2615.S56 2001
    299'92442—dc21
                                                                                    200101527
Printed in the United States of America

$\otimes^{TM}$ The paper used in this publication meets the minimum requirements of
American National Standard for Information Sciences—Permanence of Paper for
Printed Library Materials, ANSI/NISO Z39.48-1992.

National Library of New Zealand Cataloguing-in-Publication Data

Sinclair, Karen, 1947-
Prophetic histories : the people of the Māramatanga / Karen Sinclair.
Includes bibliographical references and index.
ISBN 1-877242-92-6
1. Maori (New Zealand people)—Religion. 2. Nativistic movements—New Zealand.
3. Maori (New Zealand people)—Biography. 4. Maori (New Zealand people)—
New Zealand—Rangitikei District—History.
I. Title.
289.908999442—dc 21

Published in New Zealand in 2002 by Bridget Williams Books Limited,
P O Box 5482, Wellington

Publication was assisted by the History Group of the Ministry for
Culture and Heritage.

ISBN 1-877242-92-6

Cover design: Mission Hall DGL
Cover photograph: Ruapehu at sunset, Shaun Barnett
Internal design and typesetting: Afineline/Archetype
Printed by: Astra Print

Ki a Hoana Maria me ngā Pou o te Māramatanga

Contents

Mihi

Nau mai e te taonga, hei morimoritanga mo ngā uri o te tikanga nei. He mihi hoki kia koe e Karen me tō whānau mo ngā mahi kua hāpai e koutou. Nō reira, me hoki anō ki ngā kupu e whai ake nei:

Aue te aroha i a ahau
Aue e te iwi e
E te hungaruarua puritia kia mau
Ūtaina ki runga i te waka o te ora
Ka hoe ai ki te tauranga.

Ko te kupu a te Kaiwhakaora
A Hehu tino aroha
Wetewetekia atu ngā ururua
E te hunga e mamae ana
Ka aru mai ai i a ahau.

E te iwi whakarongo ake rā
Ki te reo e karanga mai nei
Whaia kia mau te kotahitanga
He mea paihere nā te rangimārie
Kia mau ai te rongopai.

Nā mātou i runga i te aroha
Te Hungaruarua

Acknowledgments

From my arrival in New Zealand through to the present, I have received assistance, knowledge, and sustenance from sources in both countries. While many authors acknowledge their families last, my husband Michael and daughter Emily were far too instrumental in their participation to appear as an afterthought. Michael shopped, cooked, and ran the house while I worked. This went on far too long and an expression of gratitude seems hardly adequate. However, he does know how I feel and how insubstantial notions of appreciation for his efforts must be. From 1982, Emily accompanied me while I did fieldwork. As a child, an adolescent, then as a young woman, she saw things that I, the anthropologist, missed. Moreover, her affection and *aroha* for the people of the Māramatanga were so clear, that her relationships with them were less complicated than mine. Today, she is a wonderful young adult, aware of the lessons learned on the *marae* and with the notable individuals featured in this book. Both Michael and Emily, possessing talents for words and abilities both to organize and to see logical inconsistencies, carefully read several drafts. It took them a great deal of time, but ultimately together, they assisted in doing a major edit of this book.

Once I arrived in New Zealand, I was assisted by Laurie Cox (at the time the new head of the US-NZ Educational Foundation; I was his first Fulbright student), his predecessor E. Budge, Amy and Ian Brown, Michael Sinclair, and Virginia Stevenson. At Victoria University of Wellington, where I was based, I benefited from the seminars run by Joan Metge (now Dame Joan), Jan Pouwer (then Chair of the Anthropology Department) and Bernie Kernot. As instructive as I found these formal settings, I benefited as well from their encyclopedic knowledge, often given over a cup of coffee. I would also like to thank Nancy Pollock, who over the years has supplied a wealth of information.

My research could have not proceeded had it not been for the help of librarians at the Auckland Public Library, where the papers of the Rev. Richard Taylor are kept, the former Dominion Museum, and the new Alexander Turnbull Library. My requests, which would seem ridiculous even to my ears, were met with competence and intelligence. In New York, the joys of the Wertheim study and the Rare Books room allowed me to proceed for long periods of time uninterrupted. This was facilitated by Wayne Forman, who is invaluable to anyone who seeks to work for protracted periods of time. The collections at University of Michigan and Eastern Michigan University have also been very helpful. In particular, I would like to thank Keith Stanger and Rita Bullard, who arranged computer searches and interlibrary loans.

My research has been supported by a variety of sources and many individuals. My initial research was funded by a Fulbright Full Grant and extended through a National Science Foundation Grant. At Eastern Michigan University, I received financial support in the form of Faculty Research Fellowships and Sabbaticals, which gave me released time from teaching responsibilities as well as assistance in defraying the costs of travel and living abroad. In addition, I received an NEH Travel to Collections grant and then an NEH Fellowship for College Teachers, which permitted time off for writing. Eastern Michigan University's World College, run by Raymond Schaub and Geoffrey Voght, also provided assistance on several occasions. I am very grateful for the continued support of Robert Holkeboer, first at the Office of Research and Development, and then as Dean of the Graduate School. In this position, he actively oversees all research done at the university. I am also grateful for the assistance provided by Dean of the College of Arts and Sciences, Barry Fish, and a succession of department heads, who adjusted my teaching schedule to allow me to write and to travel to New Zealand. Jay Weinstein, Gregg Barak, and Joseph Rankin all provided support and understanding.

My friends and colleagues, most especially Sharon Crutchfield, Marie Richmond-Abbott, Robert Citino, Allen Ehrlich, Lynn Sipher, and Martin Shichtman offered advice on numerous occasions. Linda Stone, my flatmate in graduate school, continued the tradition of reading all I write and commenting honestly. In New Zealand, the late Amy Brown did a very thorough reading and her editing was enhanced by the very competent work of Len May and Lindsey Rogers. Bridget Williams, Dean Birkenkamp, and Terry Fischer all worked very hard and demonstrated extraordinary patience.

I hope that I can benefit from the graciousness, brightness, and dignity that I always witnessed in the people of the Māramatanga. While they were aware of the lessons they passed down in an explicit fashion, I doubt that they could understand how much I benefited just from observing their always exemplary behavior. From the beginning, they have represented the very best. I have been very lucky to have spent so much time with them. If I have not always observed it, I have, nevertheless, been taught the right way (the *tikanga*) by experts.

Me ngākaunui ahau ki te hungaruarua mo taku akoranga. Kaore ngā kupu mo taku ngākau pāpaku me taku mihi.

Karen Sinclair
Michigan, July 2002

Introduction

The Māramatanga is a Māori movement centred among the people of the Ruapehu district of New Zealand's North Island. It is essential to be specific: Māori are often portrayed as a prominent but undifferentiated race of Polynesians, indigenous to New Zealand. But Māori have always been, and continue to be, tribal, with different affiliations that are closely associated with particular geographical regions. The history of Pākehā colonization and of the Māori reaction to it is correspondingly heterogeneous, with distinctive regional and tribal histories often leading to surprising alliances and enmities.[1] The Māramatanga, the subject of this book, is grounded in a specific historical context, characterized by particular beliefs and rituals, and linked in very characteristic ways to the prophetic movements that preceded it. It does not, nor cannot, represent the Māori point of view, for there never has been a unitary Māori experience. This account of the movement is emblematic of the provisional nature of history, and of the contextual and contested nature of understanding.

All Māori, whatever their tribal affiliation and position, witnessed encroachments on their autonomy and livelihood throughout the period of colonization. For almost two centuries, New Zealand has been divided between the desires and motivations of both Māori and Pākehā. In 1840, the Treaty of Waitangi purported to provide the terms for a relationship between the two groups, but each side found different interpretations. Not surprisingly, that of the economically and militarily dominant Pākehā prevailed, serving the colonizers well for the next hundred and thirty years.

Through the nineteenth century, prophetic religious movements became an effective Māori response to their losses of land and autonomy. Both Papahurihia and Āperahama Taonui, two of the earliest prophets, came from heavily missionized areas. Like their successors—Te Ua Haumēne, Te Kooti, Te Whiti, and Rua Kēnana—they drew on the Old Testament texts of dispossession from a homeland (see chapter 1). Land and increasing Pākehā control of it have always been an important concern for Māori religious movements. For Māori, the prophets and their teachings represented continuity with their past and insulation from the intrusion of the interlopers. The emerging New Zealand state, however, had every incentive to deny the power and coherence of a religious message with intense political overtones, for the tradition of prophecy expressed an unwelcome challenge to its claims to legitimacy and authority (Silverblatt 1987; Kaplan 1995).

The Māramatanga is a successor to this prophetic tradition. From its establishment in the early twentieth century by the prophet Hori Enoka, who took the name Mareikura, the Māramatanga's ideology and ritual have sustained Māori epistemological organization in the face of dramatic and unrelenting pressures toward change. In the words of the movement's *waiata* and *whaikōrero*, and in the words of the descendants of the original founders, who have carried on the work, we see an alternative narrative in which history remains firmly under Māori control. This is a narrative that sustains Māori values and independence in the face of an overwhelmingly Pākehā society. It is no small feat for a very small minority population to remain at least partially impervious to the demands of an alien world. Yet to posit continuity is not to deny transformation. The entire prophetic tradition—and the movement of Mareikura is no exception—represents numerous examples of hybridization (see Kaplan 1995; Thomas 1994, 1997). The Māramatanga demonstrates that true syntheses collapse the distinction between what is indigenous and what is a product of the colonial presence (Kaplan 1995).

History and Context

In the aftermath of the nineteenth-century land wars, the Crown had acquired 22 million of New Zealand's 26 million hectares (Sorrenson 1990: 323); with the Māori population also decimated by European diseases, Pākehā settlers seemed justified in believing that New Zealand's indigenous people would soon cease to exist. In 1889, Edward Gibbon Wakefield, a key figure in the colonization of New Zealand, wrote that the Māori comprised an unimportant and irrelevant aspect of New Zealand's population (1889: 120). Dr Isaac Featherston, whose name adorns a central Wellington thoroughfare, talked of "smoothing down their dying pillow," never doubting that the demise of the indigenous inhabitants was soon to be an integral and inevitable part of New Zealand history. That had been the fate of other "native populations" such as the Aborigines of Tasmania, and it would soon be the fate of the Māori (Sorrenson 1981: 189). There was no reason to lament what, to many, was the convenient enactment of larger principles of social Darwinism. Dr. Alfred Newman explicitly advanced this point of view in 1881: "Taking all things into consideration, the disappearance of the race is scarcely subject for much regret. They are dying out in a quick, easy way, and are being supplanted by a superior race" (quoted by Te Rangi Hiroa [Sir Peter Buck] 1924: 362).

However, the beginning of the twentieth century saw a Māori renaissance. Māori did more than survive: although they did not overcome their differential susceptibility to European diseases such as tuberculosis, they stemmed the flow of disease and death, and saw their numbers increase. The resurgence in population restored interest in Māori traditions. On the national level, several young, talented, and educated men formed what became the Young Māori Party, whose intent was to further the development of their people. The physicians among them sought to institute hygiene reforms and attempted to ensure universal vaccination of Māori. Perhaps more effective than these measures were the efforts of local leaders—among them Princess Te Puea (see King 1977)—to improve hygiene and assure subsistence. The anticipated demise of Māori now proved no more than wishful thinking; both demography and social vigour had debunked such suppositions.

While the improvements in Māori living conditions and longevity were dramatic, there were setbacks in the second decade of the twentieth century. World War I had broken out in Europe. Some Māori went off to battle, displaying their loyalty to the Dominion government, while other tribes and *hapū* refused to support a government that had both impoverished and persecuted their people with land confiscation. For those who did go overseas to fight, it was a shock to discover that, although they met with general approval and were welcomed on their return, Māori soldiers faced a lack of employment opportunities and also discrimination (they were excluded from the soldier settlement schemes). Then in 1918 the worldwide influenza pandemic struck in New Zealand, hitting Māori many times harder than Pākehā. It was in the aftermath of the war and the influenza epidemic that the most important prophet of the twentieth century arose. T. W. Rātana became prominent in an area not far from where Mareikura and his followers lived; in fact the two prophets are closely linked by ties of kin and origin (see chapter 2). In time, Rātana moved away from religious work, turning his energy into political activism. By 1949, all four Māori representatives to Parliament were affiliated with the Rātana church and the Labour Party, an alliance that the prophet himself had negotiated.

The Great Depression of the 1930s also imposed differential burdens on Māori. The government subsidized unemployed Pākehā, but not their Māori compatriots. Most Māori lived in rural areas and, according to the controlling Pākehā stereotype, had a culture that enabled them to live off the land. While this policy was framed in ennobling, positive terms—the "noble savage" aspects of Māoridom—it increased suffering and widened the boundaries between Europeans and Māori (see King 1983: 196).

Few Māori possessed the kind of wealth that many Europeans took as a matter of course. Most of the productive land was in the hands of Pākehā farmers. That which was in Māori hands was difficult to exploit: multiple ownership made accumulating the capital necessary for efficient farming difficult; and those Māori with economic resources were expected to provide for needy relatives. Most significantly, Māori farmers, unlike their Pākehā counterparts, were not eligible for government assistance before the 1930s. Again it was argued that Māori culture would provide a suitable buffer against poverty and unemployment. With Māori occupying rural tribal enclaves, and Pākehā settled as urban dwellers or farmers, there was a real and effective separation between Māori and Pākehā. This suited Pākehā, who were interested only in Māori land: a resource that became ever more precious as the Pākehā population grew and the agricultural economy expanded. Michael King writes that Māori realized reluctantly that European colonization was "final and irreversible" (King 1983: 196).

Nevertheless, Māori were proud and eager to serve their country in World War II: the Māori Battalion fought bravely in North Africa and Italy. Yet, once again, the soldiers' return to New Zealand was problematic. Facing few opportunities for work or advancement in their rural areas, many Māori, soldier and civilian, moved into the cities. Here, for the first time, Māori and Pākehā were able to examine one another closely. Defined as always by their contrast with the Pākehā, the Māori came off second best; governmental struggles to find the most effective urbanization policy helped little. This could be identified as the beginning of Māori as an underclass. With it, I would argue, came New Zealand's reluctant, and often unadmitted, abandonment of the egalitarian ethos that had sustained the country's self-image through the Depression (others would say that egalitarianism, as an attitude and to some extent as a government policy, lasted until the New Right reforms of the 1980s). In the most telling of government statistics—those concerned with mortality, education, disease rates, and infant deaths—it is indisputable that Māori fared far less well than Pākehā.

However, by the 1970s there were dramatic changes. The Māori birth rate accelerated and infant mortality decreased, assuring a population increase, but one that would be concentrated at the bottom of the economic and class pyramid. The second Māori renaissance accompanied this increase; Māori music, language, art, and literature demanded their place in contemporary New Zealand. At the same time, the Treaty of Waitangi was re-examined and the Waitangi Tribunal was established. After thirteen decades of presumptions favoring Pākehā, the tribunal was prepared to examine Māori grievances and the distribution of resources from a more neutral perspective. At the same time, a government policy was instituted that decentralized the Department of Māori Affairs, devolving onto local bodies responsibility for Māori concerns, problems, and assets. A consequence was the development of tribal and local committees, an increased Māori activism and political awareness, and a heightened political rhetoric.

What was happening in the Māramatanga during these periods of change in New Zealand? Although the movement's origins were in the first decades of the twentieth century, its prophet Hori Enoka Mareikura did not achieve significant recognition until the 1930s. He became a healer of some renown and a conveyor of ideas and information that breached distinctions of time and space as well as Māori and Pākehā notions regarding the constitution of the world. Had Pākehā been aware of what transpired on Mareikura's marae, they would no doubt have been puzzled. Yet for Māori, he established a new synthesis. Drawing on the ancient prophets of the Old Testament, and bringing these into the New Testament, Mareikura provided his followers with new ways of understanding, new articulations that would allow them to situate themselves more comfortably in a landscape that was transformed even as they watched.

The members were responding, in very specific ways, to the intentions of the previous century and to the mandates of their current circumstances. Mareikura, his successors, and their followers in turn all understood the implications and consequences of the colonizing project that had been undertaken by the Pākehā. They understood also that these did not include the widely anticipated disappearance of Māori; nor did they include the Europeanization of Māori as urged upon them by their own national leaders. Their work, influenced by larger historical forces that were also defining other domains within New Zealand, sought to assert Māori integrity with a minimum of accommodation.

For ninety years the Māramatanga has flourished in an arena protected from the curious eyes of Pākehā. All critical communication took place in Māori, a language that ensured privacy and inaccessibility. Stories of Mareikura and other leaders continue to offer lessons to new generations, drawing on the past to accommodate ever-changing exigencies imposed by Pākehā-dominated society and government. In the complicated web of opposing moralities that is colonization's legacy, the words of the prophet, echoing through the decades, continue to bring comfort. In this new millennium—at least on the distinctly European Gregorian calendar—few members of the Māramatanga view their work as a completed project. Completion and closure consign movements—both people and events—to the past.

The Māramatanga is and always has been geographically centered in Ohakune, a picturesque rural town on the southern slopes of Mount Ruapehu. The town has a larger percentage of Māori families than is common in most North Island communities, but the worlds of Māori and Pākehā are not really separate, with one exception: the children of wealthy Pākehā tend to go to boarding school rather than to the local high school. At the same time, because the Māori birth rate is so much higher than that of Pākehā, the schools at all levels have a higher percentage of Māori children than is reflected in the town's overall population. Relations between Māori and Pākehā that I have observed in Ohakune are cordial. However, there have been relatively few intermarriages, and there is little visiting in people's homes. Instead, meetings take place on neutral ground: in the schools and on the sports fields. Pākehā come onto the marae on special occasions: for a ceremony that involves the entire town, for housie (bingo), for the monthly Catholic church service held there, and for *tangi*. When an important, influential, or beloved member of the Māori community dies, Pākehā mourners come onto the marae and attempt respectfully to follow protocol. Relations are good, but distant. Most of the people who remember that far back indicate that relations have been this way for eighty years: cordial, amicable, but not intimate.

Anthropological Matters

Studying people who negotiate the traditions of the conqueror has always raised special issues for anthropologists. How can two systems of thought, resting on different worldviews and with different moral implications, be accommodated to one another? Insofar as we can determine their differences, what do they tell us about the colonial experience and about our ability to understand the lives of those the dominant society has constructed as "others"?[2]

That Pākehā outsiders have been permitted to live with and write about Māori is not hard to understand: Māori hospitality and courtesy are widely known. Yet the strength of Māori regard for privacy and their determination not to be violated by outsiders is not often recognized. In almost all cases, half-truths, rather than untruths, have entered the academic and public record. Although an American myself, in this book I attempt to redress the balance of popular misconceptions of what it is to be Māori by giving more voice to the participants of the Māramatanga.

Māori epistemology differs from that of Pākehā, a fact that can be readily obscured because English is so often spoken, and speeches and texts are so frequently translated into English. Although most members of the Māramatanga speak both Māori and English fluently, their English reflects Māori (not Pākehā) categories and concerns. While certainly more effective in Māori, speeches of elders are meant to be instructive, and even in English they draw on the past as determinative, emphasise the importance of kinship, and stress the primordial links connecting Māori with the land of their people. Māori is the language of the Māramatanga. To use a language that the majority of Pākehā cannot understand is to invoke boundaries, to provide protection from those who have managed to intrude in most aspects of Māori lives (Lindstrom 1990: 20–21).

Māori continue to rely upon oral traditions and methods to pass down knowledge, although to a lesser extent than in the past. Trained memories and the ability to transmit what has only been heard, without benefit of writing, remain prized characteristics. But, perhaps most importantly, a culture built on the premises that attend orality—memory and a mastery of oral histories—is able to distinguish and recognize its leaders. Those who are expert, who know history because they have trained themselves through arduous repetitions until they achieve perfection, who are committed to the retention of crucial events and narratives, ultimately emerge as the select, as those most able to command prestige and attention.

Writing was certainly not new to Māori in the early years of the twentieth century. When oral cultures fear the loss of their traditions—as did Māori of the late nineteenth century—they turn to written records. This too has been the case with the Māramatanga. But for the membership, writing was always a second choice—one that clearly could not compare with the effectiveness or accuracy of oral transmission. In the early days of the movement, Mareikura strictly limited the use of writing, initially permitting only certain individuals to write down events as they transpired in the meeting-house. Moreover, discussion and debates that often followed *whaikōrero*, or, in the case of the Māramatanga, revelation, were not included in written records.

The prophet and his followers realized that writing would create multiple versions and admit the possibility of mistakes, as words or phrases were transcribed incorrectly. Later when notebooks of songs and talks became common— frequently given as presents—the old worries proved true. Writing was indeed less accurate, more fluid, and less rigorous than oral transmissions.[3] Within the movement there are now multiple and diverse histories: recollections differ and notebooks contain variations that are distinctive and work against uniformity. This book, then, is concerned with the absence of history by fiat: there is no one Pākehā history, no single Māori history, and no uniform rendition for the Māramatanga.

Many of the descendants of the original members of the Māramatanga provided me with the notebooks that had been given over to their keeping. There is an irony in this: I, an American anthropologist, have had far greater access to the accumulated written records of the movement than any member. This is true despite the fact that I have returned all the notebooks and placed them in a central location. But the library is insecure: notebooks continue to go missing, to turn up at unexpected intervals, and to elude those who most want them for specific occasions.

That notebooks are potentially available and accessible to the members of the movement is not without problems. Those who created the notebooks and diaries, in some cases sixty years ago, were sensitive to both ambience and audience. A discussion of them in the early twenty-first century can easily violate the context in which they were produced, a context that we are always wise to respect. More importantly perhaps, individuals are remembered and events are recalled through complex personal prisms. When we see them for the first time decades after words were uttered and recorded, our perspectives are, inevitably, different in the most crucial of ways; if these notebooks illuminate the past, they also have the capacity to take on new, often unintended and unenvisioned, meanings.

These journals and diaries, started by the original leaders and added to by their descendants to reflect the shifting concerns, responsibilities, and activities of each generation, comprise in their own right the history of the Māramatanga. That these notebooks are in the Māori language has great significance. On the one hand, the use of the original language mandates that in each generation there will be those who are competent to translate the past. On the other hand, the use of Māori, augmented by a history that is not widely known, ensures that precious boundaries are maintained and that, even if exposed, these treasures will not illuminate without understanding.

Fieldwork

I began research among the members of the Māramatanga in 1972. My initial fieldwork lasted eighteen months, during which time I resided at Kawiu marae in Levin. I travelled to rā (commemorative and spiritual celebration days) and went on the movement's third pilgrimage to Waitangi (see chapter 6). By 1973, the worldwide petrol shortage made it difficult for a population that was already poor to muster both the finances and the reprieve from work that such journeys required. However, by the 1990s, the mission to Waitangi had become an annual event once again. In addition, I inevitably attended many tangi.

In the early months, I lived on the marae, in the home of an elder, Ritihira, the daughter of Weuweu, one of the foundational supporters of Mareikura. Living at the marae at that time were Tikaraina, the prophet's son, whose name carried on the links between Mareikura and Mere Rikiriki (see chapter 2); Tika's wife, Aurora, a descendant of Weuweu; Ritihira's unmarried daughter, Tui; and Ritihira's grandson, Troy. In addition, Ritihira's nephew Hōhepa and his large family occupied a third house. It was, and still is, a beautifully maintained marae, with a dining-room, chapel, and meeting-house surrounding a large lawn. (The development and significance of this marae are discussed in chapter 5.)

Perhaps most significantly, Pauro, another son of the prophet and the leader of the movement at the time, made frequent visits with his wife, Hine Ataarangi. I thought this merely fortuitous, but it was planned. Hoana (whose life history is told after chapter 5), then in her forties and very knowledgeable about the movement, was not happy that a Pākehā had established herself within the environs of the Māramatanga. Worse, I was not in Ohakune, the center of movement activity, but on the periphery. The possibilities for mistakes and misinterpretations were considerable, and Hoana (whom I came to know very well in

1982) was especially concerned with accuracy and respect. Pauro and Tika, her uncles, assured her that I would be both instructed carefully and warned against disseminating the information until it had been cleared with them. I knew nothing of this until 1991.

From the start, I could not help but be aware of my good fortune when it came to my teachers: Tikaraina, Pauro, Aurora, and Hine were wonderful examples of the leadership of the movement. And their patience in explaining personalities and events was, in retrospect, very impressive. When I inadvertently heard information that was inaccurate or not for my ears, they firmly corrected it or placed it in the appropriate perspective. They gave me the basis for my doctoral dissertation. Their scrupulous teaching comforted Hoana and worked to assure the larger family's approval for my later research.

I did not go back for nine years, but I did keep in touch, most specifically by sending telegrams to all the rā. While I had not intended this particularly, the people remembered me at especially important commemorations over the course of the year. When I returned, it was the telegrams that were recalled and commented upon.

I returned for three months in 1982, with my husband and our six-year-old daughter. Since I did not yet have permission to focus on the Māramatanga, I concentrated instead on the lives of women. This proved to be illuminating as a perspective, and also provided the bases of four of the life histories in this book. The early-to-middle 1980s witnessed as well an important change in generation: Hoana, Raana, and Pinenga began to take their place as elders. Aurora passed away in 1982, to be followed by Pauro three years later. While the Māramatanga was clearly undergoing changes, the membership was now well aware of my activities.

In 1975 I had deposited a copy of my dissertation in the Anthropology Department at Victoria University of Wellington, under whose auspices I had begun my research. Because of the sensitivity of some of its contents, I had intended very limited access to it. However, friends of members of the movement spirited it away, so that when I returned, several individuals had already read what I had to say. More importantly, Bishop (now Cardinal) Tom Williams had also read it, and requested that I call upon him when I next visited New Zealand. Our visit was pleasant and informative. He urged me to write about the movement, since the rumors that circulated among various trained and untrained observers and clerics had considerably distorted intentions and activities. The members of the movement decided that they should give me permission to write about them. After Aurora's tangi in July of 1982, Hoana, addressing me, announced in public that I would be given permission to write about the Māramatanga.

In 1987, I began work on a scholarly study of the movement. This five-month period was followed up by fieldwork in 1990, 1991, 1993, 1995, 1996, 1998, and

Christmas–New Year 2000. These trips varied in length between a few weeks and several months. During this period, I elicited life histories, some of which are included here as separate narratives, and others that contribute to the chapters. I attended rā, *hui* and, sadly, tangi. I also was able to go on the Tira Hoe Waka, a spiritual and educational expedition by canoe down the Whanganui River through ancestral lands and marae (see chapter 7). It is here that all can witness the new generation, which is ready to take its place as the older generation passes on. Throughout this period, I have also been given notebooks that come from all areas of the movement and which contain waiata and messages from Te Karere (a primary spirit who guides the movement).

Note on the Text

Raana and Hoana and I discussed the issue of names for the book I was then writing. Pseudonyms were generally discarded as simply not Māori (although in a few cases they became appropriate). Hoana and Raana decided that I should as far as possible use only Māori first names, thereby employing the very barriers that they themselves have used to keep out unwanted intrusions. The use of first names (with limited references to surnames and married names) is intended to provide a degree of privacy for the individuals of the Māramatanga. This policy extends to the way names are referred to in quotations from diaries and notebooks written by members of the movement.

The text follows the current practice of using macrons to mark long vowels in Maori. Quotations and book titles, however, follow the style of the original, which frequently did not include macrons. This is true in particular of the early notebooks and diaries, which contained neither macrons nor diacritic marks.

Organization of the Book

The history of the Māramatanga spans most of the twentieth century, beginning on the banks of the Rangitīkei River on the marae of Mere Rikiriki, a prophetess who was responsible, so the members maintain, for ushering in the New Testament (see chapter 2). The members therefore see themselves as continuous with, yet crucially distinct from, those prophets who preceded Mareikura. Through four generations of leaders and followers, the ideology and rituals of the movement have been put forth, sustained, and transformed. Yet without locating the Māramatanga within a specific and precise context, we cannot understand these developments. Further, we cannot assume that their position, the space the members occupied, remained static over this time. The movement's concerns and preoccupations, as well as the responses they elicited, were all firmly grounded in a post-colonial context. This involved a set of circumstances in which the entire population of New Zealand sought to understand its position as a former colony that, as an autonomous nation, still maintained persistent ties to Empire. This is a book about confrontation and resistance as much as it is a study of accommodation and reconciliation.

The first narrative, Te Karere, introduces the movement with the definitive event of the Māramatanga—the death of Lena Ruka in 1935. Chapter 1, The Dispensation of Colonialism, sets the context for the genesis of the Māramatanga with a brief outline of the colonial history of the Whanganui, the religious influence of the Church of England and then Catholic missionaries, and the early Māori prophets' response in the late nineteenth century to these physical and spiritual invasions. Mere Rikiriki, the prophetess of Parewanui at the beginning of the twentieth century, and her role in the origin of the movement are the subjects of chapter 2, Mere Rikiriki at Parewanui: The Genesis of the Māramatanga.

In chapter 3, Mareikura, Maungārongo, and the Development of the Māramatanga, we return to the momentous events following Lena Ruka's death, and the revolutionary turn taken by the Māramatanga in the next decade. Chapter 4, Growth and the Emergence of a New Generation, tells of the continuation of the movement through the 1950s and 1960s as people of Mareikura's age pass on and the generation of Pauro and Hine step up to leadership. Continuing the chronological development, chapter 5, Expansion and Consolidation, brings the movement up to the 1970s as the members and the country revisit and rethink New Zealand's colonial past.

In the 1970s the movement began to make pilgrimages a regular feature of its calendar. Chapter 6, Pilgrimages to Waitangi, tells of the pilgrimages to the site of the 1840 treaty between the British colonizers and representatives of the Māori. The last chapter, Te Umuroa and the Tira Hoe Waka, tells of the mission undertaken by elders of the movement to repatriate the remains of Hōhepa Te Umuroa, an ancestor deported in the 1840s to a prison camp on an island off Tasmania, where he died. The chapter also covers the Tira Hoe Waka.

Interspersed between these chapters, are the narratives, or life histories, of Hine Ataarangi, Pinenga, Hoana, Raana, and Matiu, all prominent figures in the movement. Hoana, a *kaimahi* (literally, "worker")[4] and a native Māori speaker, instructed me, went over translations and meanings, and tested my understanding of the Māramatanga's history until her very high standards were at least approximated. She was a natural choice for a life history. Pinenga has become the mistress of Kuratahi (a sheep and cattle station high in the hill country northwest of Taihape, home of the most significant of the *rā*) and an important weaver. As the wife of a very senior man with an especially meaningful spiritual history, she was an affine, connected by marriage, but she was nevertheless an outsider. Her position was appealing precisely because it has been so difficult. Raana was also becoming a significant actor; she led the campaign for a *kohanga reo* and thus assured that a new generation would speak the Māori language. Raana's accomplishments, especially on behalf of children, are exceptional, but so too are her modesty and diffidence; thus I am pleased to be able to bring her to the wider audience she deserves. Hine, wife and later widow of Pauro, lived during the last years of her life in a *kaumātua* flat on Maungārongo marae where she treated me to many a wonderful afternoon and evening of reminiscence. Her life spanned generations and major transitions in the movement; she had an astonishing memory of the scenes, relationships, stories, and waiata across those times. Matiu, *tohunga*, kaimahi, gentleman, friend, and intellect extraordinary, is the subject of the final life history. These life histories offer a personal perspective on the religious, social, and political continuity of the Māramatanga movement, and at the same time permit the reader to witness the transfer of knowledge and authority across generations.

The recent deaths of Hine, Hoana, Matiu and other elders have created a vacuum that will long linger in the movement's history and narratives. Yet, even now, younger voices are being heard—voices that assure a future for the Māramatanga.

Te Karere

On November 9, 1935, sixteen-year-old Lena Ruka died suddenly. As her body lay in her coffin, surrounded in proper Māori fashion by family and friends, her wairua (or spirit) addressed the mourners. Lena's had been a troubled family, afflicted by illness, premature deaths, and a curse of barrenness that assured no offspring could survive into adulthood. That Lena had almost done so made her death that much more devastating. However, for all the mourners' pain and grief, there was little surprise among them. Lena's survival into adolescence had seemed to mock the curse; when she died, they all knew that greater forces had triumphed.

Lena's death was the latest in a litany of Ruka family catastrophes: her parents, Ruka and Anaera, had already lost a child, and throughout her extended family there had been miscarriages and childhood deaths.[1] All too frequently, pregnancies and even adoptions had ended tragically, and several women were unable to conceive at all. Barrenness and the death of children, brutal under any circumstances, were especially cruel for a population that was only now—in the fourth decade of the twentieth century—recovering from severe decline.

Whatever their travails, suddenly those assembled around the coffin or grieving in other rooms were talking to a wairua.[2] How unanticipated, how alien was such an event? The return of spirits of the dead was not new to Māori. In this case, speaking with the dead was even less unusual, for Lena's ancestors had actively followed Māori spiritual leaders, and her grandfather, Hori Enoka Mareikura, was a visionary, seer, and healer who had founded the Māramatanga movement, and was its acknowledged head.[3]

Too much emphasis could easily be placed on the uniqueness of this family. It is far from common to have a recent ancestor who was a prophet; it is probably even less common to have a returning spirit of the dead who shapes the family's future; and certainly there is a great deal that is, and has been, singular about these individuals. Yet emphasising the extraordinary allows us to mystify the way we see this family, and the way we see all Māori. To treat them as unique, to emphasise their exceptional characteristics, would be to mark and to separate them, from other Māori, and from the reader. It would make the people of this book irretrievably "other."

In the same vein, it would be easy to view the spiritual return of a beloved child as a compensation for too much loss, too much pain. But this would diminish all that followed and minimize the members' own trepidation at the enormity of the step they were about to take in 1935. More importantly, it would oversimplify the complexity of the lives that were shaped by this event. Lena's family members were neither "others" nor atypical. They were and remain an extended family with the problems and limited solutions characteristic of Māori in twentieth-century New Zealand. To represent them as somehow unique, as singular and distinct from other Māori, would seriously understate this commonality.

Many members of Lena's extended family were followers of various Māori prophets, those individuals who had recast Christianity into forms that would make intelligible the workings of the colonial establishment. For a people beleaguered and overwhelmed by Pākehā for more than a century, leaders who were able to fuse religion and politics exerted great appeal. Those gathered around Lena's coffin knew of and had witnessed the ritual prowess of her grandfather. By the time her tangi was over, doubters would be turned into converts.

Lena's wairua, speaking initially through the mouth of her aunt Kataraina, met with mixed reactions. Certainly, there were among those assembled some who were surprised and troubled, whose grief did not admit a returning spirit as consolation. But these mourners also comprised a group who had had experience with prophets, who had witnessed miracles on other marae and who could readily testify to the continuing effectiveness of the ancient world. Those around Lena's coffin that night had no doubts that spiritual intervention could alter events and change lives. Few Māori, no matter what variant of Christianity they seemed to embrace, had abandoned the notion that wairua could and did wander after death. Wairua were known to come back, to give advice or assistance when things were not going well.

Lena's return radically altered the lives of the mourners surrounding her coffin. From that day until the present, she has continued to come back, providing assurance and guidance in a world which is still troubling and which still, all too often, eludes understanding. Her name is seldom spoken: to her relatives and their descendants she is known simply as Te Karere o te Aroha, the messenger of love, most frequently abbreviated as Te Karere.

The chapel in which Lena was at rest demonstrated the apparent facility with which Catholicism could be combined with older Māori religious beliefs. In addition to the pictures of the ancestors whom she would be joining, there were flowers, candles, and various representations of Christ. Lena was buried in the family graveyard at Raketapauma; her headstone was engraved with a cross. A casual observer may have seen this as evidence of assimilation or accommodation. Yet this would be too facile and far from the entire story. Despite the overtly Christian symbols – and there were certainly devout Catholics among the congregation – there was a clear conviction that Lena had died of peculiarly Māori causes and that her wairua would traverse a path that her ancestors had been taking for thousands of years.

In spite of Lena's family's devotion to Catholicism, there was no doubt that only one legitimate ritual should be invoked at the time of death. This was the tangi (or tangihanga), which traditionally takes place over several days. During this time, the body is laid out, surrounded by pictures of the relatives and family members with whom the deceased will be united. People with the remotest of attachments to the family come from all over New Zealand to pay their respects. In turn, the mourners feed and provide housing for the arriving guests.

Tangi have always been events of great moment in the Māori community: in an intensely charged environment, friends and relatives share grief and responsibilities. However, if tangi remain distinctively Māori rituals, they have nevertheless been able to encompass many of the icons and symbols introduced by Christianity. In particular, the forms and rituals of Catholicism have been incorporated into a ritual process still viewed as holding its indigenous shape. Yet, it would be foolish to think that, as Lena's voice came forth through her aunt, the balance between Catholicism and indigenous Māori religion, the delicate mix of candles, crucifixes, pictures of ancestors, and invocations to the tribe's dead, did not require a reassessment. This had to be more than a hasty realignment of competing ideologies.

The tradition of prophecy, simultaneously encompassing accommodation and resistance, added further complications. The process of creating a meaningful space on the New Zealand political and social landscape has been continuous, requiring a flexible blend of three intellectually quite distinct traditions. The association for which Lena's tangi was a catalyst would, inevitably, bequeath to future members a burden of constant vigilance to sustain a necessary balance.[4]

The death and return of Lena Ruka transformed Mareikura and his family. Lena was henceforth known as Te Karere, sustaining contact with her family over seven decades. Anaera took over as the conduit, despite her early, youthful inclinations to avoid her father's teachings and the gravity that surrounded certain marae protocol. As Te Karere's mother, and anything but an eager kaimahi, Anaera received messages when she was asleep. Often denying any knowledge of the contents of the messages when awake, she dwelt on borders as she slept: between consciousness and sleep; between the past and the present; between ancestors and descendants. Her role here perpetuates the role of women, seen often in Māori culture, as guardians of portals. Anaera's brother Pauro and her husband Ruka were initially the only permitted scribes.[5] Kataraina, who was the first to transmit Te Karere's words to the assembled mourners, remained recognizably gifted in spiritual matters throughout her life.

Lena had not left a world that could be seen as friendly to Māori or to Māori ways of thinking; questions of power, control, and domination were always present. Yet her voice brought a new perspective, and in the process galvanized her relatives. Through more than sixty-five years, her consistent presence has opened up possibilities, reaffirmed the past and given her family an active stance in negotiating their present. She has assured that the past will continue to work its will on the future. As different commemorative occasions became fixtures in the members' annual calendars, the movement expanded to include other centres. Some rā were, and have remained, more important than others. By the 1990s five additional rā had been added as well as annual pilgrimages to Waitangi (chapter 6) and yearly trips, known as the Tira Hoe Waka, down the Whanganui River (chapter 7).[6]

Over time Pauro and Ruka ceased to be the sole scribes. Waiata and pātere were written in notebooks, which became prized personal possessions or were presented as desirable gifts. If more individuals had access to what once had been limited, there was also far more variation. But at the same time, there can be no doubt that the members' conviction that they were involved in generating their own history was strengthened in the process.

Lena's teachings brought an emphasis on equality, an insistence that wairua can and will speak to anyone in the movement. This egalitarian impulse runs counter to the ranked nature of Māori society, where even today genealogical ascendancy is given respect and where maleness continues to be valued. Nevertheless, this posited equality, as will be seen in the pages that follow, has become a means of negotiating a political stance, of challenging a world in which Pākehā superiority has been axiomatic.

Te Karere's death was a profound loss to a family that had already endured many tragedies. Her return translated that loss into an incident with critical implications, immediately altering a family's world and worldview. This event has continued, in its telling and retelling, to shape their (and our) understanding of the present. The ways in which the events of that night have been understood have framed the experience of the last sixty-five years, This is not to say that meanings are immutable; indeed, they are highly contested. But these negotiations and renegotiations of meaning allow us to see how social worlds are imbued with intention and significance.

CHAPTER 1

The Dispensation of Colonialism

Introduction

The Māramatanga is a Christian movement and the majority of its followers are devout Catholics. They also belong predominantly to Whanganui, an important and influential tribal confederation (whose history has recently been detailed by David Young [1998]). This book is about the people of the Māramatanga, British colonization and Christian missions, and the development of the Māori tradition of prophecy. Religion and politics have never been separated in the Māori world; colonialism, missionary activity, and prophecy inevitably were bound to one another. This chapter is concerned with the roots and implications of these connections—that is, with the background of the Māramatanga.

The early colonial period of New Zealand has been documented extensively, but our understanding of that history has not remained static. Through time, the heroes and heroines have changed, and we have become far more aware of how issues of perspective and politics can creep into seemingly objective interpretation. With the work of the Waitangi Tribunal in the late 1980s (addressing breaches of the Treaty of Waitangi and particularly those relating to loss of land), the reinterpretation of actions and intentions, often buried for over a hundred years, became ever more urgent. That urgency is, perhaps, a Pākehā preoccupation. For Māori, oral histories have provided narratives that have not appeared in history books, that did not become part of the larger New Zealand understanding of the methods of Pākehā dominion. While this exclusion cannot be understood as optimal, most Māori have learned to live with it. Moreover, dedicated scholars, such as Anne Salmond (1976, 1980, 1991, 1997), James Belich (1986, 1989, 1996), and Judith Binney (1979, 1987, 1995), have done much by retrieving and making accessible tribal knowledge. In the process, they have demonstrated the very specific and particular nature of Māori understandings. Such studies have also shown us how important history is to an understanding of the present.[1]

There can be no single account of Pākehā contact—religious, commercial, or agricultural—with Māori. Intermittent and varied contact of Pākehā with socially, politically, and geographically diffuse Māori led to no single or general

Māori response (Howe 1984: 225). Pākehā interests in Māori also varied, leading to conflict in the ways in which Māori were understood and constructed for British understanding. For those with a distant interest—that is, those uninterested in land—Māori exemplified the noble, if unenlightened, savage (a point made in pictorial representations of the era [see Bernard Smith 1960, Bell 1992]). For those whose interest in land was not quite so dispassionate, Māori were degenerate reprobates who did not deserve the resources of this bounteous colony.

In the early nineteenth century, the Anglican Church Missionary Society (CMS), soon followed by Wesleyans and Catholics, undertook the arduous task of converting New Zealand's natives. By mid-century, British settlement was spreading inexorably through the country. The CMS, meanwhile, cooperatively sought to "civilize then christianize" its inhabitants (Wright 1959: 40).

Missionaries may have targeted all Māori, but in most communities it was the lower ranks who had the most to gain by the possibility of a new definition of status and prestige. "Māori society which always had a healthy respect for rank therefore gave in, in its reaction to missionaries, to its healthy respect for achievement" (Howe 1984: 225). Initially, Māori were drawn to mission stations because of the range of material goods—muskets, blankets, and axes—that were readily provided. But with the arrival of Henry Williams as the new head of the CMS in 1823, the strategy shifted to the promulgation of Christian ideology; attention moved to literacy and to the translation of prayer books and Bibles into Māori. The printed word was to be disseminated and the audience at religious schools widened to encompass adults as well as children (Howe 1984: 223). Indeed, Māori desire for literacy and for books was almost insatiable and proved to be an important attraction of the missions.

Thus the means of "civilization" were literacy, trade, knowledge of horticulture, and the introduction of British weaponry. Suddenly, the hierarchy of chiefs, ritual leaders, and proven warriors that had sustained Māori society was in jeopardy from those who could read. By reinforcing a respect for achievement, which was always prominent and always at odds with the Māori preference for ascription, Christianity opened up Māori society in ways that would not be completely obvious until the emergence of the prophets later in the nineteenth century. But contact with missionaries, settlers, and sailors also made Māori vulnerable to diseases for which their own methods proved inadequate. The world, as Māori had known it, was inverted.

The 1830s, the decade preceding annexation, was a period of change in New Zealand, from Māori and Pākehā, religious and commercial points of view. Whaling, timber extraction and trade in flax, as well as the land, brought increasing numbers of Europeans (Howe 1984: 226). In the more accessible regions, European settlement impinged on and disrupted Māori, but in regions less affected (and these were by far the majority) cultural stability prevailed. In many regions, Māori adapted eagerly and creatively to introduced technologies and ideas: a situation not without ironies (see Howe 1984: 229). But social change was not entirely unilateral even in the Māori communities receiving the most missionary attention: Pākehā also learned from Māori. Owens emphasises the mutuality of any interchange (1981: 48), while Howe characterises the relationship between Māori and Pākehā at this time as "mutually exploitative cooperation" (1984: 225). For the most part, Polynesian notions of community and society still predominated: small communities governed by tribal traditions rather than centralized states with internal divisions based on class, race, and religion (Owens 1981: 53). The reactions of Britons to Māori in the first third of the nineteenth century were ambivalent. While there was humanitarian concern for native peoples (noble savages "being ruined by unregulated European presence"), the opposing view was one of non-involvement: territories such as New Zealand were to be left to traders and missionaries to operate in as they wished and at their own risk. However, the British and New South Wales (Australia) goverments were inevitably drawn into matters of trade and the real or alleged problems of relations between Māori and European. "The result was annexation of the country by Britain" (Howe 1984: 226); the Treaty of Waitangi was negotiated between the British colonial administration and several Māori chiefs, and signed in February 1840.[2]

George Grey and the Colonial Mystique

In 1845, George Grey was moved to New Zealand from Australia, where he had had a successful tenure as governor. As New Zealand's governor, he was thrown into the middle of a dispute among several combatants: Wakefield's New Zealand Company, whose interest was in settlers and land, battled with the CMS, whose interest was in souls, over land policy; Henry Williams, of the CMS, cautioned Māori chiefs against selling their land. Māori tribes had been led to the brink of rebellion over different understandings of the Treaty of Waitangi (Stocking 1987: 86). Grey called on his formidable diplomatic skills, backed up where necessary by force, to bring calm to the situation and to enhance his own position. Nevertheless, his aim was clear: the dispute between Christianity and commerce (personified by Williams and Wakefield) had to be resolved.

Grey was to some extent influenced by the idea that a more egalitarian society might be created in New Zealand. Were this indeed his goal, it was thwarted by the individuals who became some of New Zealand's early settlers. In the 1830s, there was a rapid influx of escaped convicts and ships' deserters —in short, "the veriest refuse of civilized society" (Sorrenson 1975: 102). Under the circumstances, the cause of civilization, however defined, was unlikely to be promoted.

Grey's native policy reflected his desire to create a society "free from the tyranny of the landed aristocracy" (Stocking 1987: 86). He invoked the Treaty of Waitangi to protect Māori land rights and at the same time launched major purchases of Māori lands.[3] Sorrenson (1975: 103) points out that Māori presented no long-term threat to colonization. Intertribal fighting and geographical dispersion precluded a united front against settler incursions. But, equally important, the Māori desire and capacity for civilization made amalgamation, rather than pacification or extermination, a plausible goal.

Inevitably, given the resoluteness of all sides in the conflict, Grey was forced into difficult positions, ones in which he acted impulsively, injudiciously, and perhaps at times illegally. In 1846, Te Umuroa, an ancestor of the present members of the Māramatanga, was, with several other Whanganui Māori, involved in an organized raid on a settler outpost near Wellington; they were subsequently captured by government troops. Under the prevailing law, they should have been treated as prisoners of war. Instead, Grey ordered them court-martialled as traitors, and within weeks they were convicted of rebellion against the British queen. They were exiled to Maria Island, in Australia, where the guards did all they could to make them comfortable. After two years, all the prisoners except Te Umuroa returned to New Zealand, where they were welcomed and vindicated. Te Umuroa had succumbed to tuberculosis and died during the first winter. The story does not end there: in 1989, his descendants, members of the Māramatanga, went to Maria Island to find his grave and repatriate his remains to his Whanganui people. (This mission is described in chapter 7).

The Māori Response

By the 1860s, Pākehā settlers were willing to fight for their rights to land. In this, missionaries sometimes, but not always, joined them. The land wars can only be understood through a prism of nineteenth-century ideology. Indigenous people were not seen as capable (in the strictest Darwinian sense) of overcoming the weapons and strategies of the civilized. Hence Māori victories were discounted, while less significant British triumphs were trumpeted throughout the countryside. In fact, the British could not win on their own; they were forced to rely on those Māori willing to fight for the colonial cause. Victories under such conditions hardly attested to British military prowess, but they were certainly regarded as such. It has only been in the later years of the twentieth century, as oral histories have been given credence, that British military genius has been re-evaluated, particularly in the brilliant work of James Belich (1986).

What effect did the wars have on Māori? And why were prophets seen as effective solutions to their problems? In a very general sense, Māori had been betrayed by the Treaty, which had been designed, so they had thought, to safeguard them from precisely these eventualities. Warfare, in the British mode and under the conditions that prevailed in the nineteenth century, had to be unnerving. Men of the cloth (although not all of them) who had been teachers and allies revealed Māori military positions and circumstances. To this deception and treachery had to be added the fact that Christians attacked other Christians. Whatever Christianity did for the missionaries and the white settlers, it clearly did not have the same salutary effect on Māori. Once Māori began to suffer serious defeats, they had no choice but to redefine their relationship with the all-powerful deity of the mission Bible. The challenge was to be had in winning Him over to the Māori side in their struggle against Pākehā. This required redefining themselves as separate from the missionaries and Christian beliefs while continuing to retain faith in their own past.

The loss of land and the efflorescence of Christianity among both Pākehā and Māori forced Māori to confront Pākehā power. The dispossession and despair of the nineteenth century found expression in religious movements, which manipulated the introduced symbols of Christianity both to explain Māori desolation and to offer hope for redemption. It is clear that Māori appropriated Christianity and in so doing transformed a means of submission into a weapon of resistance. The Māramatanga, a twentieth-century legacy of these movements, reveals the enduring Māori sense of grievance and injustice.

Māori prophets were a logical response to an increasingly irrational situation. For the future, this meant that the prophets were able to confer a degree of stability and continuity on circumstances that threatened to be neither stable nor continuous. For Māori, prophetic voices articulated both problems and solutions. For Pākehā, they represented the underside of a culture that the settlers and missionaries themselves had rescued from barbarism.

From the Māori vantage-point, a continuous stream of men and women, gifted and impervious to external power, has taken the measure of competing ideological systems, reconciling or choosing between them. Prophets remain connected to one another through time and space, linked by the shared gifts and interpretations that have separated them from their fellows. For Māori, this tradition is all of a piece and pays homage to those who stand above others in their capacity to give voice and meaning to Māori experience, however chaotic. For Pākehā, this tradition of prophecy is not recognized as unitary; it is seen as sporadic and unreasonable, as localized moments of frenzy.

Pākehā and Māori views of the history of colonization are not, nor can they be, the same. In the early twenty-first century, it has become insufficient to acknowledge these differences. What is now important is which group can control history. From the very beginnings of the Māramatanga, this has remained crucial, and is rooted in the legacy of Māori prophets.

The rapid growth of settlement and the Treaty of Waitangi had placed land in the forefront of the ongoing relations between Māori and Pākehā. Important in the nineteenth century, the politics of land have become ever more significant with the establishment of, and decisions issued by, the Waitangi Tribunal from the late 1970s. The issues of land, the Treaty of Waitangi, and now the Tribunal dominate the concerns of the Māramatanga, just as they dominated those movements that preceded it.

The Nineteenth-Century Māori Tradition of Prophecy

Colonization and prophecy coincided with the introduction of literacy. There is, therefore, no way for us to know with any certainty whether prophetic leaders appeared before they were written about. The oral histories of tribes describe seers and those spiritually gifted, but the prophets who emerged in the wake of conversion, loss of land, and warfare merged Christianity with their own beliefs.

The earliest recorded prophets are Papahurihia and Āperahama Taonui. Both were from the northern part of the North Island, a heavily missionized area (Elsmore 1985; Binney 1966, 1969). Each prophet queried the efficacy and honesty of the missionaries, while at the same time forming new combinations of introduced beliefs and old convictions. The readiness with which these prophets attracted followers ought to have warned both missionaries and settlers of Māori dissatisfaction. Taonui quite clearly recognized the importance of land, calling it "our father and our chieftainship" (Caselberg 1975: 48).[4]

One of the next prophets, one who was to make a durable mark on New Zealand society, was Te Ua Haumēne, a Christian convert from Taranaki. The Angel Gabriel inspired Te Ua with a solution for the difficulties besetting Māori (Clark 1975; Elsmore 1989). Gabriel revealed a new religion—Pai Mārire, "good and gentle"—to replace the teachings of the missionaries, especially those that granted favor to Pākehā. Pai Mārire expressed its anti-mission sentiment by changing the day of the Sabbath, concentrating on Jehovah rather than Jesus, and depicting a future in which Māori priests would supplant Pākehā clergy. Te Ua's followers called themselves Tiu (Jews), identifying with the exiles of the Old Testament and distancing themselves from the New Testament and the missionaries. The reversal effected by this religion was crucial: there would be no more Pākehā, yet Māori would have appropriated their accomplishments. In the exile of the Pākehā and in the supremacy of Māori, justice would have been achieved in Aotearoa (New Zealand). Once Aotearoa belonged again to Māori, the angels would instruct them in the language and sciences of the white man.

Pai Mārire ritual consisted of Te Ua and his followers standing around a set of railings painted red, inside which stood the niu (ceremonial mast), right hands held up facing inwards as if in salute, singing the hymns of the new religion. During the rites, the angels of the wind would visit the faithful, making them invulnerable to the bullets of the white men. When in battle, the soldiers of Pai Mārire were instructed to raise their right hands, palm outwards, and utter the words "Pai Mārire Hau Hau" (hence the appellation, "Hauhau"). The rite often resembled a parody of British military, thus accomplishing the appropriation of symbols of European efficacy.

Te Ua's appeal, although going beyond the boundaries of the west coast of the North Island, was never national. To a large extent this highlights the Māori dilemma: tribalism prevented the organization of effective military resistance, and traditional Māori political and social institutions were inadequate to their impending subjugation. Te Ua's movement also demonstrates that Māori were selective in rejection of European culture and technology, readily adopting elements that aided resistance (Williams 1969: 78).

On the East Coast, the spirit of prophecy was taken up by Te Kooti, the founder of the Ringatū church.[5] As a youth, Te Kooti had been well schooled in Christianity and Pākehā learning. As an adult, he was arrested as a spy, charged with sending information and gunpowder to the Hauhau during the suppression of their movement in Poverty Bay, and exiled to the Chatham Islands. While in exile, Te Kooti laid the foundation of his movement, demonstrating his miraculous abilities for an audience of admiring fellow-prisoners. While recovering from an advanced case of tuberculosis, he announced that a spirit had appeared and proclaimed: "Rise and come forth. You are spared to be made well to be the founder of a new church and religion, to be the salvation of the Faithful Māori people, and to release them from Bondage." (Quoted in Ross 1966: 31.) So impressive was his recovery that, from that moment, many people were willing to accept all that he said.

Warnings of the new religion reached the mainland, but these were, at the time, largely dismissed. The colonial government deemed it unlikely that such peaceful captives could plan a successful revolt. Te Kooti, however, was more than a match for his captors; he prophesied that soon an ark would come and deliver them from captivity. When a ship arrived at the Chathams with provisions for the prisoners and their guards, Te Kooti seized the moment to make his escape, taking 298 people with him. They reached land safely, setting up a community at Puketapu.

For Te Kooti, exile to the Chathams was parallel to an exile in Egypt, while his alliance with Te Ua was viewed as the beginning of a return to Canaan. Captivity and exile were to become central themes of the ideology of Ringatū. Te Kooti commemorated both Exodus 12 and his own escape from exile by establishing the Passover as the most distinctive festival of the Ringatū calendar. But the prophetic leader also revived elements of the old, pre-missionary Māori religion: religious officiates were called *tohunga*; sorcery once more served as an explanation for ill fortune; and faith-healing became one of the most important Ringatū sacramental acts. These invocations validated past rituals and assured a receptive audience that the ancestral sources of power and authority were still effective.

While ancestral ways were potent, they became more efficacious when augmented by Christianity. To prevail over the Pākehā, to survive in a landscape whose recognizable features were ever diminishing, the prophets had to employ all means at their disposal. The population of late nineteenth-century Aotearoa was largely Pākehā, and European law reached into the remotest of villages. And there was no doubt that Pākehā society had attractions: its advanced technology provided conveniences that Māori were eager to accept.

At the same time, Māori knew to keep their distance. Faced with dramatic population declines[6] and continuing epidemics of whooping cough, typhoid, and respiratory diseases, Māori did not find it difficult to turn once more to traditional explanations and remedies, which seemed at least to be no less effective than their introduced substitutes.

As the situation deteriorated, as Europeans became more rather than less land-hungry, two prophets—Rua Kēnana in the Urewera mountains to the east and Te Whiti in Taranaki to the west—attempted to establish self-sufficient communities that would require little or no commerce with Europeans. Once again, they chose Old Testament imagery and identified with Biblical Jews (the followers of Rua called themselves Iharaira, Israelites, and lived at Hiona, Zion). But now this identification was augmented by the distinctively Māori virtues of community life and cooperation. Peace and good living were to demonstrate obedience to divine will, which would reciprocate Māori, as opposed to Pākehā, goodness. Māori ascendancy was to take the form of moral rather than physical superiority: "The rot at the heart of much of the European way of life was rejected—the economic competitiveness and the greed, the moral laxity and the spirit-ual hardness of heart." (Gadd 1966: 450–51.) But Pākehā viewed prophets as charlatans, as tricksters determined to cheat and betray both Pākehā and Māori.[7]

The peaceful attempts of the followers of Te Whiti (whose adherents tried to obstruct the confiscation of land by removing the pegs placed there by surveyors) to block Pākehā seizure of their most critical asset were met by armed constabulary ready to shoot and kill. The chasm between Māori prophets and Pākehā officialdom has seldom been crossed by nonviolent means. The legacy is with us still, as shown by the Waitangi Tribunal's *Taranaki Report Kaupapa Tuatahi*, which revisited the events in Taranaki. Land, it maintains, has consumed all parties for the last century and a half. And there has been no resolution:

Thus the distinctive Taranaki circumstance. If war is the absence of peace, the war has never ended in Taranaki, because that essential prerequisite for peace among peoples, that each should be able to live with dignity on their own lands, is still absent and the protest over land rights continues to be made. (Waitangi Tribunal 1996: part 1, 2.)

Inevitably, racial tensions were reflected in, and increased by, these battles over land. For their part, Māori were angered by European acquisitiveness, and bitterly resented the government's willingness to facilitate Pākehā greed. Settlers, for their part, could not understand why blocks of land suitable for farming or dairying lay idle. But the heart of the matter was the Pākehā notion that Māori were inferior, and therefore unworthy, landowners. In 1905, the *New Zealand Herald*, quite devoid of shame, wrote that there was "no getting over that inherent detestation of the white races, and especially of British peoples, towards anything which savors of rule by colored or native races" (quoted in King 1981: 284).

The Māori prophetic movements of the nineteenth century attempted, with varying success, to come to terms with Pākehā domination. By referring to themselves as Jews, they demonstrated both disaffection with the Christian religious establishment that had taken over the colony, and affinity with the homeless wanderers of the Old Testament, who nevertheless emerge as God's chosen. In response to the land wars and to the treachery of many missionaries, Te Ua and his followers adopted a more militant, direct approach to the Supreme Being. Spirits and angels were enlisted to aid their crusade against the encroaching Europeans. In the East, Te Kooti created a new moral order for his disciples by blending Biblical and older teachings. In their separatist communities, Te Whiti and Rua gave their followers dignity and strength.

While Daniel and Jonathan Boyarin have described Jews as "people forever unconnected with a particular land, a people that calls into question the idea that a people must have a land in order to be a people" (quoted by Behar 1996: 146), in the Bible the Jews are the people of the promised land, and deeply connected with a particular land. Nineteenth-century prophets saw parallels between Māori and the Jews of the Old Testament. For, in Māori society, land and people are intimately connected from birth to death—first the placenta is buried on tribal land and then the corpse is interred at the end of a lifetime. Tribes are spoken of as "belonging" to land. Perhaps the metaphor of the Old Testament, while persuasive in the nineteenth century, would no longer be sufficient in the twentieth. It is not surprising, in this light, that Mere Rikiriki began the twentieth century with a new, more effective paradigm.

Throughout the nineteenth century, the cloak of prophecy was passed along as Māori leaders tried to arrest the inexorable processes of loss and dispossession. While it was often local circumstances that precipitated a crisis, prophetic leaders were aware that their concerns could not be insular. If, for the most part, their actions were directed toward parochial proceedings, they nevertheless generated a legacy by celebrating a national lineage of religious leaders who were willing to battle Māori accommodation and submission. Throughout the nineteenth century, then, there was a continuous history of resistance and a search for justice led by unique individuals. The emphasis here must be on continuity; disjuncture and rupture, terms that would well serve Pākehā as descriptions of Māori social evolution, are rendered irrelevant. The next century, characterized by Mere Rikiriki and Hori Enoka Mareikura, pays homage to these people and builds upon their work.

Nineteenth-Century Religion on the Whanganui

The Māramatanga may be rooted in the nineteenth-century prophetic tradition, but the majority of its members are also devoutly Catholic, a minority denomination among the Māori. This confluence is less strange from the Māori viewpoint than from the Pākehā. It results from the movement's ancestral origins on the Whanganui River, and the particular pattern of missionary activity in the region.

The story of the Christian missions on the Whanganui River involves distinctive personalities interacting with politics on a larger scale.[8] First the CMS, embodied in the persistent Revd Richard Taylor, and later the Catholic church, represented by Father Jean Lampila, Father Christophe Soulas, and the formidable Mother Suzanne Aubert, brought "civilization" and religion to the river. The Anglican CMS, and thus Taylor (whatever his personal feelings), were implicated in colonization and the displacement of Māori. By contrast, the French Catholics, the Society of Mary (Marists), had taken a vow of poverty, thereby absolving them of land hunger; they also originated in a country with little colonial aspiration toward New Zealand. Inevitably, the Marists raised far fewer suspicions than had Taylor and the Anglicans. At the end of the century, the Sisters of Compassion were even less suspect; in the first place, they were women, and their leader, Mother Aubert, was an avid herbalist. For Taylor and Soulas, Māori interest in prophetic teachings was evidence of backsliding, a compromise that would inevitably mar chances for salvation. The convents, the schools, and the medicines of the Sisters of Compassion offered more gentle reminders that the world beyond the river was now governed by new rules.

All these missionaries left a dual legacy: they introduced and reinforced Christian and denominational teachings along the Whanganui River; but they also left a written record for Pākehā readers. It is through such works as *Te Ika a Maui* (The Fish of Maui), by Taylor, and other missionary reminiscences that this remote part of New Zealand became accessible to European readers.[9]

Were these to stand merely as reminiscences or memoirs, their power would be diluted; instead, we have understood them as history, often mistaking them for truth. Ironically, the missionaries' insistence on a unitary worldview made their doctrine a ready object of rebellion: when prophets armed their followers with "subaltern discourses," they were not aiming at moving targets.

Richard Taylor and the Whanganui River

The Rev. Richard Taylor (1805–1873) arrived in New Zealand in 1839, a year before the annexation, and died there thirty-four years later. If sheer numbers of conversions are a measure of his success, then there can be little doubt of his accomplishment. Yet he worked in a volatile situation, made all the more complicated by his dual allegiance: he was a British gentleman, a creature of Empire on the one hand, and a sympathiser with, and champion of, native rights on the other. Even more than Grey, he found himself in difficult situations.

The Whanganui River, running from the center of the North Island southwest to the sea, was inhabited first in AD 1100. The river valley was occupied by several tribal groups, speaking different dialects and with rival interests, making warfare and intrigue common. The isolation of the area, its hilly and inaccessible terrain, and the supposed bellicosity of its inhabitants (no doubt highly exaggerated) meant that the Whanganui region was one of the last in the North Island to be settled by Europeans. The seaport town of Wanganui was established early in the nineteenth century, but relations between settlers and Māori remained tense over several decades. By the time Taylor arrived, there was a significant settler presence but little understanding.

In addition to the rigors of being the first missionary stationed in an area renowned for its ferocity, Taylor had also to find time for the demands of the white settlers. As Māori–settler tensions crystallized over land, Taylor was to find himself in the middle of two hostile groups. However, neither camp was monolithic and Taylor learned how to balance competing interests. Indeed, Murray (1969: 197) argues that Taylor's effectiveness can be traced, in part, to his ability to mediate land disputes.

Following his ordination, Taylor turned down an English parish in favor of the CMS. Given a choice between India and New Zealand, he chose the latter. After a three-year apprenticeship as a curate in Australia, he arrived in New Zealand in 1839, and in 1843 he was stationed on the Whanganui River. An able chronicler of life in New Zealand, he published two volumes of ethnography, *Te Ika a Maui* (1855) and *New Zealand Past, Present, Future* (1868). The former catalogues beliefs and rituals; the latter is a study of the influence of the Anglican church on Māori.

Although the CMS had been working in New Zealand since 1814, Taylor's arrival in 1843 signalled the first systematic attempt to convert the indigenous inhabitants of the Whanganui region. Taylor's parish, headquartered on the lower Whanganui at Pūtiki, covered not only the Māori communities along the full length of the river, but also the coastal strip south to Rangitīkei and north to Hāwera. It included Māori tribes—Whanganui (also known as Te Āti Hau), Rangitāne, and Ngāti Apa—and several settlements of newly-arrived Pākehā. For thirty years, Taylor was a major presence on the river, speaking and writing Māori, moving about with his family to serve his parishioners.

Travelling up and down the Whanganui, Taylor assiduously ministered to his parishioners, baptizing several dozen people on each of his journeys up to the top of the river. He gave names to many river villages, choosing Māori trans-literations of what he perceived as the ennobling past of Western civilization: Rānana (London), Hiruhārama (Jerusalem),[10] Koriniti (Corinth), and Ātene (Athens). Sacraments were given at hui, with often thousands in attendance. For example, there were over 4,000 present at the hui organized for Christmas 1848.

Taylor was a demanding evangelist "to whom the idea of spiritual rebirth was basic to the nature of conversion" (Murray 1969: 198). Taylor writes:

> In my district I made three requirements. 1) that they had totally renounced heathenism, had long attended the means of grace and had lived consistently . . . 2) they had given up all their wives but one and 3) had committed to memory the four catechisms.[11]

And more: Taylor also required his converts to undergo a period of probation, in which their "moral life and attendance on the means of grace" were evaluated (Murray 1969: 205). Despite these exacting requirements, by the 1850s most of the people of the region had been baptized (Murray 1969: 199).

In the early years of his missionary activity, his doubts about the completeness of Māori conversion were submerged in his efforts to foster Māori Christianity. The changes that Christianity brought about were, from Taylor's point of view, largely salutary. He writes: "*tapu* was destroyed and their heathen rites abandoned," while "their murderous wars were ended, their plundering propensities ceased." Nevertheless, he concedes that in terms of outward appearance, the Māori "were only a naked race of barbarians totally without what we should call property or domestic comforts."[12] Any unease he may have felt at the state of converts' "inner life" was not voiced in those early years.

There were troubling inconsistencies in Taylor's religious work. He could not be entirely certain about the completeness of Māori conversions; traditional beliefs, especially those concerning tapu, continued to be important. He learned early in his stay that deaths were attributed to the profanation of *wāhi tapu* (sacred precincts)—for example, by the presence of cooked food (believed to be antithetical to the presence of tapu). In the 1850s, converts became concerned about the continuing power of ancestral spirits, power that would harm those unskilled in the old ways (Elsmore 1989: 127–40). There were many attempts at *whakanoa* (removing the tapu) to protect the unwary and unwitting. In the same area, healers whose attention was directed almost solely toward Māori illnesses effected by *ngārara* (lizards) became prominent.

These movements embodied a not very subtle anti-mission sentiment with, for example, suggestions that the God of the scriptures had in fact sent the illnesses that Māori could not combat. Their hope and salvation lay therefore in healers equipped with more traditional means of coping. One important healer, Mata, wanted to take communion—suggesting that the disparity between two worldviews was much more prominent for the Pākehā than for the Māori—but Taylor refused to allow her to take the sacrament.[13] Such behavior was apt to be dismissed as a localized aberration, the machinations of ingenious individuals intent on manipulating circumstances. Taylor himself dismissed Māori healing as a "singular infatuation." In hindsight, however, it is clear that these were the first stirrings of dissatisfaction both with missionary teachings and with the new life that Māori had entered. However sanguine his dismissal of such movements appears, Taylor was deeply troubled by indications that old beliefs still held such potency. When he encountered evidence of tapu, he saw a lapse in conversion (Murray 1969: 213).[14]

Taylor's attitude toward Māori was complex. Living among them, he learned their language and was clearly appreciative of many of their ways. Yet the charm of much that captivated him was the charm of traditions that were inevitably on the wane. In 1868, he wrote: "It has always been the view I have taken and inculcated that colonization properly conducted is the natural adjunct to Christianity in civilizing aboriginal races" (Murray 1969: 228).[15] Yet his diaries (now in the Auckland Public Library) show how well he came to understand and sympathize with the Māori point of view.

In accepting Christianity, Māori were also expected to concur in the colonial enterprise, which meant giving up some of their land to British settlers. A colonial policy designed to free society from the tyranny of class merely substituted Māori as the new victims of clearly tyrannical and predatory settlers. As settlement proceeded, Taylor grew increasingly uncertain of the correctness of the colonial position. His dilemmas are understandable. Having been schooled in British orthodoxy emphasizing Māori savagery, he found himself in situations where he was forced to question, if only in the privacy of his diaries, the practices of settlers and colonial administrators (see Murray 1969: 197). Taylor's conflict is evident. The gentlemanly English principles with which he had been inculcated did not serve him well after decades in the colony.

As an administrator, albeit a missionary, Taylor was concerned about the implications of the King Movement (the Kīngitanga), an attempt to assert both tribal unity and Māori sovereignty with their own monarch. Yet the policies of the government left him with little comfort and the behavior of the settlers caused him genuine concern. That Māori should seek redress outside government process cannot be surprising. In his personal diary, Taylor writes about the *rūnanga* (congress) of 1860:

> . . . and yet it appears highly probable that had government taken any steps to make the Maori chiefs acquainted with their political privileges, the King Movement would never have taken place. They would then have felt they had a voice in the making of those laws which they were ... to obey and therefore they would have felt they were placed in the same position with the European.

By patronizing Māori, the government, in Taylor's view, ill served both the natives and its own cause. He wrote:

> Though the government have been invariably kind to them still they have viewed them rather as children, they have not condescended to ask their advice, even in those matters which more particularly concerned themselves.[16]

The hui that Taylor had initiated for conversions became forums for discussion of Māori grievances. His participation in such discussions enhanced Taylor's prestige and furthered the cause of Christianity among Whanganui people (Murray 1969: 211).

However, neither Taylor nor the Catholics could contain tribal rivalries, which were often fought out on the battlefield. Whether or not hapū or *whānau* allied themselves with the government or with resisters was motivated by a complex mix of family loyalties, tribal rivalries, and the immediate issues at hand. As land wars divided families and tribes, as well as Pākehā and Māori, the upper reaches of the Whanganui River were drawn to Te Ua, the leader of the Pai Mārire religion. Hoani Wiremu Hīpango was the main leader of the lower Whanganui Māori in their opposition to the up-river anti-government troops known as Hauhau (an indication of the settlers' and government's insistence on fusing iconoclastic religion with anti-government sentiments). The lower Whanganui Māori defeated the Hauhau forces in a fierce battle at Moutoa, an island in the river near Rānana. Hīpango was killed soon after Moutoa; his relation Te Keepa Te Rangihiwinui, known as Major Kemp, then became leader, sharing leadership with others.[17] Belich characterizes Kemp as fairly representative of those chiefs whose prestige as a *kūpapa* (pro-government) leader attracted followers (1986: 212).

Taylor accomplished much in converting the people of the Whanganui River area. Nonetheless, the vigour and gusto with which they embraced Catholicism less than twenty years after his death suggests that the conversions were never as complete as he had hoped.[18] He recognized that religious understanding did not occur in a vacuum; indeed, he was sensitive to the plight of Māori and more honest than most in his acknowledgement of government excesses. He was clearly concerned not only with the land wars and lapses from Christian orthodoxy, but also with the impact of the Catholics, even during his tenure on the river.[19] His departure from the region in 1868, and death in 1873, left a vacuum that the Catholic missionaries were, quite propitiously, ready to fill.

Catholic Missionaries

The Marists (members of the Society of Mary) sent the first priests as missionaries to Maori. In 1838 the mission, led by Bishop Pompallier, was established in the north.[20] As noted, these French priests did not have the interest in land acquisition that characterized other denominations, and had less interest in the commingling of theological and colonial policies. By the 1850s, Māori in the lower North Island were in the pastoral care of the Wellington diocese, which was in the hands of the French congregation (Bergin 1986: 2).

In 1854, Father Lampila moved up the Whanganui River, where he worked at Kauaeroa, 45 miles from Wanganui, about one mile south of Hiruhārama. He accomplished a great deal: he built three churches and supervised the construction of flour mills and the cultivation of cereal crops and orchards (Young 1998: 42–45). Moreover, he conducted a school at Kauaeroa, and was said to have converted a thousand Māori people along the river from 1854 to 1865, a time when Taylor was still active (Bergin 1986: 3). In 1868, ill and disillusioned, he was removed to Wanganui.[21]

The removal of Lampila left the Whanganui River, an area that had been quite amenable to Catholicism, without the presence of Catholic clergy. Suzanne Aubert, then lay Sister Mary Joseph, stationed in Hawke's Bay through the 1870s, argued eloquently for increased attention to Māori Catholics: Māori felt abandoned by the withdrawal of Catholic clergy; compared with its ministrations to Pākehā communicants, the meagre offerings the church presented to the indigenous population of New Zealand were an obvious slight.[22] Aubert had a gift for languages and an avid interest in herbs, but, most significantly, had throughout her life shown a daunting determination.

Aubert's argument prevailed. As a first attempt to rebuild the mission, Marist Father Eugène Pertuis, accompanied by two lay teachers, returned to Hiruhārama hoping to resuscitate the school. They failed; the two teachers returned to Wanganui and Pertuis left the area (Bergin 1986: 10). The church did, however, recognize fertile ground, Catholicism having been maintained in river communities despite the absence of a priest.

In 1883, Father Christophe Soulas was sent up the Whanganui River on an initial visit, and baptized fifty-eight people, fifty-four of whom resided at Hiruhārama (Bergin 1986: 13). On the basis of his success, Soulas requested that another priest be sent to minister to the river, accompanied by nursing sisters as well. The Sisters of St. Joseph of Nazareth, based in Wanganui, were willing to learn the Māori language and to administer a school at Hiruhārama, but they had two requests: they asked that they be allowed to return should they discover that this mission field did not suit them, and they requested the assistance of Suzanne Aubert. Thus Aubert came to the Whanganui.

This mission started well. In 1883–1884, there were 344 baptisms. The eager support of the community provided the labor necessary to build a church, which was completed and blessed in 1885. A school was founded in Rānana. As a result, the sisters were busy administering the convent at Hiruhārama, the school at Rānana, and the farm.

Yet, despite this apparent success, the nuns, except for Aubert, chose to leave the river. A year later, in 1884, four postulants of the Third Order Regular of Mary made the journey to the Catholic settlement. More importantly for the history of Catholicism on the river, Aubert headed a religious community, in which she was now "Mother." In 1892, the Third Order of Mary became the Daughters of Our Lady of Compassion; Aubert retained the senior position of the congregation for the rest of her life.

In 1888, the church burnt down; Jessie Munro, in her biography of Mother Aubert,[23] makes a convincing case that one Jimmy McDonald, the Pākehā cook for a workforce of Āti Hau, had set the blaze (Munro 1996: 177). A new church was built at Rānana, opening in 1890 as the Church of the Sacred Heart. Then the church at Hiruhārama was replaced. Father Bergin (1986: 13–14) has documented the intense desire by Māori for Catholic pastoral care. At Rānana, a community that had been Anglican, there was little further interest in the Protestant service, while there was universal participation in Catholic prayers.

Mother Aubert turned her comprehensive knowledge of Māori language and medical talents to the service of the Whanganui community. She used her increasing knowledge of Māori herbs to grow and to collect a pharmacopoeia, which was at the disposal of Māori and Pākehā alike. She worked tirelessly as a teacher, often staying up late into the night to instruct the novices in the next day's teaching. Most importantly, she expressed a desire that ran contrary to that espoused by other denominations. She said many times words to the effect: "Let the Māori keep his culture. Aid him to preserve his good qualities and his customs so far as these are good and for the benefit of his race. Christianize him, educate him too, but do not aim to make a second-rate European out of him. Help him to be a good Māori, an educated Māori, and a true Christian before all. But be sure to let him stay Māori." This attitude contrasted greatly to that of most Pākehā: waiting for, anticipating, the demise of the original New Zealand inhabitants.

Catholic Missionaries and Māori Prophets

Father Soulas was concerned about the apostates and deserters from the Catholic faith. Indeed, it seems clear from a variety of sources that Soulas, and the nuns who assisted him, saw apostasy and bedevilment in all corners not reached by Catholicism. From their perspective, Catholicism had to battle constantly against the perceived forces of evil, whether these were manifest in the persistence of traditional beliefs or in allegiance to the many prophets who arose during this time.[24] Indeed, throughout the 1890s Soulas and his assistant, Father Claude Cognet, were beset by stories about the Hauhau, and nearby Pātea (in south Taranaki) was identified as a Hauhau stronghold (Bergin 1986: 36). (At the time "Hauhau" was used to identify not only Pai Mārire but any prophetic movement.)

To the missionaries, these represented an unhealthy and political commingling of diverse religious perspectives, which could only be dangerous. These prophetic movements demanded attention and could not be viewed as benign. Cognet saw Hauhau as a hazardous mixture of sorcery and eastern religions, while Soulas recognized the political position that was implicit in the words of Te Ua. In either case, these movements needed to be discredited and undermined as a grave threat to the Church. In his 1893 catechism, "Ko Te Katikihama Kātorika" (The Catholic Catechism), Cognet addressed the challenges posed by the prophets:

> What are the "works of prophets"?
>
> Knowledge simply from man, making incantations, which are not approved by the Church.
>
> From whom do "prophetic insights" come to man?
>
> Some come ultimately from Satan, things taught by him to his disciples; some again come from man, things simply discovered by him in his own heart, and in Pakeha books.
>
> What are the "deeds with sick people"?

> Searching for cures for the sicknesses of the body in some prayers and
> some rites which are not of the Church.
> Is the aforementioned activity really a bad thing?
> It is a most seriously wrong thing, something quite out of order, without
> having any powers to heal, an activity deceiving the sick people, that their
> souls are at fault when they accidentally become ill.

Despite the priests' efforts, many of their Catholic congregants followed
prophets—Te Kooti and Tohu in particular—not, perhaps, seeing the incompat-
ibility that so plagued the priests. Their descendants today cling to a position
that asserts continuity.

Father Cognet departed for France in 1893 to oversee the production of new
prayer books and catechisms. From 1899 Mother Aubert was based in Wellington, administering to the Pākehā population (although the Sisters of Compassion
have stayed up the river to the present day). Finally, in 1904, Father Soulas, a
difficult but determined man, was transferred to Taranaki with instructions not
to return to Hiruhārama. In time, lack of funds eroded the strength of the
mission on the river.

Nevertheless, the river remained Catholic in its middle reaches. The convent
schools at Hiruhārama and Rānana have educated several generations of Māori
children, while Catholics throughout the area have been served by Marists,
among them the first Māori priest, Wiremu Te Āwhitu. And Te Huinga, the wife
of Hori Enoka Mareikura, who was born and raised in Rānana, made certain that
her family held to the faith.

Conclusions

This chapter, on events in the nineteenth century, is not of merely historical
interest. It frames the narrative that follows; the past does not disappear. The
legacy of prophecy connects Hori Enoka Mareikura and his followers to the
previous century, and so do the late twentieth-century activities: the pilgrimages
to Waitangi, and the repatriation of Te Umuroa. The members of the Māramatanga carry the past with them. Perhaps this is what it means to be Māori. But
equally the past, with its conviction of continuity and assurances of endurance,
can counter the treachery and betrayal that have been the lot of Māori and other
colonized peoples.

Māori, realizing all too soon what the Pākehā had in mind for them, defiantly
called themselves Jews or Israelites, thereby distancing themselves from the
missionaries, whom they no longer saw as benign saviors. Pākehā saw Māori
religious leaders as, at best, errant theologians; at worst, they were charlatans,

swindlers, and embezzlers. Once it became clear that Māori were not going to die off and disappear, any sign of their independence or autonomy was subject to Pākehā derogation.

The Old Testament as a metaphor for the colonial condition of Māori would not prove effective indefinitely: very early in the twentieth century, Mere Rikiriki changed this imagery, asserting that while Māori were still attached to the prophets of the last century, they were now living in the New Testament. This is, as will be seen in the next chapter, a complicated image, suggesting transition and transformation in ways that are accessible and meaningful.

In 1910, the year that members of the Māramatanga converged on Mere Rikiriki's marae at Parewanui, unemployment, land alienation, poor educational attainment and inferior health care were all seen as symptomatic of a larger Māori problem. Māori were now caught between two worlds. The world of the Pākehā, if more welcoming than it had been, nevertheless did not beckon to most Māori. The ancestral world continued to impinge on a present that most Pākehā thought was free of such influences. In short, the past did not, and would not, go away.

CHAPTER 2

Mere Rikiriki at Parewanui:
The Genesis of the Māramatanga

The history of the Māramatanga begins in the early years of the twentieth century, when a relatively obscure prophetess, Mere Rikiriki, moved away from the models invoked by her nineteenth-century predecessors. Her work, with its ritual and ideological implications, transformed the Māori prophetic tradition, shifting the paradigm from the Old to the New Testament. She is the origin, both physical and spiritual, of the Māramatanga.

By 1900 Māori were no longer in decline, numerically or culturally (King 1983: 159). European leaders who had predicted that the indigenous people would soon disappear were faced not with a diminishing Māori population, but one clearly on the ascendant. A new group of Māori leaders, educated in both Pākehā and Māori traditions, emerged to take their roles not only on tribal marae but on the national stage as well. For most Māori, the new century brought changes on all levels: social, political, and economic, but most significantly, religious.

Māori prophetic movements relying on Old Testament frameworks continued into the twentieth century. For example, Rua Kēnana (see chapter 1), who died in 1937, was a contemporary of T. W. Rātana (discussed in this chapter) and Hori Enoka Mareikura. At the turn of the century, new leaders began to address tradition, incorporating it into Christian ideology or putting it to sleep. Mere Rikiriki was such a prophet. She was a transformative agent, a woman whose fame within the movement crossed centuries, whose works bridged the Old and the New Testaments, the Māori past and the Pākehā present. The New Testament was called upon not only to buttress Christianity, but also to sustain the foundations of the past.

Events during the period 1910–1935 and instructions from Mere Rikiriki shaped the initial contours of the Māramatanga. Personalities emerged within the movement to interpret events and guide social relations. Present narratives of the movement's history emphasise individual achievement and group acquiescence. The New Testament superseded the Old Testament as a metaphor for the Māori place in New Zealand; images of exile and selection, so important to nineteenth-century prophets, were transformed but not abandoned. The history that is now told of these times refers to specific times and places—the turning century on the west coast of the North Island. But these narratives also have cosmological implications: the time scale shifts, from historical to cosmic, in the process underscoring the interdependence between divine forces and human actions.

Mere Rikiriki and her Nephew, Wīremu Rātana

Few people in New Zealand have heard of Mere Rikiriki. To most of those who have she is known as the aunt of Tahupōtiki Wīremu Rātana, and the woman who foretold the powers that would eventually overtake her nephew. At one of her hui she said (as quoted by Henderson 1963: 14):

> O ye people [of Ngati Apa], hasten to me your Prophetess of Peace. A time will come when the Child (or Chosen Man) will take action directly and strongly and with a great mission, without favoritism, he will be more than a man in his attributes.[1]

At first it appeared that one Pānau Tāmati was selected, but Tāmati failed to obey the words of God and became a cripple (Henderson 1963: 14; Young 1991: 568). In time it became apparent that the prophecy referred to Mere Rikiriki's nephew, Wīremu Rātana. Rātana was far from secure in his selection; but he trusted his aunt. She named two of his sons Ārepa and Ōmeka, signifying the beginning and the end. But her recognition of their spiritual powers led to such barriers between the prophetess and the children of her nephew that she would not touch the boys, even refusing to attend Ārepa in illness (Young 1991: 568; Henderson 1963: 23). Rātana continued to visit his aunt, seeking guidance in troubling times and becoming familiar with "the psychology of faithhealing" (Henderson 1963: 23).

A farmhand who had left school at ten, described by Henderson as "a wild and moody fellow," Rātana was an unlikely and at first reluctant candidate to assume religious authority. In 1918, the year the World War I ended and the influenza epidemic ravaged Māori, Rātana had a number of visions that would later be seen as decisive. He had been waiting for a sign, for his aunt had been certain that something would reveal itself to him. In one of these visions, on November 8, he received a spiritual message from which he took the name *māngai* (mouthpiece).

Rātana was a mouthpiece, a mediator for Jehovah, although he was otherwise firmly rooted in the New Testament. It was in Jehovah's name that he urged the Māori people to transcend tribal allegiances and unite, and with a substantial measure of success. He appealed to workers and laborers, quoting the words of Tāwhiao, "My friends are the shoemaker, the blacksmith, the watchmaker, carpenters, orphans and widows."[2] His followers were called the *mōrehu* (the survivors), people who were non-chiefly, detribalized, lacking mana and access to the prerogatives of rank in either of New Zealand's worlds.

But it was his national recognition and political success that distinguished Rātana from other prophets. Rātana has become the most influential of all Māori prophets, founding the dominant Māori political party as well as a religion. Through the formation of an eponymous church and political party, he was able to overcome tribal barriers, forging alliances that overcame ancient loyalties. And in so doing he also fulfilled both his aunt's prophecy and an early symbolic message that he would bring together two foundations, religious and political: the Bible and the Treaty of Waitangi.

Mere Rikiriki recognized the talents of Hori Enoka Mareikura as well as those of her nephew Rātana. The descendants of the people who gathered at Parewanui see no rivalry between the men. Her work at Parewanui clearly paved the way for Rātana just as it did for the Māramatanga. There is a strong conviction that the men had different destinies to follow, with each taking the path for which he was most suited. Hori Enoka, who took the name Mareikura, increased his spiritual mission when Rātana closed his, in 1928, in favor of his material works (Elsmore 1989: 389). From that time, Rātana was concerned with political, not spiritual, works. Each was caught between two centuries, between two modes of revelation, between individual demands and collective forces. Rātana bridged politics and religion; Hori Enoka Mareikura and his followers transformed their social and physical worlds.

Parewanui

The seminal event of the Māramatanga occurred when Atareta Kāwana Roiha Mere Rikiriki, prophetess, jumped forty times into the Rangitīkei River and brought forth the New Testament.[3] Mareikura was there, as were Weuweu from Levin and Merehapi from Kuratahi.

Mere Rikiriki and events at Parewanui (her marae on the banks of the Rangitīkei River) figure prominently in stories told in the Māramatanga. While most of the members who are today elders of the movement were not yet born, their parents and grandparents were present on Mere Rikiriki's marae. Their actions too are related whenever the history of the Māramatanga is reviewed, and continue to shape the experience of its members.

Mere Rikiriki is a border figure, bridging centuries, straddling modes of religious revelation, and capitalizing on the ambiguities inherent in Māori gender ideology. On a practical level, she was a healer of considerable skill (successfully treating a sick child and thereby saving an important descent line from extinction). On her marae and under her guidance, the family learned of their guardian, who has continued to serve as protector and source of revelation. She named a new generation of young Māori, including Mareikura's infant son. She gave the Māramatanga a flag, the time for prayers, and a rā—a commemorative day that enshrines the shared history of Mareikura and the prophetess of the Rangitīkei. In the retelling of Mere Rikiriki's life, these foundational protagonists and their actions are constantly present in the lives of the current membership. Buildings were named, as marae with her teachings at the forefront were developed. In the twenty-first century, this imprinted landscape reminds the initiated of the historical depth of the movement, a depth they can claim by right.

I first heard about Mere Rikiriki in 1972–1973 when Pauro, Aurora, Tika, and Hine Ataarangi related the history of the Māramatanga to me. That history was told repeatedly at rā and on other occasions at which the elder generation sought to impress upon the young the significance of their ancestors. In 1987, 1990, and 1991, Hoana, the acknowledged kaimahi, explained that history in greater detail in tape-recorded sessions.

Mere Rikiriki was born in or about 1866 (Young 1991: 568) into the Ngāti Apa and Rangitāne tribes of the west coast of the North Island; her family was well connected to the Pākehā government and to the Catholic church (Elsmore 1989: 373). Her gifts were formidable and appeared to be, at least in part, inherited. She was a descendant of Maata, who in the early years of Christianity in the Manawatū cast out lizards, ngārara. Like other prophets, she found herself looking in two directions simultaneously. And like other prophets, she was fiercely protective of her people and their destiny, which she did all she could to alter. Her own work is referred to as Te Māramatanga (the light or enlightenment), and in the conviction that they follow the path she opened, the movement's members adopted this name in honor of the prophetess.

Parewanui attracted many in Mere Rikiriki's time, including those who were to found the Māramatanga. Opposite the marae is the house of prayer, Te Wheriko (Jericho), which looks very much like a Victorian church and was built and consecrated by the Rev. Richard Taylor in 1862.[4]

Mere Rikiriki was a strong-willed, determined woman, achieving leadership stature in a male-dominated society. Evidence that Māori women could take senior roles, especially in religious innovation, was overlooked by early European ethnographers, men not trained to look for or to recognize female leadership,[5] but there were many cases of women whose powers were oracular (see Elsmore 1989; Binney 1989). Mere Rikiriki was just such a spiritual leader, and an exemplar to the Māramatanga. Her prominence indicated a new dispensation: it became evident even to Pākehā that women could be chosen and would be able to function in their selected role. Married, she was childless, another mark of spiritual ascendancy recognized by the members of later movements. For the women of the Māramatanga who were childless, what would normally be thought of as a misfortune was taken as a blessing.

But, rather than being famous, she appears to have been infamous. Recognizing her considerable abilities, King Tāwhiao, himself a prophet, summoned her as "the adulterous woman of our times." Indeed, she was described to me in this fashion in English, and in Māori as a *wāhine pūremu*, an almost exact translation. When Hoana discussed this term, she laughed, saying Mere Rikiriki no doubt deserved the appellation. Her sexual activities did not negate her spiritual potency.[6]

It was Tāwhiao, perhaps, who presented a flag to her, inscribed with the words *E Te Iwi Kia Ora* (Blessings to the People), a phrase whose significance will emerge below. Such a gesture placed Mere Rikiriki firmly in the company of prophets.[7] At Parewanui, Mere Rikiriki and her actions acquired almost mythical stature. Holy and devout, she transformed both the immediate and cosmic worlds.

The oral accounts of Mere Rikiriki's achievements that one hears from members of the Māramatanga are both more vivid and more revealing than the written record. Moreover, the oral narratives, in their refusal to see the changing milieu in stark contrasts, reveal a subtle understanding of the transformation that was taking place within the Māori world.

Many people, representing diverse tribal groups, attended the hui on Mere Rikiriki's marae. They may have come seeking cures, but they found new meaning introduced through oratory and shared symbols. These gatherings were devoted to reconciliation, not to condemnation or repudiation. Visitors at Parewanui, even if they were not already related, became intimates. On her marae, strangers became, in time, family. They not only saw one another regularly, but they also operated within an arena in which their most private, personal dilemmas emerged for public scrutiny. Alliances formed that were to carry the participants beyond Mere Rikiriki's marae and link them together in the formation of a new movement.

Weuweu from Levin, Merehapi from Kuratahi, Hori Enoka Mareikura and his wife Te Huinga, from Karioi and Ohakune, came to Parewanui. At the time, they were in their thirties and accompanied by young children. While we know for certain that Parewanui provided a meeting place, it may not have been their first encounter with one another. Each of them had attended the hui of other prophets, with several of them going regularly to the rā at Parihaka organized by Tohu and Te Whiti. By the time they all met at Parewanui, there were kinship ties that were recalled, renewed, and subsequently reinforced with arranged marriages (*taumau*) in the next generation. These were like-minded people,

readily congregating and worshipping together. Kin ties undoubtedly strengthened religious bonds, while transcendent religion reinforced kinship relations.
(Diagrams 3 and 4 in appendix 1 depict the following relationships).

Hori Enoka, who became known as Mareikura, travelled to Parewanui, as did
many of his relatives from nearby areas. Born into Te Āti Hau and Tūwharetoa,
he received his name because of an especially propitious constellation of the
stars on the night of his birth. Mareikura is the word for messengers of Io (the
supreme God).[8] His name, the surname of his descendants, maintains a link to
the substance of specifically Māori beliefs and, more significantly, to the role
played by intercessors and intermediaries.

Mareikura was a quiet and humble man. Nevertheless, by the time he
appeared at Parewanui, he had acquired a reputation as a religious leader. In
thirty years of discussion about the man and his character, his children and grandchildren have never deviated in their emphasis on his humility and modesty. He
was unassuming about his gifts and willing to extend help to the needy. His
teachings and advice, at least in the many stories that have been told to me (see
the narrative of Hine Ataarangi), always emphasized the moral high ground;
his worldview encompassed neither vengeance nor pettiness. Although he had
been brought up in the Church of England, Mareikura became knowledgeable in
the liturgies of the major denominations and, more importantly, he was also
firmly grounded in the beliefs of his people. He was, in short, both tolerant and
ecumenical.

His wife, Te Huinga, had ties to Rānana on the Whanganui River and to
Ohakune. Of three sisters, she was the only one to produce issue. She was considerably more forceful than her husband, although in a quiet way his was the will
that prevailed. While Mareikura was otherworldly, Te Huinga was more involved
in the daily lives of her children and the running of their home marae. She was a
Catholic, and when her husband began his fledgling movement, she assured his
ability to continue by giving her family land over to his cause. Maungārongo marae
(see chapter 3) was built on land that belonged to her family. As the movement
grew, Catholicism became a strong but not the only influence. The next generation were raised largely as Catholics.

Weuweu had followed many prophets, attending the ritual occasions at
Parihaka and not surprisingly seeking help for an ailing child at the marae at
Parewanui. Her tribal affiliations were Ngāti Apa, Rangitāne, and Muaūpoko,
while at least one of her three husbands came from Pīpīriki, on the Whanganui
River. She shared tribal affiliations, through birth and marriage, with Mere
Rikiriki and with the Mareikura family. She bore at least nine children with
her three spouses. At the time of Mere Rikiriki's jumping in the river, Weuweu
was immersed in her growing family. Yet she was profoundly devout, praying
regularly at seven o'clock in the mornings and evenings, urging her children in

similar directions, breaking her domestic routine to attend hui on the marae of prophets. Years later she would emerge as the outspoken, deliberate woman who would stand upright at the side of Te Karere's coffin and demand that Lena's spirit be permitted to speak.

Merehapi, already a matriarch of Whanganui's senior descent line,[9] came from Kuratahi with a sick ward. That child's recovery and the circumstances surrounding it (described below) have become understood as transformative in the Māramatanga's history. Her immediate descent line was problematic, yielding, despite many births, only two living adults. Through the marriage of her two children, Merehapi was allied to the river and to the Mareikura family. Her son Pēpene Ruka married Mareikura and Te Huinga's daughter Anaera, while her daughter Kataraina married Rūrangi. But the problems of perpetuating the descent line were destined to continue in the next generation (see chapter 4).

As the events at Parewanui unfolded, culminating in the development of Mareikura's own movement, the prophet was surrounded by forthright and bold women: Mere Rikiriki herself, Weuweu, Merehapi, and his wife, Te Huinga. Mere Rikiriki was asked, most probably by an envoy from King Tāwhiao,[10] the source of her light, the origin of her māramatanga. She replied quite readily that her foundations were Matthew, Mark, Luke, and John. To seek the Holy Spirit,[11] to bring it out of the water and to the Māori people, Mere Rikiriki jumped into the Rangitīkei River forty times.[12] After she came from the river, she said:

> Let the source of the revelation
> Be from the Rangitikei
> The three shoots
> Remain there.[13]

She also repeatedly said, "E te iwi, kia ora" (Blessings to the people), the motto inscribed on Tāwhiao's flag for her. For her followers, her proclamation of her foundations together with her diving into the water ushered in a new era.

By jumping into the Rangitīkei River, she emphasized the relationship between the land and the sea, a relationship that became metaphorically transformed into the relationship between the old and the new. Hoana explained this relationship to me thus. Mere Rikiriki had a mission to accomplish; a job whose terms she had to fulfill. It was important for her to jump into the river and thereby bring God to the people. In the process, she ended one era and allowed another to begin. This would be a new life, signified by the saying "kotahi waewae kei roto i te wai, kotahi waewae kei tua i te whenua" (one foot in the water, one foot on the land).[14]

Mere Rikiriki's dives into the Rangitīkei River and the subsequent reliance on the New Testament, with her injunction to her followers to heed the words of the Apostles, could easily suggest that the prophetess was advocating the adoption of Christianity at the expense of older Māori beliefs. It is not so. She held firmly to notions of causality consistent with the Māori, not the Pākehā, worldview; by delving into the past she sought answers and assistance for the present. In this act, Mere Rikiriki provided for a duality in Māori existence.

Mere Rikiriki's action emphasized both separation and linkage of the two domains. If the water represented the old ways, the land represented the new. But their conjunction meant that Māori could never leave the past. As Hoana recounted:

> What Mere Rikiriki did was dive in the water 40 times and when she came out she was able to put the other leg on land, which meant, into the New Testament. It is a beginning of the birth of the New Testament in the Marama-tanga, in our people, all of our people. I truly believe that the Maramatanga, Mere Rikiriki's, is the first Maramatanga to actually be the Maramatanga that's come out of the New Testament. And that's the reason why you hear talk about one leg, tonu i te wai, that's still in the water; it means the tapu, and the other is tonu i te whenua [still on the land]. It is because she couldn't get, it isn't correct to bring the two legs together and completely do away with your past.[15]

Hoana suggested that water was representative of the old ways because it "is a sign of tapu, sacredness, and all the things that we were born into and inherit as a people." In Hoana's exegesis, Mere Rikiriki's coming out of the water established a clear path, or channel, for the things that were to come. An important and critical component of these events was that they would draw on the power of the old and the new. As the nineteenth century turned into the twentieth, the Old Testament was no longer sufficient. New powers would now be needed to augment and reinforce the spiritual arsenal of the Māori.

That E Te Iwi, Kia Ora and "kotahi waewae kei roto i te wai, kotahi waewae kei tua i te whenua" are central is not surprising. Though encompassed in a few words, these are not simple stories, for they link narrators and listeners to one another and to a past that is posited as exclusive. Stories about the prophetess, about the transformation from the Old to the New Testament, have been told on the marae of the Māramatanga for over ninety years. As narrators unweave the numerous and condensed strands for their listeners, those who hear the story cease to be passive, becoming instead participants in events which continue to hold profound, and particular, meaning.

The prophetess went on to name people and places, and in this way inscribed her message upon the landscape and within the family lines of those who bore these special names. The power to name became the power to define. She placed new names on four children from west-coast families: Ringapoto (short hand, but recalling Mere Rikiriki's prophecy regarding Rātana); Whakarongo (listen); Kawai Tika (correct lineage or genealogical ascendancy); and Tikaraina (straight line, as a behavioral imperative). These names stood as a reminder to the group of their position and of their obligations. Their religious ascendancy obligated them to listen, to behave properly, and to act directly. Thus they would be assured guidance and salvation. The names also linked families of the Rangitīkei and Whanganui areas. Whakarongo was the niece of Rātana, while Tikaraina was the fourth child of Mareikura and his wife Te Huinga. Tika (who returned home in the 1920s) was raised in a Māori adoption by a couple near Parewanui who were clearly gifted in spiritual ways.[16] Whenever names were given, they were intended to recall Mere Rikiriki's work and its foundations.

The name Tikaraina was originally on a house at Parewanui. When there was an exodus in the 1920s to Rātana Pa, the house was also moved there. The meeting-house at Maungārongo marae in Ohakune is also called Tikaraina. The name Tikaraina thus links Mere Rikiriki, Rātana, Mareikura and all their followers and meeting-houses. As with so many names within the movement, Tikaraina is thick with meaning and dense with power, recalling worlds and possibilities not accessible to non-initiates. It summons forth the man, the stature of his family, the buildings which bear the name, the links to other prophetic movements, the transferred concern of Māori religious innovation from the Old Testament to the New, and the potent days of the prophetess's hui, when the efforts of a gifted leader and her committed assembly could achieve anything.

Mere Rikiriki's Importance to Mareikura

At Parewanui, Mere Rikiriki was active as a faith-healer, and stories of her abilities in this arena have become part of the movement's oral tradition. According to observers, Mere Rikiriki effected cures through prayer, most often to the Christian God. For example, one of Weuweu's daughters suffered from severe tuberculosis, a disease that in the early years of the twentieth century afflicted Māori at alarming rates.[17] Mere Rikiriki ordered the invalid, a child of eleven or twelve, to stand on the marae, to speak in Māori, and to seek help in the name of the Father, the Son, and the Holy Spirit.[18] She did as she was directed and the symptoms of tuberculosis subsided. Typically, Mere Rikiriki produced cures for illnesses that had baffled practitioners of Western medicine. Such illnesses had peculiarly Māori causes; the infringement of tapu or ancestral curses working their evil on unsuspecting descendants were often responsible. It is hardly surprising that the etiology eluded Western-trained physicians. When one woman was unable to nurture her male offspring past infancy, she sought help at Parewanui. Familiar with such misfortunes, Mere Rikiriki recognized the source of her patient's disability. The prophetess prayed over the woman, who later became the mother of a son.

While these cases provide a clear indication of Mere Rikiriki's faith-healing abilities, the following case, critical in the history of the Māramatanga, is perhaps the most dramatic. Merehapi, the matriarch from Kuratahi, brought her sick ward to Parewanui. She was understandably alarmed at the illness of yet another young boy, as her descent line had been plagued by infertility and early death. In the presence of Mere Rikiriki, Merehapi offered up the old gods of the family. In effect, she was hoping to strike a bargain: in return for the life of this sick child, her family would commit itself to the New Testament, to the Scriptures and to the God of the Bible.[19] According to Hoana, Mere Rikiriki went into a trance and began to tāpae, "to place before," "to present." In effect, the old gods, the wairua, and beliefs of Merehapi's family were placed, through the agency of Mere Rikiriki, before the Wairua Tapu.[20] As the family offered up each of their gods, the Wairua Tapu suddenly spoke, saying "Not that one. You take him back. You keep him and you take him to look after you. He is your family guardian. He is your keeper." That spirit was Tangi Wairua. Of the old pantheon, only this spirit was retained and has looked after the family for over ninety years. Merehapi's ward survived and died recently, a renowned elder of the Māramatanga.

Tangi Wairua is also known as Tū-nui-ā-rangi. He appears as a partial rainbow.[21] Hoana described him as a *wairua hiahia*, a "yearning spirit." He is both venerated and trusted. Messages continue to come through him and he has remained an important guidepost through transformations of times and places. He has overseen the world of the members of the movement through four generations.

Bronwyn Elsmore writes that Mere Rikiriki relied on prayers that are "Christian in form, patterning, and content" and that she "taught that rites and practices relating to former beliefs be abandoned" (Elsmore 1989: 374–75). But the oral histories of this time suggest that, at most, the scriptures augmented other sources of revelation, but did not supplant them. This is an important difference: Mere Rikiriki did not advocate the abandonment of the past—in fact, quite the contrary, as the story of Tangi Wairua reveals.[22]

The Legacy of Mere Rikiriki

One of the most important of Mere Rikiriki's legacies was the passing of her rā, July 27, to the Mareikura family. Since 1910 the family has met to celebrate this day. Even today, with many significant rā added over the years, this is seen as the senior day for commemoration. The July 27 rā has been held at Kuratahi since 1926 (chapter 4), when Pēpene Ruka built a house designed for the purpose.

When Mareikura returned from Parewanui to the Waimarino to tell his people about the Māramatanga, they were already committed to Hāhi Ringatū (Te Kooti's church), and therefore not receptive. However, Merehapi, who had so clearly benefited from Mere Rikiriki's talents, welcomed the Māramatanga that Mareikura offered. There is no doubt of Merehapi's influence; she made it possible for Mareikura to carry the Māramatanga to fruition.

Mere Rikiriki also gave her flag, E Te Iwi Kia Ora, to the movement. That flag, a white banner with a red stripe in which the inscription and stars appear in white, flies on the July 27 each year and on many other occasions as well.[23] For over ninety years that flag has been a clear mnemonic device, compressing the illustrious deeds of Mere Rikiriki, the legacy of Māori prophets, the ties that bind the nineteenth and twentieth centuries, and the links that connect a group of Māori in the North Island to the more cosmic concerns of Christ's Apostles, into a multivocal symbol whose meaning can only be untangled by the initiated. E Te Iwi Kia Ora, semantically dense (see Sissons 1991: 287), conveys history that is simultaneously personal, tribal, and cosmic.

Mere Rikiriki also gave Mareikura the seven o'clock bell that rings in the mornings and in the evenings summoning the faithful to prayer.[24] "Given" in this sense means "entrusted to," "given to hold and make good use of," and differs from English connotations that suggest permanent possession. It now hangs outside the chapel on the Maungārongo marae.

Mareikura's major task was to tāpae, to make otherwise tapu places safe for future generations. Mere Rikiriki reportedly said to him: "Take the straight line back to the foothills of the mountain, fill up the valleys, level off the hills, make the crooked paths straight, make the rough paths smooth." (Quoted in George 1990: 318; I have been told the same thing in Māori.) This is an injunction to make the way safe for future generations, but there is also a clear allusion to Tikaraina or "straight line." Missions and pilgrimages to accomplish these ends, to make the world safe and liveable, have marked the work of the movement since its inception and are described in the following chapters.

The figure of Mere Rikiriki does not loom large in history books. Indeed, she is seen more as an adjunct to her nephew Wīremu Rātana than as a power in her own right. She provides a perfect example of the ways in which written narratives, especially those written by Pākehā, fail to give the Māori perspective or oral histories their proper due. On the other hand, Mere Rikiriki is also an example of how individuals are seen, through stories that accumulate over decades, as pivotal players in history. Their significance often increases in retrospect. This is perhaps what is meant by the distinction, attributed to Walter Benjamin, between information and stories: information is coolly empirical, independent of the parties to the communication; by contrast, stories require the involvement of both teller and hearer. Stories that are so important that they are retold convey, for the members of the Māramatanga, far more than information. Though historical, even cosmological, they provide a heritage that both frames and justifies contemporary lives.

Discussion

Mere Rikiriki's feats and accomplishments are kept alive through their narration at rā, at tangi, and when the elders want to teach the next generation. Pauro and Hoana were convinced that members of the next generation must be conversant with the events at Parewanui in order to understand fully the work of the Māramatanga. It is said that the stories are "held by" one or two people in each generation; Hoana, who allowed me to record her telling, was such a holder. Nevertheless, there may be twenty or more who presently narrate them, and always with personal twists. Yet, over ninety years of retelling, the stories have become fairly standardized, and there are no contested areas among current narrators.

To know this history means more than to be able to recite stories of activities on the banks of a west coast river. It is to untangle the condensed and multiple meanings that are contained in names, songs, and flags, all of which provide mutually reinforcing information. For example, Tikaraina was a person, an uncle to today's elders, who lived from 1910 to 1975; but his name also appears on meeting-houses at Maungārongo and Rātana marae. Mere Rikiriki's jumping in the river is called up by E Te Iwi Kia Ora; yet this phrase also summons forth both her links to the prophets of the nineteenth century and her commitment to the New Testament. Names, phrases, flags, and songs carry varied connotations easily missed; they are mnemonic devices, that compress the personal, the tribal, and the cosmic; they permit a layering of Māori experience that facilitates its ready transmission to future generations. Any attempt to subject it to "objectification" or "historicization" would be to depoliticize it, to neutralize its potency.

Mere Rikiriki was a transcendent figure. Stories of her link the present narrators and listeners with their forebears, a process very typical of the Māori, with whom genealogy is fundamental to identity. For members of the Māramatanga, Mere Rikiriki serves as the link between them and the nineteenth century. But these stories of the past also reveal a journey in which the social landscape is reinvented, shot through with new meaning and new significance. As the Old Testament yields to the New in Mere Rikiriki's work, new names define individuals and physical locations, not creating barriers or boundaries, but mapping the contours of the present world.

One cannot help being aware of Mere Rikiriki's being a woman. Should there be any doubt, the narratives always include reference to her as a *wāhine pūremu* (loose woman). The gifts of the prophetess of the Rangitīkei are re-echoed in the later activities of several women in the movement—Weuweu, Merehapi, Te Huinga, and in later generations, Kataraina, Anaera, and Hoana. Indeed communications between wairua and the living members of the movement have often, if not exclusively, been carried on by women.

The history of the Māramatanga, which begins at Parewanui, details the lives, adventures, and exploits of powerful and heroic women. The narratives of Mere Rikiriki—removed in time and space—legitimate the role of these strong, authoritative women in framing the lives of members. For women especially, they validate their own forays into domains often seen, mistakenly, as exclusively male. But in this the stories of Mere Rikiriki are consonant with other Māori histories in which women take prominent, indeed pivotal, roles, especially in generative narratives. Mere Rikiriki stands as an exemplar of what women know women to be—thinkers, cosmologists, and creators of worlds.

The narratives of Mere Rikiriki are effective also as models of redemption for Māori living with competing traditions. Where prominent Māori leaders such as Maui Pōmare, Peter Buck, and Āpirana Ngata pressed for accommodation to the Pākehā world, Mere Rikiriki's insistence on conjunction, her simultaneous recognition of Tangi Wairua and the Four Apostles, made her place and that of her followers secure. Whatever other crises may have afflicted this group of Māori, there has been no crisis of legitimation. The Māramatanga's claim to a place in the chain of history, represented as whole and continuous, is validated through the people's connections to Mere Rikiriki.

CHAPTER 3

Mareikura, Maungārongo, and the Development of the Māramatanga

From the turn of the century through to the World War I, Māori society was transforming itself from within. It was local, tribal affairs that occupied most Māori, and tribal terms in which they addressed the many difficulties they faced.[1] For the newly declared followers of Mere Rikiriki and Mareikura, the national work of Ngata and Buck and the Māori parliamentarians remained far removed from their daily lives.

The followers of Mareikura saw themselves as having intimate ties to the Rātana church. Their shared origins in the work of Mere Rikiriki and names given by the prophetess bound members of the Māramatanga to both the Rātana church and to members of the Rātana family.[2] Members of the Māramatanga attended all the important Rātana hui. Nevertheless, the Māramatanga saw itself as distinct from the Rātana movement. The Rātana church espoused many of their own desires and aspirations, but ultimately the two groups were concerned with different aspects of the spiritual terrain. Rātana turned his concentration toward ture *tangata* (the laws of man); Mareikura pursued his gift of tāpae, and whakanoa, of making tapu places safe.

The Founders of the Māramatanga

Hori Enoka Mareikura was born in 1877 under a unique constellation of stars above Lake Taupō. Both the tohunga who bestowed the name Mareikura and his kin saw a sign of divine favor in the unusual constellation. Mareikura were messengers of Io, the Supreme Being. Thus the name maintains a link to uniquely Māori beliefs, and the critical position occupied by intermediaries, messengers.

Mareikura was raised in Karioi, an area dominated by the Hāhi Ringatū. His own family was Church of England, but Mareikura's religious curiosity was not satisfied within a single denomination: he became conversant with the teachings, writings, and practices of both the prophets and the missionaries. Whether the deity was addressed as Io, Jehovah, or God was less important to him than the relationship that was established between the believer and the divine forces in the universe. In matters of religious commitment, he was tolerant, ecumenical, and curious.[3] Having seen divine power in many guises, he avoided judgmental or doctrinaire pronouncements. His concerns were less with denominational territoriality than with metaphysical transcendence.

Mareikura's wife, Hinewaipare Te Huinga Mākere Pauro Marino (known as Te Huinga)[4] was born in 1877, the daughter of Pauro and Hoana Marino. She was brought up at Rānana in a staunchly Catholic family that had been profoundly influenced by missionary activity (see chapter 1). Te Huinga's commitment to Catholicism determined that her children be brought up within the church. Her Catholicism and Mareikura's own ecumenical beliefs proved to be a happy combination.

For much of their married life, Mareikura and Te Huinga lived in the Waimarino (the region south of the centre of the North Island that includes, among other places, Ohakune, Karioi, Raketapauma, and Kuratahi).[5] Over a twenty-year reproductive period, they had eight children, seven of whom survived. Their first child, Anaera, was born in 1899; their last child, Uira, died as an infant in the influenza epidemic of 1918. In the intervening years they had six other children, Keruihi Tūkotahi Charles (Keru), Harimate, Pauro, Tikaraina, Tekawaupango Mahinarangi, and Hoani Te Oriki. Following Māori custom, several of their children were brought up in other communities, returning in adolescence to the household of their parents. Thus Tikaraina was brought up in Parewanui and Pauro was brought up in Rānana. When Te Huinga and Mareikura were at Parewanui, they were in their thirties with a young family to care for. (See appendix 1, diagram 1.)

Mareikura had been made an heir to the gifts of the prophetess, Mere Rikiriki, who had demonstrated her approbation and confidence by giving him her flag, E Te Iwi Kia Ora, and by requesting that her rā, July 27, be celebrated under his provenance. He had witnessed the advent of the New Testament and was convinced that a new dispensation awaited Māori. In Karioi, his relations were impressed but were already firmly members of the Ringatū church. They could not help advance the work he had begun at Parewanui. For a young prophet with a new message, whose importance he could not doubt, this was disconcerting.

Yet there were a loyal few original devotees, the most important of whom were women—Merehapi, Weuweu, and Te Huinga. These women had been at Parewanui, had prevailed over personal tragedy, and believed intensely in Mareikura's abilities. The fledgling movement had practical needs—land, buildings, and workers—not available to an individual of limited wealth, however talented. These women, in their devotion to the movement, were prepared to place whatever assets they possessed (money, land, and loyalty) in the service of the prophet's mission.

Mareikura's Return to the Waimarino

Te Huinga gave her family's land at Ohakune for the movement's central marae, Maungārongo (Peace). Here July 27 was anchored, and Mareikura could carry on the work of Mere Rikiriki. Here Mareikura could raise his family according to the principles of his teaching and also have a venue for the followers he was attracting. Here Mareikura and his followers were able to locate their movement in space as well as time. Their link to the illustrious past of the prophets was secure; now they could also make their distinctive mark on the landscape. And the generosity of Te Huinga's gift cemented the Māramatanga's affiliation with the Catholic Church.

The first marae buildings were houses and a *whare puni* bearing the name Tikaraina. The name and the building, visible almost immediately to any visitor to the marae, announced the links that bound Mareikura to Parewanui and to Rātana (see chapter 2). Then came a meeting-house named Kīngi o te Maungā-rongo (King of Everlasting Peace) and a dining room whose name, Hohourongo (Unity), announced a central precept of Mareikura's teaching.[6] Soon a thriving community was living at Maungārongo. To enter the marae, to read the names on the buildings, continues to be a valorization of a history that has worked for, rather than against, Māori.

Mareikura established himself in the Waimarino as a gifted healer, attracting individuals who were sick, betrayed, or down on their luck. He gave freely and generously, whatever the cost and however little he had himself, providing the unfortunate with food, clothing, and shelter, and offering them spiritual guidance and succour. He watched over everyone's health and well-being, making sure that when necessary, sick children would have the required money for medical care. He also was concerned with his sacred undertaking of tāpae. Hine told me: "Dad's job was all the bad places. He went to smooth all those things so that they wouldn't turn around on any of the family. That was his job. It didn't matter how bad a place was, he went and talked."

By the 1920s, Tika, then an adolescent, and his brother Pauro, a few years older, had returned to Maungārongo. According to the stories told about the young boy, Tika's name accurately signified special powers. For example, his extraordinary perception enabled him to help his father heal members of the community. Many Māori believe that illness is caused by breaking rules. Mareikura was able to penetrate façades, but his insight was augmented by Tika's intuition. A patient who denied marital misdeeds might succeed in fooling his spouse, but the young Tika would cut through any duplicity, miming the very act that the patient had attempted in vain to conceal.

But Tika's powers also generated a major responsibility, especially for his father: his powerful name, which was responsible for his abilities, could have unforeseen consequences. If Tika's gifts were prodigious, his temper was dangerous; any show of anger produced, inevitably if unwittingly, a very real menace. Consequently, for the protection of all concerned—Tika, his siblings and cousins, and eventually his wife—the spirit, the wairua, of the name was taken temporarily by Mareikura.[7] Tika was therefore relieved of responsibility while his father carried the burden of the name.

Weuweu

Emily Frances Broughton Hurinui, known as Weuweu, probably first met Mareikura at Parewanui. Her kinship ties bound her to the west coast of the North Island, to Taranaki, Whangaehu, and Horowhenua; her marriage bound her to Whanganui (see appendix 1, diagram 3). As was the case with so many of the movement's members, Weuweu was personally familiar with several prophets. Her travels had led her to the marae of Tohu and Te Whiti and to Parewanui, often accompanied by her children. Her daughter, Ritihira, had vivid memories of being cured of tuberculosis during one of her mother's visits to Parewanui. Weuweu's visits to these marae led to her conviction that Mareikura was the holder of the gift in the early twentieth century.

Weuweu was married three times; her first and third husbands had ties to Āti Hau. Her second was from Ngāti Raukawa. Her third husband, with whom she had most of her children (see appendix 1, diagram 3), had been born on the Whanganui at Pīpīriki, but had been brought up in Whangaehu. Weuweu had also been brought up at Whangaehu, but the couple moved south to Levin where her family had land. By the time she met Mareikura, her children were almost all adults and she was free to travel, to follow the prophet she had come to believe in. So she was often at Maungārongo. Like Mareikura, she was very devout, insisting on the seven o'clock ringing of the bell, both morning and evening. In Levin, her house was built in such a way that a crucifix was embedded within the design. She was a determined, forceful woman, who arranged things to go according to her plans.

Together with Mareikura, Weuweu arranged the marriage of her granddaughter Aurora to Tikaraina.[8] This was a true *taumau* (arranged marriage), cemented by the exchange of mats; the two young people had no say in the matter. In fact, Aurora ran away several times, only to be returned promptly to Maungārongo by her family.[9] It would not have been easy to cross Weuweu.

Aurora moved to Maungārongo when she was fifteen and was married in 1929 at sixteen. Tika would have been nineteen. Frightened, not only at the prospect of married life but also by the family's alien beliefs, she sought refuge with Anaera. The sisters-in-law became fast friends. Soon they were joined by

Hine Ataarangi, a cousin of Aurora and a granddaughter of Weuweu, who married Mareikura's older son, Pauro, forming a powerful, if unlikely, triad.

Weuweu was thus an influential early follower of Mareikura. Familiar with the idiom of the prophets, she was convinced by her experiences at Parewanui that in Mareikura the new dispensation, the New Testament, would have a capable spokesman. She cast her lot with him, both by uniting the families through marriage and by establishing herself in residence.

Merehapi and Kuratahi

Merehapi (of Rangituhia) was at Parewanui with Mareikura, Te Huinga, and Weuweu. So convinced was she of Mareikura's gifts that she welcomed him to her marae at Kuratahi and placed her house at his disposal. Such beneficence paid homage to Mareikura and also aided him in continuing the legacy of the prophetess. Accordingly the movement's primary rā, Mere Rikiriki's July 27, is celebrated at Kuratahi.

Merehapi was no stranger to Mareikura and Te Huinga, having ties of birth and marriage through Whanganui and Waimarino. Moreover, her ties to Mareikura and Te Huinga were intensified when her son, Pēpene Ruka married their daughter, Anaera. The child born of this marriage was Kurahaupō Ruka, known as Lena to her family (see appendix 1, diagrams 2 and 4).

Merehapi had married twice. Her first husband, Pūhaki, was unhappy with their inability to produce a male heir. However, she eventually gave birth to Pēpene Ruka, who with his elder sister Kataraina would survive to play critical roles as the Māramatanga developed. His two elder daughters survived to adulthood.[10] After the death of Pūhaki, Merehapi married Paraone.

Merehapi was thoroughly comfortable in the milieu of the prophets, having visited several marae where healing took place. Later, Merehapi's ward was cured by Mere Rikiriki, so it was through her part of the family that their guardian was introduced. And it was through her intervention and persistence, as well as Mere Rikiriki's talents, that this descent line was saved from extinction.

Most significantly, Merehapi managed to hold onto land while many of her relatives and acquaintances had sold theirs to the Pākehā. Stories that her dresses were fashioned from sacking are probably more true than apocryphal, for encoded in such tales is the motif of sacrifice to retain this most precious of assets. The house that she dedicated to Mareikura for his rā, the home in which his granddaughter grew up, was a substantial holding. Over time, the Ruka family has worked diligently to reclaim Māori land, and has refused to renew leases.

Kataraina, Merehapi's surviving daughter, married Rūrangi, the brother of Poope. Before the marriage, there had been a close kinship tie, suggesting that the families knew one another.[11] This link, tentative in the early years of the movement, but reinforced in later generations by overlapping affinal and consanguineal ties—ties of marriage and descent—connected the Whanganui River valley to Kuratahi, Raketapauma, Karioi, and Maungārongo.

Kataraina's life was troubled. Her pregnancies were difficult, and she either miscarried or buried very young children. At the tangi of her daughter, Mareikura recognized that she was once again pregnant. Until that moment, she was the only one aware of her condition. Taking her aside, he asked that the baby, who would survive, be placed under his guidance.[12] The baby was given the name Tūmanako (Hope)[13] and survived to vindicate the sobriquet.[14] Even so, his birth was not easy.[15] It took Mareikura's skill to guide the baby safely through the pregnancy and childhood. In the eyes of his followers, and of Kataraina's family, the birth and survival of a son was miraculous.

When Tūmanako was five, Rūrangi left, leaving the young child to be raised by his mother and grandmother at Kuratahi. Kataraina's brother Ruka and his wife Anaera moved to nearby Raketapauma. Both houses were occupied by the Ruka family. Tūmanako spent his childhood moving between the big house at Kuratahi, the family's other home at Raketapauma, and Ohakune, where he had cousins, aunties, uncles, and the benevolent Mareikura to look after him.

Merehapi's other surviving child, Ruka, and his wife Anaera, who had lost an infant son, Walter, in the influenza epidemic, had a daughter, Kurahaupō—Lena—who thrived despite the difficulties the Ruka family faced in raising children to adulthood. Their sole surviving child was the focus of their pride and devotion.

The Early Days

In the early days of the movement, when Maungārongo was first built and Lena was still alive, there was a difference in orientation between the two generations that were in residence. The elders—Te Huinga, Merehapi, Weuweu, and Mareikura—were all devout, attending seriously to the more spiritual dimensions of their lives. Regularly, the seven o'clock bell beckoned them to prayer, to *whakamoemiti* (give thanks) or to seek divine assistance. There was a decided Catholic presence on the marae. Infants were baptized, communion and confession were routine aspects of religious observance, and, wherever possible, the children attended convent schools. Nuns and priests were respected members of the community, living outside but always invited in to officiate at critical occasions. Te Huinga, a devout Catholic, supervised the day-to-day affairs of her children and grandchildren. Nevertheless, other denominations were accepted and even welcomed. To participate in the Māramatanga, it was not necessary to be Catholic.

A considerable amount of time was also devoted to training the new generation. This must have seemed a formidable task: neither Aurora nor Hine spoke Māori and they frequently made mistakes in etiquette and the maintenance of ritual boundaries. All were subject to an intense, yet individualized, socialization that guaranteed that they would emerge competent and prepared to take over the responsibilities of what would be a much more complex movement. But the younger people—Anaera, Pauro and Hine, Tika and Aurora—took every opportunity to avoid the prayer sessions that gave their elders so much pleasure. Together they would flee over the bridge leading on to the marae before the seven o' clock bell, or even as it was ringing, making for town, to the movies, or dancing—anything but attend services and *karakia*. Anaera, the daughter of the prophet, in truth was sceptical and turned her attention elsewhere.

Weuweu's descendants Hine and Aurora had been brought up in Levin, speaking English not Māori, and in the case of Hine, avoiding in every way that she could all things Māori. Hine, who was quite fair-skinned, recounted stories of crossing the street to avoid her more distinctively Māori cousins. She told me this not because she was proud of such behavior but rather to indicate the difference in thinking about the world her new life required.

At sixteen, Aurora was overwhelmed by her marriage and her new responsibilities. And she was afraid of her new family. She did not understand their concern with omens, with dreams, and with the unworldly. She drew strength from her close ties to her cousins, Hine and Ani, and from the kindness of Anaera and Mareikura. Aurora and Hine were close throughout their lives, first as cousins then as sisters-in-law. But they each formed different alliances on the marae. In part, this is because their marriages followed very different trajectories: Hine had many children, Aurora had none. Moreover, there was a difference in their personas. Hine was enthusiastic, throwing herself into activities; Aurora, by contrast, was reserved. Hine's greatest gift was her singing. Aurora was the pet of the family, beautiful, funny, and, as it later turned out, supremely gifted in the composition of waiata. Each was to make formidable contributions to the Māramatanga, but in different ways.

Mareikura gave his daughters-in-law new names, to start them on their new lives and to help circumvent the perils of former times. Hine's father had arranged a marriage for her, but was killed in an accident before he arrived home to tell her and her family. When, in ignorance of the arrangement, Hine married Pauro, the other party was left with no bride for their groom. Aggrieved, they wished ill on Hine. Mareikura diagnosed the problem: as an individual, Hine was unknown to her affianced and his family; their malice could therefore only be directed toward the name. By changing her name, Mareikura broke the link between the spell and its object. Hine was quite convinced that had Mareikura not changed her name, she and her children could not have survived. This is an example of tāpae, of giving back, of preventing the evil of the past by laying it before the Christian God. Similarly, Aurora had been given the name of a female ancestor on her father's side, a woman who, apparently, wished ill for her descendants.[16] Mareikura divined this evil presence and changed his daughter-in-law's name. He called her Aurora, for the Aurora Borealis. Since celestial signs are especially significant in the Māramatanga, this was an important name.

Aurora could not and did not bear children. Here, within his own family, the prophet confronted one of the most dreaded of all conditions. The problem was not just Aurora's but extended across the whole family. And it extended beyond infertility: women would give birth to infants, as did Kataraina and Anaera, only to bury their children. The final, bitter blow would strike when such women, following Māori custom, attempted to raise other people's children and these children too would die.

The Return of Te Karere

Ruka and Anaera seemed to have evaded the trouble when their daughter, Lena, entered adolescence. She became the object of the special devotion of all. In retrospect, her aunt Hine suggested that Lena might have had a premonition that she was going to die. When Hine, Pauro, and their children visited her at Kuratahi, she asked to leave with them to visit her close relatives. They took her, but soon she asked to be returned home. When Hine heard about her again, Lena was in hospital. Before long, they were all at her tangi. Another version, not at all contradictory, tells that plans were being made to marry her off. This was not acceptable, for Lena was not like other young women; to prevent her marriage, God took her away.

But in the end, all that really mattered during the days of her tangi was that she was gone, that despite their best intentions, despite all their love and all their pre-emptive measures, they had not been able to protect her. And in the days that followed her tangi, all that would matter was that she had come back.

When Lena's voice was first heard, when she attempted to use her mother's body as a vehicle, Anaera wanted no part of it. There had been too much pain already; she only wanted to mourn. Her child was dead, and to Anaera there was nothing left to do. Weuweu, Merehapi, Te Huinga, and Kataraina were all present, all linked in grief to the loss of the young girl. Lena was Merehapi's and Te Huinga's granddaughter and Kataraina's niece. These women understood the implications of her death. The events of Lena's tangi and the days that followed emphasise the decisive importance of these women.

Many stories indicate that Weuweu was the most adamant of the women involved in the return of Te Karere. According to these stories, she waved her stick at Anaera and demanded that the girl be allowed to speak. But Anaera could not comply.[17] It was left to Katarainа—Kataraina who had herself lost too many children, whose husband had only months before left her and her sole surviving child—to allow herself to be the channel through which her brother's child would speak.

Here women dominated the proceedings. Following the etiquette of Māori funeral rituals, it was women who surrounded her coffin, who wept with each new group of mourners, who kept vigil in the days preceding the burial. But the importance of these particular women was much greater, for their actions effected a reversal, a destabilisation, of categories imprinted in Western theology and philosophy. European dualism elevates mind over body, and things associated with mind (or spirit) over the mundane and physical. But typically the mundane and physical (babies, nappies, feeding, clothing) are the realm of women; correspondingly, women are seen as inferior to men, the gender of mind and spirit.[18] Here on centre stage was a soul, a spirit freed from the body, freed from its physical constraints and limitations, offering what was not body, not of this world—in short, a channel to the transcendent. And that soul, that spiritual essence, was surrounded by and made manifest through women.

It would be difficult to overdramatize the effects of that night. In the midst of a bereft family, bowed by loss and pain, women emerged who, in the face of great personal suffering, were receptive to a different ordering of experience. When Te Karere came back, domains were merged, mediated, and transformed; the boundaries between the past and the present, the dead and the living, *te ao tāwhito* and *te ao hou*, seemed less rigid. Moving across these borders were women who were clearly corporeal, and one young woman now only of the spirit. It did not stay that way, but it was manifest on that first night.

Lena became Te Karere o te Aroha (The Messenger of Love), a guide to her family. For the Mareikura family, a new era began. They had known prophets, they had one in their midst, and the elders amongst them had followed others. Now, through Lena, they had a discernible route to salvation. For the next sixty-five years, her family would possess knowledge and guidance given to them by Te Karere, and in time by other wairua. Through messages, *pao* (epigrams),[19] *pātere* (chants), waiata and dreams, Te Karere o te Aroha has continued to contact and guide the family.

Kataraina, gifted in such things, provided the initial conduit. But in time Anaera became the channel, though never completely willingly and hardly ever when awake. She would receive songs and messages in her dreams, not recognizing them in her waking hours. In her later work, Anaera was assisted by men; her brother and her husband wrote down the messages and songs from her dead daughter. Anaera had never evinced any interest in spiritual concerns; although devoted to her father in many ways, she offered little support in such matters. Her own role, according to her niece Hoana, frightened her and she continued to take evasive action throughout her life. More than a decade after Lena's death, Anaera arranged for others to share in her gift.

All accounts of Anaera stress her otherworldliness, her lack of personal ambition, her kindness and generosity.[20] Anaera's difficulties in reproducing and nurturing took on new meaning: her misfortunes were seen as indications of a higher calling. The devotion of women who are not childbearers is of course seen in nuns and other religious adepts. A similar pattern is followed in the Māramatanga. Here, women who cannot bear children, or who are in some way indisposed, are often spiritually gifted. A glance at the women so afflicted—Aurora, Iwa, Anaera, Kataraina, and Mere Rikiriki—supports the contention.

Lena's death radically altered the ways in which the members of the movement lived. Her messages of guidance were eagerly anticipated and thoroughly analyzed once they appeared. In addition, the landscape was transformed as the movement began to take on physical as well as ideological dimensions.

The Transformation of Kuratahi

Lena's room at Kuratahi was transformed into a chapel. It continues to be used by the family today for quiet moments of prayer and comfort. More importantly, the landscape was altered to reflect the changing shape of the movement. A meeting-house was built onto the back of Kuratahi and named Te Karere Whare. This was the place where people would be greeted, where they could sleep together and discuss the issues at hand. As in all meeting-houses, pictures of important ancestors line the walls. The homestead, built by Pēpene Ruka at right angles to the whare, bears the inscription "Te Rua-tekau-mā-whitu o Hūrae, 1926" (27 July 1926), the date on which the movement received the flag and the rā was held at Kuratahi (see Simon 1984: 60).

Kuratahi is a sheep and cattle station high in the hill country of Rangitīkei, northwest of Taihape. The marae, located on a high hill with the majesty of Mount Ruapehu dominating the landscape on clear days, is a fitting home for Mere Rikiriki's rā. The serene and beautifully cultivated grounds contrast with the dramatic and rugged terrain. To enter this marae is to be at the centre of the beginning of the Māramatanga, for the house and the whare puni immediately summon up the past links to Mere Rikiriki, the prophetic heritage, and the legacy that Mareikura perpetuated through his granddaughter.

Songs in the Māramatanga

Although many of the messages that Te Karere brought to her people came through in the form of waiata, there were also a series of pao. These appear in Pēpene Ruka's notebooks (1936, 1937), with an indication that they have been copied. It is possible that he was acting as a scribe for his wife, Anaera, who may have been receiving these messages; or he may have received them directly himself. In one, Te Karere gives a fairly clear directive of what will be the movement's goals. She says:

> Tapaea oke o te tau tawhito
> Kia whiwhi ai ki nga hua o te tau hou ee.
>
> Let us gather and present to God that which marked our past
> So that the fruits of the new time may blossom.

Sometimes these haiku-like epigrams show Te Karere's watchfulness, and sometimes they give a commentary on the human condition from her perspective as a spirit.[21]

By far the most common form of communication from the spiritual realm was waiata—songs. Traditionally, women composed waiata, although men composed most of those directed toward prophetic leaders. In the domain of familial relations, songs that Te Karere produced and her mother received are reminders to her family to keep up their share of the work, to pay attention to her injunctions. Most songs came out over a seven-year period, spanning World War II, when the people of the Māramatanga were committed to learning from Te Karere. Hours were spent in the meeting-house discussing her teachings and searching out hidden meanings in songs that were received, messages that were communicated, and dreams that individuals had. Anaera was the primary source, with her brother Pauro and her husband, Pēpene Ruka, writing them down as she received them while asleep or in trance. Aurora also emerged during this time as a producer of songs.

Songs from spirits other than Te Karere could, however, come through men. A number of pātere came through Mareikura on themes best described as cosmological. They are attributed to Tangi Wairua, or to the Wairua Tapu, not Te Karere, and in them the worldview of the movement emerges.

Elders encouraged the memorization of pātere and waiata central to the movement so as to maintain rigor. Writing was seen as a way of losing the formal accuracy, so writing the lessons of the Māramatanga was limited to a few scribes. Nevertheless, people began to write down waiata. Often a person would write down favorite songs and present them to another as a gift. Books of waiata would circulate, and handwritings would intermingle. Songs moved among the people, and through the marae of the movement, carrying both personal and communal information. Waiata, encompassing shared experiences and histories, bound the members of the movement together, and created a barrier between them and the larger world.

The imagery in the songs of Te Karere is often of light as knowledge, enlightenment, as a passage out of the darkness; the movement is to take on the beacon of light. Themes concern familial responsibilities, of holding fast to what you have been given and to those you love. There are images of canoes, of keeping them afloat in the water, with the correct paddles as metaphors of spiritual rectitude. Natural metaphors are also important, including images of growth and fruition through nurturance and succour. There is considerable concern with articulating the relationship with the work of the past. Contemporary work is *te puawaitanga* (the blooming), but the seeds are from the past.

A number of songs and pātere were composed at this juncture that outlined the shape of the Māori cosmos. These were undoubtedly written by members of the Māramatanga in the 1940s, for I have copies of the notebooks and have seen the original handwriting. Suddenly they have entered the Māori public domain. While this is not surprising, as the songs are performed often on occasions where individuals from all over Māoridom are present, the use of what many of the younger generation consider to be their ancestral legacy by others is troubling. In particular, "Aue Te Aroha" (a waiata that marked the first generation's participation in the Hui Aranga), "Kikō," "Ko Te Rite I Ahau," "Te Kura O Kurahaupō," "Taku Taumata Tonu," "E Noho Nei Au," and "I Te Rangi Tuatahi."

Many of these themes are exemplified in the last pātere, "I Te Rangi Tuatahi," which dates from 1944. On March 4, 1973 it was performed for Dame Te Atairangikaahu, the Māori queen. An exegesis follows.[22]

1. In the first heaven, sixth and seventh, Io the parent, the all-powerful creator, selected the one to bring down the strength of God, passing on the essence which was only a spirit belonging to Him. Gabriel, the angel standing by God, was to carry the message of the Immaculate Conception.
2. To Mary, the gratified, the unsinning, a son was born, to be a messiah. Yet, the world did not yearn for him. Thus the evil wars and the jealousies. He was put to death to seek vengeance for the world.
3. His words came forth to His own Heavenly Father. "With haste, let me into the Kingdom of Heaven, staying at the right hand of God, to be called the King of Kings, and as the Holy Spirit to return to the earth for ever to be unseen, not to be taken away. The Heaven and Earth may pass away, but my words will remain forever."
4. It is the Holy Spirit from beyond that will reveal the sacredness of God and will arrest the degeneration of the world. Without God's grace, man will die in a state of sin, but the Word will clothe him with the saving

grace of God, carrying with it the mana, the salvation, that will uplift and resound through this ethereal land.

5. But should the Word go unheeded, then you will wear the cloak of blood. The oceans will heave, the striking sword will appear again, and men will wither from the winds from without. Until the sword is returned, the stubborn multitudes will continue to be torn asunder. Alas, the stream of humanity will disappear. Great will be the pain, the suffering of the people. Man, and all that is his, including his demons, will disappear. Only after this warring ceases, this chaos retreats and order appears, and the oceans calm down, only then will permanent peace be made with God.

6. Do not look outwards at the sea of Rēhua through one eye only, lest through one-eyedness you see the impression of the canoe and miss the canoe itself.

7. The sacred cloak was given to the world, hung loosely about the few and the many, extending to all. The world knew this, but refused to take heed; heard it, but refused to listen; witnessed the revelation, but refused to see. The knowledge remained with the Holy Trinity. Only from them would spring love, hope, and the faith that will allow man to be bound in truth and strength, and to know the joy of tranquillity.

8. This was not created now. From beyond the understanding of man, these prophecies, signs of miracles, come to man from the past; through the process of supplication and prayer, the whole land cried out and turned to God. At this time they were at one with God and at this time, long, long ago, the whole land bowed before Him. These signs and prophecies, that we are still using today like a delicate crown, were given to them [the ancestors].

9. Do not be excited, lest your paddle, on the return stroke, upset the canoe of the rest, and the canoe thus be lost. But, rather, see the good things that come forth—allow the race of life to be run. Only through the right things, through the final words, shall a perfect form of the imperfect world be reached.

10. Return here, the chosen, that you may look at, listen, and take hold of the canoe as a barricade against the storm. Thus, eventually, you may ascend the Holy Ladder, the sacred way.

11. My purpose, like a double-barrelled shotgun, has been wide ranging in my search for a truthful, right, way of life. Strength, thought, and knowledge may be foundations in the darkness, the darkness that takes away life, the everseeking darkness. These foundations must lead us to the light that follows the darkness, to strengthen the seed that was sown on the seed-bed of the kūmara from far away.

12. Do not provoke the right and repentant heart: hold it safe lest the wind blow it away. In all your work be alert, be watchful—distribute to the earth the strength of God. Display the keel of the canoe so that the current will flow correctly [and not cause an upset]. And to you, the chosen few, hold fast to the mana.

At first, this appears to be simply a symbolic amalgamation, a historical syncretism. Maybe so, but this pātere, written a century after the Treaty of Waitangi in a form that may well go back millennia, embodies an historical awareness of a past and a present whose relationships to one another are clearly understood. The wairua and its followers are appropriating colonial categories, giving a specificity and singularity to the present.[23] This pātere, derived from revelation, is rich with metaphors that emphasise the significance and power of revealed knowledge.

The scriptural origins are New Testament, not the Old Testament of the nineteenth-century prophets, thus reinforcing the transformation effected by Mere Rikiriki. In the very first verse, the pātere posits an almost seamless fusion between Io and the God of the Old Testament. The Māori cosmos, with layered heavens, emerges in the first line. It is Io who is the father. But Io is then incorporated into the Trinity. Io also appoints Gabriel, in this version still the herald of the Immaculate Conception. The point is obvious: Māori believed in—knew about—God centuries before the missionaries came. This undermines the novelty of the missionary message, while it invalidates any missionary attempts, familiar to members of the movement, to relegate the movement's construction of Māori tradition to a more barbaric past.[24]

In verse 2, Christ is born to an unsinning mother in a world not yet ready for the message He brings. The story of the Immaculate Conception and the birth of Christ contrasts with the degeneration of the human world; images of chaos and destruction emphasise the elusiveness of salvation for the human order.

Verses 3 and 4 emphasise the importance of words, which will endure after the earth and sky have been consumed, and which provide the route to salvation ("will arrest the degeneration of the world"). Like celestial signs that straddle heaven and earth, words occupy two domains, both past and present. Henceforth, words will bridge the domains between men and spirit, providing protection and redemption. This reflects the concern in the New Testament with logos, but here it has a decidedly Māori emphasis. Leaving behind this legacy, Christ returns to sit at the right hand of God (*ringa kaha o te Atua*), an image that reappears in a variety of pātere and pao.

In verse 5 comes the apocalypse. Only after the world has been destroyed will it be remade and peace (maungārongo) established. Here the term *maungārongo* also recalls the marae and its meeting-house.

The spirit now addresses the audience, cautioning them not to be one-eyed, for then they will see outlines and miss substance. Rēhua is the star Antares, which was regarded as the sign of summer. Here too is the introduction of canoe imagery that moves throughout the pātere. In one sense, the canoe is a metaphor for spiritual work: members are warned to keep on course, to steer straight, and to "seek shelter against the storm" in the canoe. This metaphor is blended and used in conjunction with notions of illusion and reality, form and substance. Here, the vehicle for navigation is also the word. Thus, verse 9 begins with canoe imagery and concludes "Only through the right things, through the final words, shall a perfect form of the imperfect world be reached." The metaphorical tools of navigation draw upon powerful images derived from ancestral knowledge.

Verses 7 and 8 make it very clear that ancestral knowledge continues to frame the present world and give it meaning. Indeed, this is a clear repudiation of missionary claims to Māori enlightenment: it was all known before the missionaries reached Aotearoa. Verse 7 introduces the notion of a chosen few; the cloak of knowledge, large enough to encompass all, is embraced by only a few. In the next sentence, important tenets of the movement are summoned forth—love, hope, and faith (aroha, tūmanako, whakapono)—concepts that are embodied in names given to the children of the Māramatanga's founding members. In verse 8, one of the most important of the movement's beliefs is made explicit: the conjunction of the past of the ancestors and the word of God. It was the ancestors who through prayer and supplication brought forth the precious things associated with a divine presence.

Verse 9 returns to the metaphorical canoe and links its smooth passage to the transformative power of the word. The journey is perilous, the canoe easily overturned. However, the final word (te kupu whakamutunga) will recast the imperfect world, revealing its perfect form. This verse also recalls the imagery of growth and fruition (huapai) of early pao of Te Karere. The perfect world summoned forth in the chant is a world of ripeness and fecundity.

In verse 10, the canoe again is a metaphor—this time offering protection against a storm. While the canoe carries the image of spiritual rectitude, of following the correct way (reminiscent of Mere Rikiriki's injunctions of straight lines and paths, always using the word tika), it also recalls the past and its geography. Moreover, canoes are vessels (waka has the double meaning), repositories of knowledge and power.[25] Finally, in this verse, after the importance of ancestral knowledge has been established, after the turning away of some from the word has crystallized as a critical idea, the members of the movement, the hearers of this pātere, are referred to as the chosen few (hunga ruarua).

Verses 11 and 12 indicate the shape the movement is to take. By the 1950s, new names would be given, working as foundations to the path out of darkness. The new names are mnemonic devices urging the knowledgeable to think, to have strength and to distribute the work. Here too, the word *māramatanga* (here signifying knowledge) is given a prominent place. The word *kaupapa* (here translated purpose) means "foundation," "fundamental principle," and as such lends context to notions of truth, strength, and thought. Here the kaupapa is compared to a double-barrelled shotgun, a Pākehā instrument, now used to overtake the darkness. In much the same way, this pātere overtakes and appropriates the discourse of colonial domination. The last image of this verse—a ripening *kūmara* from far away—suggests the harvest and the coalescence of past time and space in the present.

In verse 12, the various parts of the movement's ideology are blended together almost seamlessly: ephemeral work, carried by a metaphorical canoe, is the work of God, who has chosen these people to carry out His work. There is no distinction between the work of God and the work of the ancestors. With effort, with cultivation, the ancestors have laid fertile ground for the harvesting, the ripening of a new world. The effort is not in conversion but, on the contrary, in ensuring and maintaining continuity.

The endurance of this pātere is not surprising. It asserts the potency of the past, reconciling common and esoteric knowledge, and at the same time it locates the members of the Māramatanga, linking them to the past, but making them indispensable for the future. Metaphors appearing in other media—in pao, dreams, and waiata—are here linked together, ensuring a universe that is coherent, intelligible, and, perhaps most importantly, imbued with a power that is accessible to the chosen. Past time and space come together as seeds sown in ancient times in far-off places to bear fruit in a contemporary arena. Domains are crossed, through sacred ladders, through canoes, and certainly through pātere and waiata.

Waiata, pātere, pao, and dreams provided a steady source of contact with the spiritual world during the years after Te Karere died. Messages are more gravely presented in pātere than they are in waiata. In addition, pātere often came through Mareikura rather than through Anaera and the voice is generally that of a more authoritative wairua, often signed as Tangi Wairua, or as the Wairua Tapu, rather than Te Karere. Waiata reinforce the messages that are communicated through pātere, but they are far less imposing. Notebooks containing pātere, waiata, and pao attest to the steady stream of revelation and the gravity with which this activity was approached.

Names

One of the distinguishing features of the Māramatanga has been the use of names that have been given by the wairua. Individuals, communal buildings, and personal homes frequently bear spiritual names commemorating ancestors, events, or special aspects of the movement's ideology. The use of such names is by no means confined to the members of the movement, but names are used to reinforce, to insulate, and to communicate many of the Māramatanga's fundamental tenets. Names protect their bearers, bestowing and illuminating special spiritual consideration.

From the time of Mere Rikiriki, names have been given by individuals who have been inspired or by parents who feel that a particular name would be suitable for their offspring. While some (Kororia, Glory; Kāperiere, Gabriel) refer to the Christian orientation of the movement, others are injunctions (Whakaaronui, be mindful), while still others had a very specific connotation that depended on a Māori metaphor. One child was named Arorangi for a tree. This is a humble tree, rather ugly with a spiky leaf, but (revealing how misleading appearances can be) the leaves emit a very pleasant smell. Arorangi also means straight. Other names commemorate important events. Kohurangi was given as a memento of the mist that Anaera encountered on the mountain (see below). Some names were meant to enjoin or remind the followers. One child was named Whakahawea (to disbelieve, to despise), indicating that people will always be very critical and harsh in their judgments. Another was named Natura (from ngau tuāra, to backbite), intended as a warning against behavior that would not be acceptable to the wairua. Outside the very specific context of the Māramatanga, most of these names would be without meaning. But for those conversant with the tenets of the movement, names are a means through which the universe is given import and significance.

Not all names that have been given to children have proven suitable. As the cases of Aurora and Hine illustrate, family names could be dangerous. A childhood event may show the inappropriateness of a specific name. Should an individual appear to be endangered because of his or her name, the elders would discuss the issue and seek spiritual guidance. If they felt the name was inappropriate, it would be judged *tupua* (foreign, an object of terror). The name would be tāpaed, given back, and the child would be blessed and given another name.

Names condense many meanings and in this density lies their power. When Hine and Pauro's daughter died at the age of four, a song came through mentioning all the names of the children of her generation. The names were reasserted to the audience and, perhaps more importantly, her position was retained among her own cohort, despite her death. The effect of the song is to summon important ideals of the movement and to embody critical knowledge. For example, mention of Tūmanako among the children reminds listeners conversant with the Māramatanga of the painful history of loss that preceded him. Moreover, when they occur in waiata, the names of children seem to ensure that with them some knowledge will pass into the next generation. Names therefore become a mechanism through which knowledge is transferred across generation lines.

Names commemorate, celebrate, remind, and instruct. For the members of the movement, they have operated as mnemonic devices that recall important concepts and momentous events. But this knowledge is not everyone's; names contain a universe of connotations that are differentially accessible. Knowledge of these meanings within the group erects a barrier against those outside, between those who possess knowledge and those who do not. While names may recall information to those already possessed of it, their dual nature allows them to conceal as well. Histories and private narratives are condensed in, and masked by, such names. Names filled with esoteric implications are shortened into nicknames or transliterated into Pākehā names, masking their meanings, withholding them from view. It is in this manner that the private work of the Māramatanga can take place in a relatively public context. And it is in this manner that we can see the transformative power of knowledge.

New Landscapes

By the late 1930s, New Zealand was a polarized society. The experiences of Māori and Pākehā were divergent, the two populations occupying different niches within the country. Māori land development schemes had begun in the 1920s and 1930s, and prior to World War II, Māori remained rural, with large families. Pākehā were increasingly urbanized, with fewer domestic responsibilities (Pool 1991: 105). However, as the Great Depression of the 1930s deepened in New Zealand, Māori were excluded from benefits. Pākehā laborers rioted in New Zealand's major cities, while rural Māori health and welfare deteriorated.

Ohakune was by no means insulated from the effects of the Depression, although there was probably enough part-time work to sustain the community gathered at the marae. Ironically, their ability to survive, if not to prosper, during this time probably reinforced Pākehā stereotypes: Māori were somehow less civilized, closer to nature than their Pākehā conquerors, and ". . . could simply 'go home to the pa' for food and shelter" (King 1983: 200). Māori poverty and culture did not intrude on the consciousness of the larger society.[26]

When the Depression was ending, the Labour Party of 1935 made an attempt to correct economic imbalances and honor the Treaty. Housing reform led to revolutionary changes in Māori health (King 1983: 288). Labour gave Māori full equality in its social welfare legislation. A modification in social security requirements made it easier for Māori to obtain child benefit and old age pensions. In addition, the Labour government consolidated rural schools, made secondary education free for all students and raised the school leaving age to fifteen. Increasingly, native schools were brought under the control of education boards run by local communities and local tribal committees.

The decade following the death of Lena, the late 1930s through the 1940s, was a period of great intensity on Maungārongo marae. The meeting-house, Tikaraina, was devoted to the teachings of Te Karere, who initiated an intensive seven-year period of instruction. Younger people—Aurora, Hine, Tika, Pauro, and others—were being trained to take over responsibility. The spiritual world, represented by Te Karere, Tangi Wairua, and the Wairua Tapu, is everywhere in evidence, and almost constantly in contact with the membership of the movement. Te Karere's activity is apparent in the hundreds of waiata, pātere, and pao produced in this period. Most saw no lack of harmony between their beliefs in the returning spirit of a deceased child and their Catholicism. Indeed, the prophets of both centuries provided models for how introduced elements may be reconciled with other, older systems.

As the members of the Māramatanga made their way in a society transformed by the political and social currents that swirled around them, the wairua warned the members away from certain ancestral practices. Carving and *whakapapa* were to be abandoned, at least for the present (they never lost their significance and both were taken up again). The reasons given seem to emphasize the importance of turning toward the future; new generations might be unable to comprehend or manage to obey the imperatives that had guided their ancestors, such as the separation of sacred materials from food. Such rules were unyielding; breaking them brought swift, often dire consequences. The power of the ancestors must certainly inspire respect and fear, as well as *wehi* (awe).

Genealogy, with its emphasis on hierarchy, divided people. Whanganui is a proud tribe, with an illustrious heritage. Notions of rank loom large, with most people knowing the basic rudiments of genealogy, and several having a significant command. Since unity and harmony were explicit movement goals, members were encouraged not to engage in potentially divisive matches of genealogical ascendancy. The emphasis was on equality, not hierarchy; on genealogical connections, not disjunctions.

A difficult balance was being sought between the past and the present. Indeed, at this juncture, the constant presence of the wairua attested to the potency of the past, a potency that had by no means been denied or mitigated through conversion. The work of the wairua and of the people would be required to bring the past under control.

Missions

Mareikura's work was devoted to tāpae, to ensure that the powers of the past remain dormant for future generations. Conversely, it was fitting that Te Karere, a young girl, should provide leadership into a new world. One of the most important implications of the actions of both is that the past remains active in the present and requires constant vigilance and attention. Christianity generally, and Catholicism specifically, was a useful handmaiden in this exercise. But the power, the potency, derived from the Māori past. To quiet these powers, to place the resident spirits at rest, was analogous to the work of the New Testament Apostles. The 1940s was a crucial period, for there were many places whose potential for harm was exacerbated by the growing ignorance: the ability of the rising generation to traverse the landscape in safety was very much in question.

Hoana, a kaimahi in the 1990s but an adolescent in the 1940s,[27] explained the relationship between the past and present, Old Testament and New Testament, by emphasizing the flexibility of the new order. Indeed, the new dispensation brought with it alternatives that contrasted with the rigidity and denial characteristic of the past. In discussing whakanoa and tāpae, Hoana used imagery of lightening, or easing, of putting to sleep. But never are metaphors of permanent obliteration invoked. The impermanence of this changed state is an important feature of these ritual observances. As Hoana explained:

> Whakanoa is to lighten, also it's like the Creator. He and His in His time were beings so sacred there was no level . . . there was no alternative. If God said this, you are bothered by it or else . . . That's in the Old Testament. And yet when Christ came along, He gave us an alternative, didn't He? He wasn't content with what His father was doing; no, definitely not. That is how I see it in the teachings. We are able to overcome those sorts of things by doing this. The other was "you do this or else." (Interview, 1987.)

Hoana is suggesting that twentieth-century prophets and their adherents are like Christ, like those of the New Testament, who lessen restrictions. By contrast, the Old Testament God, the nineteenth-century Māori prophets, and the premission Māori cosmology all stress restrictions and confinement. Such inflexibility is viewed as ultimately dangerous. Indeed, even in the present, followers of Ringatū are seen as engaged in work whose "heaviness" and "depth" is contrasted with the "lightness" and "easing" of the new order.[28]

Concern for the past and its power also became a way of discussing crucial existential matters: what was it to be a Māori in mid-twentieth-century New Zealand? What could be abandoned with little loss? What must be retained at all cost? Debates were lengthy, prolonged, and frequently failed to attain complete resolution. For that, action was required. So began a history of missions, of pilgrimages, often in quest of particular answers, but always motivated by the most serious of issues.

In 1942 Anaera led several members of the Māramatanga on a mission to Mount Ruapehu. Aurora, Pauro, and Hemi (who was brought up by Mareikura) have all been mentioned in different accounts. Anaera had been told by Te Karere that a fog would come down and envelop her; she was to enter the fog and be carried up the mountain. Thus would a rapprochement with this most sacred aspect of the landscape be accomplished. When the time came, the fog did indeed come down, but Anaera was too frightened to allow it to carry her away.

Aurora watched her sister-in-law's struggle and tried to follow her. However, she soon was lost. She saw one hoof-print and one boot-mark—the mark of a *patupairehe* (a half-human spirit, hence the ambiguous footprints), whose footfalls led her to the rest of the group. She had feared she would be lost forever, but the spiritual footprints guided her to safety.[29]

Many on the mission, which they named Te Kohinga o te Rangi (The Gathering of the Sky Beings), saw the maid of the mountain, who appeared to them naked with long hair, clearly, according to Aurora, a half-caste.[30] Anaera had explained beforehand that the maid would be likely to appear to those who climbed the mountain. Hemi became ill and was carried down the mountain by Pauro. Neither saw the maid. Hemi remained sceptical but Pauro felt Te Karere's presence as he was guided in the perilous mist that shrouded the mountain (Hine interview, 1987). The party may have felt blessed but several members concluded that since Anaera had not gone up in the fog, and since neither Pauro nor Hemi saw the maid, more remained to be done.

That the work was, in some sense, unresolved, was not really problematic. Instead, it allowed for the necessary continuity, between generations and between the past and the present, that tied the movement to its roots and to the ancient world. For what was not accomplished on this trip would be continued at some later date, by themselves or by another generation.

Nevertheless, the personalities of the protagonists emerge. Seven years after her daughter's death, Anaera still displays reluctance and hesitation. Hemi is a sceptic, committed enough to attempt the mission, but withholding complete faith. Pauro is a stalwart—firm in his belief, unmoving under the pressure of unplanned mishaps. He is also a realist, recognizing that the job has not been done. Aurora is fearful, dependent, but trusting.

In 1945, with Te Karere as her guide, Anaera found a lake known as Rotokura, near Karioi, whose waters are believed to have healing powers. Others had looked for such waters, but had never reached them successfully. Now, members of the movement make annual pilgrimages in August, and there is always water available for the afflicted (an account of one of these missions is in chapter 5). Rotokura occupies an important place in the physical and spiritual landscapes of the Māramatanga, providing simultaneously a source of healing waters, a testament to Anaera's abilities when guided by her daughter, and an historical legacy obeyed and respected into the present.

Narratives of pilgrimages and missions are seldom self-contained. Instead, they reach out for links to other events, other times, and in so doing blur rigid distinctions, emphasizing connection rather than disjunction. Despite the very real, very difficult task of training a new generation in responsibility and knowledge, such narratives suggest a process that flows through time, blurring discrete lifetimes, transforming them into larger group concerns.

The Death of Riripeti

After the death of Te Karere, Anaera and Ruka had other children stay at their home, but they were always careful to maintain that they were not "adopting" these children nor attempting to bring them up in any formal sense. Their misfortune was not to be taken lightly. One of the children that Anaera and Ruka raised was Riripeti, the fifth child and third daughter of Rena[31] and Keru. Affinal ties (ties by marriage) linked the Gray and Ruka families, and Keru was Anaera's brother (see appendix 1, diagrams 1 and 4).

Riripeti was a lively child who especially enjoyed action songs. It is not surprising that she was taken into their households by both Aurora and Anaera. Nevertheless, in 1945, Riripeti died at the age of twelve. Her death shocked everyone, including all her young siblings and cousins, who had practiced action songs with her. On the last night of her tangi, her costume, her *piupiu* and *tāniko* top, were laid out and action songs were performed in her honor. And Mount Ruapehu erupted.

As the tangi went on, strange things happened. Flowers were rearranged, candles flickered out and re-ignited themselves, all in the apparent absence of human intercession. For many, like Riripeti's sister Hoana, these events merely reaffirmed their belief. When questioned forty years later, Hoana replied that she found them "lovely, lovely." She explained that Riripeti had kept warm for days, her cheeks remained rosy: "She was never ever painted up. She never ever looked dead." Hoana was quite sure that these events were more acceptable to the priest who presided over them, because, after all, "he was Irish." Anaera and Aurora were both stricken by guilt and stunned with grief. I asked Hoana, "How did Anaera take Riripeti's death?" Her answer was short: "She didn't." And indeed, Anaera died three years later at the age of forty-nine.

Anaera and the Challenge of Leadership

The followers of the Māramatanga have always felt a tension between their desire to preserve tradition and their perception of themselves as innovators.[32]

Their missions and pilgrimages were all designed to transform the landscape, and almost always to benefit future generations. Since the days of Anaera, participation in the Māramatanga has mandated an ability to consider both the past and the future.

In the brief hiatus between two transformative world conflagrations, issues of cultural continuity and integrity loomed large for the Mareikura family. Their travels to other marae, their involvement with Māori leaders, the waiata and pātere that exhort and persuade, all attest to the instability of the times. In the Māramatanga, hours, days, and even months of debate were held on marae to air disagreements and to search for consensus, however elusive.

Significantly, this process took place as waiata, pātere, and whaikōrero were being written down. As the critical words of Te Karere and other wairua became part of a common corpus of knowledge, the apparent flexibility of an oral culture gave way to the more rigid forms of written records. But an oral culture requires precision as a means of quality control, to sustain consistency over time. Songs were memorized with little or no variation, as whakapapa chanted to the *poi* continues to be memorized in the present. Most of the older members of the Māramatanga have clear memories of reciting waiata for hours, returning to the beginning whenever errors occurred. Mistakes were made when songs were committed to paper.[33] Indeed, for precisely this reason, in the early days of the Māramatanga, the elders insisted that only certain appointed scribes be permitted to write. Nevertheless, a notebook of songs that spans decades becomes, regardless of the intent of its compiler, a means of documenting history, of providing written records that can challenge or augment European accounts of Māori narratives.

Oral narratives appear to be more fluid. Writing may preserve them, but such narratives are seen as one perspective and understood to be frozen in time. Written renditions are not, at least in the present, granted extraordinary authority. In fact, the shifts that accompany oral renderings are considered not only inevitable, but valuable. For the most part, the relating of events to an audience in a meeting-house continues to be the most effective means of cultural transmission. The life and fluidity of such narrative transmission allows, indeed accepts, adaptivity to new social milieus, new exigencies, and new narrators (see Binney 1987: 16, 27–28). Rā are important occasions when the past and the present are subject to renewed scrutiny. The enduring legacy of Anaera's work was to determine the manner in which such discussions would unfold and the ways in which knowledge would be distributed and implemented.

Despite her reluctance, Anaera was a very effective leader, producing songs, leading missions, curing illnesses, and in time organizing the annual team preparation for the Hui Aranga (Catholic Māori culture festival held at Easter). For the most part, she was asleep at the time of her greatest spiritual activity.

Her contemporaries and those in the next generation have clear memories of her vagueness and of her unwillingness to assert or distinguish herself.[34] She followed her father both in taking over his work and in his personal style of humility and reverence.

In the mid-1940s, Anaera fasted for seven days and seven nights. She did this to open the channels for the wairua to contact everyone in the Māramatanga, so that everyone would be able to take their share of the work—its glory and its responsibility. This was a major transition. The movement now had three primary annual commemorations: July 27 (Mere Rikiriki's rā), which is now celebrated at Kuratahi; November 9 (Te Karere's return), at Raketapauma; and February 28 (Anaera's fast), at Ohakune. Other rā have come into being, and some have faded, but these three remain the foundations of the spiritual calendar.

When Anaera opened the channels to all, she caused others to bring personal experiences—revelation through wairua, dreams, and songs that took on individual meanings—to their understanding of the Māramatanga. Such a deep, individual involvement is consonant with a Māori rendering of time and place. There is a profound, often staunchly held belief that only the participant may tell his or her story. The authority to relate an event, even one known by most members of the community, belongs solely to the principal. For knowledge is a taonga that confers power. It may never be treated lightly. But there were now multiple histories to be disentangled at rā, different perspectives that could now all claim legitimacy. While this may be true of other movements in New Zealand, the Māramatanga is unique in encouraging a multiplicity of attitudes, a diversity in points of view, which may make consensus difficult to achieve, but almost always ensures a thorough airing of issues.

With the channels opened, the question of leadership seemed to be settled: there was to be none. Instead, salvation and spiritual illumination were now seen as an individual responsibility. Waiata from the period show the wairua constantly exhorting the people to be foundations, to take on the work, to go forward in their quest for spiritual enlightenment. The result was a tension in the relationships between individuals and the group. All acts had consequences for the well-being of the group, but each member was to carry his or her own burden. More importantly, Anaera's actions illuminated, perhaps unwittingly, issues involving differential knowledge and expertise. Perhaps knowledge was now to be distributed; but knowledge is never distributed evenly, and in any society there is a tight connection between knowledge and power. Experts, who "know more because they work harder at knowing more" (Keesing 1982: 161), have perspectives on the total system that are both different from, and more complete than, others. So it is in the Māramatanga. All the kaimahi since Anaera —Ruka, Pauro, and Hoana—have dedicated their lives to movement goals.

Anaera was an unwilling leader. But there can be no doubt, even allowing for the assistance and talents of her husband and brother, both of whom became kaimahi in succession after her death, that she was possessed of formidable abilities. She simply knew more than the others did. So even her most ardent demurrals could not keep her from wielding the power annealed in that knowledge. Her fast was an attempt to widen the circle of those with specialized information, to increase the commitment and involvement of individual members, to diffuse power by spreading knowledge. Knowledge had always been the preserve of elders, of leaders trained over long periods of time and very specifically for the responsibility they would bear. They were, inevitably, few. Anaera, her husband Ruka, and her father Mareikura attempted to change that.

Anaera's fast eliminated differential access to knowledge. But there was no way to mandate uniformity of understanding or of effort in seeking it. Indeed, despite an egalitarian ideology, there has been no way to abolish differences in sensitivity, curiosity, and fidelity to the movement and its history. Anaera's fast did, however, increase the sense of responsibility and participation of members who were not, and who never would be, kaimahi. The open distribution of access emphasized the importance of each individual's contribution to the maintenance of the whole. Cooking and cleaning, as well as writing, waiata, and whaikōrero, were all seen as furthering the work.

Leadership of the Māramatanga is never fully acknowledged as such. But there are clear patterns of deference, despite demurrals, to those who command language and the understanding of the histories and symbols implicated in contemporary events. Those individuals who are knowledgeable about the movement's past, who either participated in missions or know the stories that have been passed down, and can interpret the symbols on flags that fly on crucial occasions, inevitably have a worldview that differs from those who, however passionate in their belief, cannot command the body of knowledge that comprises the Māramatanga. These few bear a heavy burden, a burden that Anaera recognized.

From the time of Anaera's fast—that is, for the last five to six decades—the ideology of the Māramatanga has suggested that there are no leaders. Yet it is the vision of the kaimahi that has sustained the Māramatanga and that has engaged the membership in action that is seen as significant and meaningful. For it is the leaders who see beyond individual needs, beyond even the requirements of the membership as an aggregate, to the more pressing political and social problems that have confronted Māori. In this, as well as in the specific symbols and beliefs of the movement, ngā kaimahi have remained faithful to the nineteenth- and twentieth-century tradition of prophecy.

Hine Ataarangi

Hine Ataarangi was born in Levin in 1912, a grandniece of Weuweu.[1] Her ancestry linked her to Muaūpoko and Whanganui, although she was unaware of the latter ties until after her marriage in 1930. From the time of her marriage, she became deeply embedded in the Māramatanga community. Although her focus was on her family, her children and her grandchildren, in later life she also filled her role as a kuia, an older woman who commands respect for her knowledge. In all her adult life, she had no doubt about the importance of the prophet Mareikura's gifts. She was loyal to his memory, to his work, and to the community that nurtured both. Her ability to remember songs, to carry the pitch and lead a group was immensely impressive, even at eighty.

I first met Hine in 1972, when she was sixty years old. At the time, I thought she was overshadowed by her husband Pauro, whose quiet wisdom and astounding oratorical abilities could eclipse almost anyone. Despite their banter, however, she was mindfully observant of what he was doing, frequently interjecting, thus insinuating herself into many activities and narratives. She listened closely and observed carefully. As a result she, more than anybody else, was able to relate events that spanned close to eighty years. Her familiarity with significant times, places, personalities, and songs gave her a special place in the movement right up until her death in 1996. She did not control the esoterica known by her husband and subsequently Hoana, but knowledge of so many critical events allowed her to be an especially important bearer of the movement's history.

Hine died in Hastings. After the death of her husband in 1985, she had lived in the kaumātua flats on the Maungārongo marae, taken care of by her daughter and those of her many grandchildren who reside, at least some of the time, in Ohakune. But shortly before her death she had moved back to Hastings to escape the cold and damp of the Ohakune winter. She had outlived others of her generation by several years.[2] And from 1946 on, she had to preside too many times over the tangi of members of the generation below hers. She carried her solitary position well, relying on the richness of kin ties that had always sustained her.

I knew Hine for more than twenty years; over that time, we had dozens, perhaps hundreds, of conversations.³ These ranged easily over contemporary gossip, through to the early days of the movement and her marriage, her youth, her young adulthood, and her thoughts about current events. Her opinions were never far from the surface and she would readily supply background information. Through the years I came to expect accuracy and constancy in her accounts. She was so often gay, so ready with a laugh, or a self-deprecating giggle, that it would be all too easy to underestimate her, to belittle what she knew. Her demeanor contrasted with that of the more formidable kaimahi around her—her sisters-in-law, Anaera and Aurora, her husband Pauro, and her niece Hoana—and might have placed her, at first, in the shade. The complexities of the man she married, the sheer force of his presence, and the demands of domesticity may have, for a while, kept her in the background, and her affinal status relegated her to a space slightly off center-stage. But she had a way of inching over, of commanding the attention she richly deserved.

Hine clearly enjoyed telling her life story. In the process, she laughed, cried, and sang songs. Through hours of taping, she would close her eyes in memory and I could see that she had conjured up a tableau of decades before. In the course of her narratives, her young self, her young husband, or her children as babies re-entered her life—for a time coming into and sharing the present.

Hine's ability to adapt, to fit in, suited her well to a family with many strong personalities. But her cardinal virtue, from an outsider's perspective, was that intuitively she did what she must; propriety always took precedence over personal desires. Overcome by grief at the loss of her only son in 1972, she still stood up and chanted and danced at the end of the tangi. In the course of her life within the Mareikura family, she learned and mastered etiquette. At first frightened and awed by the Māramatanga, she grew with the movement, and like most of the members was transformed in the process.

Early Life

Hine first met Pauro when she and some of her cousins were performing with a travelling concert party. Aurora had already married Tika, but Hine was shy and unknown to many of the Mareikura family. When introduced to the young men of the area, she went so far as to give a false name. Sixty years later she found this funny, but she was also embarrassed at her seventeen-year-old self. In 1930, the young men of the area, including Pauro, worked for Pēpene Ruka on his farm at Raketapauma, digging potatoes. She was to learn later that as she and her cousin Ani performed, they were watched intently by Pauro and his friend Taumata. Their repertoire included action songs, but Hine and

Ani also performed the Charleston and the long poi. Ani did a shimmy and a hula as well. The two were great favorites with the audience, especially with the young men, who arranged a dance after the show.

Hine was reluctant to accompany the waiting young men, fearing that they might think her coterie "fast," and was also embarrassed because she would have to tell her real name. She dallied in the changing-room. But she could not put it off indefinitely; she went, danced, and had supper. She and Ani then repaired to their tent, giggling and going over the events of the night. As they did so, Taumata sneaked into the tent, terrifying both Ani and Hine. Taumata intended to be neither sinister nor menacing. In fact, the incident was meant to be romantic, and became even more so for Hine when she learned that Pauro, whom she called "Dad" throughout these hours of taping, had expressed a desire to see her. Standing on her dignity, she said, "If he wants to see me, he knows where I am." Taumata then went out and whistled for Pauro. In the morning, Hine announced that the boys were not to talk to them, that nobody should be aware that they knew one another. She was fearful of the attention that would fall on a courting couple. They went to a sports gala at Rangataua, an agricultural area adjacent to Ohakune, and Pauro excelled, winning her a big box of chocolates for her upcoming eighteenth birthday.

Their courtship was only a few weeks old when Aurora's sister died. The family returned from Ohakune to Levin for the tangi, where Taumata successfully sought permission to marry Ani. Hine and Pauro too wanted to get married, but her brother, who stood in the place of her father who had died years earlier, resisted the match. He was adamant that she not marry until she was twenty-one.

Hine looked for support elsewhere. She had been engaged to a Pākehā youth —an engagement that seemed not to have been broken while she and Pauro courted. Her family was not entirely comfortable with this state of affairs. But her grandmother argued that a match with Pauro, a Māori, was preferable.[4] Moreover, Hine confessed her love for Pauro to her mother's brother. In time, sufficient forces were joined to overcome her brother's resistance. She hastily packed her bags, jumped into a taxi, and took the train to Ohakune and her new life.

Pauro was waiting for her. But he had other plans had she failed to come. She told me that he was going to go to Pearl Harbor had she not agreed to marry him.[5] Such drastic measures were not necessary: 'Then I arrived with my swag. Golly me, and he was so glad.'

They moved into an area of the whare puni reserved for young married couples, an area already occupied by Ani and Taumata. They arrived to find their bed made up. But when they got in, they discovered that their mates had added something—in this case, shearing gear and thistle. The wedding bed was rearranged and the married life of Hine and Pauro began.

As was customary, newly married couples stayed among the elders for several weeks. Within a week of their arrival at Maungārongo, Ani and Taumata left for Kuratahi. Hine was quite happy to remain. When Anaera returned to Kuratahi as well, the tent the older woman had occupied was given over to the newlyweds. Over sixty years later, and after Pauro had been dead for six years, Hine commented: "Oh, talk about fun. That's how Dad and I got together. We got married after and I never regret the day I married Dad. He's been a wonderful husband and father to my children." From the time they met, theirs was a partnership, with his intelligence, patience, and humility at times countered, and at other times complemented, by her outspokenness, her impetuousness, and her strong convictions. They operated as a unit. Hine took it upon herself, from her earliest days in Ohakune, to learn and to accommodate to the ways of her formidable in-laws.

Married Life at Maungārongo

Hine was completely taken with life at Maungārongo and with her new family. She fell in love with their linguistic virtuosity, from which she felt excluded, and with the poipoi. Ashamed of her ignorance, she asked Pauro to intercede. Her father-in-law, Mareikura, decided that she should attend the whare wānanga soon to be held there. In addition, the tohunga, the ritual leader in charge of instruction, was her uncle and worked with the prophet.[6] She explained the conversation that took place between the prophet and the tohunga:

> He said to Dad, it's all right. You tell her when I talk to her she got to say yes to everything. Whether I understood what he said to me, I got to say yes, "ana ana" ["yes, yes"] to everything. So we went in and Dad said the karakia and then he put his, he made me kneel in front of him and he kept his hand on my head and away he went [an expression to indicate that he took off verbally]. And all I said was "ana ana." About ten minutes after, he said to Dad "finish." He said now finish off with a prayer. So Dad did . . .[7]

Hine soon commanded a range of skills; she was able to sing, to pūkana (make a stylized gesture designed to highlight women's participation in waiata), and to understand the Māori language. She rapidly assumed a leading role in waiata. Although her first child was born soon thereafter, she was sufficiently recovered to perform at the opening of a meeting-house. And yet, sixty years later she still evinced surprise at the facility with which she had been able to perform, commenting, "I knew all those things as if I knew it before. It just came to me." With the death of Te Karere, waiata would gain more importance, and Hine would find herself well situated in this changing world. Her husband

Pauro's abilities were also apparent in these very early years. Although it was decades before he would be recognized as a kaimahi, he stood as mediator between the knowledge of the old and his young and unschooled wife.

Mareikura, learned and enlightened, took charge of the delivery of new babies. For this purpose, a special house was built by the Mangawhero River, which runs along the bottom of the marae. With the sole exception of her youngest child, a son, all her children were born with her father-in-law in attendance. He would massage her, rub her back, and her children would be born.

> That's the Maori way . . . and it was simple and easy and . . . before you knew, you had your baby. I had all my babies till I had my son and I had to go to the hospital. By then Dad [Mareikura] finished, he finished doing that sort of thing. He was stopped by the wairua. No more confinement. We had to go, that's when I went to the hospital to have my son Peter.

One of her deliveries was problematic, but was saved by the intervention of divine forces and her father-in-law. Hine explained that she was so close to delivery that:

> They had to carry me 'cause I would have had her if I had to walk. I couldn't get to the place. I knew I could feel her coming. 'Course my mother-in-law had everything set for me. I just got there; I just knocked them [the boxes?] and out came the baby. Aw golly, I had forgotten that.[8]

Her problem however arose when the afterbirth would not come out. This was a problem that Mareikura resolved:

> That's when he knew I must have done something wrong. He said to me 'Did you cut your hair?' I said "yes" . . . he always said to us "Never cut your hair when you're having a baby 'cause the afterbirth . . . is affected." So he just came up and he just pulled my hair here like this and twist it and out came the afterbirth. He said to me "Never ever do that. I told you before never ever cut your hair."

Hine knew better in the future. But this example validated her father-in-law's abilities and provided proof that the wairua were acting on behalf of the family, for she completes this story with "Aw, I love it. I love the way they've been good to us." (These spontaneous expostulations praising the wairua were not at all uncommon, as members would recall their own personal experiences and the assistance that they had received.) By the time her later children arrived, Hine echoed the convictions of her elders. This family had a guardian and was in contact with the old ways, with te ao tāwhito. This was a source of succour, protection, and reassurance.

In a similar vein, when her daughter Gabrielle was an infant, she became very sick. The baby's body went rigid and she failed to respond to anything. Anaera looked in on the young family and pointedly asked Hine where she had placed her genealogy book. Hine discovered that she had placed it in a cupboard near food, something that is ritually forbidden. In this case, the transgression caused serious consequences. But because Anaera, with the help of Te Karere, had located the source of the problem, the difficulty was resolved. They had a karakia, a whakamoemiti, and the baby started to cry. Hine learned then that the wairua, the spirits of the ancestors were good, but care need to be taken lest they be offended.

Often when her children were young and sick, Hine would pray. In her dreams, the wairua revealed to her the cause of the children's illnesses. In later life, she was convinced that such advice had hastened their recovery.

Hine was matter-of-fact and casual in her narratives. But at Ohakune she had, in fact, entered a world that was radically different from that in which she had grown up in Levin. She herself noted that one of the differences lay in the fact that there were few houses (five at the time of her marriage) and two meeting-houses.[9] But beyond the physical differences, there was a different quality to the relationships that she had with her natal family and those with her husband's extended family at Maungārongo.

The dimensions of that world, even before the advent of Te Karere, were far more in keeping with Māori conventions. Karakia were said to protect, to guide, and to promote proper behavior. Mutuality replaced any notion of individualism and was seen very clearly in the behavior of Mareikura, who nurtured and succoured strangers, as well as relatives in need. Theirs was a cosmos imbued with divine forces, whose strength came from indigenous as well as introduced sources. That these were conflated added to the coherence of Hine's new world. This world demanded knowledge of Māori language, of its categories, subtleties, and hierarchies. Hine learned songs, chants, and karakia, and explored this novel universe. But within five years of her marriage, Te Karere died. She and her family now had a new source of guidance and protection, and perhaps more importantly, a new view of themselves as a select group.

Mareikura's kindness extended to her and to her young family and, in many ways, exceeded the expectations a new daughter-in-law would have of her father-in-law. Te Huinga, however, was not an easy mother-in-law. Although a woman of great beauty, dignity, and grace, she had favorites among her children and grandchildren. She showed this clearly, both by indulging those she had selected, and by subtly yet undeniably slighting those not chosen. Such disregard ranged from a trivial, unequal distribution of candies to an overt display of partisanship. Te Huinga's favorites were those children whom she herself had brought up at least part of the time. She was somewhat more distant from those, such as Keru, Pauro, Tekawaupango, and Tika, who had been brought up by other people, in other places. Pauro—brought up in Rānana— was not among the preferred.

When one of Pauro and Hine's daughters was very young, she became quite ill. Money was hard to come by and there was not enough to pay for both a doctor and medicine. Visiting his son and family, Mareikura promised assistance so that the sick child would receive the needed attention. He instructed Te Huinga to give the family money. She did not. Whatever the reason was never told, whether Te Huinga forgot or had some reason of her own for not assisting the family; Hine saw the slight as both personal and deliberate. In Hine's recounting of this incident, Mareikura found out about the child's neglect through the wairua. He was, according to her, furious with his wife.

Although Hine was convinced that her child was on the brink of death, Pauro would not ask his parents for money. While this demonstrates Pauro's pride, it also indicates that relations, at least between him and his mother, could not have been easy.[10] Hine went on, that wet afternoon approximately sixty years later, to say that the young couple would have preferred to starve rather than ask his parents for money. She would write letters secretly to her mother and received some assistance that she attempted to keep secret from Pauro. She wanted to make sure that he was not shamed.

Hine was close to her cousins and to her sisters-in-law, but especially to Aurora, who was both. Aurora was a favorite of Anaera and Ruka's and was gifted in her own right. She therefore occupied a central place in the constellation of the movement's luminaries. She also was touched by tragedy. Unable to have children, she looked after other people's children. Both she and Anaera had looked after Riripeti, and each of them endured the inevitable anguish and guilt when the young girl died. Years later, when Aurora took over the care of a kinsperson's child, she was careful to explain that she was not adopting him, only bringing him up. In time, she called him son and theirs was a close, special relationship. But she was very cautious.

Hine was somewhat overshadowed by Aurora, who with imposing gifts and the affection of her in-laws was a general favorite. But this was temporary. Hine had children, generating domestic ties that bound her to the community in a way that a childless woman could not replicate. Thus, if her position was secondary to her more illustrious cousin and sister-in-law, she nevertheless found solace in a domesticity that eluded Aurora. Indeed, in all of our conversations, and in all the times I saw the two women together, there was never anything other than pride in one another's accomplishments, and no jealousy or envy.

During the time that his family lived at Maungārongo, Pauro was cursed by a woman whom he had inadvertently offended. The young man fell ill, leaving his wife at a loss. Mareikura diagnosed his son's malady, blessed him, and he recovered. Often a misfortune was treated by "turning it around," that is, sending it back upon its source. Indeed, once Pauro had recovered, he was urged to follow that path. But he and his father, neither of whom was vindictive, and both of whom were committed to making the world better and safer, eschewed such practices. As in so many other instances, both men took the high road, arguing that to attempt to hurt the woman would make them no better than she had been. Theirs was God's work, and they would not be tempted to violate their principles, no matter how compelling the reason.

Hine saw much of her father-in-law's kindness and wisdom in her husband, Pauro. In both she saw gentleness and a willingness to help others that set them apart. She had clear memories, dating back to the years at Maungārongo, of Mareikura's hospitality to those who were without shelter. Hine and Aurora would make up beds in the meeting-house while their father-in-law looked for clothing, often for as many as six people at a time. He reminded his sceptical children that they could easily be in the place of those less fortunate. If, in the course of their stay, some of these indigent found jobs, Mareikura would urge them to save their money rather than try to pay him back. But, more often than not, the beneficiaries would disappear, taking with them blankets and clothing belonging to the marae. Mareikura would shrug philosophically, maintaining that helping them was more important than how these interludes resolved themselves. With such high-minded behaviour as an exemplar, pettiness and suspicion, if not eradicated, were removed to the background.

Mareikura exhorted his sons not to hit their wives, threatening to return the women to their people should the young men feel compelled to strike them. Hine claims that Pauro never did strike her, although probably not all his brothers obeyed their father's words. Interestingly, Hine reported that her mother would tell Pauro to "give Hine a hiding." And she confessed with a giggle that she deserved it at times for being cheeky and too smart. This is the one area in which domestic relations were seen as inviolable, as not accessible to the involvement of outsiders. If people were aware of brutality, they looked the other way. It is interesting that Mareikura attempted to prevent this by making strong statements at the outset of his sons' marriages.

Hine spent the first two decades of her marriage committed to the family and its activities. Seven pregnancies in less than a decade and the care of young children occupied her energies. She was not present when Te Karere died and returned. She and Pauro had taken Lena for a time at the girl's request. Hine is convinced that Lena knew she was going to die and therefore spent time with all her relatives, especially her young cousins. Soon after they returned her to her parents, they learned that she was in the hospital. All who could attended the tangi; most had returned home before they learned that she had come back. Hine knows the details of that night, the vividness of her description fifty years later suggesting that she listened intently as the participants told their stories of that night in Kuratahi. She could tell of Kataraina's importance, of Weuweu's insistence, and of Anaera's initial reluctance and final acceptance of her responsibility. According to Hine, Lena adored her grandfather and chose, once she was dead, to "put him on a pedestal," to turn her revelations to her mother. Anaera accepted that responsibility and handled it, perhaps because of her diffidence and hesitation, with a diplomatic fairness that undercut hostility or misunderstandings. In Hine's telling, knowledge was jealously guarded and protected. Thus when Anaera fasted and opened the channels, she defused a highly charged set of circumstances. Thenceforth there could be no spiritual domination by any one individual. In theory at least, all would be equal.

Hine prepared the senior Mareikuras for their visit to the Māori king's tangi at Tūrangawaewae, near Ngaruawahia. (This must have been in October of 1933 when King Te Rata died.)[11] If Hine herself did not go, she was nevertheless able to report on the results of the visit more than half a century later. Mareikura with his openness and honesty was pleased to be welcomed by Te Rata, then the Māori king (clearly Hine is misspeaking: it would have to have been King Korokī). He stayed some five months before returning to Ohakune. However, the women surrounding the prophet watched him to ensure that he didn't reveal movement secrets and that he returned to Ohakune with his knowledge intact.[12]

Hine did not go up the mountain in 1942 with Pauro, Aurora, Hemi, and Anaera. But again, she was familiar with events. She could relate this narrative as if through Pauro's eyes. In her telling, Pauro was frustrated at not seeing the maid and at Hemi's illness. But at the same time he realized that Te Karere had been there to guide them, and knew that further work remained to be done. Waiting at home, Hine's concern was for her husband and his well-being. I have heard these stories from Pauro and from Aurora. Listening to Hine, there is little difference.

Hine was the ideal wife for the son of Mareikura who, by dint of ability and perception, would rise to special prominence. She carried considerable responsibility early in her marriage, and it would only increase over time. She learned Māori language and etiquette. By the time of Lena's death, Hine was a proficient and competent participant in the religious activities taking place.

Although she was disinclined, by temperament, toward passivity, and despite her strong opinions, she managed never to overshadow her husband. Her inclinations early in their life together may have lain in other directions, but she soon learned to follow her husband's lead. She took her place early and definitively by his side, chanting waiata, leading the women, and nudging her husband whenever she perceived any laxity, justified or not. When Pauro was the orator of the family and a composer (with the help of the wairua) of waiata, Hine's gift for singing offered support for his words and accompaniment to his songs. Her prodigious memory, her musical instincts, and her understanding of waiata, especially as these became one of the preferred media of communication between Te Karere and her family, were sure assets to a man in Pauro's position.[13]

During the period when Te Karere was engaged in very intensive teaching, Hine spent hours in the meeting-house, singing, seeking assistance, and listening. She sang all the songs that Anaera was given and that Pauro and Ruka wrote down. She was involved in their exegesis, the illumination that such songs shed on their lives. Fifty years later, she could still remember the context in which individual songs were revealed and performed.

While Anaera was still alive, the members of the Māramatanga formed the Maungārongo culture club and competed so successfully in the Hui Aranga that they were forced to retire. Not coincidentally, the songs that they used were those that had been revealed by Te Karere. Pauro and Peehi dominated the whaikōrero, while the younger people of the day—Hoana, both the men called Rihari, Raana, Monica, Hui, Pin, and Tūmanako—were all members of the younger singing groups. Several years after their retirement they re-entered the competition, calling themselves the Ruapehu culture club.

By the end of the 1940s, Te Huinga, Mareikura, and Anaera had all died. Aurora had moved to Levin to continue the work in her home town. Pauro was suffering from asthma, so he and Hine had moved their family to the more welcoming climate of Hawke's Bay. What had been intended as a short stay turned out to be thirty-five years. It was only after Pauro's death that Hine returned to live at Maungārongo. However, the family made many trips every year, to rā, on missions, to attend tangi, and to visit. Most of their children stayed in the East Coast area. In the end, they had significant family in two places.

While she and Pauro were in Hastings, Hine found her life full with what she had learned as a young woman at Maungārongo. She and Pauro were in charge of the Hawke's Bay culture club—Waipatu—that competed in the Hui Aranga.[14] Pauro's oratorical abilities and Hine's singing capabilities made them an important couple, both within Māoridom and for the Catholic Church.

Sometime in the 1950s, Aurora got very sick. Her head was aching so that she could no longer stand up. Doctors offered no relief. Iwa took her up to Clevedon, a rural area just outside Auckland, to nurse her. Hine went along too. Weeks went by with no improvement. Hine slept with her cousin, to alleviate her pain and suffering. One night, she sat up in bed and looked at the face of the sleeping invalid. In place of the young Aurora's face, Hine saw the face of an old lady. She became frightened and moved to the couch. In the morning she told a clearly sceptical Iwa. However, when Iwa looked, she saw the same thing. Finally, over the objections of her husband, Iwa contacted a renowned North Island spiritual healer. The woman knew, even before the telephone rang, that a sick person was going to call whose problem involved a greenstone. Iwa and Hine arrived carrying the ailing Aurora. Holy water was sprinkled over her and then the cause of her problem was revealed. Aurora's brother had wrongfully taken a piece of greenstone from the South Island to lay on their mother's tombstone. Afraid that the taonga would be stolen, he told Aurora to have it cut up and distributed amongst the family. She had not got around to it, and at this time she was using the greenstone as a doorstop, often putting it on the tea trolley with food.[15] This violated the guardian of the greenstone, who squeezed the unwary Aurora's head. The healer said a prayer and exhorted her to remove the greenstone, to be certain to place it away from food. They telephoned Tika, Aurora's husband, who immediately put the greenstone into a bag and removed it to the shed. Iwa and Hine said karakia for three days at seven o'clock in the mornings and evenings. By the third day, when Hine had a telephone call requesting that she come back to Hawke's Bay to attend to an ailing Pauro, Aurora was well enough to accompany her. Once diagnosed properly, Aurora's condition could be cured quickly.

It is significant that Aurora's illness, its determination and treatment, were the responsibility of women. While gifted men could just as easily have accomplished the task, its successful execution was, in this case, in the hands of women. For the individuals involved in the Māramatanga, there was no conflict surrounding the competence, abilities, and legitimacy of women. Their individual and group experience clearly pointed to their equality, if not their supremacy.

When the women arrived in Hastings, they discovered that Pauro was quite ill with hepatitis. The doctor had prescribed medication, but Hine knew better; she treated him with a parsley infusion (parsley is a known diuretic). In several days, he had recovered completely. The doctor congratulated himself, never realizing that his prescribed medication had been flushed into the Hastings sewer system. Their faith was in their own, not the Pākehā doctor's, medicines.

Hine and Pauro's move to the East Coast effected only a minor geographical separation, and not a temporal break. They were always tied to Ohakune, where their family was, and to Levin, where Aurora and Tika took up residence and where Hine had been born. They regularly attended all the ceremonial occasions that marked the years. Hine and Pauro, and their family, remained intimate and accessible during all those years when they did not live in Ohakune.

Conclusion

Hine's life within the movement was marked by her unswerving loyalty to family and to the beliefs whose development she witnessed. She fell in love with her husband and, soon after her marriage, with his family. Eagerly, she embraced their ways of doing things, happy to learn the Māori language, to immerse herself in the whare wānanga, and to put her remarkable vocal talents to work in the service of the movement. The discovery that she was in fact a relation further cemented the partnership between husband and wife.

She was fortunate to be present when the work of the Māramatanga redefined the cultural and historical landscape. Decades later, perhaps, it no longer matters if she did not participate directly, if she was absent when Te Karere returned, if she was otherwise occupied when her husband, and his brothers and sisters, attempted the mountain. She knew the stories and she became recognized as one of the holders of these narratives. Deferring to her husband or to other participants would not have been difficult. Although by nature strong-willed, she was nevertheless always diffident and self-effacing.

Hine viewed the individuals around her with astonishingly clear eyes. Her mother-in-law's favoritism, while hurtful and disconcerting, did not detract from her love for the older woman. In her father-in-law she saw the traits that distinguished her husband. Recounting the stories of her children's birth and infancy, she was awed and grateful, fully convinced that both she and her children survived because of the intervention of the wairua. She recounted with shining eyes those days in the 1940s when Te Karere returned, when her husband and brother-in-law wrote down Anaera's somnolent messages, and when they would all practice performing the waiata and pātere. In her mind, she conjured up those early days, seeing her young husband and her entire family in their younger incarnations. She was fiercely proud of what her family has accomplished.

Hers was not a life without losses. She lost two of her offspring in their childhood, and her only son, Peter, died when he was an adult. In a context where families are very close, she watched as those around her also lost their children. She was well aware of the misfortune of infertility that had befallen men and women; Anaera and Ruka, Aurora and Tika, and Kataraina all bore the heaviness of such a legacy.[16] Hine held firmly to the notion that such women were selected to do God's work, to be distinguished within the movement. But she had no illusions about the pain they endured. She especially remembered when Riripeti died, an event marked not only by extraordinary distress but by the mountain's apparent agreement, shown by its eruption. In the 1990s, in her eighties, she lost two more children, and even some of her grandchildren died before her. Throughout it all— through the tears, the chants, the nights spent in tents with the deceased—she held her head up. It was not that she did not feel the misery, but rather that she understood its context.

Her family and her commitment to the Māramatanga gave Hine's life its meaning. She was embedded in both a system of relationships and a wider web of intention and significance. Leading chants at tangi or waiata on pilgrimages, or merely standing for old time's sake with her family as they performed songs, she took comfort in knowing that hers was a generation that changed the world for Māori. She was modest and shy, yet she knew she had played her part.[17]

CHAPTER 4

Growth and the Emergence
of a New Generation

Introduction

In the aftermath of World War II, the Māramatanga shifted from a period of revelation and transformation to one of apparent quiescence. Many important people died in the late 1940s, while others left Maungārongo: Tika and Aurora for Levin, and Pauro and Hine for Hastings. The Māramatanga was redefined in new contexts. In Levin, Aurora, Tika, and Ritihira, Weuweu's widowed daughter, started a new marae with the help of Pēpene Ruka. In Hastings, Pauro and Hine raised their family and many grandchildren, creating a culture club that partic- ipated in the Hui Aranga. Pauro became an important and respected leader in Hawke's Bay. As a result, local culture, which was of an entirely different tribe, became heavily influenced by the traditions of both the Māramatanga and Whanganui.

The historical significance of Raketapauma, Kuratahi, and Maungārongo assured their continued importance. Even as the Māramatanga developed in other directions and in other places, the commemoration of times and events celebrated in the annual rā assured that these three marae would remain focal points for the movement, as they do to this day.

The 1950s served as a transition. By the 1960s, a new generation had emerged as leaders. They were young—many were in their thirties and (in the case of the women) still bearing children. They were tentative, but eager and well trained. The decade of the 1960s, in the Māramatanga as elsewhere, witnessed the changing responsibilities of two generations.

The emerging generation undertook another mission up Mount Ruapehu in December 1962. Recorded in at least two notebooks, those of Raana and Pinenga, this mission is also recounted in meeting-houses today. This dual dependence on written and oral accounts ensures transmission to the next generation, a concern that was to become explicit in the 1970s. Fidelity to Māori traditions of orality was sustained at the same time that Pākehā ideals of documentation were appropriated.

GROWTH AND THE EMERGENCE OF A NEW GENERATION ~ 87

In this chapter, we shall see the growth of the Hui Aranga at Maungārongo, the missions that Pēpene Ruka embarked on after his wife's death, the growth of a new marae in Levin under Ruka's auspices, the second mission to the mountain, and the emergence of the generation who were children when Te Karere died.

The Post-War Years

In the years immediately following World War II, there was a significant Māori migration to the cities of New Zealand (see Metge 1964; King 1983; Walker 1990). In 1929, only 9 percent of Māori resided in New Zealand's cities; by 1951, this had jumped to 19 percent, and by 1971, more than two thirds of Māori (68.2 percent) identified themselves as urban dwellers (Walker 1990; King 1981). Employment was the lure of urban areas, as jobs that had not been available in pre-war years opened up to Māori. However, these were largely unskilled jobs, low-paid and vulnerable to economic fluctuations.[1] But at the same time, earning a living in rural areas became more difficult (King 1983: 249).

Again Māori leaders saw the concerns of the Māori people in a national, rather than regional or tribal, light. For members of the Māramatanga, the reverse was the case: their concerns remained local, with the whānau. This is not to say that individuals in the movement were unsympathetic, but their interests were dominated by more immediate problems.

For example, in the late 1950s, when the people of Whanganui had been visited by a party from the East Coast, a tragic automobile accident ended the life of a high-ranking young woman. Everyone realized that, since she died on the river, Whanganui would be held responsible and the East Coast tribe would demand *utu* (vengeance). Te Karere pointed out where traps had been laid and which areas would not be safe for the necessary mission of tāpae. According to Hoana (interview 1987), all the people from the Whanganui River were involved, whether they were committed to the Māramatanga or not.[2] The mission was led by Pauro, Peehi, and Tika. With Te Karere's guidance, they said prayers at the places that were now dangerous, and the potency lying in wait was neutralized. For the members of the Māramatanga it was axiomatic that the young woman's death would be avenged and that Te Karere would be instrumental in revealing the location of dangers; these were not individuals who were being readily assimilated into European New Zealand.

Within the Māramatanga, leadership was deliberately diffused; Anaera's fast had assured that inspiration has remained a path that could be followed by many, in a variety of ways. Individuals such as Aurora, Emere, and Iwa were given songs; Pauro dominated whaikōrero, while Hine, with her ability to sing, was to become a veritable archive of the movement's melodies and lyrics. In the next generation, Hoana—bilingual, sensitive, and talented—moved to the forefront. But others were active as well. Raana, Pinenga, Tūmanako, Matiu, Lei, and both Riharis assumed active roles as the movement developed in the following decades. The movement's ideology encouraged group ascendancy, rather than personal monopoly. Indeed, this legacy followed the opening of the channels: all were required to participate.

Pēpene Ruka: A New Order

In the years after the war, there were many changes at Maungārongo, Kuratahi, and Raketapauma. Most dramatic were the deaths of many of the Māramatanga's key personnel: Merehapi died in 1943; Te Huinga in 1944; Riripeti in 1945; Mareikura in 1946; Anaera in 1948; Katarina in 1957. Of the foundational elders, only Pēpene Ruka survived the 1950s, dying in 1960.

Pēpene Ruka occupied a central position in the early years of the Mārama-tanga's development: as the father of Te Karere, he was one of the scribes, along with Pauro, of the messages received by the reluctant Anaera. With Anaera, he had brought up several children, although he was careful to qualify the nature of his relationship to them, since his role as a parent, both biological and adoptive, had too often ended tragically. Ruka was far more than an affine to the Mareikura family; he was the son of Merehapi and the brother of Katarina. And import-antly, he was the wealthiest individual in the movement. His family farm produced an income that made it possible for him to finance many of the movement's activities. Nobody has anything bad to say about him today; the word "lovely" keeps coming up in conversations describing him. However, the financial dependence of many of the others and his independence must have made for a somewhat uncomfortable situation. His position, both genealogical and finan-cial, granted him an authority that few could question, but which nevertheless must have caused tension.[3]

In the 1940s, after the succession of deaths that could only have brought deep personal distress, Ruka took refuge in the meeting-house, spending his days writing. Hoana suggested that he was shattered; he literally wrote himself back into the world of the living.[4] But as the 1940s ended, he became more active, using his resources to finance missions of wairua. Despite the ostensible equality of all members, Ruka clearly assumed the initiative. For example, he was responsible for the creation of Levin as a centre for the Māramatanga and its adherents. The tension between a movement straining for equality and yet made up of people with different abilities and interests was ameliorated by calling individuals such as Ruka kaimahi, while leaving open the possibility for others to contribute in their own ways.

A major concern for Ruka was the mauri,[5] the spiritual essence which accompanied each of the canoes to New Zealand. One of Ruka's whāngai (children brought up by him though he was not their biological parent), Pin, who had also been raised by Mareikura and was later to become a gifted healer, joined him in this concern. Together they toured the country, knowing, with the guidance of Te Karere, precisely where to search. In addition to the words of Te Karere there was a song, revealed to Anaera in 1943, foretelling the importance of specific canoes. Songs from early in the 1940s predate these missions. On Ruka and Pin's return, the mauri was deposited in Hato Ruka,[6] the church at Raketapauma. To the individuals committed to the movement, this was a demonstration that the spirits were guiding them, protecting them and offering them the benefit of their wisdom through a variety of communications. Ruka and Pin's mission provided a meaningful lesson for subsequent generations about what was important and significant in their world. The culmination of this mission will be seen in later years (see chapter 6), when the members of the movement made repeated pilgrimages to Waitangi.

In the 1950s, the centre of the Māramatanga was drifting away from Ohakune. Motivated by his need for a healthier climate, Pauro and his family had moved to Hastings, on the East Coast. Tika and Aurora had moved to Levin, motivated by Aurora's desire to return to her people. Maru, from a high ranking Te Arawa family, had married Weuweu's granddaughter Emere, and had taken her back to Maketū, so that he could assume the responsibility of tribal elder. Peehi, who had been living in Māhia, on the East Coast, returned to take up residence in Raketapauma. However, many of Mareikura's grandchildren continued to reside in Ohakune, forming the critical core of the next generation's leadership. These individuals—Hoana, both men called Rihari, Raana, Mana Motuhake, Ruka, Matiu, Nan, Lei, and Barney—were steadfastly committed to the promulgation of the Māramatanga's basic tenets. At Kuratahi, Tūmanako and his wife Pinenga, with a growing family and developing farm, continued to lend support to the activities of the movement.

In an attempt to re-unify the movement that by now had grown quite dispersed, Ruka placed names on four more boys, prefixing each with "pou," "foundation": Pou Peka Māramatanga, Pou Horahanga Pai, Pou Kaha, and Pou Mahara Nui.[7] These four names indicated the nature of the movement as it was perceived in the late 1940s: Māramatanga was a movement based on strength, thought, and distribution of responsibility, a movement whose knowledge would be accessible to all its members. They reflected both Ruka's inspiration and recognition that the movement had become geographically dispersed, but remained spiritually intact. In choosing four new names, Ruka was self-consciously emulating Mere Rikiriki's selection of names within the tradition of four apostles. Ruka therefore chose to emphasize the ties that bound the Māramatanga to the

prophetess of the Rangitīkei, to other Māori prophets, and indeed to the development of Christianity.

In the 1950s, Horowhenua (the district that includes Levin) became a focus
of movement interest. Moving to Levin was indicated in a song of Ritihira,
Weuweu's daughter, about a bird, Pipiwharauroa (signalling a welcome for
visitors onto a marae), calling on "the currents of Rangitīkei" (a reference to
Mere Rikiriki) to merge in Horowhenua. Under Ruka's leadership, a new marae
was built on the site of Weuweu's old homestead. The meeting-house was chris-
tened Huia Raukura, a name that has much significance, with meaning on many
levels. For one, it was inspired by a song that invokes Raukura as the guardian
angel of Horowhenua. The song, Ritihira's inspiration, follows in part:

My angel	Ko taku Raukura
Dear People	E nga iwi
From the depths of Horowhenua	No runga o Punahau
Come close my loved one	Nuku a e te tahu [tau]
To help us	No [kia] piri mai
To work for the Lord	E mahi ki a Ihowa
Now my people	No reira e te iwi
Be alert to the zenith moon	Taria ra
Lest it wane	Kei popo te marama
	Kei huri ke
Until the bird call	Taria a atu ra
Of the daybreak	Kei tangi mai
	Te manu o te atatu

Raukura—here explicitly identified as the angel of Horowhenua—means
feather or plume, and refers to the huia bird, who called the people together.[8]
But for the members of the Māramatanga, Raukura summons forth the category
of guardian angels, while *kura* signifies power in its many attributes.[9] The
natural imagery of the bird-call is therefore linked to crucial indications of effectiveness and intensity in the Māori universe. The name Raukura would have
been very important to Ruka who, in his search for the mauri, believed he had
the assistance of similar guardian angels, Amokura and Pikikura. These kura,
who represent pure spiritual essence, are important sources of guidance and
inspiration because they are believed to be closer to God.[10]

Raukura, the angel, is beseeched in verses one and two, verses in which the
composer pays homage and then seeks guidance ("come close"). The wairua
turns to the people (*"e te iwi"*) urging them to take heed of the opportunity that
has presented itself, metaphorically referred to as the zenith moon. The final

stanza presents a caution that the daybreak will bring an end to the moon's ascendance and thus metaphorically to the opportunity that has been presented. Larger, natural rhythms regulate their actions, so the members' request for spiritual guidance is made within the context of a universe whose workings are familiar and in which they can negotiate their way comfortably.

This song reaffirmed Pēpene Ruka's decision to build a meeting-house on the land surrounding Weuweu's original homestead. In no small measure, Ritihira's inspirations provided vindication for his conviction that the movement should expand to the western quarter, the home of Weuweu, Hine, Ani, and Aurora. The meeting-house, Huia Raukura, was opened and the new marae was inaugurated on March 18, 1954. To this day, March 18, continues to be celebrated at Kawiu marae: for on that day each year, Levin, the home of Weuweu, the latter-day home of Aurora and Tika, and the site of much of Pēpene Ruka's work, becomes a gathering-place for members now dispersed throughout Aotearoa.

The name of the meeting-house is also related to the work of Te Whiti at Parihaka. There was a building called Raukura at Parihaka, while Te Whiti's symbol, three feathers, was similarly referred to as a raukura.[11] Moreover, March 18 commemorates the day in 1870 when Te Whiti called for the restoration of confiscated Māori lands (Gadd 1966: 448; Scott 1975).[12] This date still carries symbolic importance at Parihaka. In this context, it is important to recall that Ritihira went to Parihaka as a young girl, and the work of Tohu cast a long shadow over her childhood and the young adulthood of Weuweu, who was from Taranaki.

For all—the members of the generation that built the house and their successors—the name Huia Raukura simultaneously embodies a celebration of the past, unity of the people, and an awareness of cultural riches. Encoded here is the moral dimension of the Māramatanga: the members are to continue to work toward transcendent ends. Names that are deliberately polysemic allow for multiple representations; they permit individual variants while embracing significant variety. It is precisely because so many meanings are evoked that the house and its name can continue to be important to so many individuals.

Several houses were built on the growing marae complex—one for Ritihira and her unmarried daughter Tui, and one for Tika and Aurora. The rapidity with which the Department of Māori Affairs responded to their requests was seen as spiritual sanction for the growth and development of the new marae.

As the marae evolved, names became important features, inscribing the tenets of the Māramatanga onto the landscape, in a manner similar to that seen at Maungārongo, Raketapauma, and Kuratahi. Tika received an inspiration and named his house Tomairangi, literally "dew" but understood as meaning "shower of blessing," an interpretation frequently given to rain which occurred as members of the Māramatanga were about to set out on an undertaking of importance. The marae's dining-room was named Takeretanga o Punahau,[13] the sacred centre of Horowhenua. Ruka also planted and named two trees on the marae itself; these were called "the weeping elms" in general, but were given the more gender-specific Tama Kōrero (men speak) and Hine Waiata (women sing). Referring to the division of labor that marks marae etiquette, these names imply that the members of the Māramatanga will want for neither words nor melody, and pay tribute to the words, spoken and sung, which have inspired the members of the movement. Speech and song, men and women, living and dead, are commemorated and honored, memorialized and transformed in the permanence of the trees that grace the ceremonial ground.

Pēpene Ruka died in 1960. He had led the Māramatanga for more than a decade. This role may have been reinforced by his genealogical position and augmented by his personal resources, but he was after all the father of Te Karere and the husband of Anaera.

Ruka's work notwithstanding, through the 1950s there was a general feeling of dispersal, as leadership and gifts appeared in different arenas, and as the centre appeared to shift away from the central North Island. Through this period, the members remained devout Catholics, attended mass, ensured a Catholic education for their offspring, and participated in the Hui Aranga. Furthermore, they also kept faith with the annual cycle of rā, in which the gift of the Māramatanga (July 27), Te Karere's return (November 9) and Anaera's fast to open the channels (February 28) were commemorated, recalled, and re-enacted. The dual nature of their religious life, involving the Māramatanga and the Catholic Church, constantly involved them. As staunch Catholics, they saw little in what Te Karere introduced to contradict or undermine the teachings of the church. But priests and missioners would, in subsequent years, find the two harder to reconcile.

The Catholic Church and the Māramatanga

Throughout the late 1940s and the 1950s, there was a close relationship between the clergy who ministered to the Māori population and the members of the Māramatanga. When Māori missioners made their rounds in the district, they were welcomed most heartily into the homes of individuals who were committed to the teachings of both the Catholic Church and Te Karere. Church retreats and missions formed as much a part of the members' lives as did the missions mandated by Te Karere and the spiritual concerns of the movement.

The members of the Māramatanga were instrumental in the establishment in 1946 of the Hui Aranga, the Feast of the Ascension, which over the next five decades came to be the major focus of Easter celebrations for Catholic Māori.

The hui is a gathering of Catholic Māori culture clubs to compete against one another in all major aspects of Māori culture and Catholic theology—oratory, hymns, action songs, poi—and sports. Teams from clubs are organized by chronological age and perform and compete throughout the four-day celebration (see Pinenga's narrative). Both Māoritanga—the development of Māoriness—and Catholic dogma are celebrated at the hui. There are speeches concerned with the religious implications of Christ's crucifixion and resurrection composed and delivered in Māori. Action songs are given a Catholic subject matter, as are chants performed to the poi.

The members of the Māramatanga, who also possessed demonstrable skills in action songs, oratory, and poi, have always been eager to place their abilities in the service of a church to which they were all deeply committed. The movement's culture group was originally called Maungārongo, after both the marae and the meaning, everlasting peace. Anaera had initial charge of the group, drilling and training the young people, not only in performance, but also in a considerable amount of the Māramatanga's teachings. On a marae devoted to the Māramatanga, young people attending rehearsals would inevitably have been aware of the activities in the meeting-house.[14] In time, after winning many trophies, the club changed its name to Ruapehu, a homage to the mountain, but also more neutral than the previous appellation. Members from the Waimarino area participated in all levels of hui organization; in 1947, Maungārongo hosted the second annual Hui Aranga.

Since then, the Hui Aranga has been a major event in the annual round of rā and other commemorations. Much time and effort is spent in preparation, and has been rewarded with considerable success. But for most, Te Karere is uppermost in their minds as the songs and whaikōrero are assembled, and their success is often attributed to having a spiritual inspiration for their performances. A shield dedicated to her, inscribed in the name of Kurahaupō Ruka, is the trophy that winners of the junior action song receive. Other shields have also been dedicated by the Mareikura family over the years, circulating among the victors of the various competitions.

The Maungārongo marae has often served as a venue for retreats, in which clergy and congregates, priests and members of the Māramatanga, have renewed their faith together.[15] The members' relationship with the clergy, although warm in many cases, has not been without ambiguities. On July 11, 1962, in the course of one such retreat, a Redemptionist priest, Father Murray, presented the members with a print of a painting of Our Lady of Perpetual Succour, a representation which was to become an especially meaningful icon for the Māramatanga. The painting, and the pocket-sized copies that many members carry with them, encapsulate the ways in which the teaching of both Te Karere and the Catholic Church have worked to define and reinforce each other.

The original painting, which is currently in Rome, is thought to be spiritually charged: capable, through its long history, of working miracles. There were, in all likelihood, many copies designed to remind the observer of "the great love the faithful bore toward the Blessed Virgin under the particular form in which she appears in the image of Our Lady of Perpetual Help" (Connell 1940: 27). Ahitoro[16] wrote a narrative of the painting's rather dramatic history, a narrative that has been transcribed into several notebooks, and on occasions, read aloud. Raana related it to me as she had written it in her notebook.[17] The painting originated in fourteenth-century Crete.[18] A merchant, carrying the painting from Crete to Italy, stole it and hid it among his wares. The ship survived a storm—an event that the merchant, aware of the value of his contraband, attributed to the Virgin in the picture. The merchant sickened. On his deathbed, he asked a friend to return the painting to a church of his choice. However, the man's wife was adamant that the picture remain with him. The Virgin appeared twice to this man, but each time his wife's greed prevailed. When he died, no connection was made between their illicit ownership of the painting and the man's fate. In time, the painting, now identified as *Our Lady of Perpetual Succour*, passed to various members of the family and was placed in a church dedicated to Saint Matthew in Rome. That church burned down, but the painting was redis-covered in the nineteenth century, whereupon Pope Pius IX consigned it to the Church of Saint Alphonsus. From that time on, the painting demonstrated remarkable curative abilities. In 1867, a crown was painted on the heads of both Mary and the divine infant, indicating "a picture distinguished by miracles, antiquity, and by the extraordinary cult that is rendered them."(Connell 1940: 63.) Raana was quite specific that of course the members of the movement were aware of the Virgin Mary, in many of her guises, before this retreat, but this was something special: "from that time, we knew her as Our Lady of Perpetual Succour and that's the way we love Her the most" (interview, February 1987). *Our Lady of Perpetual Succour* has become an integral part of pilgrimages and missions. The chronicle of the painting, the account of how it (or more accurately, the copy) has come to be in Maungārongo, supports their view of history and their conceptions of themselves.

The past of both the Catholic Church and of a particular painting have become intermingled with events that define the Māramatanga's history; the members have become inscribed in a larger historical narrative that goes back to the Italy of medieval city states. The painting not only hangs in the chapel; it accompanies the members at critical times, times when their relationship to the physical and spiritual landscape is reassessed. In such a manner, members fuse traditions and write themselves into history. Five months after the painting arrived at Maungārongo, it accompanied the members to the summit of Mount Ruapehu.

The Mission to the Mountain: The New Generation

By the early 1960s, a new generation had positioned itself to assume the responsibilities of full participation within the movement. With Ruka's passing in 1960, most of their elders were dead. It was up to a new generation to prove itself. The opportunity to do so came in late 1962, with another ascent of the mountain.

This generation (comprising Mareikura's grandchildren) was, by the standards of Māori leadership, both young and untested. Those who participated actively in Māramatanga at this time were siblings and cousins: Hoana and Rihari, Raana and Rihari, and Pin, Nan and Barney,[19] Lei and Matiu, Tūmanako and Pinenga, Mana Motuhake, Whakahawea and Hiria. They were all close and all related to key founders of the movement. Yet this was far from a homogeneous group: some had married into the movement and were assuming their responsibilities as spouses of individuals who took participation as a matter of course; some were bilingual, equally comfortable in Māori or in English, while for others Māori was new and difficult; and some, to varying degrees, had grown up bearing witness to the crucial events of another generation and had been preparing for the moment when the duties and obligations of the movement would shift toward them. In some cases they were clear-eyed and eager; in others they were calm, confident and expectant as leadership and responsibility were passed across the generations. The second mission to the mountain was as significant for its validation of this new generation of leaders as for its religious and political implications.

Pinenga and Raana wrote accounts of the mission in their notebooks. Raana read hers to me, while Pinenga allowed me to copy her book directly. Reading Pinenga's renderings and hearing Raana's voice on tape illuminates their certainty that the wairua approved and guided their mission, for the presence of the wairua is recorded at every juncture. The solemn tone of the entries captures the gravity with which people approached the mission. The similarity of these two accounts, along with many people's verbal reminiscences, suggests that there is a standard version of the story, but only written in the books of those people who went up the mountain.[20]

In their narratives, both Pinenga and Raana are aware that this was their generation's initiation into the active side of the Māramatanga.[21] They were called on to take the initiative, to organize the mission, and to assume responsibility for its results. Both women referred to the journey up the mountain as the first major venture for their generation. I do not know, however, if this became obvious in hindsight, or was apparent in 1962. What has also been obscured in the intervening years is how much autonomy the elders decided to grant, how many of the decisions were purposely left in the hands of those who, until this time, were neophytes. Of course they were not entirely on their own: three of the twelve adults who climbed the mountain that day—Harimate, Hinga, and Huinga—belonged to the ascendant generation; other elders—Peehi and Ahitoro – made their appearance as the day progressed. Nevertheless, there is no doubt that the mission up the mountain marked the transfer of leadership across generational lines.

The mission had its origin in the spreading alarm over the government's plan to dam the Whanganui River. When residents from river communities understood the government's intentions, they were fearful that cemeteries and other sacred sites would be submerged or in other ways damaged. To Māori sensibilities, this would have been intolerable. A group of people from villages up the river came to the rā at Raketapauma on November 9 to discuss what could only be seen as an impending disaster.[22] Moreover, many from the river, devout Catholics who often looked askance at the activities of the Māramatanga's participants, actively sought spiritual intervention.

Raana narrated it thus:

> This mission started because our family from the Whanganui River came to the rā and said they were very worried and sick about the river. They were told the whole of the river would be dammed. All the homes along the river would be wiped out. They were worried about all the cemeteries, the church house, and all those special things that all of us think about. And they came up to one of the rā on the ninth of November and the most important wairua talk that came out was "Seek first the kingdom of God and all things shall be given unto you." Everyone went home with their thoughts and from the congregation came this idea of a mission to the mountain. This would be the second time. And it was said at that time [the time of the first mission] that that mission was not completed. Someday it would be.

This is an extremely important perception: in evoking the first mission to the mountain, the members make an explicit statement of the connection between two generations, emphasizing, in the unfinished business of the first attempt, the continuity between the two pilgrimages to Mount Ruapehu, the shared bonds of kinship and purpose.[23] The discussion in the meeting house at Raketapauma and the consensus of the members as they pondered the problem before them indicated that the time had come to go on with their work.

The members' concern with the Christian God, with the transcendent purpose of the mission, emerged in the early stages of the pilgrimage and provided a frame for the ensuing activities. Indeed, the rituals and prayers of Catholicism intermingled with intervention from the wairua throughout this undertaking. The very organization of this mission—the flags, the picture of *Our Lady of Perpetual Succour*—suggests how profoundly integrated the two systems were (and continue to be) for the members of the movement. Raana pointed out that no endeavor could succeed were it guided purely by self-interest. Service to God, through spiritual activity mandated by the wairua, was seen as an appropriate method of combating governmental plans. Prayers and the recitation of the rosary framed the mission, imparting structure to a day that was filled with uncertainties. In between times, the wairua spoke, coming through different individuals, conveying approval of the pilgrims' actions and inspiring confidence when their sureness wavered. The pilgrimage to the mountain then, involved considerable and constant spiritual, as well as physical, activity.

Raana headed her entry "A Day to Remember: Mission to Mt Ruapehu," while Pinenga inscribed it in her notebook as "Mission to God's Holy Tabernacle Mountain." The mission began with the reciting of the rosary at 7 A.M. on December 8, 1962. According to Raana's rendering, the group took holy water, the picture *Our Lady of Perpetual Succour,* and three flags: Te Waka o Te Ora (Canoe of Life), Te Āka o Te Maungārongo (Ark of Peace) and Te Tohu o Te Rangimārie (Sign of Peace).[24] The following people participated: Rihari, Hoana, Raana, Pinenga, Matiu, Lei, Mana Motuhake, and Barney, all members of the younger generation; the ascendant generation was represented by Huinga, Hinga, and Harimate, while the youngest generation was comprised of Pou Peka Māramatanga (Harimate's son), Te Rongonui (Hoana's son) and Kiwa (Hinga and Huinga's nephew). (The relationship between all these people appears on appendix 1, diagram 6.)

They drove in a truck up the mountain road and soon a message was received.[25] The message was in Māori; the following is a translation.

> Those chosen few who have come to the heights of my pinnacle, to the sacredness of the sacred mountain. You are like Moses when he also went to the sacred mountains to receive the Ten Commandments. Welcome and take back with you strength and power.

Clearly they had the wairua's approval. Shortly after, Harimate received a message—a message clearly recognized as coming from Te Karere—vividly communicating vigilance and comfort. She greeted the people, indicating that, as they approached, her hands were moving in the characteristic gestures of welcome. She assured them that she had been watching over them, guiding their truck lest something untoward occurred. In the last verse of her message, Te Karere indicated Ruapehu's stance toward Taranaki, an allusion to a separation, which has been chronicled in mythology.[26] She hinted at the ultimate reconciliation of the people who are associated with each of the peaks.[27]

When they reached the end of the mountain road, the group assembled and read out the messages that had been received and written down. At frequent intervals, the group would reassemble and go over all that had transpired. In this way, every participant knew all that had occurred, but perhaps more importantly, the telling and retelling of events as they unfolded provided a gesture toward some kind of uniformity.

The ascent up the mountain now began in earnest. From the outset it was clear that not everyone was capable of such a rigorous climb.[28] At various points individuals simply stopped, staying in place and waiting on the slopes of the mountain; others assembled in one of the huts provided to shelter hikers. Ultimately, the three men made it to the summit. But the movements of all the participants—their climbing, resting, praying, even sleeping—were recorded in minute detail.

From the end of the mountain road, the group climbed to Blyth Hut. Just how meticulous the rendering of the mission is can be seen in both Raana's and Pinenga's notebooks; each records precise distances and exact times. Thus, Raana notes that the trek to Blyth Hut, a distance of approximately three-quarters of a mile, took seventeen minutes. In a similar vein, Pinenga writes that they arrived at Blyth Hut at five minutes past nine and recommenced their journey at thirteen minutes to ten. They pay attention to times when critical points on the mountain were attained, when prayers were said, and when messages were received. These are decisive events, worth transcribing precisely.

Hoana, Hinga, and the three children—Peka, Te Rongonui, and Kiwa—remained at Blyth Hut. After a short prayer, the rest of the group continued on. At 10:20, they stopped again in order for the slower climbers to catch up with those in the lead. From where they stood on the mountain, the pilgrims could see Raketapauma, the cemetery, and a speck of the church, Hato Ruka. At this juncture the group was together, but for Harimate, who had fallen behind. At 10:30 the mission resumed, pausing at 10:45 for a drink. By eight minutes to eleven there was the first sighting of snow, and by eighteen minutes to twelve they were walking on snow. They stopped often, but Mana also fell behind. The seventh stop is recorded by both women. This is Raana's version:

> The seventh stop at 12:15, getting very steep but still carrying on. We carried on the Rosary, by this time Aunty Harimate and Mana were far behind but still climbing slowly. There were seven of us at this stage, about one mile from the top of the mountain. After our rosary, another message from the spiritual side:[29]
>
> Welcome, welcome to the sacred tabernacle.
>
> You are the seven who have been chosen. Take hold of the strength of life and distribute it to the wider world.
>
> For you, the lowest (ranking), still children, shall carry the gift given to your grandfather at Parewanui.
>
> Take it in a straight line to the highest peak on Ruapehu.
> And again I say, you are the chosen seven and God Bless you all.

This message shows the common recognition that this generation was beginning to assert itself in spiritual matters, to assume its responsibilities. The wairua refers to them as the lowest, "te tino raro rawa," and as children, "te tino tamariki," but goes on, almost colloquially, "it's all right," "e pai ana," suggesting that they are competent and will live up to the expectations set for them. Their unique and important history is telescoped in one sentence, which evokes Parewanui (and by extension Mere Rikiriki) and their own uncle, Tikaraina. And even as confidence is expressed in their abilities, these neophyte pilgrims are reminded of their position and their place in a hierarchy that is structured according to age and experience. There is an emphasis on the seven chosen individuals who are on the mountain, as well as on the fact that this message was received at the seventh stop.

From this point, there is a separation based on gender: the men go on ahead, while the women continue their ascent at a slower pace. Pinenga writes:

> We said our Rosary, so that the men, Rihari, Matiu, and Barney may go on ahead, and we women, Raana, Huinga, Lei, and myself . . . carry on slowly, as the going now was very hard, and we were holding the men back. We are one mile from the top of the Mountain.

The women persevered, but did not reach the summit. Raana's notebook narrates the women's activities, and then switches voices to describe the action on the summit. She writes:

> Three minutes to one, Matiu, Rihari, and Barney carried on ahead. The rest of us just went on, walking and sitting until we sighted the boys and they reached the first tip. The rest of us just watched them ascend until they seemed out of sight. We were then about one quarter mile from the top and after a little talk and a prayer, Pinenga, Lei, and myself found a cozy rock and had a sleep. Huinga was not far down. At three thirty spotted boys on the way down, skiing and sliding part of the way. They arrived back to us at 4:07. This was their story: at three o'clock the flags flew for half an hour, the picture and the Holy Water were placed at the foot of the pole. [Pinenga writes that the water was sprinkled over the mountain.]

In this matter-of-fact description, the elements that are merged in the Māramatanga take on meaning only as part of a distinctive whole. A picture of the Virgin Mary, reclaimed from medieval Italy, holy water, and an arduous ascent up the mountain guided by spiritual forces derived from both Catholicism and their own experience, together combine to produce an exhilaration that leaves no doubt that their mission was a success.

When the men reached the women, they sat down, discussed the mission, smoked, and took a photograph: they look relaxed and triumphant. As permanent testimonials to this mission, these accounts in notebooks, and the photographs that have been placed in many family albums, have become more important, because the mountain has been taken over by commercial interests and skiers. When they started their descent to Blyth Hut, they went as a group, "skiing"[30] where there was snow and sliding where there was not. Although Raana indicated in an aside that this was fun, sliding down a steep, rock-strewn path would probably have been more frightening had they not been so delighted with their success.

At 6:20, they arrived at Blyth Hut to discover that Ahitoro had arrived. The group had more photographs taken, drank some tea, had final prayers, and went on to the truck to return home to Maungārongo. Arriving at Maungārongo at 8:30, the pilgrims headed into the chapel where they said a final rosary. Raana:

> We finished off with Rosary in Maungarongo. An end to a perfect day. No breeze even on the mountain top. Such a day, just made for that special purpose, accompanied and guided all through by the spiritual side which left each and every one of us so full of something one cannot find words to express.

There were of course events that transpired in places other than the summit of the mountain. These too became part of the record of the pilgrimage, for no story is complete until all perspectives are taken into account. In this case, there is a clear description of the events at Blyth Hut, and an indirect description of what happened at home, as representatives from the marae came to the hut to await the pilgrim's return.

What happened at Blyth Hut during the day is explicitly recorded by Raana and is given a special section in Pinenga's rendering, *Blyth Hut Happenings 8-12-62*. As in the descriptions of other aspects of the pilgrimage, there is careful attention to detail, to specificity about the actions and thoughts of individuals.

Hoana, Hinga, and the three male children who had accompanied the adults had remained at Blyth Hut. In Blyth Hut, the pilgrims sat at the window, taking turns with the binoculars to search for the climbers, but they could not see them. They continued to pray. Soon, Ahitoro and Teko arrived. After discussion,[31] Teko and Peehi returned to the marae, while Hoana, Hinga, Harimate, and Peka went to sleep. When they awoke, a vigil began as the group awaited those who had ascended the mountain. Both Pinenga's and Raana's accounts indicate that as the group in Blyth Hut failed to spot the climbers on their descent, they became increasingly tense. They prayed once again and at 6:15 Mana was seen descending. When Mana reached the hill just above the hut, the group once again started to pray (Raana writes "carry out prayers") and suddenly Hoana spotted the other members of the party just below the snow line. This was indeed a triumphant moment, for as Raana records poetically:

They were like seven objects trailing down with silver helmets and shiny breastplates that seemed to be like glowworms. And so it was like until the group came to the last hill ascending the hut, and then everyone, to the eyes of those watching were their normal size again but with a glow that was shining in everyone's faces.

As the men exultantly slid down, they signalled a victory that the women, waiting for them, recognized immediately. Their success was obvious.

For us, the question must be what had happened on the mountain? At the very least, and not at all negligibly in a society that depends on age grading, this generation had asserted its competence. The mountain literally and figuratively stands above everyday life, above the daily struggle that can be so problematic and difficult for Māori. Here, in the messages of the wairua, in the constant prayers and recitation of the rosary, the past and the present, the distant and the proximate all become accessible. Divisions drawn along Pākehā lines are not applicable: there is no reason why the Virgin Mary cannot oversee a mission to a sacred mountain, why her portrait cannot be placed next to flags that are emblematic of a system of which she is but a part, why holy water cannot be sprinkled on the summit of a mountain to assure a providential outcome. Quite clearly, the issue of damming the river, of governmental (that is, Pākehā) control over what is recognized as a Māori resource and treasure, emerged and was contested on the summit of the mountain.

This is not to say that the whole endeavor is consistent: it is riddled with paradoxes and ironies. *Our Lady of Perpetual Succour* was introduced by the same culture that has been responsible for the appropriation of Māori resources. Was this cultural appropriation turned against itself when the pilgrims placed her at the summit of Mount Ruapehu? Certainly, the relationships of Māori to Pākehā and of past to present are both ultimately redefined; issues of control are rearticulated as history is recast in a peculiarly Māori space. The entire endeavor allowed this group of pilgrims, and all associated with them, to position themselves in a larger historical narrative, to transcend their marginalized portrayal in Pākehā accounts. On the mountain, history was re-enacted, and a major vehicle was a painting whose own history links it to other scenarios of oppression, scenarios in which control and resistance are simultaneously encoded. But that it is liberating exemplifies the essential ambiguity of the colonial, or post-colonial, situation: renegotiation or redefinition, of the past or present, is always possible. However, what these pilgrims accomplished as they stood on the summit of Mount Ruapehu, or waited in Blyth Hut, was the ability to define themselves rather than be defined.

The mission to the mountain became not only momentous but historical, recovering the history that the Māramatanga encompasses. Not only did a new generation take its place but, perhaps more importantly, the mission succeeded:

the river was not, and has never been, dammed. A new rā was added to the annual cycle: October 6 (the day they learned of the government plans), to be celebrated on a Whanganui River marae.

The 1960s: An Overview

The success of the mission was a triumph of new aspirations. In 1942, a similar journey had proved a generation worthy. Once more, twenty years later, their successors ascended the mountain to display their competence and value. Hoana, Raana, Pinenga, Matiu, Lei, Rihari, and the others all demonstrated their capacity to carry on the work. In the process they revealed their commitment to and apprehension of all that the Māramatanga encompassed.

In the later part of the decade, several of these individuals would be called upon to attend a whare wānanga where they would be taught the chants and karakia of the ancient world. Such an experience would further promote their personal transformations, emphasizing the role of the movement as a bridge between the old and the new. But nobody left Te Karere behind. Indeed the knowledge promoted at the whare wānanga, augmented by the experiences on the mountain, enhanced the competence of members in two domains. In learning the songs for the Hui Aranga, sitting and listening to their elders speak in the meeting-house, accompanying their seniors on the missions to Rotokura, and learning and then telling of the movement's beginnings in Parewanui and its subsequent development, this generation grew up understanding its past. In the pilgrimage to the mountain in the 1960s, they had become part of the very history that would be recounted and memorialized in the narratives that will entrance future generations.

Whether following Mareikura's injunction to tāpae or undertaking missions, the members of the Māramatanga continuously confront, redefine, and renegotiate history. For this generation, the first encounter with history must have been a heady experience. But in almost four decades since—three of which I have witnessed—they have never become nonchalant. They have, perhaps, become a bit more comfortable with their position: they have taken their place in a moral order insulated by inspiration from the external and intrusive world.

The members of the Māramatanga are socially and geographically specific in their actions. Even when participants are aware of the larger implications, they are careful to locate their actions, and trace their consequences, within a clearly defined political and social context. The messages received on the mountain acknowledge the particularity of the pilgrims and their mission. The songs and messages are geographically precise, leaving no doubt as to location. Yet at the same time there is a proclivity towards universality, toward endowing very specific times and places with more general and generalizable characteristics. Ruapehu, Kawiu, Taranaki, and the Whanganui River are defined and contextualized in a manner that simultaneously locates and extends the purview of the Māramatanga. The members emerge as far more than Māori creating a new marae, climbing a mountain, or fending off government intervention; the structure of revelation links them to all who have struggled, all who have taken on powers greater and seemingly more commanding than themselves.

Kawiu, the Levin marae, came into existence within a shared understanding of the history of prophecy; but its creation was located, in songs and in names, quite explicitly in Horowhenua (recalling the antecedents of key individuals). The tradition of naming that was carried on at Kawiu marae marks out a domain through which those who understand the system are separated from those who do not. Their universe has a different set of meanings, contingent on knowledge of a particular history and a specific set of circumstances. At every opportunity, whether in the placing of names on buildings or houses, in waiata received, or in the interpretation of dreams, that history and those circumstances are invoked and brought into the present.

Throughout the building of the Levin marae and the trip up the mountain, indeed, framing all the activities of the movement, the voices of the wairua were present—in songs, chants, and dreams. When a revelation was proclaimed and shared, there were no doubts about its authenticity. Other members were eager to hear what the wairua had to impart. More importantly, these messages, especially the songs that have been sung at rā and recorded in notebooks, become part of an enduring and growing corpus of knowledge, providing further evidence to the members of the Māramatanga that they were guided by larger-than-human forces.

Notebooks containing songs and precise accounts of missions became repositories of knowledge that is confined to the initiates of the movement; such knowledge forms a significant moral barrier against those not so privileged. Indeed, notebooks, which were shared, painstakingly copied, and have their contents discussed within the group, generated a community distinguished by expert learning. The songs eventually became group property, their origins often shrouded by time and by the disinclination of individuals to stand and take credit.[32] Their knowledge insulated the membership, reaffirmed their belief in themselves as privileged, and assured them that they would be offered succour in a changing, often disconcerting, world.

Women are often the transcribers of the Māramatanga, a role that fits with their position as purveyors of information across generations. Public records—for example, songs, visions, and narratives of missions that enter the shared discourse and are taken as mandates for action—are for the most part contained in the notebooks that women have assembled and maintained through decades.[33]

Pinenga was given the book that her mother-in-law Kataraina, a kaimahi, had started. Raana has kept her own notebooks for years. In addition, Harimate, Hine, Iwa, Aurora, and other women have all given me notebooks, containing waiata, pātere, and pao. They all agree that keeping notebooks and holding the knowledge they contain is, by and large, women's work.

There are other ways in which gender has emerged as critical. Virtually all the spirits who spoke were women, and it was women who received most of the messages. In a universe in which knowledge is so important, women, through this control over a valued resource, are placed in a central position. As the years have gone by, two sources of authority have remained: the oral accounts of the participants and the written accounts in these notebooks.

By the end of 1962, a new generation had arisen to take charge of the Mārama-tanga. Elders became somewhat less accessible, more remote, a situation made clear by Ahitoro and Peehi, who were now visitors rather than participants. The time of Te Karere had receded; it had been removed one generation, while those who had been present for her return, who had participated in the pilgrimages and missions led by Anaera, were recast in the role of kaumatua. Their participation clearly did not end but leadership and motivation had subtly shifted to this new generation. Nonetheless, Te Karere and Riripeti continued to be the most important sources of revelation, even as new wairua and new speakers emerged.

The movement had new centers and new concerns. Levin flourished, growing even larger with Aurora, Tika, and Ritihira holding up the traditions of the movement. Similarly, the positions of Pauro in Hastings and Maru in the Bay of Plenty gave the teachings of the Māramatanga a wider audience, and new rā. The new names, given by both Mareikura and Pēpene Ruka, gave the movement a new focus.

As members of the new generation enhanced their participation, as they enacted events that were structured along lines that they had merely heard about in their youth, the nature of their world changed. The presumptions of the dominant Pākehā society were challenged.[34] European authority and Māori passivity were clearly contestable notions, not axiomatic propositions used to structure a worldview. The government, embodying both European and colonial perspectives, emphasized the present and encouraged what were understood to be forward-looking policies. The members of the Māramatanga persisted in their contention that the past must be understood and brought to bear on the present. As the marae in Levin took form, and as new rā were established, the persistent effect of revelation through wairua, the insistent presence of the past, denied the force of government policy. Indeed, Christianity, the very mechanism the Pākehā thought would transform Māori, was inverted. The mission to the mountain encompassed an icon of colonial power that was now seen as a source of authority that would lead to Māori, rather than Pākehā, redemption.

Pinenga

Pinenga,[1] a young woman who came from a poor family, not of the Whanganui and with neither rank nor wealth, fell in love with and married Tūmanako. She came to the movement and Whanganui culture without proficiency in Māori language and as a non-Catholic. Her life has been shaped by her struggle to come to terms with these facts.

Tūmanako is the grandson of Merehapi, the son of Kataraina, and the nephew of Ruka and Anaera. Descended from Rangituhia, he is the heir to and now owner of a substantial mountain station, one of the most significant financial resources of the movement. Were that not enough distinction, his troubled birth was aided by the prophet Mareikura and led to his being the bearer of an important movement name. Tūmanako, of course, knows all this; but he is a warm, modest, and humble person, of great inner strength and intelligence, and always devoted to his wife and family. In later years, his intelligence and demeanor have brought him significant roles in the national and local communities, both Māori and Pākehā.

For Pinenga, marrying into such a family, into a new linguistic community, and into the mysteries of the Māramatanga would not have been possible were not Tūmanako the sort of person he is. Even so, it has never been easy. She could not help but feel like an outsider in the early years of her marriage. Isolated in the majesty of Kuratahi, she raised her family with only her husband's relatives as company. There were multiple responsibilities in being a farmer's wife and having a position to assume within a community that was not always open to her. Pinenga spoke of these times with a disarming openness and honesty. There was a great deal of pain as she recalled the poverty of her childhood, her family's lack of rank in a world that is still stratified, and her isolation and loneliness as a young wife and mother.

Yet Pinenga has triumphed. She and Tūmanako had six children, five of whom survived to adulthood (one, their only daughter, has recently passed away). They now have twelve grandchildren and at least one great-grandchild. For over fifty years she has lived at Kuratahi, which stands along with Maungārongo and Raketapauma as a monument to the Māramatanga and its history.

In her sixties, Pinenga is a true kuia: a loving mother and grandmother, versed in local and tribal history, competent in karanga (the call by women as they enter marae) and weaving. She takes her place beside her husband, the mistress of Kuratahi and of 27 July. But, as her story reveals, she has always felt like an outsider.

Early Years

Pinenga was born and raised in Taumarunui, the seventh of nine children born to a father from Tauranga, whose tribal affiliation was Te Arawa, and a mother from Ngāti Raukawa. The family was very poor; their house appeared so much poorer than those of their classmates that Pinenga and her siblings were ashamed to bring their friends home. Food was never wasted; all excess was canned and preserved. Older children looked after and assumed responsibility for younger siblings. Clothing was handed down; Pinenga remembers wearing an older brother's boots. Shadows of the family's poverty clearly hang over Pinenga's memories of her childhood.

Pinenga's mother had the strongest influence on her early life. She was a native speaker of Māori and spoke it in the household, although her husband used only English. She was a conservative woman, and a strict disciplinarian. She was also a healer, adept at mixing herbal remedies and setting broken bones, making her feared (and derided as a 'witch doctor') by neighbours and her family. Pinenga recalls her being especially firm in her instructions to her growing daughters. She taught them to respect men, not to step over food or men, and to avoid sitting on tables.[2] However, she did not discuss menstruation with the young Pinenga, leaving her to find out about it from an old woman in the neighborhood. Pinenga maintains that she learned much from her mother—her dedication to family and to domestic comfort regardless of material constraints, her unshakeable religious convictions—that, in turn, she worked to instil in her own daughter. Her mother became the exemplar of women in their role as teachers.[3]

When Pinenga was twelve, she was asked to join the newly formed Maungārongo culture club. Five children were invited to join the group that travelled down from Taumarunui each week. Despite any difficulties of tribal affiliation for the Raukawa woman, Pinenga's mother encouraged her and accompanied her to practices at Ohakune.[4] Pinenga was in awe of the proficiency and accomplishments of the young people who belonged to Maungārongo. In this group were Raana, Hoana, both men called Rihari, and Tūmanako, as well as many of the Akapita and Mareikura cousins and siblings. They had all been brought up within the bosom of the movement and several among them were native speakers. Already they were competent in the complex actions that accompanied waiata, skilled in the use of rakāu and taiaha, confident in haka, pōwhiri, and karanga. To Pinenga, their facility was amazing—and not a little intimidating. She was also aware of adult activities; she recalls thinking that there was something special about the people and the marae. She felt somewhat removed from the people of Maungārongo at that time. As a non-Catholic, she was uncomfortable with the karakia which would mark any meeting of the group. But of late she has grown very close. Prominent among her memories was witnessing Hine Ataarangi as she stood up to give thanks. As she watched, Pinenga felt love and affection for the people.

Tūmanako was a member of the Maungārongo culture club, but as he was five years Pinenga's senior, it is possible that they did not meet when she first joined. Her earliest memory of him is from the Hui Aranga in Taranaki, when she must have been fourteen. She was attracted to this shy, self-effacing young man, realizing that she felt an affinity for him that she did not have for the others. Her feelings interfered with her schoolwork. But she did not allow herself to hope. He was the scion of an important family, one for whom a prominent marriage offering valuable political alliances was anticipated. Yet he chose her. But two shy people don't make an easy start to a romance: even after they'd known each other for five years he could not bring himself to tell her of his feelings. He wrote to her: "I love you. Please name your first son [after me]." They married six months later.

Pinenga left school at fifteen when her mother became ill. While her sisters had gone to boarding school, there had been no money for her to attend. At fifteen she had already missed many days of school looking after her mother, so when she could she abandoned formal education. In the next four years she took the kind of work that was available to a young Māori woman with minimal education: she worked as a joiner in a timber-yard (a job that her mother strenuously opposed), in a milk bar where she learned to cook and bake, and then as a sheep-shearer with her brother. Soon after her shearing run ended, she was married.

Surprisingly, opposition to the match came not from Tūmanako's family but from Pinenga's mother. She thought Tūmanako's heritage too lofty and that he himself was too far removed from, indeed too far above, Pinenga for her to consider herself worthy to be his wife. Tūmanako was hurt by this attitude and defended his future wife against these aspersions. In the decades since, they have continued to offer such protection and support to each other, a solid romantic alliance no matter what the difficulty.

Life at Kuratahi

Pinenga married Tūmanako when she was nearly nineteen. Despite her family's poverty, the new bride came with blankets and mats especially prepared—her mother's assurance that she not appear naked in the eyes of her illustrious affines. Her mother and her mother-in-law played rather large parts in the early years of her marriage, but retrospectively Pinenga gives them a benign reconstruction. Her present sympathy and understanding, as a mother and mother-in-law herself, were probably not present in the young daughter and daughter-in-law.

The newly-weds moved into Kuratahi, the house Tūmanako's mother Kataraina had lived in for decades. Kataraina's brother, Pēpene Ruka, and his wife Anaera were only a few miles away. The young couple did not know one another well, and their early years afforded little opportunity to examine the nooks and crannies of one another's personalities. Pinenga was not comfortable with constant company and this discomfort made it hard for her to see how important to and difficult for Kataraina the arrangement was. Today she regrets her failure to make overtures, to be more welcoming. But it is unlikely that they could ever have been intimates.

Pinenga's difficult adjustment was probably not helped by the wealth and importance of the Ruka family. Such privilege bestowed a somewhat exalted position, one that several members have used to their personal advantage in dealing with other people. Justifiably or not, they are thought of as clannish and arrogant. All the Ruka family—Merehapi, Pēpene Ruka, Kataraina, and Anaera (who was a Mareikura but a Ruka through marriage)—were spiritually gifted, involved in the early days of the Māramatanga, and intimately connected to Lena. Marrying into the family with neither knowledge nor connections was a formidable task.

Not surprisingly, Pinenga's feelings toward Kataraina were a complicated mixture of wonder, respect, and suspicion. Although gifted in the ways of the Māramatanga, Kataraina did not share her knowledge with her daughter-in-law, at least as Pinenga saw it.[6] Perhaps Pinenga was too alienated, and felt too much an outsider. Her receptivity grew over time, but in those early years she was far from easy with the behaviour of her in-laws; it is hard to believe that this was not communicated. Pinenga was not a confident person, there being little in her background that would have encouraged self-assurance. At Kuratahi and in the Māramatanga, she would have found herself surrounded by competence: in Māori language and ritual, in singing, in social interaction, even in preparing the kitchen and marae for large gatherings. If all of this was daunting, as it must have been to a young bride, her sense of distance was increased because she was not a Catholic.

Pinenga threw herself into domestic work, as a way of fitting in. Even when it came to the rā, Pinenga worked rather than participated—she cooked in the kitchen, tidied up the meeting-house, and cleaned toilets. But her mother's example stood before her; she was able to make sense of the Māramatanga by seeing a parallel between her mother's prayers and the members' activities. Tūmanako readily assented to such resemblances, encouraging Pinenga to find a unity in all the forms of worship to which she was exposed. For example, her mother blessed all their children by dipping her fingers in water, summoning forth images of both Christian baptism and Māori consecration. Pinenga's early years at Kuratahi were, then, a mixture of her mother's understandings of Māori ritual, the Christianity in which she had been raised, the Catholicism that dominated the life of her in-laws, and her own tentative understandings of the Māramatanga.

Her first child, a son, Koroniria, was born in the hospital at Taihape. She was delighted, for the child emphasized her love for Tūmanako and was, so she felt, someone who was really her own. That she made this point more than thirty years later suggests how profoundly alone and isolated she perceived herself to be. Within eighteen months, she had a second child, but the baby did not live.

When her second baby died, Pinenga abandoned any hope of fitting in with, or of becoming close to, Tūmanako's family. Instead, she decided to leave. In hindsight, she recounts the symptoms of severe depression. But she was still able to discuss her feelings and wishes with her husband. Tūmanako himself was tied to the land, because this was both his chosen vocation and his children's heritage; and his substantial holdings had required great sacrifice on the part of his ancestors, especially his grandmother. His loyalties and obligations were thus in two directions: to his ancestors and to his descendants.[7] Tūmanako urged Pinenga to go, feeling that a change in environment would help her, would provide a necessary breather. When she left, he gave her money, fully expecting her to come back when she felt better. Pinenga, for her part, saw her departure not as a temporary respite but as a permanent separation: she neither wanted nor intended to return to Kuratahi. She went to the South Island, to her brother's house, and found work as a cook. However, it was not easy to support herself and her child,[8] and she dearly loved and missed her husband. So she returned to Tūmanako, to his house, and to his family, viewing her foray into freedom as part of a divine plan that was meant ultimately to unite them.

Over the next decade, she had four more children, three more sons and a daughter. She still occasionally went home to her mother, depending on her for advice and solace. She needed her family, craving an intimacy that eluded her at Kuratahi. Pinenga, in this respect at least, reflects the feelings of many young women whose lives are dominated by the demands of children and domesticity. Childbearing years were often spoken of as the most difficult, fraught with the apparently paradoxical situation in which women felt too tied to their in-laws and too remote from individuals who could provide them with understanding and genuine affection.[9]

Among the members of the movement, Aurora provided Pinenga with the most support, counselling her on the ways of the movement and the difficulties of an in-law's position. Pinenga says outright that Aurora saved her sanity; I suspect that their parallel positions made them mutually sympathetic.[10] But Aurora was a central participant, a producer of songs, and recognized by all as spiritually gifted. Pinenga felt that, by contrast with Aurora—and Hine and Raana (who arguably was raised within the movement)—she was not succeeding as an in-law, and her feeling of isolation increased. There is indubitably a divide between affines and consanguines, those who have married into the community and those connected by blood.[11] But such neutral anthropological terms ignore the pain of women at the most difficult stages in the domestic cycle, whose loneliness and solitude are compounded by intimations of rejection and exclusion.

Pinenga's growing familiarity with the movement did not diminish the difficulty. She knew, in her words, that something beautiful was going on, but she could not understand it all. Indeed, only partial knowledge of the Māramatanga, half-heard and half-understood kōrero, proved to be discomforting. Two incidents stand out in Pinenga's memory.

She had been listening, along with the others, to tales of a long dead kuia with formidable powers, who made her presence known through a strong wind. Only half understanding the meanings of the discussions, she drifted off to sleep. In the middle of the night, she left the whare puni and made her way through the fields to the outhouse, a journey that involved passing the cemetery. Suddenly, a strong gust of wind blew the outhouse door open and sent the unwary Pinenga fleeing back to the safety of the group and the meeting-house. Relating this story a quarter of a century later, she said she was so scared that she had no idea how she made it back to the meeting-house. She instantly recalled the kuia, and was frightened that she had had some kind of visitation. She has repeated this story on several occasions. It is unimportant whether or not she had been contacted by the powerful old woman. Rather, the story shows how the Māramatanga can terrorize those who have not grown up within it as readily as it enlightens. Such stories are not uncommon for affines. As they grow into the movement, such events become more rare, but their stories have common elements.

The second incident took place after Pinenga and Tūmanako had been married about twelve years. Pinenga suffered serious insomnia. Looking after four young children and her other responsibilities did not allow for sleeplessness, and she became increasingly desperate. In the middle of the day she would run out of the house calling Tūmanako's name. Something was clearly wrong, and she was prepared to take responsibility for any mistakes she might have made.

She investigated her taonga (in this case, ritual woollen cloaks used in tangi entrusted to Pinenga by her own family), even old pieces of furniture, to see if she had offended anything or anybody. She consulted with Tūmanako's aunts and cousins. She went to Rotorua to seek a faith-healer, a gifted old man among her father's people. Nothing worked, and her days and nights blurred together in a semi-wakeful nightmare.

Finally, one night she had a vision or a dream. An old woman appeared to her, "a funny looking old lady with red eyes." Only her head appeared and she said nothing. Pinenga, in remembering that vision, said that her head seemed to disappear into the corner of the bedroom ceiling. For days, that face played on her mind. She sought her mother's counsel and that of Tūmanako's family. From her description, this woman was a female ancestor of Tūmanako, a woman who had lived five generations earlier. She was concerned with the young woman's willingness to carry on, to be the recipient of the responsibilities of the mistress of Kuratahi. Once the cause of her distress was discerned, Pinenga felt better. She had received the intended message, and now her position within the family was infused with a new dedication and purpose.[12] Furthermore, her illness had brought their families together, for she had consulted experts from both sides, drawing those nearest to her and to Tūmanako closer.

For Pinenga, this was the beginning of her spiritual development, of her participation in the tikanga. To be sure, ghostly visitations in the middle of the night were alarming. But mostly she feared she was "going a bit mental," losing her mind in the isolation of her remote fortress. In the telling of these two events, Pinenga revealed the ways in which she was coming to understand her life and her role as Tūmanako's wife. Together these two stories mark her transition from fear and withdrawal to acceptance and involvement. In her construction, she had been tested for the role of Tūmanako's wife. She hoped that she had been found worthy.

Shortly before the second visitation, Pinenga had made a decision: she would become a Catholic. It was not only that being an outsider rankled; she was drawn to Catholicism, finding in the ceremonial formality a peace and beauty she wanted to share. However, the decision could not be solely hers. She had to seek her mother's approval; for her to convert, her mother would have to release her. Her mother was surprised but agreed to her request, puzzled at why someone already baptized should want to be received into another Christian church. Thus Pinenga undertook the lessons that led to her conversion.

From the earliest days of her conversion, Pinenga has been a devout Catholic, active in local and diocesan matters, an eager participant in church affairs. She has been especially involved in the Catholic boarding school that many of the movement's members, her four sons included, have attended. She has opened her home to those priests whom she has come to know through the school and through parish activities.[13] Pinenga, who is a hospitable and gracious hostess, has always been a favorite among the priests who have ministered to the movement and to the local area. Perhaps most importantly, she has framed her understanding of the Māramatanga in terms of her Catholicism.

When her mother died, Pinenga went back to look after her father and to sort through her mother's things. She divided her mother's possessions among her siblings, but, with their agreement, she kept the greenstone jewellery. In thinking about this, Pinenga was persuaded that she had been given this responsibility because, among them all, only she had stayed within the Māori fold. Her brothers and sisters had made lives for themselves in Australia and in other parts of New Zealand; she had given up her education to look after her mother, but she still was concerned that she had been a burden to her mother. She may also have been given the valuables because she never intended to keep them. She tried on one occasion to bring them back to Rotorua, only to be told to return with them to Kuratahi. When her father died, she returned them for his tangi. She retains her family's taonga. These she treats very carefully, making certain to bless them after they have been wrapped about a coffin.[14] For after a cloak is used for a burial, it is poke (unclean, polluted) and must be prayed over, lest the power of the cloak turn against the people it is meant to protect. She prays, making the sign of the cross and using holy water. For her, more than for other members of the Māramatanga, there is a direct link between her understanding of Catholicism and treatment of materials whose referent is clearly Māori.

When she had been married more than two decades, when three of her children were married with children of their own, her youngest son was away at boarding school,[15] and her daughter was also away, Pinenga fell into a protracted depression. She became unresponsive, drinking away days that were too long. At this time, she lost her faith, or her faith failed to sustain her. She said that for the eighteen-month duration of this blackness, she would have left, but she had nowhere to go; she asked herself who she was and could find no answer. Tūmanako stood by her quietly, never mentioning her drinking, never accusing her, picking up any slack caused by her inattention. Somehow she did come out of this, profoundly grateful to her husband for his understanding. Her faith was renewed. More importantly, she had found something of an answer to who she was.

Unlike Hine, who, a generation earlier, could throw herself into the lives of those surrounding her, Pinenga was very much isolated in the high hills of Kuratahi. Her faith became for her a source of solace and comfort, in many ways reinforcing her tendency to see the best in people, to find something positive in difficult situations. Hers is by far the most conventionally Catholic viewpoint of all the women in the movement. It has been a means for her to understand how the past has laid claim to her husband, and it has allowed her to constitute a place for herself in the complexity of the Māramatanga.

Pinenga's Participation in the Māramatanga

Kataraina may not have divulged the mysteries of the Māramatanga to her daughter-in-law Pinenga, but she did, nevertheless, pass her notebook on to her. This was a valuable gift, for it contains most of the movement's important pao and waiata. These songs provide a history of the movement and a chronicle of the members' concerns. The entries in Kataraina's notebook are made in several hands, making it the more interesting: the book itself has become a living document of the movement, filtered through various members and different generations for over seventy years. Although the two women were unable to discuss such matters face to face, Kataraina must in the end have had confidence in her successor's preparation. With Pinenga's own contributions taking over in the mid-1950s, the book builds on the work of Pinenga's impressive mother-in-law and reveals to a reader five decades of revelations, hopes, and anguish.

Pinenga has made the book a much more personal document, recording in it not only her participation in group endeavours, but also her personal efforts, hopes, and fears. She has recorded the illnesses of her children, and her visits to others in distress or ill health. She has also included detailed descriptions of missions and pilgrimages, recording the time and place every message was received, the name of the recipient, and the message itself. What is most striking about her notebook is her thorough intermixture of Catholicism and the Māramatanga. For example, missions of the Māramatanga and missions in the name of the Catholic Church are listed together, in chronological order, indistinguishable in religious, moral, or epistemological status.

Between December 1961, when Pinenga went on a mission to Takere, recorded as a "Good World Mission," and August 23, 1963, her notebook lists eleven "missions of Perpetual Succour"—that is, missions under the auspices of Our Lady of Perpetual Succour.[16] These eleven missions must have been especially onerous for a young farm wife with four children. In August of 1963 (around the time of her conversion), for example, she recorded three events: missions to the healing waters of Rotokura, to Ketemarae, and to Tirorangi, a crowded calendar in the lambing season. But for her there was—as there still is—a unity to her experience, indeed to her life, exemplified in her placing together missions and pilgrimages whose motivations might seem rather diverse. All events are recounted in detail; the following, of the mission to Ketemarae, is an example.

The mission to Ketemarae, which is in Taranaki, was written up briefly in her notebook. The significance of the pao at the end lies in the understood relationship of Taranaki (Mount Egmont) and Ruapehu. Several of the messages that have been received over the years indicate a rapprochement after the mountains' centuries apart. Her notebook contains the following:

Ketemarae. Crusade of the Rosary   10th Aug. 1963

Left Maungarongo by bus: Rihari, Tumanako, Huinga, Kaa, Girlie, Trina, Hoana, Raana, Tauaki, Mona, Margaret, Pinenga, and all our children, to spread the Crusade of the Rosary of our Holy Mother on the invitation of Father Durning. Arrived here at 4 o'clock. Grotto made for our Holy Mother in front of new Hall called Hoani Papita [John the Baptist]. [The foregoing suggests that they were bringing the statue with them.] Second Joyfull mystery, when Mary went to visit her cousin Elizabeth who was in child with John the Baptist. Carried out Rosary, which was so beautiful, then came over to marae. On way, this Pao was given, when we saw Mount Egmont so clear, as when first sighted, was mostly covered with cloud,

Kua ea Ruapehu
Ma taua hei mahi tahi i tenei ra ee.

Ruapehu has risen
So that we may undertake our work on this occasion.

Here Taranaki is addressing Ruapehu but using the first person plural ("we") to include the two mountains. Their task is now defined jointly, as the members of the Māramatanga (Ruapehu) travel over to Ketemarae (Taranaki).

Her entry ends with a list of the children who accompanied them on the mission. The lack of separation between adults and children continues through the most solemn aspects of the Māramatanga. Children went to all the rā their parents attended, and were routinely taken on pilgrimages and missions. In this manner they were exposed to all aspects of the movement, the language of inspiration and revelation, the rituals, and the karakia. Through such experiences, children grew into adults imbued with the solemnity and importance of these occasions.

Each year Pinenga has the primary responsibility for the practical aspects of the July 27 rā. This means preparing the marae at Kuratahi to feed and house 200 or more people, many of them for three to four days. The marae has the necessary space and equipment but it all has to be taken out of mothballs and made ready. The meeting-house has to be cleaned out, with all the sheets, pillowslips, and blankets laundered fresh for the occasion. Mattresses are prepared and set out. Some older and honored guests stay in the house, for it is more comfortable and warmer during this most bitter time of the New Zealand winter. Thus the house has to be scrubbed down and furniture rearranged to accommodate the visitors. Bathrooms and toilets have to be scrubbed and stocked. Fires are made, with barricades to protect wandering children. All the cooking and kitchen utensils have to be taken out of storage and cleaned. Planning the meals and buying the necessary stores would itself be a major undertaking, but Pinenga also bakes bread, cakes, and biscuits.[17] Little pre-prepared food is used. Of course, she has many hands once the visitors arrive; but prior to that, the day-to-day running of the farm does not abate for Tūmanako or their family. Pinenga executes this considerable responsibility with minimum help, as she has for over fifty years. And it always runs smoothly and, to a casual observer, apparently without effort. Pinenga (as she should) derives pleasure and a sense of accomplishment from the rā's successful fulfilment.

Over the years, Pinenga's commitment to the movement has deepened and she has moved gracefully into her role as mistress of Kuratahi. On missions and in organizing and attending the yearly cycle of rā, she has worked alongside Raana, Hoana, Lei, and their husbands. She has casual, joking relations with most of the people and is genuinely fond of many of them. She did point out to me the accomplishments of women who had married into the movement, who had come to the Māramatanga from the outside. But she herself has never overcome feeling like an outsider.

Pinenga as Elder

Pinenga has emerged as a kuia to respect. She will karanga or pōwhiri with the best, and execute the responsibilities attendant upon older women with calm proficiency. She has become expert at weaving, producing baskets for her friends and family, and cloaks for the clergy. She has stayed involved in community affairs, for a time being very active in her sons' boarding school, on community committees, and within the committee structure of the Catholic Church. She is always highly visible at the Hui Aranga and continues to welcome the clergy on formal and informal occasions. She has maintained a close and intimate relationship with Tūmanako, one that is based as much on an appreciation of differences as on an assertion of similarity. She has learned, after the upheavals of her earlier years, to accept, and to keep her own counsel.

She sees her life in the Māramatanga as the source of her faith; but at the same time she realises the pain she has suffered at the hands of those who, wittingly or not, overlooked and ignored many of her overtures. She has been, in her words, "outside the circle." She has also been shamed and angered at what she perceives to be misunderstandings, and underestimations, of her husband. Her marriage joined her to a particularly forceful, wealthy, and at times difficult, family. Similarly, their prosperity has elicited many predictable responses: pride, resentment, and perhaps envy. All this, although difficult, she has learned to manage with grace, humor, and dignity.

When Pinenga looks over the early years of her life, her marriage, her children, and her shifting relationships with her siblings and parents, she comes back repeatedly to ideas of responsibility and mutuality. It is especially in the context of her isolation and loneliness, her moments of despair, that these two ideas emerge. Her commitment to interdependence and obligation, despite her physical and emotional separateness, demonstrates the importance of these ideas for the members of the movement and, quite possibly, for Māori in general.[18]

Gilligan (1982) has demonstrated that American women, denied access to power, have adopted an ethic valuing relationship and interpersonal care over personal rights and aggrandizement.[19] But, arguably, it is subordination, rather than gender, that makes relationship an effective measure of self-evaluation. Abstractions are available to the dominant and to the elite; others have to take what is available as a source of moral self-worth. In New Zealand one sees the difference played out between the dominant Pākehā society and the Māori. The egalitarian ideology of the Māramatanga exemplifies the bifurcation. But perhaps Pinenga's own case shows a similar pattern even within the movement: as an outsider excluded from knowledge and its concomitant power, she has successfully taken refuge in the value of working for friends and family, the ethic of mutuality and care. Explicitly and implicitly, especially to the women in her family, she makes clear the importance of attending to the needs of friends and family, enmeshing oneself in a network of reciprocal obligations, and avoiding isolation.

Although she came to Catholicism late, Pinenga has embraced it completely; today she is a devout and dedicated congregant. The Māramatanga defines her, as the head of Kuratahi and as mistress of July 27; however, for her, Catholicism has become coextensive with the movement. Both have forced her to look inward, and enabled her to find answers to questions that eluded her in her dark periods. Today she knows who she is and she takes modest pleasure in her accomplishments. Like so many of the women in the movement, she is frank in her appraisal of others and honest about herself. She appreciates the Māramatanga, maintaining that it has sustained her through difficult times as she has moved into her present role. If there is anything that she does not know, it is that she has done as well as any outsider could reasonably expect to do.

CHAPTER 5

Expansion and Consolidation

In the 1970s, thirty-five years after the death of Te Karere, a new generation had successfully taken its place alongside their elders. Those elders—Pauro, Hine, Aurora, Tika, and Iwa—remained committed and spirited in their participation, providing both energy and continuity for the new directions in which the Mārama-tanga was to go. Moreover, the elders were no longer centralized in Ohakune, or even in the general Waimarino area: Tika and Aurora were in Levin; Hine and Pauro in Hastings. The movement grew, but inevitably become more decentralized.

By the early years of the 1970s, Māori distrust of Pākehā authority was publicly manifest. The Māori activist group Ngā Tamatoa (literally, "young warriors") put into action many of the concerns of the larger Māori community. Ngā Tamatoa agitated for recognition of the Treaty of Waitangi, demonstrated against Waitangi Day celebrations in 1971, argued for Māori language instruction in the schools, and sought the return of confiscated Māori land (Walker 1990: 212–19). Walker writes of this period of increasing activism: "The indomitable desire of the human spirit for freedom and justice cannot be denied by repression. That was the undying message of Rewi Maniapoto: the struggle will go on forever" (1990: 219). Over the next two decades, political activism was only to increase. But in its early stages in the 1970s, this new confrontational stance made many Māramatanga elders, especially those from fairly stable, rural communities, uncomfortable.

Although some members and their children moved to cities, the Mārama-tanga remained, until the mid-1970s, overwhelmingly rural both in its membership and in its focus. Māori urban migration had accelerated after World War II, but the issues it raised (unemployment, crime, and housing shortages) had not yet made a major impact on the membership. Nevertheless, they could not help but be aware of the difficulties faced by Māori in the cities; most knew or were related to individuals who had moved to New Zealand's urban areas. Increasingly the concerns of the movement paralleled the issues that emerged in the national New Zealand arena.

In Ohakune, the development of ski fields on Ruapehu brought an influx of Pākehā during the late winter, and with it a new economy not, as it turned out, very beneficial to Waimarino Māori. Children moved into the cities, but many stayed behind, supported by the large extended family around them. Some of the young members joined gangs, or Ngā Tamatoa. However, the members always kept in touch with their offspring, activating the strong kin ties that have always characterized the movement. In this manner, they were very aware of the political actions and national concerns of younger, urban Māori. Disagreements between elders and younger members were debated on marae at rā and family gatherings. This is not to say that some offspring did not break ties with family, nor that all stayed on the straight and narrow. But vigilance had its rewards; the young were monitored, nurtured from a distance, and if necessary restored physically and psychologically when they returned.

The older generation, in particular Pauro, provided a template for leadership that their successors would follow. In addition, in the late 1960s, Rangimotuhia Kātene, a respected and learned elder, led younger members in a whare wānanga, thoroughly preparing them for their new role.

In 1970, the members of the Māramatanga made the first of what were to become annual pilgrimages to Waitangi, where the original Treaty was signed. While these missions were clearly concerned with a rapprochement with the Māori past, they also took place in a highly charged political atmosphere, constituting a foray into Māori–Pākehā relations. They also gave opportunities to participants from different centres to emerge individually in the movement in confrontation with vital national issues.

With the geographic dispersal of members, localized variants of the movement's ideology emerged. New centres of the movement developed at Levin and Rotorua, and new rā were added to the calendar. Those who had grown up at Maungārongo, Kuratahi, or Raketapauma had mixed feelings about the introduction of heterodoxy. Rā provided the opportunity to air differences and consider a variety of points of view, but the geographical dispersion of the membership inevitably carried problematic ideological consequences.

The Cycle of Rā and Other Activities

Three new rā were added to the annual cycle during the early 1970s. The first was Te Aranga o te Pono at Kai Iwi to mark the faith of one of the elders, an individual whose commitment had never been in doubt (see Raana's narrative); the second was the rā to designate the opening of the chapel in Levin. The Rotorua rā was the third to be added within a few years. This kind of activity demonstrates the movement's capacity to expand, and a flexibility to lay claim to emerging events.

With three new rā, the annual cycle was considerably expanded. Now there were events on January 1 (Levin), January 3 (Kai Iwi), February 28 (Anaera's fast), March 18 (Levin's meeting-house), June 3 (Rotorua), July 27 (Kuratahi),

October 6 (Rānana, commemorating the mission that blocked the damming of the river), and November 8 (Raketapauma, Te Karere's tangi and return). In addition, members spent Christmas as a family, reconvened at the annual Rātana hui on January 25, met again at the Easter Hui Aranga, travelled to Rotokura on annual pilgrimages to get holy water, and would come together at unplanned events such as tangi or illness. Yet the critical, indeed immutable, gatherings remained the first three rā: July 27, November 8, and February 28, those celebrating the origins of the movement itself.

In addition to these movement activities, many members served on the district and central councils of the Catholic Māori Mission, and were deeply involved in and committed to the organization of the Hui Aranga. Yet the members also reached out to other prominent Māori groups during this time. Connections to Rātana, based on the shared bond to Mere Rikiriki, the name Tikaraina, and kinship linkages through Whanganui, were established as many individuals attended the Rātana annual hui. In addition, Mareikura's ties to the King Movement or Kīngitanga (see the narrative of Hine Ataarangi) were revived. The Māori queen, Dame Te Atairangikaahu, and her entourage came onto Maungārongo in March 1973. This necessitated a great deal of preparation: readying the marae, learning and rehearsing songs, and gathering and preparing food to make their important guests welcome.

With all the activity within the movement and the members' interest in other groups, involvement in Māramatanga inevitably demanded a considerable time commitment. Rā ran from midnight to midnight requiring, for most, at least three days away from home. For the young and employed, it translated into three days away from work. Perhaps for this reason, the most active members were middle-aged or older and/or not part of the labor force. (There were of course exceptions: Hoana, who worked at the army base in Waiouru, never missed a rā; nor did her uncle Pauro, who for most of the 1970s was employed in a freezing works). The consistent presence of elders assured that the narratives of the Māramatanga remained alive during a time of growth and change. Moreover, new rā brought new opportunities to come together to discuss issues of concern to the members. This helped foster unity; unlike the 1940s, in the heady days of Te Karere's revelations when all the members lived together, the 1970s were characterized by members' residential dispersion over the North Island.

Levin and its Transformation

The transformation of the Kawiu marae in Levin owes much to Hōhepa, a member of Horowhenua's Muaūpoko tribe and a grandnephew of Weuweu (see appendix 1, diagram 3). At forty, Hōhepa was not a likely or promising disciple for the movement. He was, by his own admission, dissolute, working only sporadically and drinking regularly. He lived in a beach community approximately ten miles north of the marae, but he travelled to Levin frequently to maintain the buildings and grounds and to visit his relations. At that time the marae had a meeting-house, Huia Raukura; a dining room, Te Takeretanga o Punahau; the homes of Tika and Aurora, and of Ritihira (Weuweu's daughter) and her unmarried adult daughter, Tui; and the remains of Weuweu's old homestead. On one visit to Levin, Hōhepa received a revelation that led to his changing both his own and the marae's future.

As he was cutting scrub around Weuweu's old homestead, Hōhepa heard voices that instructed him to build a chapel dedicated to the work of God. Weuweu's original home, which apparently was constructed on the foundation of a cross, was to provide the infrastructure for the new building. Hōhepa's brothers and sisters, many of whom were resident in Levin, assisted him. The chapel was erected quickly. A committee was formed to help defray the costs of the new building, and by 1972 this functioned as the Muaūpoko tribal committee, which grew through the next decade in power and prestige.

What had once been a residence was transformed into a place of worship. But for Weuweu's descendants, and especially for Hōhepa, it paid homage to their illustrious female ancestor. In a recessed nave, forming one section of the cross, are two pictures: one of Mary and Jesus, the other of Christ weeping for Jerusalem.[1] On either side, in a plane perpendicular to the area thus forming two more sections of the transept, are photographs of Weuweu and of Mareikura as a young man. Beneath Weuweu's portrait are the words "Te Pou Here o te Māramatanga" (The Guiding Foundation of the Māramatanga), while under Mareikura's likeness are the words "The Last of the Prophets." Between the two portraits stands an altar, over which are the four names given by Ruka and Mareikura—Pou Kaha, Pou Peka Māramatanga, Pou Mahara Nui, and Pou Horahanga Pai— painted in arcs in the colours of the rainbow. The imagery is clearly celestial. A crucifix lies on the altar, which is also adorned by flowers. Hand-woven mats decorate the floors and walls. The chapel itself is named after one of the four boys, Pou Horahanga Pai, signalling again the distribution of the work, the participation and responsibility of all members. Hōhepa had received another vision in which he saw Mareikura, dressed in white, seated next to God. He was reminded that Mareikura had prophezied that power would once again reside with his people. For Hōhepa, their desires and predictions were realized when his chapel was built.

Not having grown up in the Māramatanga, Hōhepa was at something of a disadvantage. But he was aware of his ancestry and the links it provided to the Māramatanga, and with all the enthusiasm of a convert he moulded evangelical Christianity into what he knew of the movement. He became far more voluble than most members, who tended to be circumspect when it came to discussing the movement with outsiders. Erection of the chapel, with its overtly blended and transformative iconography, made the Mareikura family uncomfortable. They were not happy that individuals with no pretence to anything other than mortality should be pictured permanently in a house of worship. Nevertheless, for them, as for all members of the Māramatanga then and now, primacy was granted to revelation and they were reluctant to interfere with Hōhepa's inspiration and his emerging sense of himself. They hoped it would be understood by visitors to the chapel that neither Mareikura nor Weuweu were themselves objects of worship. The distinction between those whose knowledge of the movement is extensive, who prefer mnemonic devices and metaphors, and those who are relative neophytes, and in their enthusiasm employ overt and obvious signs of the movement's intentions, was also underscored here.[2]

After the chapel was completed, Hōhepa built a home for his family on the land immediately adjacent to the new structure. This added a third house to the marae. He also added a grotto with a bell that is rung at 7 A.M. and 7 P.M., the two times of the day Mareikura and Weuweu devoted to prayers and meditation.

The chapel, Pou Horahanga Pai, was officially opened on January 1, 1970. That date inaugurated a new year, a new decade, and a new era: January 1 on the Kawiu marae joined the annual cycle of rā. Hōhepa, an individual with little or no previous interest in the movement, had through inspiration and determination established a new movement centre. The marae complex now had a meeting-house, dining room, chapel, and three houses around a large rectangular lawn, with three generations in residence. It is beautifully landscaped and maintained.

Tikaraina and Aurora had moved to Kawiu almost twenty years earlier. In 1971, they were involved in a serious automobile accident, in which Tika was severely injured. He made a surprising recovery and, after months in hospitals and nursing homes, returned home in early 1972. His brother Pauro, along with his wife Hine, spent a great deal of time in Levin, often visiting for weeks at a time. In the long discussions that Hōhepa frequently had with the four of them, the four senior Mareikuras were influences toward orthodoxy, providing checks on Hōhepa's more heterodox tendencies. Throughout the 1970s, Kawiu marae was a bustling centre of activity involved with, and possessing, its own unique understandings of the Māramatanga.

Rotorua as a Movement Centre

There were also members of the movement residing in Rotorua at this time. Maru and Emere both had strong ties to Ohakune and to Levin, and each had grown up in proximity to the movement. And their son Areke was Pou Kaha, one of the named boys.

Maru belonged to the *tuakana* (senior) line of Te Arawa, a confederation of tribes in Rotorua. He came to Karioi as a child under extraordinary conditions. A young boy from Ngāti Rangi had died. Shortly afterwards, his close relation, an elder from the tribe, was in the Arawa area attending a tangi, when he was struck by the close resemblance between the young Maru and the deceased child. He beseeched the Arawa elders, who agreed to Maru's adoption and subsequent removal to the Waimarino area.[3] As a tuakana he was understood to be important in Te Arawa's future; thus it was presumed that he would return home to assume his position. He was brought up in Karioi until he was a teenager. He was very close to Pauro. Soon he met Emere, Weuweu's niece, whom he married.[4]

Initially, the young couple lived in Levin (where Emere had grown up) and Palmerston North. They were active in and very attached to the movement. One of the reasons for this attachment may have been that when Emere had difficulty conceiving,[5] her infertility was remedied by Mareikura, who treated a similar affliction in Katariana and in his own daughter, Anaera. When the young couple had two children, Maru was called back to Te Arawa to take on the responsibilities of the tuakana line.

For Emere, life in Rotorua was complicated. Although she had married into the tuakana line of Te Arawa, she was still an outsider. During their early years in Rotorua, she focused on performing the tasks that were expected of her, finding little time for the religious aspects of her relations' lives in the Māramatanga. But neither she nor Maru ever abandoned their commitment to the movement or their devotion to their relationships with its members. Their children were not so committed; Pou Kaha was indifferent to the implications of his name, using the name Areke in Rotorua.[6]

All of this changed when Areke, by then a young married man with two children, was involved in a harrowing automobile accident. It happened on a stretch of road that had been a Māori cemetery and was considered for that reason to be especially dangerous to Māori. As if to prove the point that only Māori were at risk, Pou Kaha's brother-in-law, the Pākehā husband of his sister Ruth, emerged virtually unhurt in the accident. Pou Kaha's injuries were so severe that the doctors prepared his parents for his imminent death. Rather than accept a medical verdict, Maru and Emere summoned their family from Ohakune, Levin, and Auckland. When the family arrived, they spent their days praying, maintaining a steady vigil until Pou Kaha rallied.

Hōhepa asked for a sign; it came when he saw Jesus at the foot of Pou Kaha's bed, nodding his head.[7] When Hōhepa relayed this message, the family all knew that Pou Kaha would survive. His long convalescence was marked by remarkable deeds, not the least of which was his wife Pane's pregnancy in bold defiance of the doctor's predictions that he could father no more children. The entire incident was viewed as a miracle; it is generally believed that Pou Kaha's spiritual name and the prayers that were offered saved his life, his recovery having exceeded the expectations of modern medicine. The movement holds him up as an example of the efficacy of prayer, their special position in the eyes of God, and the beneficence of the wairua.

In mid-1972 when I met him almost two years after his accident, Pou Kaha was a semi-invalid. Although he attended all the rā, he remained quiet and allowed his mother and father to do much of the talking on his behalf. Emere had become a major force in the Māramatanga. Reputedly, Emere had struck a bargain with God, saying "Give me back my son, and I'll work for you." She remained true to this promise. Outspoken and direct, she had a commanding personality, especially when it came to songs and to her obvious gift for lyrical inspiration, both of which she would demonstrate for the assembled members of the Māramatanga. Her position was buttressed by the fact that she was the mother of Pou Kaha and by her close relationship to several women who had moved to the top of Māramatanga's hierarchy, namely Aurora, Hine, and Iwa. She showed that she was indeed their peer.

Until her death in the early 1980s, Emere organized the rā established in Maketū (a coastal town connected to Rotorua, with a strong Catholic Māori presence) to commemorate the occasion of Pou Kaha's recovery.[8] Her considerable talent for songwriting emerged during this period.[9] For example, in April 1971, Emere composed a song in which a bird calls out to the people in the first stanza, extending greetings and seeking their attention. In the second stanza, the names of the four boys are used simultaneously as both injunctions and as mnemonic devices, as reminders of a concealed history whose meaning may be readily unravelled by the initiated. Both the quality and aptness of the song and Emere's personality thrust the four names into the forefront of movement interest.

Emere took an active role in Māori affairs within the Arawa community, her presence and participation complementing her husband's position as elder. As Hine did in Hastings, Emere became the leader of the culture club, appeared on nationally televised Polynesian festivals, and participated in the Hui Aranga. Her grace and voice made her an exceptional performer, and her inspiration often provided the words for songs used in competitions. But here her divided loyalties surfaced in an interesting way; the words to her songs, concerned as they often were with issues germane to the Māramatanga, were given not to the team from Rotorua, but to their competitors from Levin and Ohakune. Maru too had conflicting allegiances; he referred to people from the Waimarino as "my family," those from Rotorua as "my people."

Others in the Arawa community were drawn to the rā held at Maketū and then to other events that concerned the Māramatanga. But this is not a proselytizing movement, as members believe it to involve the *hungaruarua* (the chosen few). In fact they were welcoming to outsiders or visitors; if there was discomfort, it was never meant as personal. Those who demonstrated sincere commitment would find themselves accepted. Such was the case with Hemi and his wife Roimata.[10]

Hemi was a close relation of Maru; thus Maru was able to vouch for him.[11] Hemi had a penchant for drinking, which he abandoned when he turned to the Māramatanga. Listening to a song composed by Aurora, Hemi was moved in a novel way, forcing him to re-examine his life. The result was a significant transformation of his behaviour. Roimata was delighted and embraced the movement enthusiastically; she believed that her marriage had been restored, saved because of her husband's new-found devotion and domesticity.

Hemi went on to assume many of the prerogatives of leadership: in addition to writing many songs, which he performed at rā, he took on the role of orator; he coached the local haka team; and he was active in the local Māori Catholic club. Roimata similarly was involved in community organizations, and had a repertoire of songs which she sang to support her husband's orations. Their commitment to the Māramatanga and to one another was most obvious in the names they gave their children. These names were deemed "spiritual" and were meaningful within the context of the movement. One child was called Rosary Paeroa (a sacred wind, a good omen),[12] while the other was named Hine Waiata, recalling the tree on the marae in Levin and the division of labor between men and women, as well as the gift of song.

The rā at Rotorua illustrates the flexibility within the ideology of the Māramatanga. New events are encompassed and understood in a way that allows them to become part of the movement's history. Within a few years after Pou Kaha's accident, the rā, the telling and retelling of his recovery, the participation of Emere, Maru, Hemi, Roimata, and the Rotorua contingent—all were integrated into the annual cycle. It was all cast in terms that made it seem inevitable. Inspiration and intervention had saved a young man who bore a specially designated name. Such an event confirmed the members' view of their role and validated the movement's ideological basis.[13]

The Māramatanga and the Māori Mission: A Cautionary Tale

Priests have always been invited to rā; most members seemingly speak freely in their presence. One such priest, Father Gerald Arbuckle, working for the Marist mission, only partly understood the rituals and ideology he witnessed at rā, and wrote an alarmist, and in truth alarming (if for nothing other than its ignorance), version of his perceptions. Most unfortunately, his "confidential" report, intended only for dissemination within the Catholic Church, became accessible to the Mareikura family, who were bewildered and mortified to have been characterized in such a manner. The section devoted to the movement comprises a very small portion of a full report on the Marist mission in the Diocese of Wellington. But Arbuckle takes an epistemological stance that does not countenance variation: divergence is understood as ominous and as profoundly threatening.

The report begins by stating that Māori are migrants experiencing cultural and individual frustrations—a bitter irony given the growing prominence of Māori issues of land rights, sovereignty, and autonomy. Such a premise, referring to the indigenous population in terms of exile and dispossession, was certain to lead to difficulties. So it was for Father Arbuckle.

He refers to the Māramatanga as the "Mareikura cult." The term was devastating to the members of the movement. For in one blow, Mareikura—the man and his work—was diminished and trivialized. The word "cult" conjures up the embodiment of otherness: primitive, bizarre, irrational, and marginal. The followers of Mareikura never thought of themselves in this manner. Moreover, their centrality in the whānau, in the Catholic Church, and in national affairs belied such a definition. But so characterized, their successes in other domains seemed not to matter; they were profoundly humiliated and shamed (*whakamā*).

The report is inaccurate, sometimes with mistakes that are almost humorous. For example, Father Arbuckle barely contains his alarm in his description of the statue of Our Lady of Perpetual Succour at Maungārongo.[14] His dismay increases at Levin, where he clearly was given a great deal of (mis)information.[15] Describing the inside of the renovated chapel, he mistakenly characterizes Weuweu as Mareikura's wife. But he is concerned with the symbolism, and worries, quite erroneously, that a system has emerged that supersedes the Bible and the hierarchy taught within the Catholic Church. He writes:

> Above the doors are four fans. The significance of these fans could not be satisfactorily obtained. One said that they are supposed to represent four archangels. Are they the biblical archangels? Or do they symbolise the four men contained in the revelations of the cult and who are above archangels? The writer would tend to favor the latter assumption.

Of course in Māramatanga's cosmology no individuals, whether they bear names or not, are above the archangels.

Father Arbuckle's alarm gets the better of him as he attempts to understand what a rā is and what happens on such occasions:

> It has been difficult to find out what exactly is done on these days. One member of the family said that there are prayers and then members present rise when the Spirit moves them to speak of their problems. She mentioned

that they pray for good health and feel united to the ancestors. It may be that when they stand the ancestors are thought to speak through them. But one can only speculate on these points though there are sufficient indications to assert that the day is permeated by forms of spiritism.

Father Arbuckle clearly attended rā. Yet the prism through which he filtered his information permitted him only to see an alien, arcane form of worship. His interpretation reveals far more about his attitudes than it does about the Māramatanga's beliefs.

Perhaps the most egregiously incorrect, and the most painful to the members, was Father Arbuckle's contention that the movement was using the Catholic Church as a shield, as a means of achieving a legitimacy that was not deserved. This is clearly incorrect. The members of the Māramatanga are proud of their history, their ancestors, and their connections to a source of inspiration that is, to their way of thinking, not in the least inimical to Catholic belief. Almost all consider themselves devout and loyal Catholics, and feel deeply betrayed by Arbuckle's imputation. Such a representation trivializes them and minimizes the hospitality that was extended entirely in good faith.

Ultimately, the existence of the movement forced Father Arbuckle to issue a warning to the Catholic Church:

> It would be most imprudent to ignore this cult. Its significance must be understood:
> (i) It indicates that the faith as explained to them fails to reach them at their point of crisis. It is not totally satisfying. Therefore, they look elsewhere for satisfaction.
> (ii) Maoris have in their midst a cult already equipped with a messiah, a dream of a new world of justice, and a structure to support the cult.

The members of the Māramatanga were mortified by this document. By 1972, when I began my research, many of them had read it and felt both betrayed and humiliated at being seen as a cult and as a problem that the church had somehow to solve. Individuals with little knowledge had spoken too freely to the priest, who possessed no context in which to place such information.

It is very easy, more than thirty years later, to argue that Father Arbuckle could have, or should have, done things differently. In fact, he did attempt to write off-the-record and to keep his findings confidential. That he thought he might succeed in this seems naïve, given communication networks within the Māori community. His research and writing were no doubt motivated by his religious convictions and his desire to improve conditions for Māori under the pastoral care of the Marist mission. However, he had only a partial understanding of the belief system, of its history, and of the place within the Māramatanga of those who may have spoken to him.

The incident inevitably aroused suspicions on all sides. The members of the Māramatanga were quick to grasp the implications of being labelled a cult, and an opportunistic cult at that. Plunged into a new definition of themselves, one that separated them from a church to which many were devoted, the members had to rethink the ways in which they could reconcile their Māoritanga, their Māramatanga, and their Catholicism. They had to re-examine the relationship between official Catholic doctrine and revelation. And, to make the task even more difficult, this had to be accomplished in the context of a world whose very foundations were being questioned and transformed.

The movement was fortunate that Pauro, Mareikura's son, a kind, intelligent, and insightful individual, was the kaimahi. He was able to straddle the boundaries between generations, between the Māramatanga and the Catholic Church, between religious inspiration and political activism. He found common ground in situations where few would have seen any possibility for reconciliation; relations with the church were sustained, if subtly altered. Pauro guided the movement through some very difficult, yet decisive, times.

Leadership: Knowledge, Genealogy, and Cultural Negotiation

In a time of increased activity, and problematic relations with the Catholic Church, Pauro, who was then in his early sixties, emerged as a clear leader. Pauro saw the Māramatanga as an auspicious gift, something that both set Māori apart from Pākehā and made their living together easier. He was proud of the history of the movement and of his family's implication in that history. He had been very close to his father and they had consulted one another on many issues. The two men were also similar temperamentally: both were humble, despite their impressive accomplishments, deeply committed to helping others, and, each in his own way, profoundly bound to, and knowledgeable about, the Māori prophetic tradition. Tikaraina, Pauro's younger brother, bore an important name, but it was Pauro who followed in Mareikura's footsteps. A native speaker of Māori, Pauro shone in oratory, weaving images that invariably moved his audiences. This was true whether he was addressing mourners at a tangi, the young people who were under his care in the local culture club, or the faithful in the Māramatanga. Pauro's leadership coincided with the second Māori renaissance, a time when interest in things Māori was resurgent.

Pauro was the person most responsible for transmitting the teachings of the Māramatanga to, and instilling Māoritanga in, the next generation. He understood how revelation worked (he was his sister Anaera's scribe) and wrote messages down, often in the middle of the night, both to preserve them accurately and to make them accessible when they were needed. He trained the Hui Aranga teams from Hawke's Bay, providing far more than words to the waiata, haka, and poi. He instructed a new generation in the complexities of etiquette, emphasizing the cohesion of a system that depended on both form and content. Pauro also relished the long discursive interpretative sessions that sometimes occurred at rā or when the family got together. On these occasions, the words of messages were scrutinized, contextualized, and made meaningful to the members' current circumstances.

The interpenetration of the Māramatanga and Māoritanga was, to him, evident in Te Karere's messages, in the manner in which the teachings of the church were to be followed, and in the structure of his personal life. He said often, "Your Māramatanga is to be found in your Māoritanga; your Māoritanga is to be found in your Māramatanga." The two were obviously interwoven. Knowledge and training were required for competency in both.

Pauro was a devout Catholic. His messages were frequently concerned with the Father, the Son, and the Holy Spirit. When his thoughts carried him back to Mere Rikiriki, it was to invoke the four foundations, Matthew, Mark, Luke, and John. Fluent in two languages, committed to Catholicism, and devoted to the Māramatanga, Pauro was probably the person most able to navigate the difficult relationship between the Māramatanga and the Catholic Church in the wake of Father Arbuckle's report.

Pauro had many claims to an ascendant position. Yet the Māramatanga had become a movement that was bent on egalitarian impulses, as the name Pou Horahanga Pai (emphasizing "distribution") indicated. In fact, many of Pauro's messages emphasized the importance of other members' contributions. Nevertheless, as with Anaera before him and Hoana after, the crucial aspect of his role as leader lay in his unequalled knowledge, not only of the movement's ideology and history, but of the people involved, their genealogies, and of the history of Ngāti Rangi and related sub-tribes. But the role entailed more than that: Pauro and his niece Hoana, the two kaimahi I came to know and respect, both had an enthusiasm for knowledge, for wanting to find out what things mean and why, that distinguished them within the movement (in fact among humans in general). And all the leaders of the Māramatanga who have emerged in an era that was ostensibly leaderless have been distinguished by their commitment to the movement; they never missed rā. Moreover, Pauro, Anaera, and Hoana were all kind and sensitive, wielding the sceptre of leadership modestly and benevolently.

The responsibilities of such leadership should not be underestimated. Members of the Māramatanga turn to their leaders for advice in all matters. Moreover, a leader can no longer treat dreams or even thoughts—their own or others'—as merely random occurrences: they must scrutinise each as a possible communication from the wairua. At rā, Pauro would stand and tell or sing to his audience the precise details of any message he had received. But, sensitive to issues of consensus and equality, he would encourage the group's participation in arriving at a satisfactory interpretation. Such leadership requires awareness of the sentiments of other members and special care to direct events in ways that do not cause conflict or give offence. Indeed, Pauro counselled peace (*rangimārie*) and harmony in all interpersonal relations. While he certainly encouraged accord within the group, he also advocated that members take the high road when wrongs were committed against them (see the narrative of Hine Ataarangi).[16] Pauro was comfortable in his role as kaimahi, a characteristic that was obvious whenever he stood in the meeting-house on his own or others' marae. This sense of himself is equally apparent in his notebooks, in which he recorded dreams and messages, at times pondering their meanings.[17]

Pauro's wife, Hine, had a remarkable ability to remember songs, and a clear, beautiful voice with which to sing them. This was important not only to the Māramatanga, where messages from Te Karere or wairua are often in the form of songs, but for the Māori custom of following a speech with a supportive song. On any marae they visited, whether they were considered home people or visitors, Hine supported Pauro by offering a song for all his speeches. They were a formidable couple, reinforcing their words with their actions on all marae, and representing the Māramatanga in an exemplary fashion in other tribal areas.

Several of Pauro's notebooks recount the history of the movement, bringing it up to the time of his death. One of the most impressive aspects to emerge is his modesty;[18] he never links himself to the line of prophets or even to the kaimahi. Genealogical position is a means of defining and attributing status in the Māori world; yet when Pauro's dreams refer to his father (Mareikura) or brother (Tika-raina), they tend to emphasise the more familial aspects of their relationships. Were a reader unfamiliar with Pauro's genealogy, it would be impossible to discern it from his writings. In the years in which I heard him speak, he similarly declined to use his illustrious position to prove a point, relying instead on the construction of his argument.

His notebooks reveal a concern with retrospection and with Te Karere. He was far from fixated on the past. However, understanding its importance, he saw the works of previous prophets as a means to make sense of the present, to disentangle its roots, and to contextualise events so that they were never isolated from their antecedents and so that current members never lost touch with their ancestors. In this way, people, places, and events were part of a universe whose coherence was revealed to them through Te Karere.

In one of the messages, signed by Te Karere,[19] she begins by saying "Ask the questions, think the thoughts," assuring them that the knowledge so gained will permit light to flow from their eyes. In another, dated June 4, 1971, he demonstrates not only his role as kaimahi, but his previous experience with the early teachings of Te Karere, and times in which questions were asked and answers debated.

He posits four questions, and while these appear in Māori in his notebook, Pauro labelled the message in English, "Fruits for Thought":

1. Who is the senior, highest ranking of the four boys, Pou Kaha, Pou Maharanui, Pou Peka Maramatanga, Pou Horahangapai?
2. Who is the senior of those foundation names, who we all rely upon: Whakarongo, Tikaraina, Ringapoto, Kawai Tika?
3. Who is the senior of the four major foundations [literally, upoko or head], Matthew, Mark, Luke, John?
4. Who is the senior member of the trinity, The Father, the Son, the Holy Spirit?

These questions are interesting independently; but in the context they reveal a movement from, and therefore a linkage through, the present (the time of Pou Kaha and the other Pou) to the Trinity. The intermediate steps are of course Mere Rikiriki's four foundations, and their source, the four apostles. The appearance of these names, spanning centuries and modes of revelation, reveal their ultimate significance for the members of Māramatanga.

These disparate threads came together when the growth of the movement, both in its members and in its centers, and the emergence of new activist leaders, became part of a pattern that began in the 1970s and extended into the decades that followed. The pieces did not always fit. It was not easy, for example, to reconcile the activist stance of youth with the more conservative position taken by some elders. Yet this lack of neatness was not a cause for concern. On the contrary, at rā, and on other occasions when members of the movement met, debates would go on into the early hours of the morning, with individuals exploring diverse perspectives and the group benefiting as the spectrum of possible positions was set out.

The Whare Wānanga

Sometime in the 1970s, Rangimotuhia Kātene,[20] a tribal elder and respected tohunga from Whanganui, called upon a select group of young people to come to a whare wānanga in Patiarero,[21] to learn tribal wisdom crucial to the preservation of tribal identity.[22] For several years, key members of the Māramatanga— Hoana, Raana, Matiu, Lei, Pin—and others spent their weekends at Patiarero learning genealogy and whaikōrero. The perpetuation of knowledge was not to be left to chance. At this whare wānanga, Matiu began his training as a ritual specialist, a tohunga (see the narrative of Matiu).

Whanganui is geographically remote, and its people have a distinct dialect[23] and unique knowledge and history. Whanganui iwi and hapū are known collectively and generically as Te Āti Haunui-ā-Pāpārangi or, as a variant, Te Āti Hau.

There are many sub-tribes. But Ngāti Rangi encompasses all the important relationships from the early years of the Māramatanga.[24] The elders were insistent that their tribal traditions remain among descendants of the tribal area. This included settlements on the river itself and descendants who belonged to —that is, had strong genealogical claims to—the Whanganui River iwi. The whare wānanga was therefore established both to pass down knowledge and to retain the boundaries that made Whanganui distinct. Those selected from Ohakune were either native Māori speakers or were eager to master *te reo* and knowledge and to establish their commitment to the perpetuation of a Māori perspective.

Thus a new generation was trained in the most esoteric aspects of Māori ritual and ideology. All members of Ngāti Rangi were aware of the existence of the school of learning; so the participants would inevitably see their fame grow within the larger tribal community. That they were almost all members of the Māramatanga surely transformed the view of the movement, common on the river, as different from their staunch Catholicism. But, this was a new generation —one whose prominence and influence would be carried beyond the movement and affect the larger tribe.[25]

That the participants in the whare wānanga sought knowledge rooted deeply in the Māori past would seem at odds with a movement ideology focused on the present and eschewing the very demarcations of the past that separated Māori from Pākehā, most specifically, genealogy, carving, and ancient karakia.[26] But in their missions up Mount Ruapehu and to Mount Taranaki, and in their yearly pilgrimages to Rotokura, they displayed enthusiasm, not reluctance, at coming face to face with the past. From the teachings of Te Karere and from their kaimahi—Anaera, Ruka, and Pauro—the members of the Māramatanga had been taught that the insinuation of the past into all aspects of Māori life in contemporary New Zealand was axiomatic. So they welcomed the opportunity of the *whare wānanga*. And in a time marked by early, unexpected deaths, this preparation of a new generation assured the continuity of the movement.

The children of the participants were given special ritual consideration while their parents pursued their weekend studies; they were trained in the poipoi, which accompanies the recitation of genealogy, and the taiaha.[27] Although neither gender nor rank were assigned ascendant positions, it was the children of Hoana, Matiu, and Raana, and other novitiates, who were pre-pared for their turn at leadership. Hoana, Matiu and Pauro were not genea-logical seniors.

The attendance of a new generation in the whare wānanga, led by a respected tohunga, attests to the continuing vitality of an institution many thought had been abandoned for over a century. This is more than a correction of Pākehā ignorance of a critical Māori institution that many thought had ceased to exist, if they thought about it at all. Through its teachings, manner of instruction, and selection of novitiates, the whare wānanga demonstrates the enduring importance of a Māori way to organise and preserve knowledge. At the whare wānanga, information and wisdom are conveyed across generations on Māori terms—knowledge may be held by, but does not belong to, any individual—undisturbed by Pākehā conventions, presumptions, or protocol.

This generation's participation as students in the whare wānanga and as pilgrims was to endow them with the confidence to move beyond their marae, to negotiate a place for themselves within the wider Māori community and in so doing to rub shoulders with oft-times suspicious and unhelpful Pākehā. In the whare wānanga, they were taught to reconcile potential with plausibility and to frame the most mundane aspects of their lives in ways that would remain consistent with the teachings of their ancestors and Te Karere.

The activities of the 1970s and 1980s continued the work begun by earlier generations. The movement's calendar filled up, with new and old rā and with the additional endeavors that called for members' attendance and commitment. These latter often involved activities outside the Māramatanga: the annual Rātana hui, the yearly Hui Aranga, and attempts at rapprochement with the King Movement. Once more, the relationship of the Māramatanga to other Māori groups in New Zealand was re-articulated and re-examined. While activists in urban centres proposed new pan-Māori models of identity, so too did members of Māramatanga move to transcend local arenas. Nevertheless, the movement remained staunchly tied to a very specific place (the land of the Whanganui tribes and hapū) and history (that of the prophets). If anything, their tribal allegiance became stronger over the years.

The whare wānanga came at a propitious time for national as well as parochial reasons. As the Treaty of Waitangi came to have increasing implications for both Pākehā and Māori New Zealanders, as the official policy of New Zealand moved toward biculturalism, the defenders of Western civilization became increasingly intransigent.[28] As movements like Ngā Tamatoa carried the Māori position to the national political front, the whare wānanga erected and sustained boundaries around the movement's ideology and membership at the local level. In a situation where Pākehā and their claims appeared to be omnipresent, where privacy and inaccessibility for Māori were increasingly rare, the whare wānanga, conducted on a distant marae on the remote Whanganui River, provided the participants with knowledge that was insulated from Pākehā appropriation. Combined with Catholicism and inspiration from the wairua, such knowledge provided a blueprint for action that would redound to the benefit of not only the members of the movement but all Māori.

Conclusion

Relationships with the Catholic Church improved gradually as the members continued their activity on committees and councils at all levels of New Zealand society. In the mid-1980s, a delegation of Māori Catholics went to Rome to petition the Pope for a bishop who would be concerned with Māori issues. Several members of the movement were chosen to go. They were successful: Takuira Mariu, a Māori priest known to the movement over his entire lifetime, became the first Māori to be elevated to bishop. A native speaker of Māori, Bishop Mariu is very aware of what goes on within the movement; he visits people in their homes, is frequently billeted with one of the several competing groups affiliated with the Māramatanga at the Hui Aranga, and attends as many rā as he is able. He is an ally, and an important one. Members of the movement have come to accept the fact that the clergy are no different from other people—some are sympathetic and understanding, others are dogmatic and judgmental, and there are many in the middle.

Community discussions at rā, or on other occasions, provided the opportunity to transform personal revelations into public knowledge and to incorporate these into the growing corpus of events, both historical and revelatory, which comprise the characteristic and unique narratives of the movement. Pauro's leadership was especially successful in this arena. He frequently received messages, which could be encompassed within the Māramatanga's larger history. Perhaps as critically, he knew how to present these revelations to other members and how to elicit a response from them. In this manner, Pauro involved all the members in the process through which individual inspiration was transformed into something larger and more enduring. In short, he managed to lead without appearing to do so. And in taking this approach (whether consciously or not), he was able to sustain the movement's emphasis on equality and distribution.

Throughout the 1970s, as questions of sovereignty and land ownership became more prominent, the members of the Māramatanga confronted these issues. The return of alienated Māori land had become a national concern by the mid-1970s, but in 1970 inspiration took the members of the Māramatanga to Waitangi on the first annual pilgrimage, a mission they saw as involving the whole of Māoridom. But they did not see this as something novel: they had climbed a mountain to save the Whanganui River from a government dam; a journey to Waitangi was simply the next piece of work. As they journeyed north, in what was to become an annual pilgrimage, they were accompanied, as they had been before, by *Our Lady of Perpetual Succour*, Te Karere, and other wairua who revealed themselves in order to provide support.

In the decades since Te Karere's death, a new generation of elders had emerged to carry on the work begun by Mareikura and his predecessors among the prophets. As their social and political worlds changed and became more complex, there were, to be sure, contradictions to be confronted and reconciled as effectively as possible. And yet, as they embarked on their journey to Waitangi, the members of the Māramatanga surveyed the larger picture and understood that this time they would not merely employ history, they would make it.

Hoana

I first met Hoana in 1972, at a rā in Rotorua. She was then forty-two years old and already a powerful force in the community. We were not especially close in the early years of my fieldwork, not only because I was based away from Maungārongo, but because she was less than happy about having an anthropologist in the midst of the Māramatanga and did not hesitate to make her feelings known. When I returned in 1982, I stayed with her some of the time, and devoted my work to the study of women. At the end of that period, she granted me permission to write publicly of what I had learned. Until her death in 1994, she was then very generous with her time, a generosity for which I am especially grateful in light of all the commitments she had undertaken.

Knowing that I was writing this book, Hoana took special care that I should get it right. We went over the history and location of major events of the Māramatanga's development and the contributions of individual members. We went over waiata, pātere, and the many stories in the Māramatanga's history. Hoana was a clear and lucid storyteller, but one who was careful with Māori notions of the ownership of knowledge. She would recount events in which she herself was not present only if none of the original participants was still alive. Similarly, while her knowledge of genealogy was substantial, this was a domain that belonged to men in general, and especially to her brother, Matiu. It was, therefore, an arena she would not enter, except to clarify very basic relationships for me.

Hoana was a woman with distinct opinions and notions of rectitude, even as she traversed the junctures between Māori and Pākehā, past and present. She was introspective and thoughtful, and she recognized the difficulties that often eluded others. Her reactions emerge clearly on tape recordings as she snorts ill-concealed indignation over mistakes—her own and those of others—and revels in recounting difficult undertakings that end as triumphs.

Her nascent leadership, already visible at our first meeting in 1972, emerged indisputably as she grew older. By the 1990s she was clearly one of the most important figures in local and regional Māori developments and in the movement itself. Like kaimahi before her, she insisted that the marae be governed by Māori rules, but at the same time took precautions to protect those untrained in, and ignorant of, the subtlety of these rules. She relied on women who had been her friends since adolescence or young adulthood, but, as her family matured, also formed alliances with her daughters and many of her nieces, all of whom earned her confidence.

Because of her sense of responsibility, she took on the task of instructing the next generation how to perform as competent Māori in a world surrounded by Pākehā rules and conventions, a world to which, in all reality, they would have to make concessions. To the extent that she and her peers were successful, a new generation has emerged to take their place as participants in the movement and as leaders in the wider Māori community. However, while eager to transmit her knowledge to the next generation, she was less than forthcoming, although always polite, to those she decided had best remain ignorant of the rituals and ideology that attended the Māramatanga.

Hoana did not passively transmit knowledge: she created it. She wrote songs and, through her interpretations and narratives, shaped and constructed the ways in which the Māramatanga came to be understood by two generations. She lent meanings to movement waiata precisely because she could make them public without violating the meaning for the select, chosen few. Songs for the Hui Aranga—and indeed other songs—were so often captured on video and audio recorders that we must see them as having entered the public historical record. Years after their initial presentation, many songs and their accompanying actions can be replicated effortlessly by those who have participated in and listened to their continuing performance.

Hoana was steeped in oral tradition and uncomfortable with writing as a means of carrying information over space and time; in her youth, writing was prohibited in the movement, except in the case of selected scribes. Yet she herself wrote journals of special events such as missions and rā, and she willingly allowed others to see them. This reflected her growing sense of responsibility for ensuring that the movement endure. She recognized that her writings would never be taken lightly; like the kaimahi who preceded her, she was writing history, an endeavor that could only be treated with respect and gravity. Hoana therefore ensured that her voice would be heard and that her interpretations would become part of the record, as information was transferred across generations and, at times, over great ravines of understanding.

Childhood on the Whanganui

Hoana Maria was born in 1930 in Rānana, the second child of Keru (the second child and first son of Mareikura and Te Huinga) and Rena, whose father, Poope, was Kataraina's husband's brother. Keru and Rena had nine children, of whom six survived into adulthood. One of the three who died in childhood was Riripeti, discussed in chapter 4. Five of Rena and Keru's children were raised elsewhere.[1] Their first two children—Rihari and Hoana—remained in Rānana when Keru and Rena moved to Ohakune.[2]

After the difficulty her mother endured giving birth to her older brother, Hoana came into the world relatively easily. She was given the name Hoana for John the Baptist, but her full name—Hoana Maria—replicated that of her great-grandmother, thus binding the young infant to the people and history of Rānana. Hoana heard that Te Karere wanted her own parents, Anaera and Ruka, to raise her; instead, after Te Karere's death in 1935, Anaera and Ruka raised another of Rena's daughters, Riripeti. Looking back, Hoana thought that Rena deferred too much to the wishes of others.

Hoana was raised by her grandmother's sister, Wiki (Wikitoria), whom she called her Kui or Granny (to be distinguished from Te Huinga, her grand-mother), and Wiki's husband, whom Hoana called her Koro (grandfather). It was a home in which only Māori was spoken. Her older brother Rihari stayed with another family near by in Rānana.[3] Hoana explained that, in these cases (known as Māori adoption), it was not that parents did not want their offspring, but that so many others clearly desired the presence of a young child, frequently the child of a particular favorite.

Wikitoria and Te Huinga were daughters of Pauro, whose land facilitated the development of the Māramatanga. Wikitoria was a devout Catholic, main-taining an unswerving and exclusive faith in the church.[4] Despite the events through the 1930s and 1940s at Raketapauma, Kuratahi, and Maungārongo, involving her closest relatives, Kui Wiki found the beliefs of the Māramatanga incomprehensible. Hoana learned little about Te Karere or the Māramatanga during her childhood in Rānana. And it was not until she was older that she came to see how the followers of Mareikura were understood by their relations. According to Hoana, however, on her deathbed Kui Wiki fully accepted the range of possibilities generated by the Māramatanga.

The rules of the household and of the marae at Rānana followed Māori conventions of correctness. Kitchens were always erected outside, thereby main-taining the separation of food preparation and storage from other aspects of domestic life. Areas designated as tapu were kept distinct from those recognized as noa. Aches, pains, and illnesses were treated with herbal medicines,[5] and if necessary by a tohunga. All physical crises were handled through bathing—a pattern that continued when, as a child, Hoana fell from a horse, as an adolescent, her hip collapsed, and as an adult, she suffered miscarriages. Water was healing and redemptive. Most importantly, Hoana was taught that the spirit of the river—a spirit once more invoked in the Tira Hoe Waka (chapter 7)—was protecting her and all its descendants. The persisting importance of genealogy pointed to the continuity of her own life and the history of her people.

As a devout Catholic, Wikitoria was not pleased to have a tohunga involved in critical events. Yet when Hoana, as a young child, fell ill and medicines proved ineffective, the tohunga was called in and traced the cause of her sickness to a singularly Māori source. The young child had inadvertently brought food into contact with Kui Wiki's suitcase containing whakapapa books. This disturbed an important boundary of the Māori world: food and sacred items (whether genealogy or carved treasures) could not be placed in close proximity. Hence the separation of the kitchen from other arenas of social and ritual life.

Hoana recalls that both Granny and Koro spoiled her; she never "got a hiding"—at least not from her granny. They owned a shop in which they stocked basic food supplies for the community. Hoana recalls being poor, although their house was quite large: four bedrooms, a passage, and a "lovely verandah." Granny, who was placid—in contrast to Koro, whom Hoana remembered as loud—tended to keep both the house and the shop running smoothly. Yet there was no doubt that Koro was the man of the house. Indeed, Hoana learned basic women's behavioral rules, such as never to step over a man. As female she was poke, while men were understood to be tapu. She saw this as meaning "I'm defiled," and felt that she had been taught this to ready her for her place as an adult Māori woman.

In fact, it is clear from Hoana's recollections that, while obeying the external commands of male competence and control, her grandmother was very much a dominant figure. Granny became, in the eyes of young Hoana, her first model of a strong, competent woman. And indeed, little Hoana—bright, quick to grasp implications, and an eager pupil—must have been wonderful company for Kui Wiki.

The primary school in Rānana was maintained and taught by nuns. Hoana could recall only two Pākehā pupils, two boys from the other side of the river. She pitied them for their minority status. In hindsight, she could recollect no difficulties between Māori and Pākehā. She did remember her Granny referring to the Pākehā from time to time, but she had no perception of difficulties between the two groups. However, she herself was taunted for being very fair, for in fact resembling a Pākehā. For the most part, her recollections of primary school days sound quite idyllic, riding horses over the hills with friends and playing at the river.

Hoana's only recognition that life might be different elsewhere came on a school trip to Wellington, going down the river by steamboat.[6] She was acutely aware of the differences that divided them from the sophisticated urban dwellers that she now saw for the first time. She was curious and interested in the city, but also felt very much "a country hick." Almost fifty years later she conveyed a feeling not only of discomfort, but of exposure, of being looked down on because of who and what she was. She carried this vulnerability with her throughout her life.

In 1940, when Hoana was ten, her Koro became ill and had to move with Kui Wiki to Wanganui for medical care. Hoana and Rihari returned to live with their parents in Ohakune. Rānana has remained an important part of her life, never left behind. She was also very close to her brother Rihari, a tie that intensified when they returned together to Ohakune.

Return to Ohakune

This was a very busy time, both on Maungārongo marae and in New Zealand. World War II had just begun. For the followers of Mareikura, these were years of intense teaching. The marae at the time contained only a dining room and two meeting-houses, but there were also the private residences of Te Huinga and Mareikura, Harimate and Ahitoro, Rena and Keru, Aurora and Tika, and Hine and Pauro. In addition, although they lived at Raketapauma, Anaera and Ruka were frequently present, as were the members from Kuratahi: Katāraina, Merehapi, and a young Tūmanako. Weuweu was also present.

The elders at Ohakune were not especially welcoming to the two children; Hoana never forgot how unwanted she was made to feel. The village at Rānana was primitive compared with Ohakune, making Hoana and Rihari feel like bumpkins, and indeed Hoana recalls being referred to as a "river brumbie."[7] Matriarch Te Huinga played favorites, among grandchildren and children alike, and Rihari and Hoana did not come within her circle of beneficence. Not surprisingly, they were soon regarded as troublemakers.

To a perceptive and vulnerable ten-year-old, to be treated as a suspicious stranger must have been very painful. She was mocked by children her age for her initial inability to speak English fluently; adults, sceptical of her ability to speak Māori, must not have realized that she could understand their often caustic characterizations of the two returning children. It was a distressing transition, from indulged and beloved mokopuna to somewhat suspect interloper. Her sole ally in those early months was her brother, Rihari.

At Maungārongo, Aurora and Anaera took charge in ways that seemed harsh and arbitrary to the frightened young girl. At Rānana, children would climb the rafters in the dining-room, and eat freely from other people's gardens (Hoana laughingly remarked that it was true that stolen goods are sweet). At Maungārongo, children who engaged in such activities were roundly taken to task by Aurora. And Hoana and Rihari, understanding where other children did not, knew that they were held responsible for any wrongdoing: they were the backwoods ruffians who led their playmates astray. Fifty years later, Hoana commented: "I grew up with that thought. I became bitter with that thought."

Frightened and bewildered, she lived up to their worst expectations and for a time became the town bully. In discussing this time, she said that she was "rude," a term that she would use to characterise herself throughout her life. In fact, she was seldom rude, and always polite, especially to strangers. She was, I think, recognizing the price she paid for not being silenced, for having the stamina and fortitude to hold on to her convictions and not lose her voice. She made a choice not to be silenced by either the language barrier of her peers or the barriers erected by the elders. She bravely spoke out and would continue to do so throughout her life, often with painful consequences. The strong, determined woman she became had her source in a frightened girl's return to live among her unwelcoming relations.

But being privy to the Māori of adult conversation in the meeting-house had other consequences: Hoana also understood their discussion of the Māramatanga. Here she found her attitudes undergoing a curious reversal. From distance and distrust, she was, in her words, "falling in love with the people." By the time she went to high school, she felt a clear affinity for the movement and its beliefs. At about the same time, she began to demonstrate her own gifts.

Hoana's schooling in Ohakune, at St Joseph's Convent and later at Ohakune District High School, did not go well. On the river, in a one-room schoolhouse where she knew every other student, she felt confident and capable. There was no such connection for Hoana in Ohakune. During her first year at high school, she continued to feel lonely and apprehensive. To make matters worse, her hip collapsed; one morning she was simply unable to get up. The family treated this by bathing her, but she stayed out of school for some time, increasing her isolation and her discomfort when she returned. But she did form a close friendship with another young girl, Pin. Both Pin's parents had died when she was still very young; she was brought up by the senior Mareikuras, then by Pauro and Hine, and ultimately by Anaera and Ruka.[8] Hoana's memories of their youth together suggest that they were playful and adventurous. But over the years, they grew into firm allies, attending the whare wānanga together and sharing in the more esoteric aspects of the teachings of the Māramatanga.

In her first year at high school, Hoana had fainting spells, something the old people attributed to the onset of menses. However, when she lost consciousness, she would see Te Karere. She explained that she would be playing marbles and "something would come over me." The elders would carry her into the house and listen intently to what she said at this time. Regaining her presence, she could not help realizing that she had been uttering things the elders understood to be significant. Perhaps most unsettling to a young girl, she had no recollection of events that took place while she was unconscious. She found her first experiences *of being in a trance unnerving—in her words, she was "petrified"—despite her devotion to Te Karere. Far from encouraging such events, Hoana went out of her way to avoid their repetition. Like her aunt Anaera, she was a reluctant medium.⁹ Only many years later did Hoana see herself as a channel for Te Karere's messages; Te Karere continued to appear to her throughout her life, providing guidance, comfort, and inspiration.*

This was a turning-point in her relations with her people of Maungārongo. Far from the rural ruffian they had all thought her to be, she was emerging as a gifted, shy adolescent. Nevertheless, her conviction that the elders had not welcomed her or her brother and had thought of them as vaguely unsavory invaders persisted, even as she was becoming part of, and immersed in, the occurrences on the marae. A lifetime later, those memories still were capable of inflicting pain.

On the marae, the young and receptive Hoana was impressed by the women and their work: Weuweu, Te Huinga, Aurora, Anaera, and Hine were all competent and active in multiple arenas. Marae etiquette prevailed at Maungārongo, but in the meeting-house, women were permitted to speak. Here, the major producers—Katataina, Aurora, and Anaera—were clearly in their element. Songs and talks that came through these women were discussed long into the night, as the group made concerted efforts to tease out all meaning from the messages. Hoana explained that while the family would get together for morning and evening prayers, the talks would take place more commonly in the evening. Often, groups of people would meet beforehand to plan what to say and what topics to bring up when the family congregated that evening. The wairua always let them know if they had wandered off the proper track. She recalls one session in which the question was posed, "Which is the greater: the word, strength, or water?" They debated all day, finally arriving at an answer, which was presented to the wairua—who chastised the listening audience for not understanding that all three depended on one another. Through this debate, and in the many others on similar topics, the wairua allowed the people to grow, to develop. Such metaphors of growth and development were very important for Hoana, as they had been for Pauro, her uncle who preceded her as a kaimahi.

By the time she was in the middle of her high school career, she no longer was, nor did she understand herself as, a rowdy outsider. Brought up Catholic, she apprehended connections between the Māramatanga and Christianity, which reassured her of a larger unity. She was committed to the people, to their beliefs in Te Karere, and to a Māori identity in a Pākehā world; yet she never abandoned her outsider's perspective completely. Perhaps because she had not been embraced and heartily welcomed immediately, she could listen to Māori discussions, take stock of the speakers and what they were saying, and analyze what she heard. She formed alliances warily, but her caution was rewarded; she formed lifelong allegiances.

At this time, Hoana also witnessed her aunt Anaera's distinctive way of leading without appearing to lead. Here was a woman committed to the message but not in the least to her own role in its delivery; Hoana understood her auntie's modesty and diffidence. Thus from a young age, Hoana's command of the Māori language and her personal connection to Te Karere gave her privileged access to the inner workings of the Māramatanga. But, just as important, she earned her position because she knew when to be quiet, when it was wiser to listen, and when she had to obscure awareness of her own understanding.

In 1945, Hoana's sister Riripeti died. Riripeti was loved and admired not only by Hoana but by all who knew her, and her death was sudden and overwhelming. Hoana saw for herself the events of Riripeti's tangi (described in chapter 4), but far from being frightened, she became more convinced of the singularity of the marae and her family. This point marks the completion of Hoana's difficult transition from a protected and indulged childhood at Rānana to her adult participation in a movement imbued with a strong sense of mission and purpose. It was also at about this time that she began to pay attention to a young man named Rihari.

Marriage and Childrearing

At first Hoana thought Rihari arrogant and did not want to know him. Even years later she could not tell why or how she could have made such a misjudgment. Rihari was always modest, kind, and gentle. He always worked hard, gaining the approval of his elders and, over his life course, the respect of his juniors. He was also an excellent athlete, playing rugby for his province and continuing well into his forties. There would have been a decided contrast between Hoana, the outsider, suspicious and the source of suspicion, and Rihari, the darling of aunts, uncles, koro, and kui. They were separated for several years when Rihari went with his family to Wanganui. This gave Hoana time to overcome her initial negative feelings and, in her words, to "learn to be herself."

At first they kept their relationship secret from the family. Before their marriage, it is unlikely that anybody would have anticipated their union.[10] They were first cousins, so their nuptial mass required a special dispensation. However, when the romance became public, it was opposed by their parents and Kui Wiki. There were several reasons for Granny's discontent. Most obviously, the closeness of the couple's kinship connection was a source of discomfort; but also to Kui Wiki, a firm believer in Hoana's capabilities, even Rihari, the almost universal favorite, was not good enough for her mokopuna. Additionally, devoutly Catholic Kui Wiki was suspicious of the Māramatanga; she could not be happy at the prospect of a union between Rihari and Hoana and the resulting conjunction of two seemingly disparate ideological systems. Indeed, the people of the middle reaches of the river referred to their kinfolk at Maungārongo as "the dream people." Some found that appellation amusing in the last decade of the twentieth century, but half a century earlier its barbs were no doubt felt acutely. Kui Wiki eventually came around, acceding to the marriage, and, ultimately, to the values of the Māramatanga.

Things were still not settled with their parents when they decided to force the issue by having a baby. (In retrospect, it is not clear whether this was a planned strategy or an after-the-fact justification.) That the elders could still refuse consent was a possibility; in such a case, the young couple would have had no choice but to leave the marae. It was certainly a gamble. However, the pregnancy and the consent of the clergy allayed any remaining opposition. In June 1952, they were married by a priest in the chapel on Maungārongo marae.

Their first child was born in the hospital at Raetihi. Hoana spent twelve hours in labor with only nurses for company. In those days, fathers were not permitted into the wards with women in labor. Her aunt Hine and uncle Pauro named the baby Te Rongonui.[11] (Babies are named alternately by the mother's and father's sides of the family.) Hoana was nervous at the responsibility, but they were both fine and returned home to be looked after by her assembled relatives and by a wonderfully engaged father. Te Rongonui had a bassinet in Hoana and Rihari's room, but in fact would sleep on top of his father. When Rihari went off to work, he was shifted on top of his mother.

Yet this was not an easy time for Hoana. She found herself married to a man whom she certainly loved but who managed to eclipse her effortlessly in the affection he commanded. In the face of such overt favoritism, indeed adoration, displayed toward her husband, the issue of her own problematic acceptability raised itself once again. She avoided certain of her aunts and uncles, convinced that it was Rihari they sought and fearful that she was tolerated only as his inevitable, and unavoidable, consort. Apart from her husband, through these early years her Granny Wiki was her one exclusive supporter.

It was the birth of Hoana's second child, Mākere, named by Rihari's father Ahitoro, that brought Kui Wiki's complete acceptance of Hoana and Rihari's marriage. As a result, Mākere spent much time on the river with Kui Wiki, who was by then widowed. Their third child, a son, Hemi, died of pneumonia when he was six months old.

There was little work in Ohakune at this time and Rihari was forced to seek jobs in neighboring districts. As a result, he was able to be at home with his young family only on the weekends. Once there, his Saturdays were often devoted to rugby. For her part, Hoana found this painful, but felt strongly that she must learn to accommodate Rihari, who worked very hard during the week and who, everybody agreed, deserved time for sport and relaxation. For a time Hoana worked for the railway, but she was forced to stop after her second miscarriage. With only Rihari's income to support them they were very poor. At this time, with a growing family and with Rihari moving in his own, predominantly masculine, arena, Hoana learned to depend on the other women on the marae, Raana, Pin, and Monica.

Hoana later described herself as "troublesome" in these early years of marriage. When she and Rihari had rows, their uncle Pauro would approach Hoana and counsel rangimārie (peace). This would only infuriate her: why was the admonition directed solely at her? And in this, too, she stood up to her elders and held her ground. She knew she was difficult and demanding; but she also knew that Rihari's kindness, gentleness, and willingness to help everyone obscured from all but herself his tendency to be headstrong and stubborn. Theirs was a complex and profound relationship. In the forty-two years they were married, they had some mighty quarrels, but these never diminished their understanding of, and devotion to, each other. In the last years of Hoana's life, the couple took very good care of one another.

When she was pregnant with a fifth child, a girl, Rihari's sister Mana and her husband requested the baby. As a sister who was unable to have children, Mana clearly had a lien on their offspring. Hoana wanted to keep the baby, to ease her sorrow after the recent loss of her baby; but she could not bring herself to say no to her sister-in-law. This is but one example in which she clearly subordinated her own will to that of the group, or to what she felt was a higher purpose. The baby that Mana and her husband took, Rongomau, died. Hoana was soon pregnant with her next child and once more Mana requested that she be allowed to raise the child. This time Hoana and Rihari did not immediately give up the child, a boy, Te Rangimārietanga, but brought him through infancy first. It must still have been a difficult decision, but Hoana found it was made easier by the child's obvious fondness for, and desire to be with, his aunt and uncle. He stayed with them until he reached secondary school age, when he returned to attend Ruapehu College in Ohakune. Hoana went on to have two other daughters, Maurea and Maharanui, and then, with no planning, her family was concluded. She had had nine pregnancies in thirteen years, producing five surviving children. Her last child was born in 1963. She was pregnant with Maharanui when she went on the mission to the mountain.[12] In addition, Rihari and Hoana raised two other children.

The Māori universe in which she had been brought up in Rānana was sustained in Ohakune. Respect for the mauri of the marae was axiomatic, as was compliance with kawa (tribal etiquette). Hoana taught all her children respect for the rules of marae protocol, waiata, pātere, and karanga. She taught her daughters how to conduct themselves, paying attention to notions of poke and especially how to behave around men. She told me that women of a certain age group tended to raise their children in a particular way. She and Raana raised their children closely and together, with each of them often assuming responsibility for the other's offspring.

From her earliest years on the marae, Hoana was also learning. She learned not only how to karanga,[13] but also how to work in the kitchen preparing food, setting the tables, and waiting on the guests, visitors, and elders. She was always active in the preparation of the marae—the cleaning of showers and toilets, and the arrangement of mattresses, pillows, sheets, and blankets. She and Raana became the mainstays of the marae when the elders were gone. Her competence must have been obvious to Pauro, who as kaimahi, spent a great deal of time with her.

In the late 1950s the marae was undergoing a change as elders either moved away or died. A new generation was taking their place. As their families grew, the bonds between the women of Hoana's generation intensified. Years later, she explained to me how important visiting was, for in these times spent with other women, she learned she was not isolated and that her vision was not a solitary one. For Hoana, both Māoritanga and the Māramatanga were gifts from God, gifts that required vigilance to nurture, and consistent gratitude. Her commitment to the Māramatanga assured her participation in pilgrimages and missions and her attendance at all rā.

Hoana was introspective, understanding both her own and others' motivations. When she did speak out, it was because she had weighed the matter carefully and felt something important would be compromised by her silence. She learned at this point that it was women's responsibility to pass down knowledge. This was a duty that she took very seriously, teaching confused children (she and Rihari spent the rest of their lives looking after wayward young people), and looking after her own and others' offspring. She also took it upon herself to intervene on behalf of individuals from the marae who ran afoul of rules and regulations. For example, when her son Te Rongonui was expelled from boarding school, he was said to be responsible also for the expulsion of several of his friends. His mother had no doubt about his culpability but had strong suspicions that his comrades were rather more innocent. She argued vehemently with the priest in charge, but to no avail. She felt, despite his vocation, that the priest's behavior could hardly be considered Christian.

As a native speaker she was inevitably a teacher of Māori language, but her engagement with the movement and her understanding of issues and events also placed her in a central position. With seniority, she became much like her aunts Aurora and Anaera. However, while these women of the senior generation had been deferential to authority and, in the case of Anaera, shy and retiring, Hoana confronted problematic situations and individuals directly. Her abilities earned her respect, but approval was hard won.

Hoana as Kaimahi

It is not surprising that Hoana, in time, became the kaimahi of the movement. She was the granddaughter of Mareikura, and the niece of Anaera and Pauro. But it was not merely kinship that qualified her. She had always taken a greater than usual interest in the movement and its beliefs; she had direct and personal experiences with Te Karere; but perhaps most important she had the ability to understand the subtlety of leadership in an ostensibly egalitarian movement. Even in the time of her koro Ruka's leadership, she was already consulted as a relative equal, despite the fact that she was still in her twenties and had a young and growing family. She was gifted and committed in ways that distinguished her from her peers and brought her to the attention of her elders. If Te Karere appeared to her unsummoned in dreams, in time Hoana would seek out this special form of spiritual guidance, becoming increasingly confident of special assistance. Pauro was especially interested in Hoana's interpretations and reactions. As both a native speaker and a disciple of the movement, she was one of those most capable of understanding the context and content of messages. And without explicitly saying so, Pauro also relied on her assessment of people. Although she was slow to pass judgment upon them, Hoana was an accomplished student of people's motivations and reactions.

Hoana participated in the mission to the mountain in 1962 (see chapter 4). Pregnant at the time, she was unable to climb the mountain. But she was vigilant and dedicated, watching the proceedings, praying, and far surpassing her explicit role as cook. Years later, she understood and articulated the mission's importance in validating her generation's performance and commitment to the movement. She explained that those who went up the mountain became "firm soldiers of the wairua."

From the late 1960s on, she, Raana, Pin, Matiu, Lei, and selected others attended the whare wānanga, where they learned the rituals, chants, poipoi, and cultural specialties of the people of the river from a most learned elder (see chapter 5). In the early 1970s, she, her husband Rihari, Matiu, Pauro, and Hine became the core of those who made yearly pilgrimages to Waitangi (see chapter 6). As the rā expanded beyond the original four days of her youth and young adulthood to include celebrations at Rānana, Maketū, Kai Iwi, and Levin, her own time became more committed to activities centering around the movement. There were also yearly trips to Rotokura for holy water, as well as the culture club's annual participation in the Hui Aranga. Hoana was involved and active in all contexts, as a teacher in some, as a student in others. She had become a filter of knowledge between generations.

When I came to stay with Hoana in 1982, her children had become adults, several of them had become parents, and she was more free to move beyond the world of the marae. She had already been to the Philippines on church business and was active in the various levels of diocesan affairs (as was her husband). Her involvement in the culture club included, for example, her composition and instruction of songs for the Hui Aranga. She would pore over old notebooks, search her memory, and work along with her sister Wenerau and Raana to compose songs that each of the three teams (midget, juniors, and seniors) would present. She would then work out the actions to accompany the waiata. She attended and supervized practices. However, her major occupation was in the Māramatanga. Her yearly round was punctuated by the movement's activities, but she was always available to consult with Raana and with anyone else from the family whose needs required her special assistance. She was enthusiastically engaged in the movement and its history; with great facility, she could recount all the movement's commemorations and their meanings. But she especially paid attention to the education of the young.

The demands of protocol were never shirked. Even in bitter cold and rain, parties were to be assembled to come onto a marae for a tangi. Hoana felt that all individuals—of her own and other generations—should be willing to assume the most mundane and lowly responsibilities if that was what it took to get them done. Both she and Raana, in their sixties, would clean toilets and scrub floors and appliances to ready the marae for visitors. There were to be no shortcuts, no concessions made to human discomforts. To compromise kawa would be to show disrespect for the very things in their universe that most deserved reverence.

Hoana was especially supportive of her brother Matiu, a tohunga. They possessed complementary knowledge and the presence of two of them on a marae, often preceded by a conversation with Raana, represented considerable power. Inevitably, however, as Matiu's authority and prestige increased, the dynamics within their family changed. As he was called upon to travel around New Zealand—not only in a ritual capacity, but as a member of various Catholic organizations, and Māori commissions—he depended on his wife Lei, his children and grandchildren, and increasingly his brother Dean and Dean's wife, Mona. The running of the marae and tending to the young were still priorities, but this burden fell increasingly on Hoana, Raana, and Rihari.

This period, which began with the whare wānanga, saw the emergence of Hoana as a kaimahi. She had become adept at blending all available sources of knowledge, building bridges between the teachings of the Catholic Church and the teachings of her elders. She understood herself to be a connection between generations, moving into territory grown familiar throughout her adult years, as she worked hard to explain in English things which to her made sense only in Māori. She experimented with different perspectives from which to blend together new understandings. Her relationship with Raana sustained her during this period. The two women would talk about everything and each lent her perspective to the other's musings.

Political Activity

In the 1980s the New Zealand government developed a program to eliminate the Department of Māori Affairs and devolve its operations onto the local (and iwi) level, administered by the Iwi Transition Agency. This meant a growing number of committees were needed to run marae and Whanganui affairs.

Hoana, Raana, Pinenga, Tūmanako, Rihari, and Matiu found their participation increasing in a number of separate, albeit related, arenas. The larger family worked to consolidate control over their land through a number of trusts, and several claims were lodged before the Waitangi Tribunal. All this activity meant that the older members served on many committees. For example, Hoana served on committees dealing with the management of the river, with trusts concerning land, with the administration of the marae; she also served on the district and central councils for the Hui Aranga. Tūmanako worked to reclaim leases on Māori land, and served on the local hospital board, on the central council of the Catholic Church, and on land trust boards. At the same time, their participation in the affairs and management of the Catholic Māori mission grew with the appointment of Takuira Mariu as bishop. Members found that their tribal interests and their activities within the Catholic Church coalesced.

As Hoana ventured further afield, travelling throughout New Zealand and beyond to attend committee meetings, hui, tangi, and missions, she grew to be more dependent on spiritual support generally and upon Te Karere specifically. Whether she went to Australia, Waitangi, or Wanganui, she knew that she could count on the assistance available in another domain. As her political experience and mastery grew, she began to resemble her uncle Pauro and all the Māori leaders who had preceded her; she understood, both intuitively and explicitly, that religion and politics were not discrete categories, and could not be separated.

This was hard work and the travelling was difficult, especially when she felt that she was needed at Maungārongo. Nevertheless, as at so many other junctures in her life, she had to choose between competing demands and expectations. If she was needed by the whānau on the marae, she was also claimed equally by the larger Whanganui iwi. Her sense of responsibility frequently outweighed her own personal needs for calm and respite from the intensity of political negotiations. Unfailingly devout in her observation of both Catholicism and the Māramatanga, Hoana would stay at rā from midnight to midnight, considerations of work and other responsibilities notwithstanding.

Yet despite the great increase in her workload, there was a perceptible continuity in Hoana's experience. While striving to improve the position of her family and iwi in New Zealand through negotiations with the Pākehā, Hoana began to see that recovery of land and victories in court would be bleached of color and significance if the next generation lost the Māori language, history, and culture. Her sessions with adolescents, especially her nephew (Wenerau's son), became more devoted to the transmission of very specific knowledge. Hui Aranga songs, which she composed and taught, were designed not only to impress the judges, but to instruct the young on their heritage.

As Māori identity became a crucial theme, Hoana discovered intersection and connection, not divergence and opposition, in the ways that the Māramatanga, Catholicism, and Māoritanga were constituted and understood. The unity that Hoana was able to achieve brought together two domains, religion and politics, that were never separate in the world of her childhood. If the instruction of Te Karere was meant to guide future generations, then the fusion of Hoana's apparently disparate interests would be inevitable. More than anything substantive and concrete (and there was much of that), this unity, fidelity, and devotion distinguished the quality of the knowledge and information she possessed and passed on.

Travelling took up a great amount of Hoana's time in the last ten years of her life. Not only were there the annual missions to Waitangi (see chapter 6) and Tira Hoe Waka (see chapter 7), but in 1988 Hoana, along with other elders, undertook the repatriation of the remains of their ancestor, Te Umuroa, from Tasmania (see chapter 7). In addition, Hoana journeyed, under church auspices, to the Philippines and to Singapore. She also accompanied the new Māori bishop to Australia. Thus, in addition to all her other responsibilities, Hoana found herself travelling on pilgrimages whose results would strongly affect the next generation.

The Next Generation

In 1982, there was a Tū Wairua (spiritual instruction period) at the marae. Young people related to the whānau came from all over the country to learn about their heritage. Although this was initially to be Pauro's responsibility, his ill health forced him to remain in Hastings. Hoana had to step into the leadership role. Despite the respect in which she was universally held, she was clearly nervous, although this is not surprising given her natural diffidence. In preparation she worked on organizing the food and sleeping arrangements.

E Te Iwi Kia Ora was flying over the marae. Hoana explained its history to the assembled children and teenagers and its importance to Mere Rikiriki, referring to the work of the nineteenth-century prophets as Mosaic Law. Despite her misgivings she did a wonderful job, accomplishing the task so well that Rihari commented to me at the time that she was truly gifted. And indeed, she was a natural teacher, dividing the young people into groups so that they could talk among themselves, then bringing the larger group together to check on the accuracy of the smaller discussions. She used these group discussions as a platform from which she could teach both marae etiquette and the history of the Māramatanga. She told the gathered young people about the nature of mauri and how the guardian of a marae was a source of protection, but at the same time must not be offended. The gifts of their ancestors had been handed down through a chain of prophets and prophetic movements, through Pai Mārire, Ringatū, Te Whiti, Mere Rikiriki, Rātana, and Mareikura. Although all connected to the Mareikura family, these young people were led into the larger tradition of Māori religious thinking. They were also told explicitly that the missionaries did not give the Māori all the teachings of Christianity; they were known already.[14] Because the Tū Wairua overlapped with the rā in Rotorua, Hoana had to leave; before she went, she explained to the young people her commitment to the rā and to the teachings of the Māramatanga.

When the Tū Wairua was over, Hoana was clearly relieved. There could be no doubt that the day had gone well, with information transmitted across a generation to an audience that was generally eager and receptive. Thenceforth Hoana was understood by all, and came to understand herself, to be a teacher. Her knowledge as well as her linguistic skill had prepared her, and from then on she took the pedagogical role everybody had come to expect of her.

Hoana and other elders, especially Matiu and Raana, trained members of the next generation to take their place. Young women have learned to karanga and mihi (welcome visitors); young men have learned taiaha and oratory. The mainstays of the marae kitchen are now of a new generation. At rā and other hui, young women will be seen organizing the dining room and meeting-house, cleaning the bathrooms and other facilities, ordering stores and cooking in the kitchen. Young men are now involved in the major cooking, hangi, and the jobs that require food preparation for large crowds. Several younger people have distinguished themselves in their interest in, and their curiosity about, the history and the tenets of the movement—as she herself had done in the past.

Hoana was a strict teacher and expected that her instruction would redound to the credit of the larger family. When one of her nephews, Mikaere, a talented and gifted orator even in his teens, went to Nepal on a youth program, she explained to him that she had not trained him to stand on mountains, but to stand tall on his own marae. Similarly, she made it clear that whatever he was to learn at university was to be used for the good of his people.

In many ways, then, Hoana's last years were spent mediating the concerns of two different generations: as concerned as she was with overseeing the regulation of ritual events, she was equally concerned with transmitting her knowledge to a younger generation. But as well as substantive knowledge, Hoana was always attentive to attitude: for her, gratitude for spiritual guidance was axiomatic. In return, precision and rectitude were to be the hallmarks of individual conduct, coming onto marae, in meeting-houses, observing rā, at tangi, and in that most precious of all gifts, knowledge.

Conclusion

In telling her story, Hoana inevitably revealed a great deal about herself. But through this process, she illuminated important cultural themes. Since she saw herself as a teacher, her conversations with me unavoidably took on a didactic component. Yet her narrative was much more than an expert teaching a novice, an insider patiently going over details for an inquisitive stranger. In telling and retelling the events that had come to shape her world, she simultaneously gave that world shape and contour. She emerged as a comfortable actor in a world she had participated in creating.

From her earliest years, Hoana had contact with pivotal figures in the two older generations. Many of them were women: she heard stories of strong women such as Mere Rikiriki, and she knew Anaera, Katenraina, Weuweu, Te Huinga, and Merehapi. She observed as women ran the marae and as they produced the songs and inspirations that marked the Māramatanga. She forged links with women of her generation—Pin, Raana, Monica—and these placed her in the center of the forces that were converging in the movement. Over time, she became the figure most responsible for the transmission of knowledge and hers became the commanding narrative of the marae and of the movement.

As her generation reached maturity, there was a critical change in personnel when elders died or moved on. Concurrently, there was an expansion in the move- ment's activities. Hoana saw missions—to the mountain in 1962, to Waitangi through to the present—as a means of fortifying and revivifying her dedication to the movement's works. At the same time, she was responsible for the marae, for her own children and other offspring of members of her generation, and for dealing with the Pākehā whose incursion into their world was strongly felt. She learned and taught the importance of knowledge, respect, and gratitude.

She understood that Te Karere, by bringing the members of the Mārama- tanga close to their origins, was a means to knowledge and a source of strength that could be built upon. Using the metaphors of growth and development she had heard as a young child, she continued to urge her people to build themselves up, to fortify themselves through knowledge, and to erect an edifice upon which they could stand. She taught the young people that theirs was a heritage in which they were to take pride. In teaching them respect for the kawa of their own and other marae, she was instilling her firm conviction that forces at work in their universe could insulate and protect the people, if only they were understood.

Her own children, if less articulate, realized this. Increasingly, they understood that their mother was gifted, that her dreams often carried meaning, and that she understood what motivated people and events. More importantly for their future, they came to see that their family was implicated in a part of Māori history that they would have to sustain. Hoana and her close friend and ally, Raana, along with their husbands, and Tūmanako, Pinenga, Matiu, and Lei have, by word and example, inspired a new generation to continue.

Hoana understood that Mareikura and Te Karere together were to clear new paths. This imagery, along with that of building, informed her life. One of her favorite statements was that we all stand on the shoulders of those who came before us; we are guided by their knowledge, and only by looking to the past can the present be seen clearly. Hoana understood that the very act of sharing knowledge, history, and meaningful events would weave relationships across and between generations of women and men. Kinship prepared the way, but the essence was transmitted through time and space in shared tellings and retellings. In articulating the interlocking, interwoven relationships that have maintained and sustained the Māramatanga, Hoana herself cleared the path for another generation.

Hoana died suddenly in May 1994. She collapsed at a meeting north of Wanganui, was rushed to the Wanganui hospital and flown from there to Wellington where she was operated on, but died of "a bleed of the brain"—an aneurysm. Among her things were strong prescription medicines to help her through the headaches she had been having. She had kept working and told nobody but the doctor; as her bereft husband, Rihari, said, "It was typical of her." She left behind a chasm that refuses to close. Years later, with other deaths occurring in their midst, those closest to her remain dazed and unsettled by their loss.

CHAPTER 6

Pilgrimages to Waitangi

By the late 1960s and certainly by the 1970s Māori political awareness had esca-
lated rapidly as activists became more assertive and expressed more resistance to
Pākehā control (Walker 1984, 1987, 1990). Perhaps the most notable group of this
period was Ngā Tamatoa, who were idealistic, educated, and urban. Demon-
strations, pickets, and petitions became part of the arsenal of Māori activism.
In 1975, another group, Matakite o Aotearoa (The Seers of Prophetic Vision
of New Zealand), led a march of 30,000 from the northern tip of the North Island
to Parliament in Wellington. Their slogan, "Not One More Acre of Land," pub-
licized the passion with which Māori viewed the issue of land and its alienation.
This passion was demonstrated repeatedly throughout the decade, and with
reasonable success. The 1975 Treaty of Waitangi Act, and its amendment in 1985,
opened up the possibility of redress and compensation for Māori grievances. The
Waitangi Tribunal (created by the act) held hearings on marae, an arena governed
by Māori conventions. Suddenly the control and ownership of resources, and
mutual protection and obligation, were under discussion and negotiation.

But the new mode of activism did not sit comfortably with many older
members of the Māramatanga. Elders persisted in the conviction that the past
continued to intrude upon the present, that wisdom derived from the ancient
world remained efficacious, and that spiritual revelation was to be accorded a
privileged place in any contemporary epistemological system. For their part, the
young relied on the Treaty of Waitangi, with a focus on legalistic interpretations
and political implications. To engage in such a discourse requires familiarity with
and facility in Western styles of argumentation. For many of the younger generation, especially those who were attending university, these differences bespoke
the divide between themselves and their elders. But by the last decades of the
twentieth century, many of the elders were also concerned with the treaty and its
inclusion in national legislation, avidly following the Waitangi reports as they
were released to the public.

In this social context, the Māramatanga initiated a tradition of pilgrimages to
Waitangi, a headland at the mouth of an estuary in the far north of New Zealand
where the 1840 treaty was signed. This tradition has continued through three

decades of radical social change in New Zealand, and the missions involve three generations. While elders were looked to as interpreters of events and signs, members of the middle generation (the generation of Hoana, Matiu, and Rihari) were placed in positions of significant responsibility. Over the course of the first missions, a policy developed to concentrate on the legacy to be left to the younger generation; young adults, adolescents and children became the focus of later pilgrimages. The disparate beliefs and approaches of these generations came together on the pilgrimages. In particular, the disjuncture between young and old became a focus: while the early pilgrimages were clearly intended to be instructive for all who participated, they were also meant to bridge the gap between generations by ensuring the safety of a landscape that had rapidly, and recently, eluded Māori control.

The Treaty of Waitangi, in some understandings, made New Zealand a Crown Colony of the British Empire and turned the Māori into subjects of Queen Victoria. But the Treaty was in two languages, Māori and English, yielding two rather different understandings.[1] As a seat of Māori–Pākehā contention, Waitangi was a destination fitting to the Māramatanga's tradition of visiting places of ritual power and political potency. Where better than the very location of the treaty's signing to learn how a document understood to protect Māori had left them so vulnerable?

Those members who went on the first of these missions anticipated the controversy that came with renewed interest in the treaty. But although the middle generation was comparatively young, it was neither unprepared nor inexperienced: most had been trained in the tribal whare wānanga and, more importantly, had exhibited knowledge and competence, climbing Ruapehu only a few years earlier. Fortified by this experience, these individuals emerged as the leaders and stalwarts of the missions to Waitangi and of the movement itself.

Early Missions to Waitangi: Inspiration and Action

It is a common belief in New Zealand that the ancestors of the contemporary Māori arrived in seven canoes from a legendary Hawaiki.[2] The tribal divisions found among Māori today are held to be derived from these canoes; indeed, many Māori who know little of their genealogy can readily name their ancestral canoe. The Whanganui tribes are associated with the Aotea canoe; however, they also have subsidiary links to Kurahaupō.

When Pēpene Ruka was kaimahi, accompanied by his ward Pin and guided by the wairua, he identified all seven sites of the initial landfalls of these ancestral vessels. This brought him into contact with the mauri, the life forces of the canoes. One purpose, of the early missions to Waitangi especially, was to replace the mauri of the Māori people and so recast their history of migration.[3] In retrospect this endeavor appears intrinsically problematic, and as late as 1995 some members felt that the mauri had been returned to Waitangi, while others felt that this had never been accomplished. Some felt that it was unseemly for the group to have the mauri of other canoes, while others felt it had given them spiritual power and had been returned to its rightful place. But whatever construction is placed on it, mauri, as a life force of the Māori people, became an important metaphor for the trips to Waitangi.

According to Hoana, the wairua had for several years been sending messages to prepare members for signs of the right moment to begin. Two messages to women of high credibility precipitated the first pilgrimage. Raana dreamt about Hone Heke, a Ngāpuhi warrior,[4] who on four separate occasions between 1844 and 1846 chopped down a flagpole erected by the British settlers. Both Māori and Pākehā understood erecting the flagpole as an assertion of sovereignty. Heke, though fighting an ultimately losing battle, became a national hero, renowned for his courageous rebellion. That Hone Heke was among the first to sign the treaty may be a reason why his anger at subsequent events was so extreme (Sahlins 1985: 66).

Concurrently, Hinga, Peehi's wife, received a vision that would galvanise the group. Situated in 1840, the year the Treaty of Waitangi was signed, Hinga's vision revealed indecision and disputes among the paramount chiefs gathered to discuss the proposed treaty. Contention was inevitable in light of the mana of the assembled chiefs, but at the centre of this disputation was the wisdom of signing the treaty. In the midst of the argument, a tohunga from Ngāpuhi attempted to settle the dispute: he argued that pride and politics were inevitable concomitants when individuals wielding such personal power were forced to take concerted action. To facilitate the necessary decision, the tohunga urged the chiefs to give up their *mana*, and make their decision unencumbered by vanity or parochial concerns. The chiefs acceded and in yielding their mana demonstrated their commitment to concerted action. The tohunga subsequently buried this source of prestige and planted a karaka tree to mark both the place and the significance of the leaders' actions. It was to remain there until claimed by a future generation. This karaka tree, rooted in the mana of the Māori people and their chiefs' personal sacrifices for the general good, had to be tapu, sacrosanct. Hinga's revelation provided both insight into past events and a narrative that gave a distinctly Māori turn to New Zealand's colonial history.

Loss of mauri was an apt way to describe the sense of deprivation felt by most Māori in 1970; a treaty, that had proved problematic for numerous reasons, had left Māori powerless, their source of strength buried, yet not entirely inaccessible. Ritual action had proved productive in the past; now it seemed both suitable and inevitable. While the members of the Māramatanga surely depended on widely circulated histories of the Māori settlement of Aotearoa, revelation offered a much finer, more nuanced, and ultimately more familiar means to contact and to understand the actions of their ancestors. Revelation had helped them articulate the dilemma, providing the members with a coherent construction of the past (intelligible in terms of both chiefly and settler motivations) and a means to provide relief for their present situation. For, if they could prevail in retrieving and restoring the mauri of their people, they would be armed with a potent weapon against the colonial interlopers.

The First Two Missions

There were approximately fifty pilgrims on the first mission, all prepared by dreams and messages. In 1970, Pauro was the kaimahi, but Rihari supervised the organization of the pilgrimage. The cars travelled in convoy, stopping frequently to ensure that all members were well and comfortable. Pauro, Peehi, and Aurora were in touch with the wairua, although they were in different cars. When late that evening they compared messages, they were not surprized to find that they were the same. They reached Whangarei in time for evening karakia in a local church. By midnight, they were on the road again, and they reached Waitangi in the morning.

As they discussed their mission in the church-house at Waitangi, they concluded that the mauri was to be maintained in keeping for all Māori people. But the wairua told them that God could not help the people, for their mana, tapu, and wehi (awe) were buried. The difficulty had originated in the past, but these pilgrims, with the *hunga wairua* (group of spirits), would be able to return to redress the situation. Pauro and Matiu both used ancient karakia while at Waitangi, melding the wisdom of the ancestors with introduced teachings of the Church and inspiration passed on through the wairua.[5]

The pilgrims' first task, after their talks in the church-house, was to approach the karaka tree. There was inevitable trepidation as they came near. Suddenly, Aurora was seized by a desire to reach out, touch the tree, and shake its hand. To her surprise and relief, the tree responded by grabbing her hand and shaking it back. The pilgrims then prayed and recited a rosary. The old and the new were not merely blended; each was transformed by the other. For those who witnessed and for others who heard of the event, this was strong evidence that peace had been made at last with the karaka tree. Indeed, on subsequent visits the tree has blossomed and borne fruit. There can be no doubt that for these pilgrims their reconciliation with the tree was the beginning of a new accommodation to the past.

The second mission in 1971 continued the themes of the first, but with an emphasis on children and their emergent Māori identity.[6] Both the early missions attempted a reconciliation with a past that is clearly problematic. Beliefs about a past untouched by the Pākehā merged with ideals of Christianity and contemporary revelation. As in other missions, all forms of knowledge, derived from all possible sources, were assimilated and transformed into an instrument of reconciliation. The image of the karaka tree, rooted in the buried power of their ancestors, and transformed in the present by Māori chants and Christian prayers, is especially compelling—remarkably apt for a people who are navigating the treacherous seas of identity politics as they renegotiate their past.

The decision to go to Waitangi demonstrates that these pilgrims were able to engage complex yet interwoven traditions that depended upon the authority of both biblical discourse and spiritual revelation. Their activities, their movements, and their discussions designate the extent to which political modulation relied upon such a mixture. With each successive trip, replete with revelations and reassertions of spiritual privilege, the pilgrims to Waitangi laid claim to, and established their responsibility for, their past.

The Third Pilgrimage: 1972

The third pilgrimage, in 1972, was the last of the "big trips." The number of pilgrims was considerably smaller on subsequent trips. The adults who went were, for the most part, the leaders or future leaders of the movement. With them were children and young people—the "next generation"—to whom this mission was dedicated. In addition, the mission had special meaning, perhaps especially so for Pauro. Pauro and Hine's only son Petera had died suddenly a few months before, and the anniversary of Pauro's sister Harimate's death occurred while the group was at Waitangi. Both wairua were to figure in this pilgrimage. This, also, was the first of the pilgrimages to be accompanied by an anthropologist.

In the weeks preceding our departure, there were doubts about the wisdom and viability of this particular expedition. The concerns of those who were opposed induced those who were committed to going on the mission to establish strict rules of conduct. Cars remained together in one convoy; karakia were said at the appropriate times of the day regardless of where on the road the pilgrims happened to be; most participants fasted and refrained from smoking during the journey between Auckland and Waitangi. Such strictures were not exceptional during pilgrimages; but in this case they also ensured that the pilgrims were, to some extent, immune from the recriminations of those who had chosen not to participate.

The group assembled at Ohakune on Thursday of the first week of the school holidays and journeyed to Auckland the next day. We travelled from

Auckland to Waitangi and back on Saturday. Sunday was devoted to discussion, in the Auckland home of Whakahawea and Hiria and their young family. Leaving in the late afternoon, the party travelled home through much of the night.

Adjustments were necessary from the very beginning. The unexpected death of a distant relative delayed our leaving Ohakune as the pilgrims first went to the tangi. As a result, we arrived in Auckland at approximately 4 A.M. Saturday and were on the road again to Waitangi shortly after seven o'clock karakia.

Visions began almost immediately, giving heart to the pilgrims who had chosen to persevere. Ani had the first that I recorded. Ani was a granddaughter of Weuweu and had married into the family at Kuratahi. In her fifties at the time of this journey, she had frequent visions throughout the weekend.[7] While waiting to be picked up, she had watched a tree materialize in her living room. An aeroplane hovered around its upper branches before the image dissipated. When she described this vision to the other pilgrims, all readily concurred that this signalled spiritual approval for the mission. The tree, so reminiscent of the karaka tree in Northland, assuaged whatever doubts may have occurred to the participants.

Before departing, the group gathered in the chapel for an especially solemn service designed to ensure spiritual support. Discussions continued in the meeting-house; messages were analyzed and examined for their broadest, most encompassing meanings. Individuals stood to speak (much as they would for rā) and explained their personal ambitions to the attentive audience of pilgrims. While there was clearly an overlap of interests, something that Pauro would work to crystallize in the discussions at the end of the mission, there was also variation in the pilgrims' quests. Some had purely personal motivations for going, such as seeking better health or the welfare of their loved ones. Others sought assurances that the movement would flourish over time, and become a means through which a new generation would prepare to take their place. Still others went in quest of benefits for all Māori, searching for some redress for over a century of colonization. With spiritual guidance, the pilgrims all sought to continue the work of the movement and to promote and refine their own conceptions of Māoriness, their own version of the history of Aotearoa.

While it would be necessary for the pilgrims to discuss symbolism and meanings as the mission unfolded, such deliberations could never be precise. This was a journey designed to encompass all desires. Pauro, who was Hoana and Matiu's uncle, was clearly in the forefront of this undertaking; everyone seemed to look to him for direction. The entourage derived both directly and indirectly from Maungārongo, emphasizing the importance of the marae in the movement's history and the crucial role that its contemporary residents played.

There were five cars to our convoy, each with several adults and a number of children wedged in between. I was a passenger in the car carrying Hoana,

Matiu, Lei (Matiu's wife) and several of their children. Discussions were solemn, centering on the mission and the spiritual aspects of the participants' lives. Matiu, who because of his marriage to a woman from the north was a leader for this expedition, clearly looked to his older sister Hoana for knowledge of the movement. His contribution to discussions was tentative, if eager. Nevertheless, he knew a great deal about the history of the movement, about Tangi Wairua, and about the work that brought him, Matiu, as a descendant of prophets, to this juncture. Moreover, both he and Hoana, in the opening discussions, sought peace of mind, a tranquillity that would permit them to absorb all that they must. Over the long ride between Ohakune and Auckland, brother and sister sang songs from decades past and recalled the lives and actions of their aunts and uncles, their grandmothers and grandfathers. We were accompanied by *Our Lady of Perpetual Succour.*

We arrived in Auckland close to 4 A.M. After greeting relatives who were already there and tackling the usual meal given to guests, most of us dozed for an hour or so. Seven o'clock karakia officially began both the day and the pilgrimage. From Auckland to Waitangi, approximately six hours, the cars remained together. Inside, the people were solemn, moved by the impressiveness of their undertaking. Most adults fasted and abstained from smoking. There were frequent prayers, both in Māori and in English and, other than children, no one chattered idly.

When we approached Waitangi, the convoy pulled off the road for final prayers. At this time, those pilgrims who had received messages or visions recounted them to the reassembled group; pao of welcome from wairua, most especially Harimate (one of the older generation who participated in the ascent of Ruapehu in 1962), complemented visions of the Virgin Mary, assuring the pilgrims of their success within two traditions. The frequent cloudbursts that had marked our travels were seen as "showers of blessing"—yet another heavenly sign of approval. As these pilgrims had been wont to expect, the express assent of the heavens was an integral part of the pilgrimage process.

At Waitangi

Once in Waitangi, we stopped at the Anglican church, where members offered thanks for a safe journey and expressed hope for a successful mission.[8] In keeping with the harmony of the occasion, Anglicans (often husbands of women born into the movement) and Catholics both led the service. At this time, several people reported visions. Iwa's husband, Tuck, who characteristically kept his own counsel, addressed the members. The mauri, he said, must be returned, repatriated to those descendants of the canoes visited decades before by Pēpene Ruka and his ward, Pin; early visions had made this mandate clear; they had, perhaps, been unfaithful in failing to return it in previous years. Those present at the time agreed vigorously; many even maintained that the disputes and controversies that had disrupted their personal relationships were a direct consequence of these past failures.[9]

From the church, we moved to the karaka tree. The picture of *Our Lady of Perpetual Succour* was placed on the tree's branches and held there by one of the children. The pilgrims bowed their heads while one recited the rosary in Māori. Several proudly indicated to me how much the tree had grown since the missions had begun. The tree was clearly a metaphor for the past, for here all the chiefs, with their mana and tapu, had made a critical decision, one that would affect all Māori for generations to come. At the same time, the growth of the tree indicated that this group of pilgrims had come to terms with the past: the tree's ability to thrive was a tangible demonstration of this reconciliation.

Following this we moved to the flagpole and to the treaty house, both of which have become tourist attractions.[10] Again, prayers were said at the flagpole while those of us who had not attended previous missions were taken to the beach to see the original landing place of one of the seven canoes and to hear the narratives that motivated the first pilgrimage. After a brief tour of the treaty house, where a replica of the treaty is encased, we started our return journey to Auckland.

When we arrived once more at Whakahawea and Hiria's home, Manukorihi, prayers of thanks for the safe completion of the trip were followed by a good meal.[11] We deferred discussion until the following morning, when we would all be refreshed from a good night's sleep. But that night several women dreamed of holding babies or giving birth. These women were past childbearing, so the dreams were interpreted as images of rebirth, regeneration, and the emergence of a new era.

Karakia at 7 A.M. on Sunday initiated nearly ten hours of discussion. Pauro played a major role both as moderator and as a critical speaker. More than anyone else, he was adept at using and interpreting metaphors and symbols. Moreover, his ability to understand the members' complex personalities permitted him to defuse arguments before they surfaced. Perhaps most significantly, Pauro was able to move seamlessly between individual concerns and the larger issues that the Māramatanga confronted—the education of a new generation and a rapprochement with the past. By emphasizing the positive aspects of concerted action, he brought everyone, even those whose interests appeared to be relegated to a secondary position, into sharing in the achievements of the larger group.

Presentations of the pao, waiata, and haka that had been received were a measure of the movement's success. Pauro received one of the haka, which addressed the general work of the movement but which, in a key metaphor, became especially emblematic of all that the pilgrims hoped to achieve. The wairua addresses the people:

> Our love welcomes you,
> The builders.
> Cast your fishing line and
> Anchor it to Waitangi
> So that it may be pulled up by Tangi Wairua
> The mana, the tapu, the power, and the awe
> Bind us to one another.[12]

This haka, sent to the pilgrims by a wairua, defined their task in nautical images. Their line was to be placed and anchored in Waitangi, to be drawn out for the benefit of them all by Tangi Wairua, a spirit already recognized as their guardian and whose link to the past was known to all. The haka then asserts spiritual connection while it links present preoccupations to their guardian from the past. Moreover, the invocation of mana, tapu, *ihi*, and wehi—all pre-missionary concepts—establishes the enduring vitality of a past that the Pākehā has not been able to transform. Pauro's skilful use of metaphors assured the pilgrims that their journey had been both successful and momentous.

During the day, the discussion was highly charged, defined by the liminal characteristics that distinguished it from mundane concerns and daily constraints. Pauro brought out the renegotiation of the relationship between past and present; continuity with the past was proclaimed and unity, which had seemed so elusive a mere forty-eight hours previously, was asserted. The purpose of the pilgrimage, as Pauro explained it, was to find roots to the past, to set down an anchor and by so doing make their descendant's claims to history.

> Some of us are ignorant of the fact that the anchor is there. The anchor has to be pulled down. The anchor of a boat is useless when left floating. But once down, it holds. Cast your line and anchor it to Waitangi.

He called the work an octopus and the followers tentacles, which must return frequently to the nurture of the main body. The octopus was a metaphor for the importance of interdependence: for the organism to survive, each tentacle must support the others. He described the rā and the pilgrimage as refuges, suggesting that while members might live in the world of the Pākehā they would be able to draw the necessary strength and sustenance from such occasions. This talk, one of many he gave that day, provided imagery for consensus and cooperation and an understanding that the past would never loosen its hold on the present.

Many spoke that day, celebrating personal victories and championing the overall benefits conferred by the pilgrimage. However, repeatedly it was Pauro who placed this particular journey within the context of the movement's pilgrimages and the movement's origins with Mere Rikiriki, making the members conscious of the history that had prepared them and their ancestors for this undertaking. By the time we left for home in the late afternoon, there was a general feeling of achievement and release. As we left Auckland, there was a brief shower and a brilliant rainbow, Tangi Wairua's sign of pleasure.

We drove for another twelve hours to Levin, stopping for seven o'clock prayers, for gasoline, at Ohakune to call in at the chapel, and for an entirely unanticipated occurrence. A young man of about nineteen was driving one of the cars on the way back to Ohakune. Suddenly there were frantic motions that we were all to pull over. A very shaken youth emerged, pale and at a loss for an explanation: as he was driving, Petera's face appeared before him. (Petera was Pauro and Hine's recently deceased son.) This young man was one of the new generation—that is, part of the generation brought to Waitangi so that their Māoritanga would be strengthened. He was a sceptic and saw himself as a driver for his elders and a mate (friend) for his cousins. He did not know what to make of the vision that loomed before him as he drove.

For Pauro, Hine, and the other adults on the pilgrimage, there was neither difficulty nor contradiction; the dead appeared and continued to influence the living. Indeed, Petera's appearance to this young man—a young man who, to understate the case, had serious doubts about the concerns of his elders—made it clear that a new generation was indeed on the right path.

We arrived in Ohakune, where prayers were said in the chapel and Hoana, Matiu, Lei, and Rihari ended their trip. The rest of us would continue until close to 5 A.M., when we reached the chapel at Levin. Here, during prayers of thanksgiving, Aurora had a vision: She saw two baskets on the altar, both overflowing with gold stars. Levin, their last stop, thus completed the transformation of the pilgrims from a community of exiles into a community of the triumphant.

The pilgrimages to Waitangi continued into the present. They now take place, however, after the November 9 rā, in commemoration of Te Karere. The pilgrims felt that for the time being at least their work at Waitangi had served its purpose: there was now a national Waitangi Tribunal reviewing claims from iwi all over New Zealand; history was being revisited.

Discussion

> Histories told and remembered by those who inherit them are discourses of identity; just as identity is inevitably a discourse of history. (White 1992: 3.)

The missions to Waitangi augmented rather than replaced the themes of the movement. The persisting, if problematic, importance of the past was confronted, as it had been before on Mount Ruapehu; specific emblems of Catholicism were melded with revelation and inspiration derived from Māori sources; a generation now fully equipped to lead began in turn to train its successors. The social conceptions and arrangements that emerged at Waitangi speak as much to continuity as to innovation.

Pilgrimage is an especially appropriate vehicle to return to the past and to subject it to the scrutiny of the present. The pilgrims were in a liminal state, more than—and different from—their usual selves. Yet when they were mistaken for a visiting football team, they chose to allow the misperception to persist. There were constraints on neither their position nor their mobility; the past and present were easily negotiated with the assistance of their visions, dreams, and contacts with the wairua. Metaphorically, they enlarged their public personas in ways that emphasized determination, courage, and a willingness to place themselves at risk. In short, they became what they knew themselves to be: the heirs to the prophets.

The thorny problem lay in presenting new dilemmas in familiar terms. In this sense, Pauro's eloquence and mastery of the conventions of oratory provided the necessary means to weave these strands together. More importantly, the challenge to colonial authority was now waged on the movement's terms. The imagery used so skilfully by Pauro and other kaimahi suggested the nature of the confrontation that occurred at Waitangi, and asserted unequivocally the persistent link between religion and politics that exists in the Māori world.

History converges at Waitangi: the history of colonialism merges here with the tradition of Māori prophecy, and now with the history of the Māramatanga. Waitangi is the site of the treaty that, for a century and a half, gave a patina of legality to Pākehā colonial subjugation of Māori and expropriation of Māori land; but it is also a locus of Māori power, represented by the mana of the chiefs buried under the karaka tree. Here, the tree shakes hands with the Māramatanga on their first mission, and then goes on to blossom for later missions. Can there be any doubt that what is understood here is reconciliation with the past, a marshalling and anchoring of its potency? The songs that link the past of the prophets to the present activities of the movement and Pauro's emphasis on anchoring, stability, and continuity suggest that reconciliation is possible and was achieved here. Moreover, the image of growth, fruition, and blooming (puawaitanga) more than suggests a reversal of Māori decline. The relationships between past and present, proximate and distant times, and religion and politics are resolved, as the pilgrims and we learn that each is incomplete without the other.

Pauro, as always an eloquent and important leader, gave expression to the complex events that unfolded. A modest and humble man, he would never point to the importance of the movement's work or to the abilities of the kaimahi to give voice to the extraordinary. Hoana and Matiu, as grandchildren of the prophet, as individuals with recognisable gifts, and as participants on other missions and in the whare wānanga, clearly stood out from others of their generation. As they observed Pauro—his fluency in two languages, his ready interpretations, and his command of both biblical verse and the history of revelation within the movement —they also witnessed the effortless, almost invisible, display of competence and influence.

The knowledge that members of Matiu and Hoana's generation gained in the whare wānanga validated the importance of ancestral traditions. Combined with Catholicism and inspiration from the wairua, such knowledge provided a blueprint for action, one that would redound to the benefit not only of the members of the movement, but to that of all Māori. Perhaps the whare wānanga's main importance is to be found in the fact that members now felt able to scrutinise and re-examine tradition and custom. Their activity at Waitangi suggests that such an examination served a more national identity, in a desire to move beyond purely local, tribal concerns. Such revelations present these pilgrims with a privileged view of a crucial historical event, which can then be subjected to interpretations encompassed within their own distinctive belief system. The ancestors—those connected to all Māori, to the descendants of all the canoes—are presented as noble, if misguided, forebears who left a hidden legacy for their descendants. This legacy provides a means of separation from Pākehā.

The missions to Waitangi took place at an especially propitious time in the histories of both New Zealand and the Māramatanga. The former was on the verge of a significant re-evaluation of land rights with the establishment of the Waitangi Tribunal. The members of the movement, some primed by their experiences in the whare wānanga or on the missions to the mountain and Lake Rotokura, were prepared to be spiritual pioneers.

The pilgrims to Waitangi in the early 1970s were, as Māori, members of a minority in their own land. However, it was precisely and ironically this situation that gave strength to their position. In their journey to Waitangi, they left behind local parochial traditions. But they wilfully maintained the constraints of kinship. For them, unlike for most other Christian pilgrims, salvation is a corporate, not a personal, issue. The moral unit continues to be the social group; under these circumstances, individual concerns yield to the larger goals of the group.

This very stance is in opposition to the dominant values of New Zealand Pākehā culture. In fact, the entire pilgrimage process is a celebration of those aspects of Māori culture most valued by Māori and least prized by Pākehā. Good fellowship and hospitality are exalted; the importance of the past and the enduring spiritual contacts with the dead are emphasized. All these are important in themselves, but it is the contrast between Māori expectations and Pākehā behaviour that heightens their significance. The celebration of distinctively Māori aspects of social life in a situation that is free of structure, and free of Pākehā constraints, permits liberation from a profane social world and from a problematic social identity. Pilgrimage can and does arrest the inexorable process of accommodation. For it is only by confronting their past that the members of the Māramatanga may define themselves anew.

These are not the hapless would-be warriors nor reckless rebels of New Zealand history books. Rather, they are heroes, resisting the imposition of a foreign will, using all the weapons at their disposal. Perhaps most importantly, they have communicated through the centuries by distinctive Māori means. A refusal to accept Pākehā domination of history is encoded in the imagery that is always present in pilgrimages to Waitangi. Rather, Pauro and all the participants assert Māori control over the narration and interpretation of critical events.

The imagery of the mission to Waitangi is condensed and multivocal: for the initiated, the flagpole conjures up Hone Heke, British domination, Māori rebellion, previous missions, and current treaty negotiations. The karaka tree elicits notions of reconciliation and fruition, which in turn are linked to a Māori past populated by resolute and strong-willed leaders. Here, as in the trips to Mount Ruapehu, the past and the present were brought together; the lines between exclusively Māori beliefs, colonial impositions shared by most of the country, and Christianity were deliberately blurred. Yet again the pilgrimage provided a forum in which disparate traditions were merged and transformed.

Here the pilgrims were able to lay claim to the Virgin Mary: her placement in the leaves of the karaka tree as they simultaneously said a rosary in Māori effectively removed Catholicism from a legacy with undeniable links to colonization. Far from superseding the beliefs of their ancestors, Catholicism had been transformed, through the process of pilgrimage, into a weapon against encroachment, against dispossession and loss. The tree and the Virgin became woven into a narrative that was comfortably able to encompass both the history of colonialism (and all that meant for Māori displacement) and the continuing effectiveness of indigenous notions of power. Clearly, the work of the pilgrims, the Virgin Mary, and the rosary, as well as invocations to and signs from the wairua, ensured their future by establishing roots in the past.

The retelling of events through the years also validates the importance of oral, as opposed to written, history. These are not mutually exclusive, for members of the Māramatanga preserve accounts of their missions in notebooks. But the reliance on narrative—on the gathering of people together as events unfold and waiata, pao, and haka are performed—emphasizes the priority of oral representations. Here at rā those accounts are elaborated and interpreted by the kaimahi. Words on paper carry neither the potency nor the flexibility of oral narratives. The songs revealed during particular events become part of the movement's repertoire and are extended in time and space beyond those who were present; history comes alive for those who were not present and is relived for those who were. Far more effectively than a written document, these events become integrated parts of individual and group histories.

The visions that characterize these journeys to Waitangi join with other voices from the Māori tradition of prophecy in pointing out that ground that has been regarded as immutable has, instead, shifted and its meaning is no longer certain. Such revelations inevitably raise doubts as to how we in the West understand history. They make clear that the stories of conquest, confiscation, and dispossession cannot be merely linear, but must involve divergences, returns, and missed opportunities (Clifford 1988). This is as true for Pākehā as it is for Māori, with one critical difference. Māori have often been trapped by the stories that can be, and have been, told about them.[13] Visions and revelation not only keep faith with past Māori reliance on orality, they grant authority once again to Māori.

The conversation between Māori and Pākehā has also been enhanced by the privileged discourse initiated in movements such as the Māramatanga. Here the difference between Māori orality and Pākehā reliance on a text is at its most obvious. It is no accident that the text is the Treaty of Waitangi. However, the members of the Māramatanga, motivated by private, orally transmitted revelations, respond both with legal disputation and with religious action. The Waitangi Tribunal, which ostensibly bows to Māori convention by holding its forums on marae, has, nevertheless, been influenced by Pākehā notions of justice and of history. The pilgrims to Waitangi knew better. They realized that they had to be present at the site to be effective.

Raana

Raana is one of the most important and respected members of the Māramatanga. Her knowledge, perseverance, and personality have brought her leadership and authority. She is a stalwart of the Maungārongo community, and has managed the marae for decades. But her reputation extends beyond the movement and beyond the Waimarino: she is an outstanding example of what a local woman versed in tribal knowledge can accomplish in arenas beyond the marae.

Raana's life—she was born in 1932—has been heavily involved with children. She has looked after her own twelve offspring and supervised the development of many of her nieces and nephews. Like many women, she has been actively involved in her grandchildren's upbringing, raising several in her own home. Her children and grandchildren gravitate to Raana in times of stress, knowing they will receive both emotional and practical support. She has instructed children at the local primary and secondary schools and established the marae educational institutions. In 1986, with Hoana, she started the kohanga reo at Maungārongo, and in 1993 she initiated a kura kaupapa (primary school), both of which are conducted entirely in Māori. In 1996, she received a formal Te Kohanga Reo certificate from the Māori queen, Dame Te Atairangikaahu, on the marae at Tūrangawaewae.

Raana is an habitual journal writer, compiling over several decades a repository of both church business and the concerns of the movement. Her meticulous descriptions of missions provide documentation of her generation's experiences for all who will come after her. She also writes stories for young children, which she illustrates with her own excellent photographs; these stories make experience within Māoridom meaningful to children who must grow up in the Pākehā world.

Such an intense involvement in the movement, the marae, and the development of young people has provided Raana enduring satisfaction, but it has come at a price. She has tended to neglect herself—fairly easy to do in the relative poverty of Māori since the breakdown of the welfare state in New Zealand. Regular medical care is too expensive for limited budgets so most ailments, whatever their gravity, are minimized, dismissed as minor for as long as possible. Māori women suffer disproportionately from hypertension, respiratory illnesses, and cancers of the stomach and lung (Pōmare and de Boer 1988). Despite her outward calm and matter-of-fact competence, Raana has dangerously high blood-pressure.

Raana now has outlived almost all her generation; she is, in her words, one of "the last leaves on the tree." Widowed since 1991, she was faced in May 1994 with the death of Hoana, her sister-in-law and lifelong friend. When I saw her in late December of that year, Raana was still in shock, the bruises of mourning and memory as yet overwhelming. One afternoon, looking about her, she could not help but notice the vacuum and imbalance created by the loss of Hoana (and others). Her social world was off-center, clearly diminished, and she remarked: "Either there's too little of them, or too much of us."

Sixteen years separated our first recording in 1982—in which we went over the early years of her life and the meaning of being a woman in the Māori world —and the most recent recording, in 1998. Over this time she has become one of the most respected and knowledgeable elders in the Wanganui region. The growth of her authority and prestige in the intervening years reflects not only the ascending position of women as they move through life, but also her competence in, and devotion to, all she undertakes. Indeed, her influence derives at least as much from her personal characteristics: integrity, knowledge, warmth, and desire to strike a balance, regardless of the strength of competing factions. With the losses of Hoana, Matiu, and finally Rihari, she has stepped, however reluctantly, to the forefront. Since Rihari's death in 1999, her burden has become singular. A naturally modest and reticent woman, Raana has marshalled her resources and dedicated herself to what lies before her, as she has done many times in her life.[1]

Early Years

Raana was born in Karioi in 1932, the second of five children, and lived there until the death of her mother. The family then split up, with Raana moving to Kuratahi to be raised by Mere and Tei.[2] Her affiliations by birth, marriage, and adoption linked all the major kinship units encompassed within the Māramatanga. Not surprisingly, she has always identified herself as Ngāti Rangi, a more inclusive kinship designation than a specific hapū such as Rangiteauria. In the household, in addition to Raana, were Hōhepa (not the Hōhepa of Kawiu marae) and Dick, and Tony. Raana refers to all those who shared the house with her as her siblings. They lived in a large, gracious dwelling, with three bedrooms, a sitting-room, a kitchen, and a bathroom that had hot and cold water. Tūmanako and Peehi lived next door. Raana arrived in Kuratahi several years after Te Karere died there, but she overheard the conversations of her elders who were present, and participated—indirectly when she was young, more directly as she matured—in the development of the Māramatanga.

The children at Kuratahi attended Ruanui primary school and the Catholic school in Ohakune. Raana delights in memories of her childhood. As a group, they explored the countryside on foot and horseback, swimming in creeks and streams, venturing into caves and wandering great distances. With a glint of pride, she said they had been in all the bushes around Raketapauma and Kuratahi. Their elders, especially their Auntie Anaera, believed firmly that the children were protected and watched over by their spiritual guardians; Anaera reputedly always knew their whereabouts. But this freedom was limited to rural activities; going to dances or the pictures in town was strictly forbidden. Raana's recollections of her childhood are of liberty combined with security, care, and shelter.

In this bucolic freedom, the children became familiar with bush lore, plants, and birds, and learned from their elders to rely on herbal treatments for illness and affliction. Specific leaves and roots had properties that were effective for a variety of maladies, ranging from local injuries to systemic disease. This knowledge has served her well. While she will certainly avail herself of Western medicine, she will just as readily, depending on the illness, scour the bush for the appropriate remedy.

These sojourns across the countryside, as well as regular journeys to other marae of the Māramatanga at Ohakune and Raketapauma, created bonds that would continue throughout their lives. Raana's childhood ties with Tūmanako, the Waretinis, and many of the Mareikuras and Akapitas proved durable alliances. Perhaps as importantly, their ventures seldom involved any separation based on gender. The parity with which boys and girls roamed over the landscape characterizes the nature of interpersonal relations in the movement. Young and adolescent girls fit comfortably into leadership roles, never thinking to defer to their male cousins merely on the basis of gender. This generation came of age within view of one another, establishing early and clearly patterns of interdependence, leadership, and female equality.

Nevertheless, the division of domestic labor was based upon gender from early childhood. Raana recalls helping with the dishes as soon as she could stand on a stool. Her grandmother was especially strict, teaching the young Raana how to sew, wash, cook, and clean. It is no surprise that in her adult years she has exhibited exemplary organizational and culinary skills. As a young girl, she was also taught the stringent rules governing personal cleanliness and the maintenance of bodily boundaries. In particular, she learned to restrict her movements in the presence of men and to be especially careful when handling food. She was instructed, and in turn prepared her own daughters, to adjust to the rules that governed their ritual universe. It was the responsibility of women, Raana stated emphatically, to sustain these gender divisions.[3]

Raana's childhood memories are of minimal Pākehā intrusion. There were Pākehā leaseholders on nearby farms, but she lived surrounded by Māori families. Her days were spent attending the convent school, working about the house, and exploring the bush, a routine punctuated by trips to neighboring communities for rā. For all that New Zealand and its Parliament were dominated by Pākehā, Raana's world was controlled by Māori conventions and instilled with meanings that were specifically and exclusively Māori. In her childhood, when Māori perspectives vied with Pākehā, Māori triumphed.

In 1944, her grandfather became ill and Raana moved to Ohakune. Her formal schooling ended with her grandfather's death in 1947. Raana took a job nursing in a maternity home near Taihape. Her grandmother missed her and did not approve of a young girl's living on her own. But in the absence of paid work, Raana had no choice but to seek her livelihood elsewhere. By this time she was active in the Maungārongo culture club and had formed lasting bonds with the core group of her peers—Hoana, both the young men called Rihari, Monica, Huinga, Tūmanako, Pin, and Riripeti. The club, with its rehearsals, preparations for the Hui Aranga, and deep commitment to the words and ways of the wairua, strengthened their ties to one another as they grew into adulthood.

As she took on adult responsibilities, Raana became increasingly involved with Rihari, the charming and good-looking brother of Hoana, and oldest son of Rena and Keru. Like Raana, the two eldest Mareikura children had arrived late at Ohakune and had had to learn to balance the tension between being both insiders and outsiders. And they had to find their proper place in the younger, subordinate generation. Like their predecessors, Raana and her peers were more interested in romance and their Hui Aranga performances than in the more serious concerns of the wairua.

Yet, as was so often the case with young people who grew up within the purview of the movement, the intentions of the wairua and of the elders intervened to shape their lives. In 1946, Riripeti died. Many of the adults were devastated, but her loss was also deeply and personally felt by the younger members of the group, who had been her companions and teammates for years. Monica, Riripeti, and Raana were all the same age. The mountain's eruption demonstrated the obvious—this was no ordinary death. Riripeti came back and has been, since her earliest days as a wairua, a special source of inspiration for Raana. Fittingly, at Riripeti's tangi, Raana learned to karanga.

Marriage, Children, Domesticity

Raana married Rihari soon after an Easter hui and moved onto Maungārongo marae. Hoana was married to her husband (also Rihari) at the same time.[4]

The elders did not approve of these matches, for the kaumātua were not convinced that intense attraction was a sufficient foundation for an enduring union. The elders were wrong: both these marriages lasted for lifetimes, and Pinenga and Tūmanako have been married for more than fifty years. Raana's marriage to Rihari united several families. Although born in Karioi, she was brought up by the Te Kooro family, thereby connecting her parents' people to the Ruka and Gray families. Her husband, a Mareikura, was also the son of a Gray (Rena). Raana therefore connected the critical families of the movement—the Ruka, the Gray, and the Mareikura families.

More than any other affinal woman, Raana's position is unique. She has never felt or been treated as an outsider, and other women who have married into the Māramatanga have included her in their number. Of course, she was brought up very much in the heart of the movement at Kuratahi, and as a native Māori speaker, she participated throughout her lifetime—albeit only on the fringes as a child—in almost all crucial events. She is intimate with Kuratahi, Raketapauma, and Maungārongo; for her, more than anyone else, all these marae are "home." The ways in which Raana is able to negotiate distinct family domains are reproduced, through her understanding and empathy, in the personal arena; she has maintained close contact with individuals from all areas, both geographical and philosophical, of the Māramatanga.

It is not surprising, then, that unlike other women who have married into the movement (Aurora, Hine, Moana, and Pinenga) she has always been much less unsettled by the interpenetration of the mundane and spiritual worlds. This is familiar territory, known from childhood, offering neither the terror nor the awe it has inspired in other affines; she is both comfortable with and committed to the Māramatanga 's teachings. Similarly, since the early years of her marriage she has lived among her husband's family, and there has been a degree of comfort in her relations with them that no other woman "outsider" could claim.

Raana bore twelve children, something she accomplished by being pregnant nearly every year for over a decade. She commented wryly that if she missed a year, it was only because she had been pregnant so late in the previous one. The large size of her family was all the more startling to her because she and Rihari waited several years for their first child. Two of their children died, and two were brought up by others. It was not easy to raise so large a family. Their difficulties were compounded by a lack of work in the area, causing Rihari's frequent unemployment. Raana remarked that in retrospect she did not know how they had managed. Those were difficult times.

It is too facile fifty years later to ask why, in the face of so many difficulties, she stayed: a young Māori woman with a large family had few options in the New Zealand of the 1950s. But far more importantly, she was increasingly committed to the Māramatanga, and with each year she grew ever closer to her sister-in-law Hoana. The two women shared virtually all aspects of their lives. They married at the same time, lived in adjacent houses, had children, and moved through the life cycle together. They visited and confided in one another, sharing the responsibilities of child rearing, generating over time the intimacy that was to make each so important to the other. Their bond, based initially on kinship, developed into intellectual and emotional camaraderie. Through the years, they would turn to one another with a regularity that by middle age had become unconscious and automatic; abbreviated sentences and twitches of eyebrows were sufficient to bridge a separation of days or even weeks. Most decisions, mundane and momentous, were made in consultation with one another. Both possessed unflagging loyalty to the Māramatanga and to Catholicism, insisting that the two could and must be reconciled. They sought and found continuity between the ways of the ancestors and those forces molding the new world. Raana and Hoana were each purposeful and resolute when it came to transmitting knowledge and competence to the next generation. Together their authority was beyond question and they became the decisive voices behind concerted actions.

Missions and Pilgrimages

Raana is especially committed to the teachings of the Catholic Church, and has always treated members of the clergy with singular respect. Although she depends on the wairua, she was characterized lovingly by Hoana as "a real Our Lady fan." Her world exists with two interrelated sources of revelation, springing from the same source but holding out different aspects of salvation.

Raana's devotion to both the movement and Catholicism and her commitment to their reconciliation emerge clearly in her participation in pilgrimages and missions. In her journal accounts, she demonstrates that the two ideological and ritual systems are readily merged and understood more effectively as part of a larger coherent entity. Raana chronicled the many pilgrimages in which she took part with an eye for detail, recording the names of all the participants, the nature of the messages sent by the wairua, and the names of the flags that so often went along with the pilgrims. Her notebooks also record in great detail the narrative of the priest's presentation of Our Lady of Perpetual Succour, and she always noted explicitly the presence of the icon. From the earliest years of her marriage Raana has been on as many pilgrimages as she was able, frequently accompanied by one or more of her children. Since the 1960s, she has gone faithfully to Rotokura to replenish her family's supply of curative water. She was also present on the slopes of Mount Ruapehu in December 1962. Many other missions and undertakings, especially the Tira Hoe Waka (see chapter 7), bear her distinctive mark.

The following is from her account of the movement's second mission to Ketemarae, Taranaki, in 1964.[5] (The first mission, in 1963, had a predominantly Catholic orientation; a brief account of that mission is in Pinenga's narrative.) It shows how church business, Māori traditions, and the ways of the wairua are blended so as to support, rather than compete with, one another. Taranaki, isolated from the other mountains, has stood for centuries in lonely splendor on the west coast of the North Island.

The second mission to Ketemarae sought a reconciliation between the two mountains, Taranaki and Ruapehu, as foretold during the 1962 mission to the mountain (see chapter 5). This was a trip framed by narratives that preceded the advent of the Europeans by hundreds of years, a peculiarly Māori context that extended the boundaries of the Māramatanga's spatial and temporal domains. The pilgrims were to place a plaque on the house of an elder in Taranaki, one who had been an especially fervent adherent of the movement's teachings. This plaque, Te Aranga o te Pono (The Rising of the Faith), would imbue the dwelling with recognizable personal and social significance.

Raana understood the mission to Taranaki as an attempted rapprochement in which the tribal groups acted as representatives of their respective mountains. The tribal area on the route to Taranaki is adjacent to that of the sub-tribes of Whanganui, with resulting proximate and overlapping kinship relations. A reconciliation was therefore sought on ground that was simultaneously removed and familiar. By the completion of the mission the pilgrims were certain that a new mutuality and harmony had been established between the mountains and between the people who lived beneath them.

With Tikaraina leading, the mission started at 6:30 A.M. with a recitation of the rosary. Accompanying the pilgrims were three flags and Our Lady of Perpetual Succour. Eighteen went, including members from three generations, with Raana's in the middle. Messages began almost immediately, to reinforce the pilgrims' determination and conviction.[6] In describing this mission to me, Raana stressed that signs from the wairua, however they manifested themselves, were to be treated respectfully and with proper awe. Should something out of the ordinary occur, it was, in the context of these sacred, charged moments, perceived as evidence of spiritual intercession.

The wairua were there with greetings when the pilgrims arrived at their destination. As they made their way closer to Ketemarae marae and the elder's house, where they stopped briefly, the words of the wairua's song came through. But it was when the pilgrims approached the mountain that the mission was transformed. For now, the wairua did not greet them, but instead, the mountain himself hailed the pilgrims, indicating that he, Taranaki, had waited for a long time for an accord between the two mountains, a reconciliation of the two peoples so strongly allied to each of them.

The behavior of the pilgrims demonstrated that they had carefully planned their time on the mountain. They moved to an assigned place, carrying with them the three flags, Our Lady of Perpetual Succour, and holy water. As they walked, they said the rosary. The picture of the Virgin was hung on the branch of a tree, the flags were draped over a bridge, and the pilgrims were in the space between these boundary markers. Once again, two traditions, on either side of them (in both literal and figurative senses), were summoned forth to lend authority to their activities. Then, as Raana writes:

> After completing the rosary, we gave thanks to God for the guidance and strength. The spiritual side also came amongst us with greetings. After all was finished, everybody bathed and drank of the water, which was clean and ice cold.

They had brought water from Ohakune, symbolising its place of origin, to be mixed with some from Taranaki. Collecting water from a source near the mountain, the pilgrims returned to Ketemarae.

From the mountain to the marae, they said the rosary, which was also said as the plaque—Te Aranga o Te Pono—was placed by Tikaraina on the residence. Close by, Our Lady of Perpetual Succour watched over the proceedings. Marae etiquette was followed: speeches and a short service attended the mutual greeting of the people, who then adjourned for tea. The wairua emerged with commentary as they were discussing the many events of the day, in particular (in a pao) the wrong turn taken by some of the travellers. Ultimately, Raana drew strength from this, realizing that the wairua had been with them, even when they had strayed from the prescribed path. And the themes of peace and appeasement would resonate for Raana, who in her personal, more mundane activities sought similar resolutions.

Beyond Domesticity

Many women who are married, have several children, and live in rural areas find their lives dominated by domestic responsibilities. To be sure, with eight children to bring up, Raana was thoroughly engaged in household tasks for the early part of her married life. But she took the organizational skills of the domestic domain into a wider context. Over a period of thirty years, she moved from the care of her family into national prominence.

By the 1960s, Raana had added the organization of the marae to her list of responsibilities. Her duties included buying and overseeing supplies for tangi, rā, and hui, and assuring that proper amounts of food were prepared and served in timely fashion. Toilets and showers were to be cleaned. Bedding was always to be in readiness; sheets and pillowcases, mattresses, and blankets were to be available on short notice. Such arrangements are a major undertaking for even a small marae. For Maungārongo, where it was not uncommon for hundreds to gather, the tasks were that much more formidable. Hoana and Raana worked together in this for many years and over time trained several of their children and other young men and women to form a reliable core that could be depended upon. Raana's responsibilities did not stop at the kitchen and whare puni. One would see her busy in the kitchen at one moment, then she would suddenly appear transformed in front of the meeting-house to karanga and pōwhiri arriving visitors. Visitors were made welcome at Maungārongo in the proper Māori fashion. Along with her demanding supervision behind the scenes, Raana made certain that all undertakings were accomplished according to the strictest Māori etiquette. Her abilities were called upon as the group moved beyond Maungā-rongo. It was her voice, for example, that punctuated the dawn at the opening of the whare puni at Rānana. But her karanga are not planned; she has always depended upon her feelings to guide her.

Together with Hoana, Raana organized a kohanga reo on the marae for pre-school Māori children. Their goal was to produce a new generation that would be entirely bilingual. By the time it started she had several grandchildren who, along with other children in the community, formed the core of the kohanga. Hoana and Raana named the school building Manu Kōrero (Speech of the Birds). When the two women were travelling, the words of a song from the 1940s came to them, and they knew this was to be the name for their kohanga.

Creating the kohanga took considerable organization, but the task yielded to Raana's skill and determination. First the building had to be constructed (and later added to) and supplied with equipment for teaching and tending to the needs of infants and teachers. Once the kohanga was started, students had to have materials, mothers needed to be enlisted to supervise infants and toddlers, and breakfasts, morning teas, and lunches had to be prepared five days a week. The kitchen had to be stocked with food, dishes, and other supplies. Raana effectively managed all this, creating a roster of mothers who would shop, pre-pare food, and look after the children. In addition, she has run the kohanga in such a way that it has become an exemplar of how to teach and instil Māori language and Māori perspectives. In this, she was greatly aided by the Mārama-tanga and her strong religious convictions.

The children learn to start their days in prayer, often derived from Catholic-ism, but always in the Māori language. They say grace in Māori before all meals. There is a sign instructing all participants to speak only in te reo, and when Raana is in the room, no English is spoken. Some mothers in attendance are at a disadvantage in this, but they attempt to obey by using sign language or relying on their limited vocabulary and getting help from the children. When Raana is not present, English is heard rather more frequently.

The children spend their days doing what most pre-schoolers do: they color, play, eat, sing, nap, and simply enjoy one another's company. But the distinctiveness of this kohanga lies not in the fact that songs are sung in Māori, but that these are often songs derived from the Māramatanga. Elders who hear the words understand their significance; the majority of children who have mastered the Māori language also apprehend their meaning. Children are taught to recite a basic whakapapa that they repeat every day. In the kohanga, the children not only learn Māori language and attitudes; they are given a strong sense of being embedded in a far-flung kin network. They are told stories of their ancestors, both immediate and far removed. And they are taken to any ceremony that takes place on the marae, learning by example the rules of Māori marae etiquette and propriety. The kohanga is far more than a nursery school; it has become, in the case of Manu Kōrero at least, a training ground in ritual competence.

When children graduate from the kohanga, they are frequently bilingual. Raana discovered that children lost their facility in the Māori language soon after they began to attend the local primary school. This was true even if they attended the bilingual unit, which was established at the local primary school to accommodate the needs of the marae and staffed by teachers and assistants who coordinate their activities with Raana. For several years, children would return to the marae early each day to reinforce their Māori language skills. This proved unsatisfactory, however. In 1993, Raana and the whānau established a kura kaupapa conducted solely in Māori. She was assisted in this by Moriana Hancock, a former assistant-principal at the primary school, who had in recent years devoted her considerable abilities to administration of marae projects. To have established this primary school—to have secured funds, land, building, and coordination with the local education authorities—was impressive. To this achievement can be added that in 1997 the school became entirely autonomous, responsible to the marae and the Māori community, but no longer tied to the primary school. With a kohanga reo and a kura kaupapa on the premises, Raana has ensured that their children's education is under the control of Maungārongo.

Raana taught in both the kohanga and the kura kaupapa, and also taught evening classes in Māori for adults, both Māori and Pākehā. In addition, she has written several books, often complemented by her photographs. Those for children tell stories of the nature of the Māori world and their specific place within it; she establishes the children's knowledge of the Whanganui River, of the guardians that protect its descendants, of relations between generations. The narrative, always in Māori, is entertaining, witty, and captures the children's delight at playing in leaves, frolicking in the swimming pool, or climbing the mountain in the snows of winter.

Merely listing her accomplishments gives scant recognition to the authority Raana has exerted for the half-century she has lived on Maungārongo marae.

Her presence, from the earliest years of her marriage, has shaped the contours of Maungārongo. Almost effortlessly she translated the skills developed for domestic purposes onto a larger arena. The two schools, carrying her devotion to her children to a much greater population, are only the most obvious examples. Raana pursued her interest in the training and education of children beyond the marae schools to national committees dedicated to these issues. Through the entire process, she negotiated judiciously with predominantly Pākehā local and national school authorities.

As she has moved through middle age, Raana's activities have taken her beyond the borders of Aotearoa. She has travelled to Canada and the United States as an Aotearoa delegate to conferences for indigenous peoples, and to India and Australia as a representative of the Catholic Church. As her confidence has grown, she has become less inhibited about showing her abilities, but she is still remarkably modest and diffident for one so accomplished.

It is difficult to write about Raana without writing about Hoana as well. Always close, the two seemed even more drawn together in the later years of their lives. In both cases, they were sustained by, and in turn sustained, the Māramatanga and the marae's commitment to Catholicism. As members of the younger generation watched them, they could not help but be impressed by the gratitude shown by the two women for what had been revealed to them by the two sources of knowledge that had guided Maungārongo since its founding.

Conclusion

Today, Raana is one of the most important elders at Maungārongo, a job she handles with apparent effortlessness. It is only those close to her who can recognize the cost and the loneliness that her ascendant position has brought her. While women frequently move beyond the domestic realm in middle age, she continues to be deeply involved in the lives of her children, her grandchildren, and now, her great-grandchildren. In part this is because she seems incapable of turning her back on situations where she might be needed. And the needs are as real as her desire to answer them. Māori are particularly vulnerable to the vagaries of the New Zealand economy, where the unemployment rate averages 6 percent or higher. Unemployment, with its attendant drug use and marital discord and violence, destabilizes domestic relationships. When marriages fail or jobs are lost, it is women such as Raana who step into the breach, taking care of grandchildren, cooking for extended families, and attempting to ensure some degree of stability for her grandchildren and others of her grandchildren's generation.

To see Raana today is to think that she has always assumed such an eminent role. In fact, she has only recently taken over this position with any conviction.

While her sense of responsibility has been evident from her earliest days at her grandmother's sink, she has, until the present, been content to remain away from center stage. Watching her in 1995 at the Tira Hoe, I witnessed an important transformation. Hoana, who would customarily have worked with the younger generation, had only just died. Raana had no choice but to become the spokesperson of her generation. As a public speaker, Raana was always shy, reluctant, and self-effacing. Now, as I watched her, I saw her take a deep breath and then move on to center stage. She filled the room with her stories of the first Tira Hoe. The youngsters listened in rapt attention as she told of that pioneer voyage, and of discomforts that were borne in the face of the acknowledged importance of the trip. She stood as the group sang "Pōkarekare" and then told her audience how she and Hoana had come to write the song.[7] One could appreciate the cooperation of the two women, their ability to synchronize their thoughts. In the humor that accompanied the story of the song's origins, some of the pain of Hoana's recent death was allayed. For those who did not understand the Māori version of the song Raana translated it and placed it within the wider context of the Tira Hoe's purpose.

Raana, whose early preference was for writing, has emerged as an accomplished storyteller. Her linguistic facility would surprise no one familiar with her written work, but in maturity, her instincts for situations and personalities enable her instantly to modulate her language and her insights to suit diverse audiences. In accepting the role of storyteller, Raana has shifted the balance of power, realizing for herself and her listeners the authority of narrative dominance. She commands words beautifully and she now possesses an audience.

But Raana is more than a chronicler; she is a visionary. Her life involves themes that emerge in the lives of many Māori women: reconciliation, responsibility, and the transmission of knowledge through generations. Speaking to a desire for parity if not equality, her efforts for Māori self-respect if not Pākehā admiration go beyond the anticipated or expectable. In this Raana stands apart; her vision and the steps she has already taken towards its realization are "beyond the ordinary," for it has fallen to her to understand mercy and redemption (Ozick 1994: 224, 232). She is a crusader, pilgrim, and explorer in all senses of the words. She has become a woman who makes decisions and assumes responsibility, a woman of courage and grace.

CHAPTER 7

Te Umuroa and the Tira Hoe Waka

This chapter concerns two undertakings: the mission to retrieve the remains of an ancestor, Hōhepa Te Umuroa, from Australia in 1988, and the annual Tira Hoe Waka, the "coming together to paddle" down the Whanganui River, begun in 1989. Obviously these are quite different missions. Yet within the movement they have interestingly similar functions: they both revisit the past and insist on its insertion in the present; and in both, the paths of religion and politics are inseparably intermingled. The participants were well aware of these phenomena within the movement and Māori society, as they saw the reactions of the society around them. And, again, knowledge with its attendant power was to be transferred to another generation so that it might prosper as Māori. At the same time, such knowledge must be protected from inquiring and suspect outsiders.[1]

In these two undertakings, the place of the Māramatanga within Whanganui becomes more apparent. The people of Maungārongo are joined to Whanganui by a shared history and important ties of kinship, but they have their own separate history and indeed are seen by others on the Tira Hoe Waka and among the other hapū of the river to occupy a privileged place. They bring to these undertakings an additional sense of a history imbued with guidance from Te Karere. Moreover, many of the Māramatanga's teachings were integrated into the instructions of the Tira Hoe. For individuals brought up within the movement, these teachings are so much part of their way of thinking, of organizing their world, that it could not be any other way. The elders of Whanganui who were not from Maungārongo were aware that the members of the Māramatanga possessed knowledge that was special and a history that had, over eight decades, set them apart. But they were content to watch the commingling of the teachings of Te Karere with the traditions of Whanganui. How aware others were of references to Te Karere or the implications of flying E Te Iwi Kia Ora with hapū flags on the various marae visited by the Tira Hoe is a matter of speculation. Surely most of the wider audience that heard waiata from the Māramatanga on the return of Te Umuroa would not have caught their significance. But the younger generation, by habitual exposure, will come to regard such movement symbols as part of their lives.

The Context

The return of Te Umuroa and the first Tira Hoe Waka took place in the late 1980s. This was a period of overt readjustment in Māori–Pākehā relations in New Zealand, a readjustment not entirely pleasant in its process and to this day neither congenial to many Pākehā nor effective for many Māori. As the nation struggled with its identity, these missions addressed what it means to be a Māori in New Zealand at the end of the twentieth century.

In 1985, the Treaty of Waitangi Act was amended to make possible retrospective claims over confiscated land and resources, making ownership of many resources contestable before the Waitangi Tribunal. At the same time, Aotearoa was declared bicultural and Māori was given the status of an official language. These developments led to a more assertive Māori public stance and varying responses from Pākehā: some felt more threatened and became more defensive, while others were more tolerant and supportive. Hitherto, the treaty had at most been a minor incident of Pākehā domination; now it was being used to redress a century and a half of inequity. All Māori were familiar with biculturalism, and many Māori with bilingualism, but both concepts were alien and threatening to almost all Pākehā. Deterioration of economic links with "mother" England placed this upheaval in a period of economic readjustment and exacerbated Pākehā insecurity (Walker 1990: 29).

Māori aspirations were given further voice by radical leaders, many of whom had been university educated, who commanded Pākehā attention by the force of their rhetoric. In the universities, a new generation of scholars (Sissons, Salmond, Binney, Belich, Ballara, and Howe) re-examined early relations between Māori and Pākehā. Inevitably, the basis for "historical truths" and the ways in which New Zealand history had been constructed and understood were subject to re-evaluation. Undertaken by both Māori and Pākehā scholars, these studies documented a Māori perspective on events of the last two centuries that was widely divergent from that taken for granted by most Pākehā.

Internationally, Māori culture was recognized in *Te Maori*, an exhibition of Māori art from New Zealand collections that travelled to the Metropolitan Museum in New York, museums in St. Louis and San Francisco, and the Field Museum in Chicago.[2] The acclaim that both the art and the people received vindicated Māori in their contention that theirs was indeed a worthwhile culture. It proved hard to ignore in New Zealand.

The Pākehā backlash to a renewed Māori sense of pride and assertiveness was virulent. It can be seen in the treatment of Māori in the media and the willingness of Pākehā to make overt, negative reference to the indigenous population. There was a demonstrable Pākehā disregard of Māori achievement and indeed a pervasive distrust of Māori generally. For example, in 1987 after *Te Maori's* triumphant travels in the United States and return to New Zealand, Auckland's monthly glossy, *Metro*, showcased an article written by Carroll Wall, a senior writer for the magazine. The article, entitled "Te Pakeha," ostensibly laments the failure of Pākehā to have an identity, a failure that is brought into much greater relief when contrasted with the efforts of the author's indigenous compatriots. The real intent of the article, as anyone who reads it can see, was to mock and diminish Māori identity. Wall (1987: 36) attributed the exhibition's success to its being "presented in the grand manner and with all the media hype, PR, sponsorship and advertising and expensive and fastidious mounting of the Pākehā." The article ended on a somewhat conciliatory note, but the cultural misunderstandings and the fear of Māori it revealed were startling.[3] All this tension and dissension raised the stakes considerably.[4]

Maungārongo marae, with a kohanga reo and a kura kaupapa, had become a place of concerted effort to prepare children to take their place as Māori in a bicultural New Zealand. That some individuals privately queried the government's commitment to biculturalism only attested to their political sensibilities. Indeed, people avidly followed the Waitangi Tribunal on the television news (especially *Te Karere*, the Māori news program) and in newspapers. It continues to affect their lives as they have several land claims waiting to be heard.

Changes in central governmental bureaucracy in the 1980s also had a significant effect. In October 1989 the Iwi Transition Agency superseded the Department of Māori Affairs. Many members of the Māramatanga and of Whanganui found their lives dominated by committee meetings and committee concerns. In addition to the local committees running Maungārongo marae, an infrastructure was established to regulate the kohanga reo and the various work schemes that were subsumed under the Kōkiri Centre (community administration). Raana, Hoana, Matiu, and their spouses were all given new responsibilities, and new people were hired. Their duties also extended beyond the local community, to encompass work done for the larger Whanganui iwi (Te Āti Haunui-ā-Pāpārangi), and for the Whanganui River Trust Board. As elders, they also served on hospital boards, social welfare committees, and community councils, and they became active, to varying degrees, in the newly formed Māori Congress. The elders conducted their work with the same seriousness of purpose that characterized their approach to every endeavour. Most were busy with various community and tribal responsibilities six or seven days a week.

Thus, life in Aotearoa changed considerably in the 1980s. Māori became stronger, more forceful, and seemingly more unified in exerting claims for equity and a new balance. For their part, Pākehā were uncomfortable with a dispensation that would put Māori participation on a par with their own; despite the official pronouncements of the government, few Pākehā were knowledgeable about Māori culture, and fewer could speak Māori. Moreover, they were not eager for their children to change this situation. In the media, there was strong evidence of a backlash as negative stereotypes were asserted and reinforced. It was in this context that elders of the Māramatanga went to seek their lost ancestor, a former "enemy of the state," and revisited their own history and traditions on the river they so loved. Their work clearly concerned the larger Whanganui iwi, but the manner of their participation demonstrated their unequivocal commitment to the teachings of the Māramatanga and of Te Karere.

The Journey to Maria Island: The Return of Te Umuroa

The story of Hōhepa Te Umuroa began in 1846 and was completed in 1988, when his remains were repatriated to New Zealand.[5] Such an undertaking involved cooperation between Whanganui and the government of New Zealand, and between both these parties and the governments of Tasmania and Australia. There were the inevitable, and time-consuming, bureaucratic maneuverings, but finally Te Umuroa was brought home to Wanganui, where he was laid to rest at Patiarero.

The New Zealand of 1846, six years after the signing of the Treaty of Waitangi, contrasts with modern Aotearoa New Zealand and its avowed goals of biculturalism. But there are critical similarities between these two times. While New Zealand is no longer a colony, it would be a mistake to overlook Māori resistance in both periods. Pākehā misconstructions of Māori behavior have, unfortunately, been common for two centuries. The Pākehā viewpoint, better documented in English texts, has had official currency; but the Māori perspective has always existed, both in written and oral accounts, and is becoming increasingly accessible (see especially Salmond 1991).

Hōhepa Te Umuroa is thought to have been born in the early 1820s into Ngāti Hau, a hapū from the middle reaches of the Whanganui River.[6] A man "of over six feet, with a fine, large head and an incomplete moko on the left side of his face,"[7] he worked as a laborer and never married. In 1846, along with other Whanganui Māori, he joined Te Rangihaeata of Ngāti Toa who "was regarded as being in arms against the government" in the Wellington area.[8] He participated in at least one action against outpost settlers, but within a few months, Te Umuroa and several of his compatriots were captured.[9] Tattersall (1973: 4) writes:

> It was near midwinter. The inhospitable bush clad hills were cold and wet and provided little in the way of sustenance to moving parties. To the Wanganui Maoris they were, in addition, [in] strange country . . . On 13th August a party of friendly [to the colonial government] Ngati-awa, at Pari Pari, on the coastal lands near Paekakariki took prisoner eight Maoris of

the invading force. They were said to be starving and had come down from the hills looking for food, probably a potato patch.[10]

Te Umuroa and his comrades were captured without violence, and taken first to the police station at Waikanae and then to the prison ship Calliope.[11]

At the time—late 1846—the Wellington area was under martial law so, according to some, Te Umuroa and his colleagues should have been treated as prisoners of war.[12] However, Governor George Grey had them court-martialled. Wards writes (1968: 73):

> If it is difficult on the information and needs of the time to justify Grey's insistence on these courts martial, how much more difficult it is to view with anything but distaste the explanations he made to the Colonial Office. Here he stretched truth to the point of falsehood, not from ignorance of the facts but from a calculated attempt to mislead.

The prisoners had no legal representation and, as Māori speakers, were unlikely even to have understood the charges let alone offer a defense; in any event, they all pleaded guilty. Thus, on October 12, 1846, they were convicted of armed rebellion and sentenced to "transportation for life": banishment to a penal colony in Van Dieman's land (Tasmania) to reside there as "felons for the Term of their Natural Lives."[13] The harsh and public punishment suggested that Grey sought to create examples rather than justice, hoping that his tactical decision would bring other recalcitrant chiefs into line.[14] But so doubtful was the legality of the charges, and so unjust the procedure, that even the Wellington Pākehā public was brought to protest.[15]

Te Umuroa and four of his colleagues[16] along with other convicts arrived at Hobart, Tasmania, on November 16, 1846. There was great interest in, and sympathy for, the Māori prisoners; the public were aware of the nature of the criminal proceedings against them, and Australian newspapers were filled with praise for the prisoners and condemnation for the treatment they had received at the hands of the New Zealand government.[17] Norfolk Island would ordinarily have been their prison destination, but these were no ordinary felons. Heald (1988) writes that the citizenry, as well as the administrators of Hobart, were against placing the Māori with other prisoners in such a harsh institution. Perhaps recognizing that they were indeed political prisoners, the authorities sent them to Darlington Station, on Maria Island off the Tasmanian coast. Maria Island was generally thought to be a more humane institution (Wilkie 1991). Once at Darlington, the Māori prisoners were provided with a residence apart from the main dormitory, which housed several hundred convicts. Australian interest in them continued; the noted artist John Skinner Prout painted portraits of all the Māori prisoners. These portraits are at present in the Art Gallery of

New South Wales.[18] A copy of Prout's portrait of Te Umuroa is presently in the meeting-house at Maungārongo marae.

Te Umuroa did not survive for long on Maria Island. He succumbed to tuberculosis in his first autumn, and died in the middle of winter. Apparently touched by the man and his illness, J. J. Imrie, the prison foreman, wrote in his diary on July 19, 1847: 'At 4 a.m. visited the Maoris. Found Hohepa very nearly gone. At 5 A.M. he breathed his last without a struggle.'[19] Te Umuroa was buried the next day in the public burial ground, not in the convict cemetery. Imrie read the funeral service in Māori at the graveside. An anonymous benefactor later erected a headstone over the grave, whose inscription read (as reported by Tattersall 1973: 22):

Here lies the remains
of
HOHEPA TE UMUROA
Native of Wanganui
New Zealand
who died July 12th
MDCCCXLVII[20]

To bury a foreign prisoner in the public cemetery and erect a headstone was, to say the least, unusual. However, it accords with the contention, maintained for one hundred and fifty years, that there was outrage in Tasmania at the conviction, deportation, and confinement of these Māori (Heald 1988). It accords, too, with the continued action of Australian authorities; in less than a year the remaining Māori prisoners were released, and returned to Auckland in March of 1848 (Wilkie 1991: 288). This was remarkable in the context of the colonial government's attitude to Australia's own indigenous people.

Hōhepa Te Umuroa had clearly touched the people of Tasmania. It should not be surprising that he had a similar effect on his descendants more than a century later. What is surprising is the degree of rancour the repatriation of a Whanganui ancestor aroused in the Pākehā population of Wanganui in 1988.

Retrieving Te Umuroa: Preliminaries

From 1985 to late 1987 correspondence moved between the Australian government; Robin Gray, then Premier of Tasmania; the Department of Māori Affairs; the Whanganui people; and the New Zealand High Commissioner in Canberra. By the end of the first year the requests of Whanganui elders to "release the sacred remains of our honored ancestor" had drawn no response from Robin Gray. Australia's internal politics, rather than personal or official recalcitrance, may have caused the delay. Australian Prime Minister Hawke had expressed his sympathy for Te Umuroa's repatriation. However, Gray, whose relationship with Hawke was strained, responded neither to memos from the Prime Minister nor to letters from Koro Wetere, then Minister of Māori Affairs, until January 1987. He wrote that the remains could be repatriated on certain conditions: the expense of the operation was to be met by either the New Zealand or the Commonwealth government, including the cost of the archaeological excavation as well as the conservation and curatorship of any remains or artifacts.[21] Furthermore, Gray stipulated that such materials recovered were to remain in the hands of the state archaeologist until tribal elders could take responsibility for them. With all these provisos, it was another eighteen months before Te Umuroa's descendants undertook the trip to Tasmania.

The preliminary cost analysis by the Department of Māori Affairs included the following: transportation for ten elders, their accommodation and meals in Hobart; an overnight stay in Wellington; costs of the excavation, conservation, and curatorship; and expenses incurred for air freight of the remains and the tangi in Patiarero, as well as contingency money for the accompanying archaeologist and for unforeseen exigencies. The total came to $32,845.80. Te Āti Hau was informed that the Māori community in Tasmania had offered support and hospitality for Whanganui tribal elders, who should be ready to embark on their trip as soon as the various levels of government acceded to their request.[22]

As arrangements were being negotiated, the tribe received word from the Australian government that the integrity of any findings could not be guaranteed. Gravestones had been moved about in the intervening years, suggesting that the placement of Te Umuroa's headstone might be nowhere near his actual remains. Furthermore, graves had been robbed and it was entirely possible that there would be no remains. Success was far from certain. However, Christopher Heald, an expatriate New Zealander who had researched the repatriation saga back to 1846, and who in 1987 was working for a special minister of state in Australia, sent a cable to the Department of Māori Affairs expressing his confidence in the integrity of the site.[23]

Maria Island: The Search for Te Umuroa

In August 1988, six elders from Whanganui went to Tasmania to seek out and repatriate the remains of their ancestor.[24] Matiu and his wife Lei, Hoana, and Te Otinga (members of the Māramatanga) were accompanied by two Whanganui elders, Joe and Nohi. Another individual raised within the Māramatanga, whom Hoana refers to as "brother," came too, representing the New Zealand Broadcasting Corporation. David Cresswell, a representative for the Department of Māori Affairs, also accompanied them.

Hoana kept a detailed diary. This was meant not to supplant but to supplement the oral accounts she and the others would bring back with them—narratives that would be told and retold at rā, hui, and tangi. However, by writing down the events, Hoana did more than provide a permanent record; she appropriated Pākehā methods for making and recording history. Her chronicle, written as well as oral, could stand as a competent counter to Pākehā attempts to interpret what was, after all, an essentially Māori experience. Moreover, the narrative structure of the diary reveals a great deal about how she and Matiu had come to regard themselves, the responsibilities they felt obliged to bear, and the spiritual assistance that they had come to rely upon. Hoana's diary is written with authority and without self-consciousness. She details the songs that were sung, the uses to which revelation was put, and the actions that Matiu initiated as he struggled for control in an undertaking that was far from secure. While conscientiously cataloguing events as they unfold, she brings immediacy to the story by interjecting personal reactions—of delight, sorrow, satisfaction, or dissatisfaction.

While Hoana's narrative would certainly be intelligible to anyone, it is enriched by the evocative recasting of the past as an arena that is so unknowable and apparently, for the moment at least, askew. She was in a foreign land, with the task of finding the remains of an ancestor in grounds that had been violated for over a century and a half. Her voice reveals that she saw herself as a colonized person, but one who, in finding success where failure would have been a reasonable presumption, managed to upset, to destabilize, the calculus of power that separates Māori from Pākehā.

The early entries in Hoana's diary tell of the farewells in New Zealand, the send-off by well-wishing friends and family, and the greetings received in Hobart from Aboriginal leaders and Māori residents who had come to meet their plane. The pōwhiri and action songs brought tears to her eyes. The waiata with which they responded ('Kikō') was drawn from the Māramatanga and had been revealed in the 1940s; despite the revelation of new waiata, this was a staple for members in dealing with other groups. A kinsman, then resident in Tasmania, who had travelled five-hundred miles to meet a relative from up the Whanganui River, particularly moved her.[25] In addition, Chris Batt, a member of the Tasmanian Parliament, was present to greet the party from New Zealand and to present them with a photograph of Te Umuroa. Such enthusiastic warmth would lend support to them when they were forced to confront the less receptive reactions of their Pākehā compatriots in Aotearoa.[26]

When they arrived in Tasmania, leaders of the Aboriginal community presented them with an Aboriginal flag, which is red, yellow, and black. They were told that the red spoke to the Aboriginal blood spilt, an explanation that resonated with Māori. The pōwhiri that they gave in return referred to greeting and crying for Te Umuroa, ill-treated (tūkinotia) by the justice system of the interlopers (*e ngā ture tauiwi*), a reference that would recur over the next few days. The words referred to the past. But within that waiting-room at the airport, many recalled experiences of injustice in a way that made it an electrifying moment. Certainly there were many tears—of greeting, of shared loss, and of pain for the young man who died and remained unconnected to his family for so long.

The entire history of Te Umuroa is one of high-handedness: it is surely an account that evokes the present? The primary concern was the successful return of their ancestor to Whanganui, but these were politically sophisticated elders who were meticulous in their choice of words. That they chose to sing "Kikō" is surely no accident. To the knowledgeable, "Kikō," sung to old melodies, offers Mareikura's view of the world; to all, it suggests the continuing importance of the past.

From Hobart they moved to Louisville, on the east coast of Tasmania, whence they would start the boat trip to Maria Island. On July 31, the night before they were to leave for the island, the members of the Whanganui party were told what to expect on the next day's journey. Their activity had moved into an unanticipated spotlight so they would be accompanied by archaeologists, cameramen, journalists, and government officials. Yet throughout her diary, Hoana stays focused on the task before them, indifferent to media coverage. She and her brother Matiu existed as though there were an impenetrable membrane surrounding them. When either received a message or inspiration through a dream, the other was readily available. Their accommodation—in which Hoana, Matiu, and Lei shared a room—facilitated their almost-constant communication. Such intense mutuality (as with Hoana and Raana) strengthened the confidence of key actors and no doubt aided their analysis of events as they unfolded.

Hoana's entry for August 1 begins with a message from Te Karere explaining that she has cleared the road of harmful influences. At the same time, the message alludes to those who have been ill-treated, a direct reference to Te Umuroa but encompassing also those sent to retrieve their ancestor. Their job is to carry their thoughts with them, so that they may once again be on the sacred road of the Trinity, moving towards spiritual living without end. Here Te Karere, with her specific ties to family, both connects and merges with the major tenets of Christianity.

At the break of dawn, a prayer was said over the boat and the waters that would link them to their ancestor. This attention to protocol—an attention that shows up repeatedly and frequently even under difficult circumstances—sustained them, providing balance, stability, and comfort in an uncertain and insecure situation. They were domesticating this event, demystifying it; the search for a long-dead ancestor in a foreign land became encompassed in the familiarly Māori. As is the case with so many of their other missions and undertakings, this process was transformative: what was foreign and treacherous became knowable, even intimate.

Once on the boat, Hoana called out in Māori, linking the sea and the land, praising the Earth for its power to embody the words that are uttered on the sea. This was the first day of their search. Two schoolgirls had located the gravestone, but its connection to Te Umuroa and his remains was unclear. When they landed on the island, Hoana called out again to Te Umuroa, greeting him as a respected ancestor and assuring him that they had come to bring him home. As the group approached the area of the tombstone, Matiu initiated the formal ceremonies with a karakia in Māori. Hoana writes in her diary:

> Matiu began the karakia as the powhiri continued. Very moving. Also very moving when we sighted Hohepa's tombstone standing upright on the hillside which sloped towards the sea. The warm breeze from the East Coast winter seas was there to greet us. As we approached Hohepa's grave, the sun shone to make us very welcome. Karakias still continued along with the Powhiris.[27]

Showing unusual sensitivity, the press and television reporters did not follow them as they greeted their long lost ancestor. Hoana wrote in her diary that this sacred time was not to be witnessed by outsiders. As the greetings ended, reporters were invited forward. Hoana continues:

> When all was over they came forward so that what the world would see was an open prayer and tangi. The two girls who found Hohepa were with us along with their parents. There were many people present because of their feelings for Umuroa and us; schoolteachers, archaeologists from Australia.

Matiu had had a dream the previous night, which indicated where he was to find Umuroa's remains. Hoana, knowing that Te Karere was there to guide them and that Matiu had had a dream whose import was unmistakable, felt no uncertainty. She, along with the other members of the party, was fulfilling an important obligation, a task for which she might anticipate and indeed receive spiritual assistance.

However, for the press corps, the events that unfolded were truly extraordinary. Chris Heald wrote about the events for the *New Zealand Listener* (September 10, 1988):

> The Pakehas stayed out of sight and earshot as Hohepa's relations approached his grave. After their chanting and prayers, the first sod was turned by a Maori hand. A signal brought us from our waiting down to the graveyard. The dig commenced . . . Attending the dig affected all present, even the supposedly hardened and cynical journalists. The solemnity and dignity of the occasion remained constant. I remember finishing a cigarette, dropping it, and in that instant reflexively thinking "No" and before my foot could mash the butt I had

picked it up, ground it out with my thumb and slipped it into my jacket pocket. For the first time I totally understood that I was standing on "sacred ground."

Although Hoana wept for joy that day, there was still some ambiguity about what the party had uncovered. On August 3, however, it was indisputable: the Whanganui contingent, digging without the aid of the state archaeologists, had undeniably found Te Umuroa's coffin, identified by the "H" for "Hōhepa" that through the decades had remained discernible. The coffin was opened the next day and the remains, almost an entire skeleton, were revealed.

The press probably attended out of curiosity, in the hope of watching a human interest story unfold as contemporary Māori searched for an ancestor wrongly displaced from his homeland. But if the media documented the event in search of the exotic, they found instead dignity, purpose, and humility. The gathered reporters could not help but be moved. Chris Heald describes the drama of the moment as the coffin and its contents were revealed:

> It was time to take up the lid. Matiu Mareikura and Joseph Nihi Wanihi knelt at the edge of the grave. The Pakehas stood back. In the trench, Richard Morrison and Brian Prince [the state archaeologists] carefully lifted sections of the lid, and placed them on clear plastic for wrapping.
>
> All present were hushed. Never in any church or at any European ceremony have I been so moved. We waited.
>
> Again a wordless communication, this time from Nohi Wanihi, a blink and a little nod from me. Exultation rushed through me. Just 20 CM down from the headboard, exactly where it should have been, Richard Morrison had found a tooth, and we had found Hohepa.

Hōhepa Te Umuroa's bones, along with the mat on which he had lain and the cloth in which he had been wrapped, were placed in a casket for the journey home from his land of exile.

What is most in keeping with the character of Hoana and Matiu, and of the other people who had come to find Te Umuroa, was the absence of triumph, vindication, or smugness. All of them saw themselves as performing a job that had fallen to their generation. In turn, they had duly called upon the necessary sources of aid and assistance.

Nevertheless, there is gratitude and humility, as expressed in Hoana's entries for the days that followed:

> Morning prayers together. Matiu spoke of his dream. Plans were made for our arrival on the mainland with Umuroa. The suggestion is that on Thursday we will directly take him to Hobart Catholic Church and from there to Christchurch Catholic Church, fly to Wanganui then travel up river to Hiruharama where he will be buried in the family cemetery.

On August 4 and 5, she writes:

> Karakia, kai, and all ready to leave . . . David [the Maori Affairs representative]
> having problems about clearance for Umuroa's remains. God bless him. I miss
> the family—try not to think too much; I believe the Hunga Wairua helps me
> a lot. . . .
>
> Karakia. Our family has left to prepare for our coming back to Hobart. They
> are dear lovely people.

The Journey Home to Whanganui

On the night of August 5, Te Umuroa was brought back to Hobart, the first step
in his return journey back to Whanganui. There he was laid in St. Joseph's
Cathedral. The success of this mission, and their recognition of it, was clearly
marked by their observance of protocol: Te Umuroa, like all the deceased, was
accorded full personhood and hence was not permitted to travel alone. Indeed,
all the restrictions demarcating the sacred, the ways of dealing with a corpse and
with an ancestor, were called into play. That their triumph had transformed
them can be seen in Hoana's entry in her journal for that night, in which she
describes the events in Hobart:

> Our Maori people were there to pick us up. Powhiri and mihimihi were
> exchanged because of Te Umuroa. They in turn, with heartfelt aroha said
> "take our tupuna home to Aotearoa." "Take him to rest in his beloved
> Whanganui River." "Go and return with the love of the people who remain
> behind." (Haere, haere e hoki me nga aroha o te hunga e noho ake nei.)

This was a night of celebration and culmination. There was a feast, replete
with special Māori dishes. The party of elders gave gifts to those who had assisted
them; woven kits and ornaments were given to the state archaeologists and to
Chris Heald. The songs in support of the speeches given by the elders all came
from the Māramatanga.[28]

Hoana's diary reveals a general lightening of the mood. While always important, kinship and solidarity with Māori on both sides of the Tasman became a
primary focus. Individual celebration was transformed into community ceremony.
The return of Te Umuroa was understood not in terms of individual achievement
but as a group accomplishment and shared honor.

From Hobart the party flew with their ancestor to Christchurch, where Te
Umuroa rested overnight in St. Mary's Cathedral and the others stayed with
family. A huge welcoming party greeted them the next day in Wanganui. Hoana
rejoiced in the people and in the protocol that would lead the final way:

There must have been 100 people there at the airport. We were most elated and grateful for our people being there and the "Kapa Haka" was so good to see, especially for Koro Te Umuroa. Knowing he had landed back on to his beloved Aotearoa. Aunty Moke's Powhiri was most heart rending.[29]

The confluence of loyalty, aroha, and protocol sustained Hoana, affirming her view of her world and her circumstances. They had a karakia before they began the journey up the river road to Patiarero, making a mournful procession with the hearse of Te Umuroa in the lead. Once on the marae, a full entourage of mourners and a complete observation of protocol—haka, taiaha, whaikōrero, and waiata—greeted them. Here Te Umuroa was laid out for a tangi, which would last until the next day's burial.

On the next day, when Te Umuroa was buried, there was great ceremony, as all the Whanganui people seemed to recognize the importance of what had been accomplished. In the rain, his body was borne with precision and ceremony to his final resting place. Women, wreathed in leaves to signify mourning, recited his genealogy and in so doing bound him once and for all to the people of Whanganui. Hoana writes:

> The service was conducted by Reverend Father Te Awhitu. Three separate groups of pallbearers as they carried Umuroa to his grave to lie forever with his family in Aotearoa on the banks of Te Awa o Whanganui i runga o Patiarero iraro o Pukehika te Maunga o Ati Hau [on the banks of the Whanganui River, on Patiarero marae, in the shadow of Pukehika, the mountain of Ati Hau].

Here Hoana placed her ancestor through his identification with a river, a marae, and a mountain, the means of identification for all Māori. Hōhepa Te Umuroa had come home. The members of the party said a special prayer, for in bringing their ancestor home they had disturbed bodies and graves—disturbances that could not be treated lightly.

The burial ceremony was carried out under the guidance of Matiu, Hoana, and Raana, the next generation, who in 1962, as neophytes on the top of Mount Ruapehu, had demonstrated the ritual competence to proceed. But their children also played significant roles: Hoana's Mākere, Matiu's Corinna, Raana's Charles, and Hoana's Rongonui used the taiaha as the body was brought onto the marae. The daughters and daughters-in-law of all the important senior people joined with their elders in chanting Te Umuroa's genealogy, while their sons and affines were pallbearers as the coffin made its way to the cemetery. Thus emerges the presence and participation of two generations.

The *Wanganui Chronicle's* photographer Steve Paul ran a fine series of photographs that captured the importance of the occasion, the strict adherence to ceremonial rules (despite the rain), and the gravity of the task that they had so successfully accomplished.

However, even with their long-exiled ancestor buried in Whanganui soil, there was not yet closure. Their responsibilities—both ceremonial and political—were to continue for some time. For example, Delphina Crapp, a Māori woman who had been living in Melbourne for over a decade, realized that a *tokotoko* which she had purchased at an Australian auction must belong to the man whose descendants had crossed the Tasman to retrieve him. This supposition was vindicated when an expert on Whanganui carving confirmed that the specific design could only have come from Whanganui. The stories that accompanied the stick as it made its journey across the Tasman and then up the Whanganui River became part of the narrative of this pilgrimage.[30] The tokotoko became the focus of Chris Heald's article in the *New Zealand Listener* (1988), in which he wonders at the difference between Māori and Pākehā: "The Maori presence and way of life and thinking is an unknown quality to most Australians." To be sure, and to most Pākehā New Zealanders too. However, not all differences in perspective were as benign as Chris Heald's.

Reactions in New Zealand

In the letters to the editor section of the *Wanganui Chronicle*, a respected newspaper that serves the entire Whanganui–Waimarino region, several voices were raised in dismay. These letter writers expressed outrage that government monies should be spent on the repatriation of the mere remains of a possibly suspect Māori, who had been dead for almost a century and a half. In a few letters, the gulf between Māori and Pākehā understandings became evident. Māori notions of the past, of history, and of the mutuality between individual and kin group, were dismissed. For example, on August 8, 1988, IPA, a frequent correspondent, wrote to the newspaper:

> They state it as a matter of mana within the family or tribal group to which they belong. Surely it would have been more fitting to accept an apology from the Governor-General or Prime Minister Lange.
> It shatters me to hear of the money that is being spent on wasteful Maori claims and complaints.
> I am fully aware of the problems facing all genuine New Zealanders who are being kicked in the guts, but the ones who think it is their God given right to bludge off society should be the ones who should suffer. It could or should be a proud nation of all people.

Clearly, to this writer, the success of the mission to Maria Island was not a matter of pride to the nation. On the contrary, for him, such actions showed that Māori were keen to spend government money on "wasteful Maori claims and complaints."

Rhetorically, the author conflates this specific case with the generalized stereotype of Māori as "welfare bludgers." Could understandings of what happened have been any more different?

If the members of Whanganui understood their mission as a return (in time and space) to right a grievous injustice, what was their reaction when they found themselves insulted and their work belittled? Moreover, how were they to understand it when a mission that they viewed as a necessary preliminary to reconciliation was met with rhetoric designed to effect their exclusion, suggesting that the participants were not "genuine New Zealanders"?

Once again, in an ironic replay of events from the last century, Māori found that sympathy for their position and an understanding of the integrity of their culture was more forthcoming on the other side of the Tasman. After the consistent support the party had received during an especially difficult time, Matiu became uncharacteristically confrontational when he was interviewed for the *Wanganui Chronicle* (August 9, 1988). The story as it appeared quotes Matiu's disappointment:

> The general public didn't know about it, or didn't care. And the ones who did know said it was a waste of time and money. But the Tasmanian people were tremendous. We were overwhelmed with their love and generosity.

Matiu expresses simultaneously the irreparable nature of the iniquity perpetrated against his ancestor and his gratitude for all the help received along the way. That there is an edge to his appreciation for Tasmanian assistance is not in question: "We can never rectify the wrong which sent him from his home, but at least we can say thank you to all the people who helped us get him back."

Implications of the Journey to Retrieve Te Umuroa

The consequences of the repatriation of Te Umuroa were quite different for the two populations of New Zealand. To the writers of letters to the editor, the entire enterprise constituted an indulgence whose end was unfathomable. To the members of Te Āti Hau, commitment to the past made the trip across the Tasman not merely feasible, but necessary and inevitable. Repatriating Te Umuroa was consistent with their view of themselves as Māori. Perhaps most importantly, their journey indicated that history is not something that happens to people, but something they make; meaning is invested by social actors. The trip to Maria Island, Hoana's diary, and the oral narratives that have kept the mission alive allowed the participants to map their experience for others and give it significance.

The very difference in the ways in which some Pākehā and some Māori understand history emerges quite clearly: Pākehā have used the past to discredit

Māori, while Māori seek the past to lend meaning to their present. Indeed, their belief that the past and present commingle sustained them and made their task possible.

As Te Umuroa was laid to rest at Patiarero, the chanting of his genealogy resituated him among his kin while he found his final presence on ancestral land. The members of Te Āti Hau were similarly resituated, having achieved a rapprochement with a past that held out the possibility of future reconciliation. Their narratives reconstituted and renegotiated the past as much as their actual journey retrieved and reversed an error—a Pākehā error—committed in the previous century. That dreams, revelations, and inspirations guided them assured them that the forces that have been with Māori since before the nineteenth century have not lost their effectiveness. They brought Hōhepa Te Umuroa home, but they also justified their position in the present.

If one of the lessons of this is that there is continuity in change, there is also the lesson that Māori can relate a narrative or generate a history that is not dependent on colonial categories and colonial conventions of discourse. On the contrary, the history that emerges is governed entirely by Māori conventions. At a time when meanings are contestable, open to variable interpretations and put to different uses, the ability to understand this, and to use it to their own benefit, has provided a point of vantage for the members of Te Āti Hau. In seeking an ancestor, they have laid claim to their future.

The Tira Hoe Waka

The Tira Hoe Waka was begun in 1989 with no notion that it would become part of the yearly cycle of events and rā. Superficially, it is a waka trip down the Whanganui River from Taumarunui to the lower stretches, with overnight sojourns on marae or camping. Above Pīpīriki the land is very rugged and beautiful, but inaccessible by conventional means. Thus the trip is undoubtedly a vacation adventure for many of both the young and older participants. But this is the land of the tūpuna of the members of the Māramatanga, the location of their tribal history. The elders who lead the Tira Hoe introduce the new generation to their homeland and re-explore the narratives about the life of the old people. In recent times, they have also focused attention upon contested areas along the river. As with the return of Te Umuroa, the Whanganui iwi is committed to these annual journeys down the river. Some of this is public knowledge, with events being written up in the *Journal of the Polynesian Society* (Moon, 1996), as well as in various newspapers. I shall not discuss anything in this section that is not already in the public domain.

The members of the Māramatanga, to be sure, belong to Whanganui, but there is not a complete correspondence in belief and ritual between the move-

ment and the larger tribal entity. The members command respect for their knowledge, and while others of Whanganui are aware of the history and significance
of Maungārongo, Kuratahi, and Raketepauma, they do not necessarily share all
the movement's beliefs, nor participate in the annual round of rā. (Hoana's story is
indicative of the different perspectives that existed between the river villages.)

The Tira Hoe is marked by memory, a concentration upon and reconstitution
of the past, and the desire of the elders to transmit to a younger generation the
importance of their heritage. Emphasis is on oral traditions, those narratives
passed from one generation to another, which simultaneously challenge Pākehā
written history, and create a boundary about those whose shared knowledge
insulates them. Indeed, one of the most important characteristics of these
annual river trips was their general inaccessibility to Pākehā;[31] this was private,
tribal knowledge, transmitted within a context that was not to be violated. To the
extent that these journeys were meant to encourage the participation of the
young and to foster an understanding of their heritage, it is hard to think of a
better way in which this could be accomplished. Days out in the sun and on the
water were ended with long communal talks around the fire, often lasting into
the early hours of the morning.

The Tira Hoe blends the Māramatanga with the larger traditions of the
Whanganui tribes and with the Catholicism that has characterized the population of the river since the end of the nineteenth century. The success of this
confluence may be attributed to the leaders of the movement, especially those
prominent in the Tira Hoe—Matiu, Lei, Hoana and Rihari, and Raana. Plural-
ity of belief does not, in this case, lead to conflict. Finally, the pressing problems
that confront Māori today—the proper education of a younger generation, the
passing down of oral traditions, and the continuing contest between the government and tribal entities over land and valued resources—transcend ideology and
require attention on many fronts.

The participation of central members of the Māramatanga inevitably affects
the nature of this annual journey. Revelation and inspirations may be shared
with everyone, but with obviously different understanding. Songs and allusions
to the prophetic tradition may not, indeed probably do not, resonate with all the
listeners. Yet for those who understand their meaning, an extra dimension is
added to an already moving and important experience. Perhaps the most important aspect of all this is to be found in the clear authority of Rangitihi, Matiu,
Raana, Hoana, and Rihari, whose visions of the world have been imprinted onto
the shape of the Tira Hoe.

I was on the trip that took place January 6–20, 1995. This was perhaps the
most sad and poignant aspect of my fieldwork, for Hoana had died in May of 1994.
So strong had her presence been in the earlier years that, almost daily, people
would stop and gasp at her loss. For there was so much to remind us of her: the

song she composed with Raana, which is now sung as the official waiata of the
Tira Hoe, her instructions to the young, and her simultaneous enthusiasm for
and fear of the river. Hoana's death had occurred eight months earlier; yet the
sense of loss remained raw and immediate.

I was not the only Pākehā on the journey that year. Jenny McLeod, a composer with an international reputation who had become involved with both
Hoana and Raana through their choral work, was making her second trip down
the river. She has written about the experience.[32] In addition, friends of young
adults, who had been told about the Tira Hoe, joined in and participated. For
some, a Pākehā presence was a nuisance that could easily be forgone. Indeed,
"intellectual property" was often invoked as a means, I suspect, of ensuring that
we did not spread about knowledge that was specific to Whanganui. This was an
especially charged political time, a time of occupations[33] and negotiations about
the treaty and the fiscal envelope. A Pākehā presence, if not unwelcome, was at
the very least a constraint on how open discussion could be. Some ignored us.
But they were young. The elders were more vigilant.

Jenny McLeod has, however, written eloquently and for a mainly Pākehā
audience about these undertakings. Through their writings, a new generation
of Pākehā, one brought up with an official national position of biculturalism
and the Waitangi Tribunal, have become exposed to a Māori way of doing
things. At the same time, McLeod has argued that there is indeed a distinct
and distinguishable Māori perspective. Is this not then a validation of pilgrimages and missions? Is there an extra dimension added because members of the
Pākehā intelligentsia witness and lend their approval to such activities? Or do
Māori want or need such validating? I do not know that these questions can
be answered.

The Whanganui River: The Instruction of a New Generation

Each year, those who have gone on the Tira Hoe Waka are younger. Each year,
they arrive shy and diffident but leave confident in their abilities. Timidly on
the first day, they would repeat: "I am the river, the river is me." By the last days,
their voices rang out in confidence. They had confronted their heritage and forever more their past would be part of them. For young Māori, this is a powerful
means of distinctiveness; Pākehā are not involved with nor committed to their
history in the same manner.

On the first trip, Hoana and Raana wrote a song together, which has come to
be sung every year. This was especially difficult in 1995, when Hoana's photo was
brought down the river, and everything conspired to remind the group of their
loss. The song, "Pōkarekare ana ngā wai" (The Churning Up of the Water) refers

to the *tira hoe waka* (the company of canoes) and hence has given the mission its name.

Here differential knowledge is perhaps most obvious: some young men, who are now clearly leaders, had been selected by Hoana and Matiu. By the time I met them in 1995, they were fluent speakers of te reo, although only one had been brought up on the river and was a native Māori speaker. Moreover, there were those who knew about the Māramatanga, and were therefore able to recognize the mnemonic devices that signalled the movement and its history. For example, as we travelled to different marae, different flags were flown. While it is common to have flags waving on important occasions, their meanings may not be obvious. To see E Te Iwi Kia Ora is to understand the invocation of Mere Rikiriki and of the prophetic tradition.

Similarly, the names of meeting-houses have stories, which are not apparent to the uninformed. In Pīpīriki, the meeting-house is called "a rat of a deal" and its name is inscribed in Māori on a flag waved frequently. This refers to a late-nineteenth-century land deal, and the constant display of this flag on the marae assures that the travesties of the past are never forgotten. The Tira Hoe also took us to more recent sites of Pākehā disregard for Māori rights. A new generation, with tendencies to be more militant and to refuse any less-than-adequate dispensation, are now informed. They are not likely to let these incidents go.

There are two important aspects to these voyages: first, by taking place every year, they enhance continuity and tradition for a new generation; secondly, regardless of the weather or other circumstances, no lapses in protocol are permitted. If mourning is to take place on a marae, the speeches are made and all listen; leaves signifying loss and bereavement are wrapped about the head and placed on certain rocks, whose history and importance have been explained as the journey began that morning. These are time-consuming events. But they will go on in rain, sleet, and gales, and also on idyllic days for canoeing down the river. For this is what makes individuals Māori, and the young cannot afford to bypass the lesson.

As with much that goes on at rā and pilgrimages, there is a significant political element in the discussions. In 1995, the settlement of particular Waitangi Tribunal cases was on the agenda. The elders were already well informed on the issues; they were, in many cases, active in tribal and national political organizations. But the younger members were being educated by the discussion, and this was invaluable.

Discussion

The Tira Hoe Waka will continue to educate new generations in the ways of the river, in the etiquette of their people, and in the history that makes them distinctive. What is most impressive is that there will always be a generation that is in a position to pass on knowledge.

The differences between Whanganui and the Māramatanga become especially obvious during a mission where members from both groups overlap and participate together. Their disparities are signalled in many ways—in verbal allusions, the positioning of flags, and the singing of songs—but these signs are recognizable by very few as specific to the Māramatanga. For those who bring two histories to bear, the canoe trip down the river has additional meaning.

On the river, history and politics are direct and accessible. This is crucial for those of a younger generation who will be future leaders. They not only learn on these trips, they are inspired; they are proud to be Māori and eager to learn all they can. They create ties to one another, that will serve them well in the future, when individuals from different sub-tribes must unite and govern.

But, certainly unanticipated when I went down the river in 1995 and unexpected as recently as the tenth anniversary in 1998, a generation has passed over. Very few of the generation of Hoana and Matiu survive. Of these, even fewer are competent in the complex rituals and narratives. Yet there is a new generation, trained by Hoana and Matiu, who, although they have assumed responsibility prematurely and perhaps reluctantly, stand on a marae and instill pride in their people.

Both the mission to retrieve Te Umuroa and the pilgrimages down the Whanganui River appear at first glance to deal with history. This they certainly do. But it is in revisiting history that the future is assured.

Matiu

Matiu's life history quite fittingly comes at the end of a narrative that began almost a century ago—a story whose origins can be traced to decades before he was born. He was one of the youngest members of a generation who today, as the successors of Pauro, Tika, and Ruka, are seen as elders and as important sources of knowledge. Part of this knowledge and its attendant responsibilities is a keen awareness of the past's influence on the present and the importance of preparing the rangatahi, to ensure that distinctively Māori views of time and place will be perpetuated.

Matiu grew from a much prized, if somewhat spoiled, younger brother, cousin, and son into a religious and political leader, active and sought after throughout Māoridom. His development coincided with the transformation of the wider New Zealand society and the renegotiation of relations between Māori and Pākehā. Even allowing for the atypical historical context, this is not the life history of a typical Māori man. It is the story of a man who, at any time and place, would be judged extraordinary. Matiu became a mediator—transcending generations, negotiating past and present, old and new, Catholicism and the Māramatanga. His biography yields an insight into the ways in which different sources of knowledge can be combined and reconciled to ensure effective and continuous cultural transmission.

Within the Māramatanga, Matiu assumed two roles: that of an elder, and that of a tohunga. The two overlap somewhat, most notably in the necessity of preserving and transmitting special, reserved knowledge. Matiu shared this responsibility with other leaders of his generation, and like them was instrumental in the instruction of the young. He taught the children and younger people of his tribe by holding wānanga so that the young would enter a world in which the landscape was familiar. He was a repository of tales of ancestors and natural phenomena.

As did all the individuals whose life histories are told in this book, Matiu had a heightened sense of self, of what he was doing, and of the implications of his actions. In many ways, his tasks became harder as he became aware of the influence of the past—both the ancestral past, with its axiomatic claims on the present and future, and his personal past and its bearing on his adult decisions.

His life diverged from those of others in his generation in many ways. Initially, this divergence was marked most strongly by his youth. He was the youngest of a generation that, as grandchildren of the prophets, spanned over a decade between the eldest members, born about 1927, and Matiu, born in 1942. Nevertheless, as that generation became elders in the 1980s, Matiu himself, although scarcely forty, moved into position to assume responsibility. He had attended the whare wānanga and he became a tohunga. He was trained by a tribal leader who commanded universal respect. As a result, Matiu became an elder well before he was chronologically in that category.

On a more personal level, Matiu grew up the youngest of a generation. He alone among his siblings witnessed his mother's relationship to his stepfather. Inevitably, his perspective on some of the major figures of the movement differed from those of his siblings.

As a tohunga, Matiu possessed a great deal of specialized ritual knowledge, which also set him apart from other elders. This knowledge made him responsible both for ritual and spiritual crises and for the transfer of knowledge, general and sacred, between generations. Increasingly, as he gained recognition as a tohunga, his role moved beyond the Māramatanga. Since his knowledge was esoteric, his skills were difficult to acquire. That he performed so well is an indication of the dedication and intelligence which characterize his family in general, and which were so important in the respect that he earned. At Maungā-rongo, he was a much-needed master of ritual. He was there to open buildings, to protect the belongings of the ancestors, to lead visitors onto the marae, and to protect all that is Māori from Pākehā incursion. It is not surprising that, politically, he was aware, active, and sophisticated.

With all these accomplishments he was, nevertheless, humble. He knew when it was necessary to defer to his sister Hoana or to his sister-in-law Raana. In matters concerning the movement, he often bowed to their judgment. But his knowledge about the Māori past and about ritual protocol was beyond question. He also maintained, at times against all odds, a sense of humor. This has characterized all the leaders I have known; they have inserted levity into their actions and narratives, steadfastly refusing to take themselves too seriously. One woman suggested to me that perhaps Matiu's sense of humor was a saving grace: that he could not, after all, deal with such grave events and momentous occasions without a touch of waggery. Certainly, his self-mockery redeemed him socially; it obscured differences in position and the reality of hierarchy.

This is not to say that his position was entirely without problems. Indeed, the tension between the Māramatanga, which is forward looking, and his role of tohunga, which is more concerned with the distant rather than the proximate past, created a conflict that was often difficult to negotiate. He was, as well, a participant in a community where some degree of friction is inevitable. Seven original children have produced well over fifty cousins. Not everyone could get along, and it fell to the elders to mediate disputes. Remarkably, they accomplished this with grace, always permitting participants to maintain their dignity.

In relating the early years of his life, he was careful to define himself in terms of his relationships with his whānau. Matiu would refer to himself, his siblings and cousins as "the olds," a humorously irreverent term, less ponderous than "elders," or the Māori "kaumātua." Nevertheless, he grew into the roles of tohunga and koro well.

Early Years

Matiu was born in August 1942, the last child of Rena and Keru. He was raised on the marae in Ohakune, surrounded by cousins and siblings. In addition, many of his aunts and uncles, emergent leaders in the fledgling movement, were present with their families.

Matiu recalled the environment as being specifically Māori; nevertheless, as a child he would speak only English, even when addressed by his elders in te reo. Unlike his siblings Rihari and Hoana, who were raised as native speakers, he did not learn to speak Māori until he was in his thirties. Moreover, during the years of intense spiritual activity in the movement. Matiu was still a child and thus largely removed from the concerns of the meeting-house and the adults.

Matiu and the other children were surrounded by an impressive group of elders. Matiu's memories of his grandparents, Te Huinga and Hori Enoka Mareikura, were weakened by his youth at the time of their deaths. Te Huinga died in 1944, when Matiu was still an infant. Her strength, however, lived on with him. Years later, when his granddaughter was born with spina bifida and given little chance of survival by the doctors, Matiu insisted upon medical persistence and he gave the baby his grandmother's name. He said that he knew the kuia would pull the baby through— and she did survive childhood with minimal problems.[1]

Mareikura, however, lived until Matiu was four years old. Like everyone else, Matiu remembered his grandfather as loving, kind, and generous. He did not remember his Auntie Anaera nearly so well as he recalled others who lived into his adolescence and adulthood. He recalled her as a woman who had special attributes, although he couldn't be specific.[2] His words were vague, noting that she was very spiritual, a woman who saw and ministered to the needs of the people, a kaimahi who led the people through momentous times. This combination of her unspecific abilities and her own reluctance to assume a leadership position make her both more elusive and more convincing as somebody with extraordinary abilities. Furthermore, Matiu suggested that she might have died so young because she was so committed and devoted to spiritual work. He saw her dedication as in effect giving up her life.[3]

Matiu had a somewhat different perspective on Pēpene Ruka—a man who was sometimes resented (by the Mareikura family at Maungārongo) for his outsider status, for his money, and for his ownership of land. But Matiu is grateful to him, seeing him as a figure of central importance in his youth. In the late 1940s, Ruka would have been omnipresent, organizing missions in search of the mauri, writing all the time, and seeing to it that people held to the tenets of the movement. It is probable that the first real glimpse of multiple interpretations would have arisen at this juncture. But Matiu would have been far too young to realize this. From Matiu's vantage-point, Koro Ruka was financially well off but used his money to help the people. It is interesting that this was Matiu's interpretation, for those who are older are far more suspicious of the wealth and land differentials between the Ruka and the Mareikura families.[4] In addition, Ruka supported Rena, Matiu's mother, during the time when she was widowed. Rena was a Gray, and a niece to Kataraina. These kin relations can be reckoned in two ways: one accords equality between the Mareikuras; the other grants genealogical ascendancy to the Rukas. Yet despite a pervasively egalitarian ideology, it is almost always accounted for in the way that favors the Rukas.[5] This may well explain some of the strain between the two branches of the family. While his older sister probably would have been uncomfortable with this, Matiu was grateful. He recalled Koro Ruka as an individual who got things done and who worked with the other elders in harmony.

Koro Ruka also looked after Keru during the latter's final illness. Keru died in 1949 at the age of forty-nine from the effects of rheumatic fever, a disease he had contracted years earlier. Decades of hard work had exacted a toll from which his body could not recover. He left a young widow and young children—the youngest, Matiu, was seven. Like his daughter Hoana, Keru had been brought up at Rānana and raised by Wiki and her husband. Keru's last sojourns took him to the hospital in Taihape, to Raketapauma, and then finally home to Ohakune.

Matiu's uncle Tikaraina was shy but witty, with a wicked sense of irony. As the bearer of a highly charged, sacred name, he nevertheless was willing to defer to his older brother's oratorical abilities. There was no animosity between the two men, despite the prestige gained by Pauro. I think Tikaraina handled the importance of his name, its gravity and significance, by emphasizing wit and humor. Matiu handled his rank and significance in much the same manner. I have seen him grim and serious, but somehow, however briefly, the gravity is broken with a quip that relieves the tension.

But Matiu told of another side to Tikaraina, his Uncle Dick, one more in keeping with the general persona. Matiu knew from his early years that his was a special family, but his knowledge was not specific. His memories were much clearer about issues that involved his age group. When he was very young there was talk about St. Cecilia coming to baptize his two cousins, both of whom were named Felicity. Matiu realized that some individuals were sanctioned by the wairua: singled out for special treatment. These children, often given names to demarcate their special position, seemed to be even more chosen. Matiu wanted such a name.

In those days Tikaraina was in charge of the taiaha, a task that Matiu later took over. Tika put the recruits through a rigorous workout, involving all manner of contortions. (Matiu always thought of his uncle when he himself took over taiaha training for the next generation.) The older man told the young boy that if he lifted a bar above his head, Tika would reward him. Always anxious for presents, Matiu was especially delighted. When he accomplished the task set for him, and his uncle announced that he was not to be given candy but a name, Matiu was truly thrilled. Tika looked at his nephew and intoned solemnly, "I'm going to call you 'Stuart Frosted Balls.'" Matiu started to cry. The adults, however, could not help but laugh. When Matiu's younger son Hemi arrived, Tika looked at him and called him "Little Frosted Nuts." Because everyone was laughing, the young boy laughed, too. For the rest of his life, Tika called Matiu and Hemi "Stuart" and "Little Stu."

Both of us laughed as Matiu related this story. Nevertheless there can be little doubt that the experience, though daunting, showed the young Matiu an important side of leadership. The story has become incorporated into the corpus of stories that have come to characterise Tika as irreverent and whimsical. At the same time it demonstrates that Matiu always possessed the ability to lampoon a system, to satirize it at its very core. This was not scepticism or cynicism, but a profound understanding of the way the system operates. Tika's sense of humor was a critical counterpoint to the reverence that his name engendered. From Matiu's perspective, Tika taught him the importance of easing the most solemn occasions by wit and self-deprecation.

The mid-1940s were traumatic times. Deaths and disasters were so frequent even young children were permanently affected. As World War II went on, Merehapi died in 1943 and Te Huinga in 1944. The following year brought Riripeti's tangi and the eruption of Mount Ruapehu. The next year Mareikura died. In 1948 Anaera was dead. Loss and grief marched across the marae. Tears and whaikōrero marked all these occasions. No Māori child, allowed to enter the meeting-house and required to be silent during all the adult conversations, would have failed to perceive the significance of what was going on around him, nor failed to see the exhaustion and suffering of the survivors. For Matiu, the pervasive sense of loss became more immediate with his father's death.

Matiu was also distinguished from his older siblings because he lived with his mother and stepfather, Mick, after the death of his father. By the time his mother remarried, he was twelve; he alone among his siblings bore witness to his step-father's brutality, a brutality he was to recall with a shudder four decades later. His stepfather was kind to the children, but cruel to, and violent with, Rena. It was very difficult for a young boy to witness the violence that his mother endured. With obvious pain, Matiu recalled one incident when Mick hit Rena so hard that the kettle came off the fire, burning her badly. Matiu watched all this and wanted to retaliate, to save his mother, but he never could. Nobody, it seemed, could do anything about it. This is a pattern that has recurred, but even today there is little community intervention in domestic violence. Clearly, it had an effect on Matiu, who commented that this was a terrible part of his life.

As a child, Matiu, along with his cousins, realized that strange, often inex-plicable things happened. He knew that his elders communicated with the wairua and he claims to have seen them materialize in the meeting-house. His descriptions, years later, were of children observing while the elders participated. However, on one occasion, a number of the children attempted their own explor-ation of the supernatural. With their parents asleep, the children attempted to replicate their parents' actions. This went on for a few nights without any adult being the wiser. One night, however, the children evoked a spirit who refused to identify itself as good or evil. The next night everything started to move. The elders rescued them, by a propitious placement of the rosary. The children were chastised; Matiu wryly commented that no physical punishment was necessary, as the hair-raising terror of the evening would sufficiently deter a repeat per-formance. While certainly terrifying, such an incident clearly brought out the privileged position his elders commanded.

Matiu told me that as a child he could not learn at school: no matter how hard he tried, he simply could not understand what was going on. Moreover, he claimed that he was both naughty and dumb. This is so unlike the man that Matiu became that I cannot help but feel that the process itself must have been at fault. Because of what he viewed as his own shortcoming, Matiu felt over-whelmingly whakamā, a word that means not only "shamed" but literally "made white," "drained of color."

Not surprisingly, Matiu ran away from school as often as he could. His teachers told him that he was naughty. He stuck up for what he believed in, but he claims, quite credibly, that he was not a bad boy. When Matiu attended the convent school, he ran away so frequently that it became necessary for his mother to hire taxis to take him to school.[6] However, this would seldom work, as he fled the convent on the heels of the taxi. In desperation, Rena had a local policeman talk to her errant son. Forty years later, Matiu could mimic the policeman's inton-ation: "Now listen here boy, make sure you don't humbug around." This officer of the law tried to exact a promise from the young boy that he would stay at school. This was a vow that Matiu could not make, for he had learned that a broken promise paved the way to hell. Young Matiu had no intention of lingering in the school grounds, nor of going to hell for making a pledge he could not honor.

It seems not to have taken long for Matiu and the establishment of the school to square off against one another. As he told the story that follows, he was not really able to make sense of what had happened forty years before. Apparently, he aimed his slingshot, quite successfully, at the bottom of a young girl. Her screams brought the nuns, who were quick, indeed eager, to mete out punishment. Matiu realized it was futile to plead innocence. Instead, he chose a tactic that would only have infuriated the nuns. Called an "ugly, useless little imp,"[7] Matiu replied by saying "thank you." Strapped, rapped on the knuckles, and insulted, he faced it all with unremitting gratitude. The priest, Father Tom Fuouy, was called. Matiu then apologized and found, to his surprise, his apology rejected. Without discussion, in fact with a great deal of abuse, Matiu was dismissed from school.

The Mareikuras had been stalwarts of the Catholic mission in the Whanganui River valley and the surrounding Rangitīkei–King Country Area. To have treated the young son of such an important family in this manner was very high-handed. Father Dan Fuouy, a cousin to the offending Father Tom, was called and came immediately. He too thought the dismissal precipitate. Yet, despite a multitude of pleas and interventions, Father Tom would not listen. Matiu was not permitted to attend the convent school. Father Dan asked Matiu if he wanted to go to Hato Pāora, a Māori boarding school. Matiu declined, knowing that his mother could not possibly afford to send him. Father Dan offered to pay the expenses out of his own pocket and alluded to a trust that could see Matiu through secondary school. Matiu declined it all, instead entering the Ohakune primary school.

Matiu decided to make a new start in his new school. He knew, certainly as an adult, but most likely as well as a child, that he had hurt his mother. He vowed to make it up to her. And indeed at primary school things were better. He was happier and found school easier to understand. Suddenly this became an environment in which he was willing to apply himself. Those last months of primary school remain his fondest memories of his academic experience. It is not surprising that he fared so much better in primary school. Rather than being told he was naughty and horrible, he was inspired to go on. Whether the new environment, his shame about his mother's humiliation, or a combination of both prevailed, the Ohakune primary school had a very different Matiu in attendance from the Matiu the convent school had had.

Matiu started high school reluctantly; he was convinced that he would not benefit from further schooling. As a result, he entered in February and dropped out in April, thereby ending his formal education.

Throughout his youth in the 1940s and 1950s, Matiu seems not to have been especially involved in the discussions that were taking place about the Mārama-tanga. Yet he maintained his commitment to religion and to the Catholic Church, despite his experience with the nuns in the convent school and with Father Fuouy. When asked if he was ever cautioned about revealing anything about the Māramatanga to the priests, he emphasized that he had never been told to censor his remarks. However, he knew that he could be ridiculed by the priests. In all probability, those members of the clergy who were half-aware of the beliefs of the Māramatanga indicated their contempt or suspicion.

Nevertheless, Matiu always felt good about himself and his relationship to the Catholic Church. His commitment to Catholicism had sustained him while he endured convent school, and his devotion did not seem to dissipate as he matured. But by nineteen or twenty, he was aware that the Māramatanga offered an alternative view. This undermined forever the position of Catholicism as a steadfast truth. Matiu had become a relativist, the critical first step in assuming all his adult responsibilities.

Adult Life

When Matiu left school, he was unskilled and had few aspirations. But finding work was not a problem. He had a series of jobs: scrub cutting with his older brother Rihari, shearing and working on the farm at Kuratahi with his cousin Tony. But it took some time for him to settle into a permanent job with the railway and learn a skill.

Shortly after his eighteenth birthday, Matiu married Lei, a woman from the north whose brother Barney had married Matiu's sister Nan. Lei and her family had moved to Ohakune some time ago, after Barney and Nan had married. Lei and Matiu began their family almost immediately, having five children in as many years. They later had five more, four of whom survived into adulthood (although one died as an adult), and also raised the son of one of Matiu's nieces.

In those early years, however, domestic economics for a peripatetic unskilled worker often made life difficult. It became easier when Matiu was employed by New Zealand's national railway in the highly skilled job of laying electrified tracks. This was an excellent job, and it ensured lifelong employment. Its liability lay in the fact that there were lines to be laid and repaired throughout the country so Matiu and his young family had to move often. For this reason, they spent a period in Wellington.

While he was at work on the rail in a hilly Wellington suburb, he and his fellow workers noticed a figure climbing toward them with a cross on his back. This turned out to be Father Tom Fuouy, the very priest who had thrown Matiu out of school so many years before. The other workers were quite impressed with the penitent's devotion and hard labor; Matiu was unmoved but maintained his silence. He knew what the man had been and remained skeptical of any spiritual transformation. But Matiu took no joy in Father Fuouy's newly reduced lot; rather, it taught him to separate the creed with which he had been brought up from the persons who were responsible for passing it on.

Matiu was homesick in Wellington, even though he and Lei welcomed visits from relatives. Finally Lei's illness, attributed to homesickness, convinced a doctor to see that the couple was permitted to return to the centre of the North Island. Ironically, Lei is from the far north, so the story has the apocryphal conclusion that Ohakune so draws people that even those from distant regions of the country are inexorably bound to it.

At this point in his life, Matiu was an avid rugby player. Although clearly devoted to his family, he was so intensely involved in the sport that a game could involve him even when his wife was delivering their new baby. When I spoke to him about this period of time, he rather sheepishly admitted his propensity for rugby over everything else, including family and the burgeoning of the Mārama-tanga movement. However, he did seem to feel, even then, that his grand-father had left a legacy to him and his siblings, and that they were obliged to fulfill it.

In these early years of married life, Matiu maintained his Catholicism but was not heavily involved in the Māramatanga. At this time he also could not yet speak Māori. He did, however, continue to participate in the rituals of the move-ment, even to the extent of ascending Ruapehu in the mission to prevent the damming of the Whanganui River (see chapter 5).

Ritual Training

Soon after Matiu and his family returned to Ohakune from Wellington, Matiu and several members of the Māramatanga began to attend the whare wānanga. Here they learned more fully the culture of their tribe, including genealogy, songs, history, and whaikōrero (see chapter 5). Most of them (Hoana, her hus-band Rihari, and her brother Rihari, and Raana) were native speakers of Māori; for those (like Matiu) who were not, it was also a total immersion school of Māori language.

Whanganui kawa (loosely, etiquette or body of knowledge) is unique in Aotearoa. Moreover, it is closely guarded. The tohunga who presided over the whare wānanga, Rangimotuhia Kātene, wanted to train a member of the younger generation to succeed him. Originally Matiu's brother Rihari was chosen, but he demurred and said "take my younger brother instead," a significant passing over of the prerogatives that older brothers possess. Matiu was reluctant, in part because of the magnitude of the required commitment, and in part because it was his older brother's right. Even then he was reluctant to bypass protocol.

Matiu did not seem a likely choice. While he had been on pilgrimages with other members of the group, he preferred rugby to almost all other activities, he did not speak Māori, nor was he familiar with the strictures of etiquette demanded of a tohunga. He always maintained that he was chosen in the absence of a superior candidate (modesty and self-effacement are important Māori virtues). This view is not easy to sustain: tohunga do not pass on their knowledge cavalierly. Rihari clearly had insight into his younger brother's character and ability, and one cannot doubt that wise Rangimotuhia must have shared that perception before taking Matiu on as an apprentice. Matiu's performance in the role more than vindicated his choice.

After the whare wānanga, Matiu travelled regularly to study with the tohunga in the river hamlet where he lived. As the teacher neared the end of his days, he moved in with Matiu and his family at Ohakune, ensconced on the sofa. Matiu sat at his feet and learned the sacred knowledge of the ancient world. He learned the chants by which buildings are opened, the prayers over the sick, treatment of illness, including a complex pharmacopoeia of herbal medicines, and a mastery of genealogy.

Clearly, Matiu did not master this knowledge over a short period of time; rather, he was involved in a process that took place over years. Inevitably, Matiu himself changed. He grew in authority and stature. This ascendency came at a particularly propitious time. Not only was a generation turning at Maungārongo and in the Māramatanga; throughout New Zealand a change was underway in Māori–Pākehā relations. Sometimes viewed as part of the "Māori renaissance," it involved an increasing political awareness on both sides, the recognition of the Treaty of Waitangi as a guarantee of Māori rights as much as of Pākehā sovereignty, and the legal implementation of that recognition through the Waitangi Tribunal. While studying the wisdom of the past, Matiu became sophisticated in the present, politically astute, well versed in land issues and conflicts between Māori and the government.

Matiu's transformation involved more than a shift in personal interests; it situated him at the center of fluctuating Māori self-definitions. His life reveals much about the changing nature of Māori culture from the middle to the end of the twentieth century. His historical perspective and personal interpretations illuminated current social and political events.

Tohunga

To be a tohunga, to hold this kind of specialized knowledge, is to invoke respect bordering on awe. At the same time, such a select individual is asked to bear tremendous, at times almost intolerable, responsibility in his day-to-day work. Matiu was called upon to do a number of things. He ministered to the sick, and sought the reasons behind illnesses that eluded European doctors. He opened houses at dawn— task that carried with it not only knowledge of specific prayers, but also the requirement that the lights never go out and the principals remain awake until the ceremony is completed the following day. He was in charge of training the young in poipoi, taiaha, and whakapapa, and held periodic wānanga. He was often called out in the middle of the night to offer solace and advice in his own comforting way. His knowledge had to be encyclopedic: no errors were permitted and each event required a different incantation. Through all this he remained devoted to the Māramatanga, and was prominent at all rā, on the missions to Waitangi, and on the Tira Hoe Waka.

Increasingly, as his reputation spread and as trained tohunga became increasingly scarce, Matiu was called upon to perform ceremonial tasks for other tribes. He was active on a variety of committees dealing with the Whanganui River and at the end of his life he was working for Te Puni Kōkiri, the government department devoted to Māori affairs. In short, Matiu was responsible for the spiritual continuity of the Māori world in contemporary New Zealand.

Apart from the everyday tasks of a working tohunga, Matiu also took responsibility for special disruptions in the continuity of the Māori world. An example was his making peace with the mountain in 1991 after a fatal accident. There has been a ski field on the northwest slopes of Ruapehu since early in the twentieth century, but only in the 1970s was the southern slope commercially developed. Of course this violation of their mountain offended the Māori of the area,[8] but for over a century the government had controlled it as a national park and so could license its commercial exploitation. The roads for the Turoa ski field made these parts of the mountain accessible for military alpine training, and in one such exercise troops were caught in an avalanche, with many injured and one killed. The death and injuries defiled the sacred mountain, so Matiu went up there alone for a day with appropriate prayers of purification, healing and restoring Ruapehu.

He was on call at all times for children and teenagers in distress. When teenagers had psychotic episodes—whether from drugs or other causes—he would always go to them, no matter what the time or place; and no matter what the cause, he would set them at peace.

An example of his work on the national level occurred in 1993 in Seattle. An exhibition of Māori art required closing,[9] and he went as a representative, not of

Whanganui but of all Māori, to conduct the ceremony. His son Whetu and brother Dean went with him and both participated in the formal closing.[10] *Matiu said the appropriate prayers of appeasement and purification so that the art works could be safely removed and returned home.*

Matiu was keenly aware that he himself was the source of the knowledge that informed his decisions. He knew he was both chosen and especially gifted, but it never detracted from his humanity: in fact, quite the contrary. In 1993 his granddaughter Hinewaipare, whom he had worked to save as a baby with spina bifida and had named after her powerful tupuna, died of kidney failure. In 1994 his sister Hoana died suddenly, and worse: at Hoana's death Matiu's daughter Wiki died as well. Matiu was utterly devastated. His vocation involved just such interstices, but no matter what his powers, he knew and felt just how limited they were.

One cannot properly portray Matiu Mareikura without mentioning his remarkable looks, which must have affected his relations with others throughout his life. He was as handsome as a film star. Indeed this, together one presumes with the self-possession that made performing natural, brought him significant roles in films. He had a major role in Pictures *(1981), appeared in* Wild Horses *(1983), and had a substantial part in* Te Rua *(1991).* Te Rua *represented New Zealand in the 1991 Montreal Film Festival, as did Matiu.*[11]

Conclusion

His taking part in movies and representing his country in an international film festival shows just how well Matiu was able to bridge the apparent gulf between different worlds. The key to this ability was that he did not see these worlds as disparate: his worldview was one of continuity, not of division, a distinctly Māori perspective. But it seems remarkable when one considers the disparities. At the general level, his work depended on knowledge from a past long preceding the British colonial presence, but was carried on in the late twentieth century in a country dominated both numerically and culturally by Pākehā. He was a devout Catholic, and yet he summoned Māori spirits. He was integral in the Māramatanga, but that is a movement that looks to the future, while his special ritual skills drew on the past. Even within his own family he was a younger brother and yet took on the most senior of ritual roles. And in a society and movement in which reciprocity, interdependence, and personal humility are so prized, his work required him to take responsibility in a manner that was solitary and independent. Ultimately, Matiu's ability to straddle, indeed to unify, these diverse arenas validated the desire of all Māori to live in a world that is continuous and whole. Ancestral times, the colonial encounter, and modern Māori experience can thus be conceived as all of a piece: as integrated rather than fragmented.

Matiu's conflicts reveal much about the problems that all Māori face, dilemmas that Māori as a minority ethnic group must confront when dealing with the dominant culture. For despite official nomenclature, New Zealand is a society in which the present, not the past, is valued. It is a society in which Pākehā privilege is sustained, often at the expense of Māori advancement. Matiu's narrative reflects the ways in which biography and history must reinforce one another; history is encapsulated in biography, while biography is a way of waging a battle against death—not only individual mortality, but the passing of a culture.

Matiu's life and actions provided the opportunity for an indigenous people to respond to a history that, for the most part, has been generated, written, and propagated by Pākehā. Moreover, his very existence and potency attest to an alternative interpretation of events and an entirely different epistemology. His biography offers an important counter to notions of Māori cultural demise, for it asserts the continuing strength and vitality of exclusively Māori knowledge and ritual. Matiu was an exemplar to young people, who could see what they might become and who could not help understanding the effectiveness of knowledge that is exclusively Māori. To older people, as well, Matiu provided an example of a man who was able to weave the many strands of his life into one coherent whole. Matiu demonstrated the possibility, indeed the necessity, of being true to Māoriness.

Matiu stood at a threshold where everything is possible, everything has happened, and yet everything has still to happen (Behar 1995). He was, like most tohunga, a guardian of time. This was a fearsome responsibility, but one which he bore without flinching to the end of his life.

CONCLUSION

The Tradition of Prophecy in the Nineteenth and Twentieth Centuries

This book is the result of over thirty years of fieldwork. Inevitably, events at the turn of the millennium are very different from those I witnessed when I first began my work in 1972. I can no longer regard the Māramatanga or Aotearoa New Zealand through the eyes of a student. For their part, the members of the Māramatanga no longer see me as a naïve young American. Since we first met, I have married and had a daughter whom they have seen grow up, I have a professional life, and unmistakably I, too, have aged. These things have all changed the ways in which people talk to me. People of an age that used to call me "Karen" now call me "aunty" or even "kui." We are intimates; we have come to know one another well.

In Aotearoa, there have been changes on all levels. The replacement of the Department of Māori Affairs with Te Puni Kōkiri (the Ministry for Māori Development) and the devolution of some of its functions to the iwi has affected both Māori and Pākehā. The Waitangi Tribunal has led many Māori, including those from Whanganui, to believe that their share of resources may well be greater in the future. Within the Māramatanga, there have been major shifts in personnel and roles. Since 1972, an older generation has passed away, as have very many members of its successor; children have grown up and become parents, even grandparents. Some members have become less active, while others have astounded us all by their virtuosity and abilities. Most importantly, there is a new generation—one placed there prematurely and not entirely willingly—which has not only learned the ways of the Māramatanga, but also learned to negotiate in the ways of the Pākehā. Although inexperienced and nervous, this generation is likely to be formidable.

This book covers almost a century, through which generations have turned over several times, responsibilities have changed hands, and missions and pilgrimages have ushered in a different world. Nevertheless, there is circularity that is both comforting and ultimately very much in a Māori mode; the movement today stands, literally and figuratively, at the place where its origins are to be found:

Waitangi and marae of the Waimarino and the Rangitīkei. There are certainly different interpretations and different meanings in the present. But insistence on the legitimacy of specific polities has, in fact, been the driving force in Māori–Pākehā relations.

The prophets of the nineteenth and early twentieth centuries live on in memory and constitute a meaningful past for the members of the Māramatanga.[1] They have become components of a history that has denied rupture and emphasized continuity. In their arguments with the government about polity and autonomy, Māori have been served well by these prophets.

The nineteenth-century prophets were steeped in the Old Testament—hardly surprisingly, given its chronicle of dispossession. Prophets of the early twentieth century such as Mere Rikiriki changed the metaphor: Māori had now entered the New Testament. But just as the Judaism of the Old Testament was encapsulated by New Testament teachings, so too the early prophetic movements on the west coast of New Zealand's North Island were absorbed in the new. One of Mere Rikiriki's followers, Hori Enoka Mareikura, became a leader himself. His powers were enhanced when his granddaughter died and became Te Karere to the adherents of the movement. The prophet knew this was a new dispensation, but the movement has been scrupulous in asserting its nineteenth-century past.

The history of prophets, especially of Te Kooti and T. W. Rātana, makes a compelling narrative in the general conversation between Māori and Pākehā. However, the history of the Māramatanga is a localized history, whose context cannot be violated. Māori, in their concern with tribal etiquette, certainly insist on this point. The larger stories are diminished in the absence of their location in space and time. By treating Māori as the generic colonized, the generalized "other." Pākehā have denied Māori the specificity that has always been so important to them.

Far from disappearing and leaving room for a completely British South Pacific state at the onset of the twentieth century, Māori have had a resurgence in health and population. There have been two Māori renaissances, and at present, the Māori population is growing at a much faster rate than Pākehā. Their minority status is no longer axiomatic. Māori activism has produced a literature that has gained international renown, including a Booker Prize (for Keri Hulme's *The Bone People*). Māori have actively gone before the Waitangi Tribunal, and in the process have garnered financial and moral victories. If the abuses of the last two centuries cannot be undone, Māori have at least revealed them to the world's eyes. Perhaps the change with the greatest consequence has been New Zealand's declaration that it is officially bilingual and bicultural. For many Pākehā, this means merely that there are now book titles to go with many place names they can neither pronounce nor understand. For Māori, however, the kohanga reo have flourished, with the result that many Māori pre-schoolers are comfortably bilingual. There are daily news programs in the Māori language on the radio and television. Few talk about Māori as a dead language, although it is still a long way from being an established part of New Zealand's discourse.

If Māori experience has sustained some continuity, it does not mean that prejudice and antipathy do not exist in New Zealand. On the contrary, Māori have emerged on the worst side of virtually every comparison that can be made: they have higher infant mortality rates, die decades earlier, attend school for fewer years, make less money at less secure jobs, and are more likely to be laid off in harsh economic times, which unfortunately have characterized New Zealand for over a decade. References to a "backlash" against Māori resurgence encompass prejudice and an unrelenting insistence that New Zealand prefer, retain, and sustain all that is British (see Thomas 1994: 183–84).[2]

Appropriation as a Māori Device

Post-colonial studies have correctly insisted that we permit those who have been silenced to speak. For an anthropologist working with the Māramatanga, this is almost shamelessly easy: they possess diaries, journals, and notebooks, and each year at rā they actively recall the major pilgrimages and events in the life of the movement. Moreover, they are generous with their time and with their personal narratives. In effect, they have done much of my work for me. But what did it mean to convert to Christianity, to take up literacy, to interpret the signs and symbols of the Catholic Church?

It has been argued that there was little choice in the matter (see Wright 1959; Ballara 1986): that, given the differentials of power, Māori would have to yield sooner or later. But if Māori absorbed Christianity, they also transformed it, creating their own mythic structure and their own hierarchy (Taussig 1980). Under these conditions, it is reasonable to question who has control, who are the appropriators? Religion got many Māori out of a tight spot in the two centuries of colonization. They were not taken over; Māori made this new, strange religion work for them.[3]

Literacy, which was to draw Māori to the churches, clearly produced unanticipated results. Written words can be hidden, or not revealed, as they have been for generations in the Māramatanga. Yet at the same time, oral narratives need not be repeated to suspect audiences. Therefore, both writing and orality have sustained boundaries; they protect Māori and preclude their violation. It may have been the Bible that they learned, but the intentions of the Catholic Church were not to keep the clergy at bay. Precisely what is important has remained inaccessible, but now in two modes. Each increases the possibilities of memory. For the members of the Māramatanga, stories that are so important that they are told on all available occasions and written in private notebooks cannot be viewed as disposable pieces of information (Benjamin 1978). Records, be they oral or written, can be controlled; they belong to the realm of both the historical and the cosmological, providing frames for contemporary lives and justifications for the pasts of the movement's members.

Māori are the appropriators. The introduction of new modes and languages did not make Māori subservient; on the contrary, these new skills allowed them to exercise dominion and power. By writing about the pilgrimages and the stories that link *Our Lady of Perpetual Succour* to medieval Italy and contemporary Aotearoa, the members of the Māramatanga inscribe themselves into a history that already exists. Their trips up the mountain and to Waitangi permit them to participate in a history that has yet to be written.

The major questions they ask and answer concern where they fit in and what they are doing. These are powerful questions in a landscape that is far from stable. To answer them, they turn to self-reflection. As the members scrutinize their past and examine the narratives of others, they illuminate and explore their predicament. Ultimately, what appears as unique is profoundly human: as they write themselves into history, they enlarge all they have undertaken.

Anthropology and the Moral Domain

There is a tendency in any kind of analysis to reveal more about the critics and their times, context, concerns, preoccupations, and longings than about their subjects. In contemporary anthropology, the third-person omniscient narrator who favors the passive voice is tending to disappear in favor of the committed and implicated individual whose vision must be partial and itself situated and located, and colonialism tends to be seen as a global form of victimization. Certainly, any colonized state will reveal a history of treachery, duplicity, and broken promises. Equally undebatable is the fractured dispensation that was left to indigenous peoples as they lost land and political autonomy. But victimology not only presumes the diminution of moral agency, it also presumes to describe the inner feelings and motivations of a people. In the decades that I have worked with the members of the Māramatanga, I have learned that they have been angered and have felt betrayed and humiliated on particular occasions, but they do not see themselves, nor have they ever seen themselves, as victims. Their will is too strong and their confidence in their past too great. It is anthropology, in its current crisis of conscience—not wholly unwarranted—that is concerned with colonial casualties and with victims. However, as a description of the members of the Māramatanga—a group that has sustained kinship relationships over decades and that has generated a counter-history—"victim" is profoundly incomplete.

The members of the movement derive a great deal of satisfaction from the structure of the Māori community and the trust, obligation, and security that a society based upon kinship confers. In addition to their participation in the Māramatanga, individuals are mothers, fathers, brothers, sisters, nephews, and nieces. The pull of kinship and the ideology of the movement work against individual glory and personal vanity, whatever the nature of accomplishment. Bragging and pride are not tolerated; humility and a matter-of-fact persona are expected and required. The differences between those who are ordinary and those who are extraordinary are not obvious at first glance.

The past, both proximate and distant, is critical for the members of the Māramatanga. But its meaning is far different for Māori than it is for those of us who live within the purview of one or two generations and are ignorant of ancestors beyond grandparents. Actions taken generations before an individual was born have an immediate and influential impact; ancestors can cause shame decades after their infamous activities. For those of us in other cultures, there is no immediate connection between lives separated over time. By contrast, the Māori kin group encompasses all its members, living and dead. Under such conditions, it is essential to behave well, for a negative legacy will besmirch a descent line. Māori are thus held hostage to history in a way that Pākehā are not, while at the same time, history works to define, protect, and demarcate each new generation.

The Māramatanga, like all such groups, is comprised of some individuals who are quite conventional and others whose abilities elevate them above all others. This has caused surprisingly little discomfort for a movement that is predicated on equality of knowledge and access to spiritual revelation. Despite this ideology, inequality has been manifest, since the time of Te Karere, in a series of kaimahi. Yet not every kaimahi has happily or readily assumed the role. Anaera remained asleep as her daughter contacted her, and Hoana admitted freely to being afraid of the dark. Abilities that distinguish one from the group can also bring terror and feelings of isolation—uncomfortable feelings for the kaimahi, who were raised in group settings and dependent upon communal actions and approval.

It is the job of the kaimahi to sustain faith with the past. To do this is to ensure that etiquette is followed, ritual imperatives are obeyed, and the correct prayers and songs are at hand. It is easy to overlook how difficult this aspect of their task can be: there can be no concessions when speeches must be made, even in a howling gale and rain storm; on pilgrimages, cars must pull over for karakia at 7 A.M. and 7 P.M.; following Whanganui etiquette, coffins are closed at midnight the night before the burial, but the lights remain on as the group farewells one of its members.

Another necessary source of their leadership is to be found in their ability to smooth social relations. Expertise in social relations—humility, lack of arrogance, and willingness to yield—is seen in the West as a feminine trait (see Gilligan 1982). Why then is it common among both men and women kaimahi? The answer, I think, lies less with gender than with subordination. These are the characteristics of those who are not dominant, be they women or Māori. However, even if they do not command respect in all social contexts, these abilities are essential when personalities, wills, and agendas clash. Those more assertive but less sensitive would, in this context, be far less successful.

Intense curiosity and intellectual appetite have also distinguished the kaimahi. They did not settle for the obvious, nor were they content with partial answers. In each case—Anaera, Ruka, Pauro, Hoana, and Matiu—there was intensive preparation. Ultimately, what distinguished these individuals was their command of knowledge that others could not fathom. This required memorization, fluency in the Māori language, and constant repetition that finally yielded to mastery. This was not a task for the lazy or unwilling. Furthermore, they all took it upon themselves to teach a future generation. At times this meant writing and teaching songs for the Hui Aranga (in the case of Ruka, Pauro, and Hoana); for others (Pauro, Hoana, and Matiu) it was holding wānanga; and for all it meant iterating history at rā, and leading missions. To be a kaimahi was to be willing to go without sleep and food, to answer all who called upon you, and to remain, through it all, committed to the family and to the Māramatanga. It is no wonder that these were exceptional individuals; they had to be. A great deal was asked of them, and they were the few who were both able and willing to come forth.

The Māramatanga has thus carved out a domain that has been, and remains, independent of the Pākehā. It has had its own set of moral imperatives and has remained, to a very large extent, untouched and unknown by the larger society. It was not easy to establish this isolation, but there is no doubt that this was their desire. The movement demonstrates the falsity of the notion that moral agency is lacking in colonized peoples.

When I was concluding this book in 1998, I was notified that Matiu had died suddenly on July 19. This could not have come as a surprise to anyone, as he had suffered two major coronaries and yet persisted with his demanding and certainly exhausting routine. I flew to New Zealand for the tangi and burial. Matiu and I had met in our twenties; although he was older than I, we had, nevertheless, known one another for most of our lives. The tangi lasted five days—several more than usual—in order to allow people time to arrive from all over New Zealand, a testament to the regard in which Matiu was held. For days, with no pause, groups and buses arrived on the marae to pay their respects. The numbers were so overwhelming that a brigadier-general of the New Zealand army, who had known Matiu in their younger days, insisted that the army provide for the unprecedented crowds, numbering over ten thousand. Dozens of tents were erected to house overnight guests and portable showers and facilities were also put into place.

The army took over the cooking, thereby freeing the people from Maungārongo to take care of their visitors.

As I walked onto the marae, my eye was drawn to the flags that were waving to the right of the tent in which Matiu was laying in state. Here were flags representing the iwi of the Whanganui River, Mere Rikiriki's E Te Iwi Kia Ora, and Maungārongo's flag. Encompassing the river, the Māramatanga, and the local family, these flags signalled Matiu's multiple responsibilities and commitments.

While this was certainly a very large tangi, it was also unique. A leader had fallen and there were questions about who could or would take his place. These questions have not yet been definitively answered. Replacing Matiu will be a considerable task and is unlikely to be undertaken by only one individual.

However, at Matiu's tangi, we saw that his and his sister Hoana's work and their commitment to the next generation had borne fruit. Young men, often nervous and unsettled, gave their first speeches on the marae and the young, trained in chanting, singing, and genealogy, performed in his honor. There can be no compensation for the knowledge that was lost when Matiu died, although a surprising amount—passed down to various young individuals—surfaced in the days of mourning. Under the watchful gaze of elders, the young displayed their abilities; through a difficult time, these young people demonstrated that the Māramatanga was not, after all, in jeopardy. It would prevail.

Despite unanticipated contingencies and unexpected deaths, the movement has survived since Mere Rikiriki named Tikaraina in 1910. To be sure, it has changed over time, as each generation has produced new leaders. Matiu's death was shocking and alarming. But his life and his work, and that of other kaimahi and dedicated members of the movement, offered assurance that the Māramatanga can and will be sustained.

Kinship Diagrams 1–6

DIAGRAM 1: **The Children of Hori Enoka Mareikura and Te Huinga**

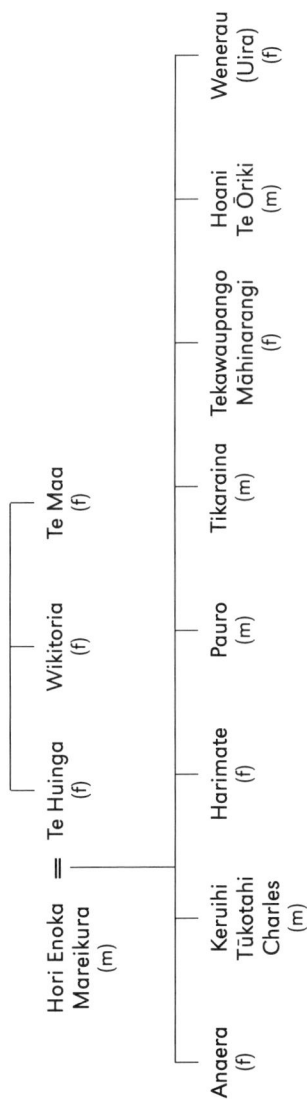

Hori Enoka Mareikura (m) ═ Te Huinga (f)

Te Huinga (f) — Wikitoria (f) — Te Maa (f)

Anaera (f) — Keruihi Tūkotahi Charles (m) — Harimate (f) — Pauro (m) — Tikaraina (m) — Tekawaupango Māhinarangi (f) — Hoani Te Ōriki (m) — Wenerau (Uira) (f)

Note: In Te Huinga's generation, two brothers are not shown.

DIAGRAM 2: **The Ruka Family**

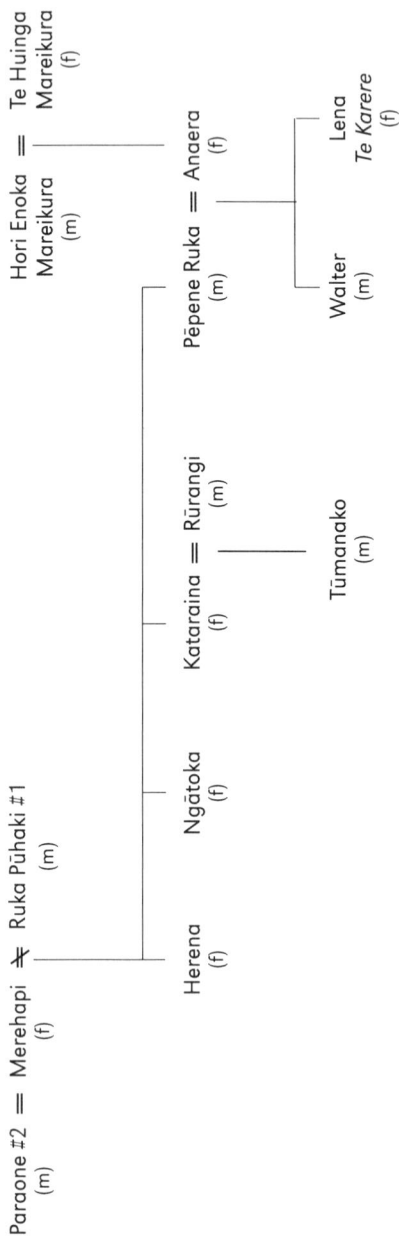

Paraone #2 = Merehapi ≠ Ruka Pūhaki #1
(m)   (f)   (m)

Herena   Ngātoka   Kataraina = Rūrangi   Pēpene Ruka = Anaera   Hori Enoka = Te Huinga
(f)   (f)   (f)   (m)   (m)   (f)   Mareikura   Mareikura
                                                                     (m)   (f)

                              Tūmanako   Walter   Lena
                              (m)   (m)   Te Karere
                                                                   (f)

Note: Walter and Lena died as children.

DIAGRAM 3: **Weuweu (Emere Frances Broughton Hurinui) – Descent Line and Marriage Ties to the Mareikura Family**

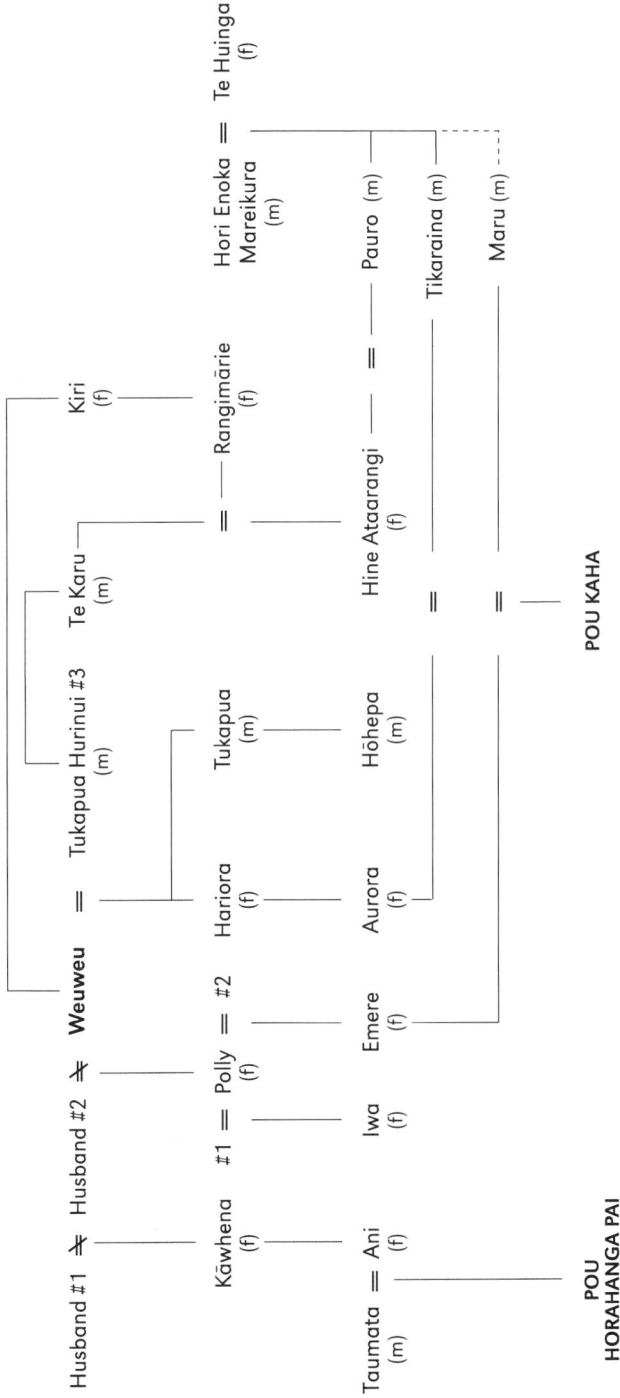

Husband #1 ⚡ Husband #2 ⚡ **Weuweu** ⚡ Tukapua Hurinui #3 ─ Te Karu ─ Kiri
(m)   (m)   (f)

Kāwhena #1 ═ Polly ═ #2   Hariora ═ Tukapua ═ ── Rangimārie ═ ── Hori Enoka ═ Te Huinga
(f)   (f)   (f)   (m)   (f)   Mareikura   (f)
                                                                      (m)

Taumata ═ Ani   Iwa   Emere   Aurora ═ Hōhepa ═ Hine Ataarangi ═ ── ── Pauro (m)
(m)   (f)   (f)   (f)   (f)   (m)   (f)   Tikaraina (m)
                                              ═   ═ POU KAHA   Maru (m)

POU
HORAHANGA PAI

Note: Maru was raised in Karioi by Hori Enoka's relatives.

DIAGRAM 4: Affinal Links between the Gray, Ruka, and Mareikura Families

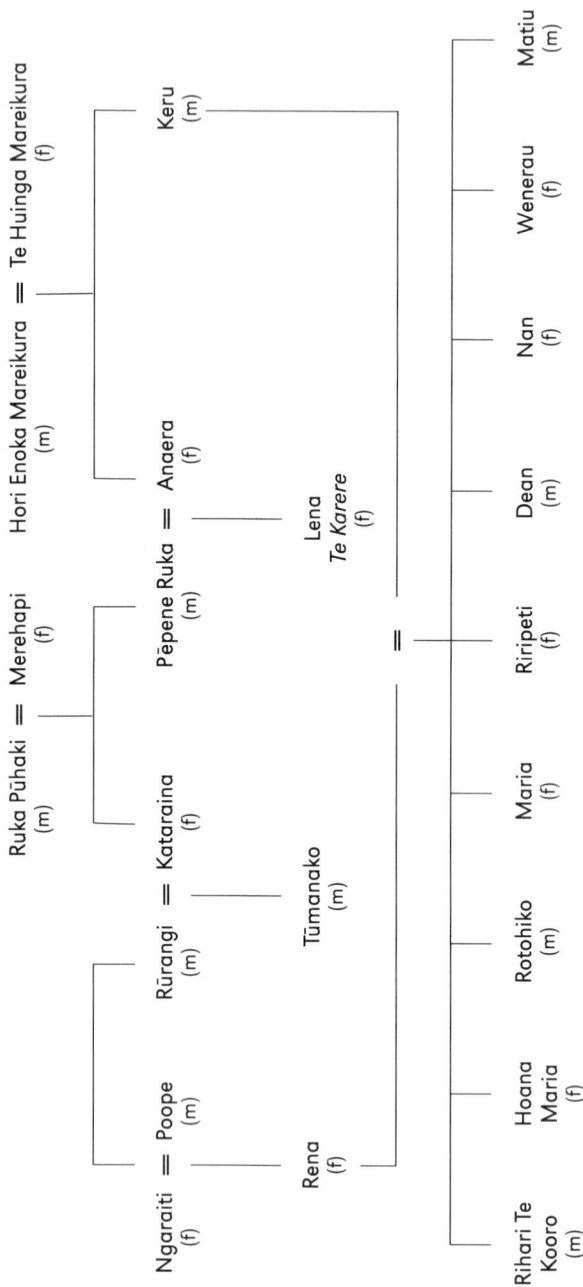

Ruka Pūhaki (m) = Merehapi (f)

Hori Enoka Mareikura (m) = Te Huinga Mareikura (f)

Ngaraiti (f) = Poope (m)

Rūrangi (m) = Kataraina (f)

Pēpene Ruka (m) = Anaera (f)

Keru (m)

Rena (f)

Tūmanako (m)

Lena
Te Karere
(f)

Rihari Te Kooro (m)

Hoana Maria (f)

Rotohiko (m)

Maria (f)

Riripeti (f)

Dean (m)

Nan (f)

Wenerau (f)

Matiu (m)

Notes: Rūrangi and Kataraina were also descended from a sister and a brother, Te Rewha and Koroniria. Rotohiko and Maria died as infants.

DIAGRAM 5: **Akapita Family**

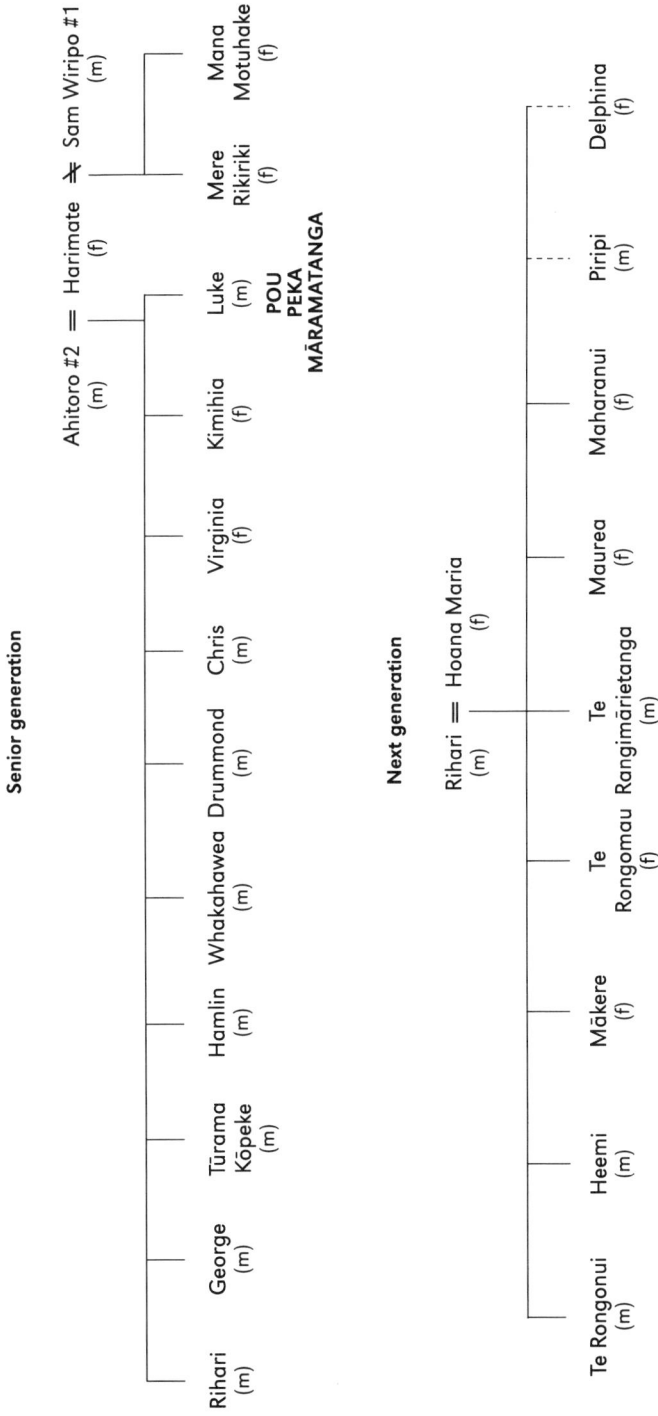

Senior generation

Rihari (m)

George (m) — Tūrama Kōpeke (m) — Hamlin (m) — Whakahawea (m) — Drummond (m) — Chris (m) — Virginia (f) — Kimihia (f) — Luke (m) **POU PEKA MĀRAMATANGA**

Ahitoro #2 (m) = Harimate (f) ≠ Sam Wiripo #1 (m)

Mere Rikiriki (f) — Mana Motuhake (f)

Next generation

Rihari (m) = Hoana Maria (f)

Te Rongonui (m) — Heemi (m) — Mākere (f) — Te Rongomau (f) — Te Rangimārietanga (m) — Maurea (f) — Maharanui (f) — Piripi (m) — Delphina (f)

Notes: Heemi, Te Rongomau and Mere Rikiriki died as infants. Piripi and Delphina were brought up by Rihari and Hoana; this is indicated by the broken line.

DIAGRAM 6: **Participants in the Mountain Mission, December 1962**

A brother and sister marry a brother and sister

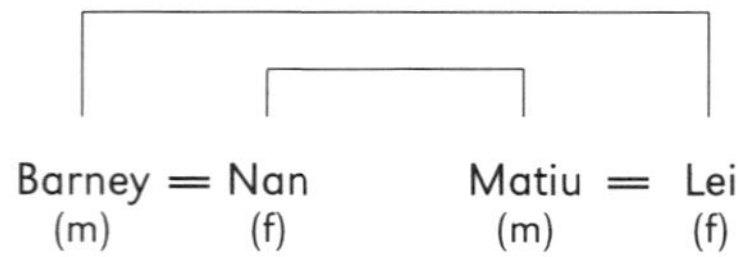

Barney = Nan   Matiu = Lei
(m)   (f)   (m)   (f)

On the mountain, December 1962

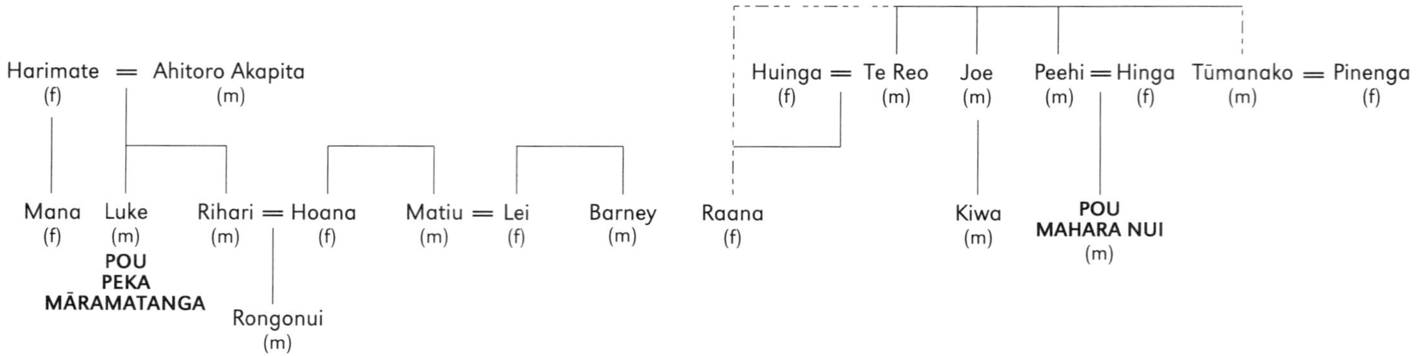

Tūmanako = Pinenga
(m)   (f)

Peehi = Hinga
(m)   (f)

**POU
MAHARA NUI**
(m)

Joe
(m)

Kiwa
(m)

Huinga = Te Reo
(f)   (m)

Raana
(f)

Harimate = Ahitoro Akapita
(f)   (m)

Luke
(m)
**POU
PEKA**

Rihari = Hoana
(m)   (f)

Rongonui
(m)

Matiu = Lei
(m)   (f)

Barney
(m)

Mana
(f)

MĀRAMATANGA

Note: Age and seniority are not represented in these diagrams.

Nationally Recognized Waiata from the Māramatanga

This is a list of some waiata from the Māramatanga. These waiata are widely used within the Māramatanga and are also sung nationally by other tribes.

Aue te Aroha i Ahau
Waiata-ā-ringa
This is acknowledged as one of the key waiata-ā-ringa of the Māramatanga. This waiata-ā-ringa is generally recognized as a Whanganui national anthem and is also sung by other tribes. It was chosen as the mihi to this book.

Ki kō (Kikō)
Pātere – 3 August 1948
This pātere was originally composed as a tauparapara but was then changed to be sung as a pātere (sometimes accompanied with a single short poi—this style of poi dance is typical of the Aotea area). In the 1980s Queen Victoria Māori Girls' School were given permission by Pauro to use the words of this pātere as a contemporary poi, which is now sung nationwide. The traditional pātere is also frequently sung throughout the Māramatanga and also the greater Whanganui iwi.

Ko te Rite i Ahau
Waiata-ā-ringa
This is another key waiata-ā-ringa of the Māramatanga and also the greater Whanganui iwi. This waiata is also sung in the Taranaki region. A slightly different version is sung in the Waikato region.

Te Kura o Kurahaupō (Ngā Kura)
Pātere – 16 September 1943
This pātere is generally referred by its shortened name—Ngā Kura. Sung throughout the Māramatanga, it was through the kinship ties of the Weuweu branch of the movement that the pātere was shared with Ngāti Pikiao and Te Arawa.

Taku Taumata Tonu
Pātere – 22 July 1942
This pātere encapsulates the original answer Te Mareikura provided to the King Movement in response to King Te Rata's invitation for Te Mareikura to reside amongst the king's people. This pātere is referred to by the Waikato people as Ngā Tongi and they sing it to a different tune.

E Noho Nei Au
Pātere – 16 September 1942
This pātere is sung throughout the Māramatanga and the greater Whanganui iwi. The men of the Māramatanga also chant this pātere in the tauparapara form.

I te Rangi Tuatahi
Pātere – 22 July 1942
This pātere is sung mainly by the Maungārongo and Hawke's Bay branches of the Māramatanga (though other branches also sing this pātere less frequently). Generally, the Maungārongo branch will sing the first verse only and the Hawke's Bay branch will sing the second verse only.

Flags of the Movement

E Te Iwi Kia Ora (Greetings to the People) harks back to Mere Rikiriki and her plunge into the Rangitīkei River. Originally given to the prophetess by the Māori king, the flag passed into the hands of the movement. Today it is one of the major links between the Māramatanga and the King Movement. It is a white banner, with red stars, and red inscription.

Te Āka o Maungārongo (The Ark of Peace) was inspired by Ritihira, and recently redone by her son John. On a light blue background, a white picture of a dove and crucifix appears. This is a conscious connection between the ark of the movement and Noah's ark—a vessel built with divine guidance that led the faithful to a new life. In a song received by Ritihira, there is an exhortation by the deity to "hold the peace." Kīngi o te Maungārongo (King of Peace) is the name of the meeting-house in Ohakune, Mareikura's home.

Te Tohu o te Rangimārie (The Sign of Peace) comes from an inspiration by Peehi. The flag is white with a rainbow; the lettering is in red and white. Here the rainbow motif exemplifies the movement's ideal of spiritual communication. Rangimārie means tranquillity, harmony, while maungārongo carries connotations of truce, cessation from conflict.

Te Waka o te Ora (The Canoe of Life) is a navy blue flag with a white crucifix and a brown boat. The flag was Ruka's inspiration and was used to open the meeting-house in Levin. Here the imagery calls forth the seven canoes of the original migration, but suggests in its Christian imagery concern with the new order. The different connotations of waka (canoe, vessel, transporter) and ora (life, health, well-being, fulfilment) make for a very potent image.

Ko Ahau te Ārepa me te Ōmeka (I Am the Beginning and the End) is a white banner with red lettering and a red crucifix, recently remade by John Paki. Here the biblical imagery is obvious, but it also recalls Rātana, who (assisted by Mere Rikiriki) named his two sons Ārepa and Ōmeka (Alpha and Omega).

There are also two flags that always fly at Levin during tangi. Together they affirm local tradition and their people's inclusion in the wider society. Although not directly related to the movement, they illustrate the use to which flags are put in Māori life.

Muaūpoko is a blue flag with the Union Jack, symbolizing the inclusion of the tribe into the Commonwealth and the Dominion.

Tutere Moana (Rock of the Sea) refers to Kapiti Island off the west coast of New Zealand, where Muaūpoko ancestry is believed to have its origins.

Interviews, Research, and Notebooks[1]

1. Research and Interviews

March 1972–July 1973 Interviews in Levin with Hine, Aurora, Pauro, Tikaraina, Hōhepa. Taped interviews[2] with Ritihira; mission to Waitangi; Hui Aranga (1972 Porirua; 1973 Christchurch).

May–August 1982 Taped interviews at Kuratahi with Pinenga, and at Ohakune with Raana, Hoana, Rihari.

January–May 1987 Taped interviews at Kuratahi with Pinenga, and at Ohakune with Hoana, Raana, Hine and Rihari. Interviews with all major figures in Levin and Ohakune. Attended rā, 18 March; attended Hui Aranga at Palmerston North.

May 1990 Interviews at Kuratahi with Pinenga and in Ohakune with Hoana and Rihari, Raana, Tūmanako, Mākere, Rongonui, Merrilyn George. Research in Auckland Public Library.

May–August 1991 Interviews in Ohakune with major participants in the Māramatanga—Moriana Hancock, Mākere, Gabriel, Rongonui, Ngāwai. Taped interviews with Hoana, Pinenga, Hine, Matiu. Attended 27 July rā.

1991 and 1993 Meetings with Matiu in the US, when he attended the Montreal Film Festival (1991) and the closing of the Māori exhibition at the Burke Museum in Seattle (1993).

April 1993 Research in Ohakune and Hawera: attended Hui Aranga and Hui rehearsals; taped interviews with Matiu after Hui; billeted with Maungārongo. Interviews with most major figures.

5–20 January 1995 Participated in Tira Hoe Waka.

March 1996 Research at Alexander Turnbull Library. Interviews at Ohakune with Matiu, Lei, Mākere, Ngāwai, Raana, Rihari.

1–15 July 1996 Attended tangi for Amy Brown. Research at Maungārongo.

21–26 July 1998 Attended Matiu's tangi. Interviews with Mākere, Rihari, Raana, Aroha Clarkin, Mikaere.

Christmas–New Year 2000 Christmas at Ohakune.

2. Rā, Missions, Notebooks

Rā recorded: June 1972; July 27, 1972; October 6, 1972; November 9, 1972; January 1, 1973; January 3, 1973; March 18, 1973.

Missions attended: Waitangi, August 1972; Tira Hoe Waka, January 1995.

Notebooks referred to: Aurora (4); Auta (1); Harimate (1); Hine Ataarangi (2); Hoana, diary of the trip for Te Umuroa; Iwa (2); Kataraina (2); Pauro (3); Pinenga (1); Raana, on Tira Hoe Waka (1); Raana, selections of notebooks read into tape recorder; Ruka (3).

Glossary

Note: Māori words do not add "s" for plurals; verbs are conjugated by adding particles; the same word may be used for different parts of speech (as in English); long vowels are indicated by a macron. The names of some waiata, pātere and flags from the movement are explained in appendixes 2–3.

Aotearoa	New Zealand
ārepa	beginning (Māori transliteration of 'alpha'). The name Ārepa was given by Mere Rikiriki to one of Rātana's sons.
aroha	love
E kui	grandmother (form of address for respected woman elder)
E pai ana	It's all right
haka	men's war dance
hapū	sub-tribe, extended family
hoe	paddle
hohourongo	unity, to unify through peace. Hohourongo is the dining room at Maungārongo.
huapai	fruition
Hui Aranga	Catholic Māori culture festival held at Easter
hui	gathering (formal and informal)
hunga ruarua (hungaruarua)	chosen few (term given to the members of the movement)
hunga wairua	those of the spirit realm
ihi	authority
iwi	tribe
kai	food
kaimahi	worker; within the movement, closer to leader
karakia	prayer
karanga	distinctive call given by women
kare or karekare	ripple, rippling
kaumātua	respected elder (male or female)
kaupapa	foundation, fundamental principle or founding philosophy, purpose
kawa	tribal etiquette, protocol, body of knowledge
kāwai tika	correct lineage, genealogical ascendancy

Kīngi o te Maungārongo	King of Everlasting Peace—the name of the chapel at Maungārongo
koha	donation, gift to defray expenses
kohanga reo	Māori language pre-school; literally, language nest
kohurangi	mist
kōkiri (Kōkiri Centre)	community administration
kōrero	talk
Koro	respected male elder (addressed as E koro)
kororia	glory
kuia	respected female elder, grandmother (addressed as E kui)
kūmara	sweet potato—a root vegetable brought to Aotearoa by Māori
kūpapa	Māori who assisted the government cause; traitor
kura	school, education course, power (in its many forms), red feather
kura kaupapa	primary school
mākutu	evil doing, spell, sorcery
mana	prestige, power, salvation
māngai	mouthpiece
manuhiri	visitors (in contrast to the local people)
marae	communal focal point of a hapū
māramatanga	light, enlightenment, knowledge. The name Māramatanga is shared by the current movement and Mere Rikiriki's movement.
Matakite o Aotearoa	The Seers of Prophetic Vision of New Zealand (the name of a group)
maungārongo	peace, maintained peace. Maungārongo is the name of the movement's marae at Ohakune.
mauri (mouri)	life-principle, spiritual essence
mere	short war-club (generally made of greenstone or whalebone)
mihi	greeting
mokopuna	grandchild
mōrehu	survivors
ngā	the (plural)
Ngā Tamatoa	The Young Warriors (Māori activist group)
ngārara	lizards, reptiles
niu	ceremonial mast
noa	opposite of tapu, common
ōmeka	end. Ōmeka was the name given by Mere Rikiriki to one of Rātana's sons. A transliteration of Omega.

Pākehā	New Zealander(s) of European ethnic descent
pao	epigram (often directive)
pātere	chant
patupaiarehe	a half-human spirit
piupiu	flax skirt
poi	flax ball
poipoi	beautiful, rhythmic movement with flax balls suspended from each hand (most often used on ceremonial occasions for genealogy)
pūkana	stylized gesture designed to highlight participation in waiata and haka
pōkare	churn, stir
pōwhiri	welcome song
puawaitanga	blooming
rā	commemorative celebration day(s); also known in the movement as Rā Wairua
rākau	staff, tree, stick
rangatahi	youth
rangimārie	peace
raukura	feather, plume; guardian angels
ringa kaha	strong hand. Ringa Kaha was one of the four original names given by Mere Rikiriki.
ringa kaha o te Atua	right hand of God
ringa poto ringapoto	short hand. Ringapoto was one of the four names given by Mere Rikiriki.
rūnanga	congress, council
taiaha	spear-like weapon about five feet long (used in ritual challenge and to clear the way for visitors)
tākere	main part of the hull of a canoe, centre, chief, or important part of anything
tamariki	children
tangata	the law of man
tangi tangihanga	loosely, funeral; ritual mourning period lasting several days, to which family, friends, and acquaintances come from all over New Zealand (and beyond)
tāniko	ornamental weaving, Māori tapestry
taonga	valuable, treasure
tāpae	to present to God, to give back to God, to place the power of the past in God's hands, to neutralize
tapu	sacred, sacrosanct, sacredness, forbidden by religion
tauiwi	alien, foreigner, interlopers

taumau	engage to be married, arranged marriage
te ao hou	the present-day world, the living
te ao tāwhito	the old ways, the ancient world
te aranga o te pono	the rising of the faith. Te Aranga o te Pono is the name of a house, inspired by a tribal elder.
Te Karere o te Aroha	The Messenger of Love (often abbreviated to Te Karere) —the primary spirit who guides the movement
te kupu whakamutunga	the final word
te reo	the (Māori) language
te tino raro rawa	the lowest
te	the (singular)
tika raina or tikaraina	straight line. Tikaraina is one of the four names given by Mere Rikiriki; it is also the name of the meeting-house at Maungārongo.
tika	correct, usual
tikanga	custom (deriving from tika)
tira	touring party
Tira Hoe Waka	the movement's annual spiritual and educational expedition, made by canoe down the Whanganui River through ancestral lands and marae
tohunga	specialist in Māori ritual, religious officiate, expert
tokotoko	carved stick
tonotono	to serve or order around
tū wairua	literally, let the spirit stand tall; (spiritual) instruction periods like wānanga
tuakana	older brother, older sister, senior; senior descent line
tūkino	ill-treat
tūmanako	hope, expect, desire something that is absent
tupua	foreign, an object of terror
tupuna/tūpuna	ancestor/s
ture	justice system
utu	vengeance
wāhi tapu	a sacred place
wahine pūremu	loose woman
wahine/wāhine	woman/women
waiata	song(s)
wairua hiahia	yearning spirit
Wairua Tapu	Holy Spirit
wairua	spirit(s)
waka	canoe(s), vessel(s)

wānanga	classes of Māori esoteric knowledge. Wānanga is now commonly used for tertiary education but it still signifies special and separate types of learning.
wehi	awe
whaikōrero	speech(es), art of oratory
whakaaronui	to be mindful
whakahāwea	to disbelieve, to despise
whakamā	shamed, humiliated, made white, drained of color
whakamoemiti	to give thanks
whakanoa	to neutralize tapu, to remove ritual restrictions
whakapapa	genealogy
whakapono	faith
whakarongo	listen. Whakarongo is one of the four names given by Mere Rikiriki.
whānau	family
whāngai	literally "to feed"; foster-child (a child brought up by people other than his/her biological parents, although these are almost always known to the child)
whanganui kawa	etiquette, body of knowledge
whare puni	sleeping house
whare wānanga	school of esoteric learning (also, university)
whare-ngaro	literally, house destroyed; barren, sterility

Endnotes

Introduction

1. Ballara (1986, 1998), Belich (1986, 1989, 1996), Salmond, (1980, 1991, 1997), Binney (1987, 1988, 1990, 1995), Sissons (1991), Young (1998)—and other historians and anthropologists—have in recent years paid particular heed to the specificity of Māori histories.
2. The understanding of Māori as "others" has a long history, going back to the first English contact, as Salmond's analysis of Cook's correspondence shows (Salmond 1997: 27).
3. In examining notebooks from the period 1936–1975, not surprisingly I found many of the same songs, but with some differences in the words. These inconsistencies have always been recognized by those most knowledgable: Hoana and Hine would look at others' notebooks and shake their heads.
4. Kaimahi means worker in Māori. For the movement, the word carries this connotation, but also clearly invokes leadership of a spiritual nature. This is altogether fitting, since the kaimahi are workers whose dedication gives them special prerogatives.

Narrative: Te Karere

1. The history of the movement has been marked by barrenness. While traditionally it was believed to suit a woman for her destiny as a spiritual leader, this has nevertheless been very painful for the individuals involved. Judith Binney (1986: 26) has written:

   > The experience of childlessness, *wharengaro*—literally house destroyed—is the thing most feared by Maori women, because of its remorseless frequency in the recent past. Infant mortality, which is higher among Maori than Pakeha, is directly related to poverty.

   Binney was writing about the followers of Te Kooti, a different context, but the meaning and devastation of this experience is of more general application.
2. In a fundamental sense, of course, no one will really know what happened that night (if an "objective" account were even possible). There is the obvious time lapse, the discriminating reconstruction that goes with all remembered events and the fact that "texting the past—and by that making history—is always one sided and selective" (Dening 1988: 9). An event of this magnitude is possessed in different ways, the variety of which is revealed in journals, notebooks, and diaries, as well as personal recollections.
3. Hori Enoka Mareikura, whose kinship relations were with Ngāti Rangi in Karioi and Tūwharetoa, frequently had hui on his marae. During these occasions he healed those who were ill, frequently diagnosing Māori sources for their lack of health. His ties to the prophetic tradition go back at least to the time of Mere Rikiriki (see chapter 2). So impressed was she with his abilities that she bequeathed him her rā and her flag (E Te Iwi Kia Ora), named one of his sons Tikaraina, and gave him the power to tāpae. (All these matters are explained in greater detail in chapter 2.)

4. One of the ironies of contact is that we have information only for a time when much had already begun to change. It is likely that Māori religion was never static, but always changing according to many criteria, not least being political.
5. This was a complicated process. Only these two men were permitted to write Anaera's messages down. Some of the notebooks survive. Much of my information comes from notebooks that survived from the 1930s in Ruka's hand. There are further books, again written by Ruka, who was an important person in the history of the movement (see chapters 3–6), which have become known as *kaupapa*, "foundation" books. These have been kept at one of the movement centers and I did not see them.
6. In such forms, history is told, retold, and in the process remade. In a predominantly oral culture, events are enshrined in the telling; children and the uninitiated learn, inevitably, through repetition. New songs and new inspirations become part of the ever-increasing corpus of the movement's works. Written documents appear, disappear, and reappear, allowing the "past to suffuse [the] present in . . . transformed, translated, interpreted, encapsulated ways" (Dening 1988: 2).

Chapter 1: The Dispensation of Colonialism

1. More recently, many of these themes have been expressed in literature. For example, Witi Ihimaera has examined the history of his East Coast people and their differences with Pākehā in several novels.
2. The existence of two nonequivalent versions of the Treaty (one in Māori and one in English, but neither an exact translation of the other) led to problems that persist into the present. Settlers saw the Treaty as authorising annexation, an assurance that New Zealand had become a British colony and was there for the taking; Māori believed they had ceded governance while retaining sovereignty.
3. Stocking maintains that the goal was "to carry out a checkerboard policy of racially integrated settlement."
4. Taonui was reported to have spoken out against a governor, understanding that the office symbolised Pākehā hegemony. On February 12, 1840 the prophet stated, "No, we are not agreeable to give up our land. It is from the earth we obtain all things. The land is our father; the land is our chieftainship; we will not give it up." (Caselberg 1975: 48.)
5. The best sources on Te Kooti are Binney (1987, 1988, 1990, 1995), Elsmore (1985, 1989), Greenwood (1942), and Sissons (1991). In addition, Witi Ihimaera's *The Matriarch* (1986) and its sequel *The Dream Swimmer* (1997) are excellent fictional accounts of the events of the nineteenth century and their legacies. Te Kooti's relationship to Whanganui is related in Young (1998: 79–97).
6. According to Parsonson (1981: 161), the Māori population in 1857 was 56,049. By 1896 it had dropped to 42,113.
7. This is illustrated by a 1914 article published by the *Auckland Star Supplement*. Written by Colonel Porter, the article is entitled "'Te Kooti Rikirangi: The Real Story of the Rebel Leader with an Account of the Maori Fanatic Religions Pai Marire, Ringatu, and Wairua Tapu."
8. David Young (1998: 14–73) provides a richly detailed account of Pākehā and Christian penetration of the Whanganui River.
9. *Te Ika a Maui* (referring to the myth in which Maui, the culture hero, fishes up the North Island of New Zealand) detailed rituals and beliefs. The veracity of Taylor's reports is still a topic of discussion more than a hundred years after his death.

10. Today, in large part because of its connection with Taylor, the area known as Hiruhārama is called Patiarero.

11. GNZMS 297/33 Part I, Auckland City Libraries. In this section of Taylor's diary, his handwriting is particularly hard to read.

12. GNZMS 297, No. 13, Note Books on New Zealand and its Native Inhabitants, Auckland City Libraries.

13. In so doing he may well have provided the impetus for her retraction, for within two months she "humbly confessed her sin" (Elsmore 1989: 110).

14. Murray also notes that Taylor didn't always take public issue with this belief. When Māori men were involved in building churches, he was perfectly happy to go along with the rules of tapu that mandated the separation of food and construction. (Elsmore 1989: 205.)

15. In this he was echoing the view put forth by Samuel Marsden (the head of the CMS in the Pacific), Williams, and Grey. See Stocking (1987: 86).

16. GNZMS 297, Letter, 2 July 1860, Auckland City Libraries.

17. Te Keepa was from Muaūpoko (a tribe from the southwestern sector of the North Island). His father was a Muaūpoko leader, while his mother was linked to tribes on the Whanganui River. When Te Rauparaha and his followers invaded and conquered Muaūpoko territory in the 1820s, his mother managed to survive by swimming to safety across Lake Horowhenua with her son on her back. They sought refuge with her people in Pūtiki, where he quite possibly was given the name Te Keepa (see Dreaver 1984). His fighting qualities distinguished him early on, as did his allegiance to Durie, a major in the colony's Armed Police Force. Te Keepa's fortunes were tied to those of Durie. When the latter moved to Wanganui to be magistrate, Te Keepa went with him. By 1862, Te Keepa and his relation Hīpango were seen as leaders of the Wanganui pro-government Māori.

Feeling for Te Keepa continues to run high on both sides. I first became aware of him in early 1972 when I stayed at the home of one of his descendants. She was very proud of her ancestor, although for feats accomplished in places other than Moutoa. Other people, whose allegiance is more directly tied to both Rānana, in the middle reaches of the river, and to the prophetic tradition in general, saw him as a reprobate who had sold out his people in return for what the Pākehā government could offer. He went on to negotiate land purchases, attempting—not always successfully—to maintain Māori control.

18. However, it is entirely possible, indeed likely, that Māori were far less concerned with the intricacies of denominational rivalries. Christianity meant abandoning many of their native practices, at least for appearance's sake. It is quite probable that their reaction to individual denominations depended more on their response to individual missionaries than on clear positions on doctrine, which seemed never to have been explained especially well.

19. Catholic lay readers were already proselytizing along the river during Taylor's time, and Father Lampila arrived at Kauaeroa in 1854. Taylor found Catholicism such a significant threat that he wrote a pamphlet in 1863 to be distributed among his river congregants. Entitled "Te Hahi Matua: He Pukapuka Ki Nga Tangata o Wanganui Na Te Teira Minita" (The Father Church: A Book for the People of Wanganui by Reverend Taylor), his booklet challenged the Catholic Church's claims of earthly supremacy.

20. The lack of attention paid to Catholic missionaries has been aptly characterized by Thomson (1969: 166): ". . . they were unknown because unsuccessful and unimportant." Her main points are that, between 1838 and 1860, Catholics failed to gain a foothold in New Zealand because they arrived later than other missionaries, as a rule they were poor

and unworldly, and the mission was plagued by administrative inefficiencies. Indeed, the next phase of missionary activity, centered in the central and western sectors of the North Island, were far more successful. History and personalities assisted in conversion efforts. Thomson (1969: 174) notes that even in the 1860s (the time at which her study concludes) only Lampila was working full-time as a missionary on the Whanganui River.

21. The reasons for his disillusion are not hard to find. Bergin (1986: 1–2) writes:

> However, the Wanganui River mission had been devastated by the wars and racial conflict of the 1860s. One of Lampila's Marist assistants, Brother Euloge Chabany, had been killed at the battle of Moutoa in May 1864, along with a number of influential Catholic chiefs and catechists. Other young Catholic men had left the Wanganui River with kupapa forces of Major Kemp in pursuit of Te Kooti Te Turuki Rikirangi. Poor crop cultivation and the spread of disease had also had a demoralizing impact upon many River villages. The move by some Catholics to the Pai Marire religion, the destruction of the Kauaeroa church, and Lampila's painful double hernia, were further influences on Bishop Viard's decision to withdraw a disillusioned Lampila from Kauaeroa to Wanganui, where he was appointed as the second resident priest from 1868 to 1872.

22. According to Bergin (1986: 7), Aubert's letter contained the following:

> "In what part of the world does the Bishop live who came to see us two years ago, and promised us a priest? He is like the others. He forgets us! We believed that he would love us, but no, nobody loves us. Everything is for the Pakeha, nothing for the Maoris. We were told that Christ was born in a stable, that he lived a life of poverty, that he died for all men. If that is true, why are his ministers concerned with the Pakeha only, and abandon us so completely? . . . Is it because we are poor and ignorant? . . . They bring the light to those who are sitting in the sunlight, but they refuse the light of a candle to those who are sitting in the shadow of death. Our hearts are broken. We weep and lament. We desire to be good, and we have nobody to help us. Everything for the Pakeha, and let the Maori go to the devil." I confess, my Reverend Father, I was unable to speak for grief and shame.

23. *The Story of Suzanne Aubert* (1996) is dedicated to the memory of, amongst others, Hoana.

24. This attitude does not simply fade away; it is still apparent almost a century later. In a booklet put out by the Sisters of Compassion, the anonymous author (n.d.: 3) wrote:

> Until the Catholic Mission was established in Jerusalem, it had been notorious for devil worship. Although the Maoris always believed in a Supreme Being (Atua), they had no formal worship of Him. But they had great fear of evil spirits, and had strong ways of placating them. Sr. Anne's first boy pupil was a weird looking creature whom his parents had dedicated to the devil—probably to safeguard their other children. His hair had never been cut, and it hung in wild-looking spikes about his face. No one attempted to guide or control him at all. He was about twelve years old when Father Soulas took him in hand, instructed him and baptized him.

This is all too typical of the attitude towards Māori. Of course, there is also the political agenda of representing Catholicism as a civilising influence upon hitherto barbaric souls. We can also presume that the anonymous author of this pamphlet did not fabricate this story, although quite possibly she added her own interpretation. Such stories came either from correspondence or from the oral histories that would comprise any society similar to the Sisters of Compassion.

Chapter 2: Mere Rikiriki at Parewanui

1. The inclusion of "Ngati Apa" in parentheses is Henderson's. Arguably, however, Mere Riki-riki intended this message, whose strength and origin were beyond human affairs, and in a mission designed to overcome parochial concerns, for a wider audience. In Māori it is:

    > E te iwi, kia tere mai ki ahau ki te mea Wahine. He Rangimarie Taku. Taro ake nei ka eke ki runga ki te Tamaiti Tane: he ringa poto, he ringa kaha, e kore e whakahoa, kahore ona whanaungatanga ki te Tangata [ringa poto and ringa kaha relate directly to Mareikura's time at Parewanui].

    Two other prophets, Te Kooti and Āperahama Taonui, produced prophecies that could fit Rātana. Te Kooti had spoken of a star that would rise to herald a new leader and set upright the capsized canoe of the Māori, a prophecy taken by Rātana's followers as confirming his selection. Āperahama Taonui said, "There is a man coming, however, who will carry with him two books: the Bible and the Treaty of Waitangi. Listen to him." ("He rā anō kei te haere mai kite koutou i tētahi tangata e mau mai āna e rua ana pukapuka: ko te Paipera me te Tiriti o Waitangi. Whakarongo koutou ki a ia.") (Quoted in Binney 1990: 180–81.)
2. Quoted in King 1981: 292. In the 1940s, Mareikura was inspired with a pātere (chant) in which he invokes the same imagery.
3. It is not clear exactly when this happened; it could have been as early as 1890. In her prophetic mission Mere Rikiriki had contact with King Tāwhiao, who died in 1894.
4. According to Morvin Simon (1984: 74), a descendant of the Whanganui people and a student of marae for the region, the building preceded Mere Rikiriki's birth by some four years, indicating that the marae was named before she started her work.
5. Among the Ngāti Porou, an East Coast tribe, there are many documented examples of skilled and powerful women who have given their names to sub-tribes. Seniority of descent and ability, rather than gender, seem to be the critical issues in this case. With the choice involving descent, primogeniture, and gender, a high ranking first-born woman would be considered qualified for many positions. European males who were the first observer/ writers of Māori probably did not fully understand the scope of women's participation. Also, there is some reason to believe that the actual authority of women declined through the nineteenth century (Binney and Chaplin 1986: 189).
6. Her sexuality has to be significant, whether as an allusion to generativity, or to emphasize her femaleness. While often males were reprobates before they became enlightened, their sexuality is never discussed. That it is with her, and often, cannot be accidental.
7. She achieved this status also because of her ability at faith-healing and foretelling the future.
8. There is debate about whether Io is a post-contact phenomenon or existed before the missionaries (see Hanson 1989; Simmons 1976).
9. Whanganui are believed to be descended from two brothers and a sister: Rangituhia, Rangiteauria, and Uenuku. In this case, the male line possesses ascendancy.
10. The chronology is problematic; it is possible that these events took place close to 1910. Hoana told me that Tāwhiao was prescient, that the deeds of Mere Rikiriki had been foretold. I believe Tāwhiao had given her the flag and that the phrase "E te iwi kia ora" was on it. That may have been why she chose to say those words when she came out of the water. According to the people of the Māramatanga, the questioner was an envoy of Tāwhiao (who had died in 1894).

11. Wairua Tapu is understood and used, by Pākehā, to mean Holy Ghost. However, Māori understand it as Holy Spirit. This is a subtle difference, but it does accommodate multiple meanings, and permits the blurring of two distinct cultural traditions.
12. Forty is a number with Biblical significance. The forty jumps probably symbolize the Israelites' forty years in the wildnerness, though forty was also the number of days of rain that produced the great flood, of days Christ fasted alone in the desert, and of days in which he was made manifest after his death. The invocation of Christ and four disciples shifts the emphasis onto the New Testament.
13. The three shoots are presumably the Father, the Son, and the Holy Spirit. See Elsmore 1989: 374.
14. It is important to note here that Mere Rikiriki did not say this. The words were understood to be those of the Wairua Tapu. This Spirit clearly did not mean that the past should be abandoned.
15. The metaphor is an old and common one, but in English literature at least it does not have the same unifying effect. Shakespeare, for example, employs it to imply duplicity and treachery. In *Much Ado About Nothing*, Act 2, Scene 3:

> Sigh no more, ladies, sigh no more
> Men were deceivers ever,
> One foot in sea, and one on shore,
> To one thing constant never.

16. This, again, is a problematic chronology. It seems, judging from both the oral and the few published sources, that these names were bestowed somewhere around 1910. Tika would have been just born, although Hoana maintained that Tikaraina, her own relation, was named before Mere Rikiriki jumped into the Rangitīkei. When pressed, most members could not say if Te Huinga was pregnant with Tika, if he had already been born, or if the name existed waiting for a child to assume it.
17. At the turn of this century, Maui Pōmare, a medical doctor, reported that 12 percent of his patients had tuberculosis, while a whopping 46 percent had respiratory infections (*AJHR* 1909 H-31, p.37, quoted in Pool 1991: 85). Pool reports that "54–55 percent of Maori deaths were from infectious diseases . . . [compared with] 12–13 percent of Pakeha deaths" (1991: 116–17).
18. In addition to the insertion of a decidedly Christian element, this procedure afforded women the opportunity to speak publicly. In meeting-houses throughout the movement's tribal areas, women get up and speak, but they generally defer to the tradition, which keeps women silent on marae.
19. I was told quite emphatically that ancestors knew the difference between good gods and the "other element." In this case they were prepared to give them all up.
20. The idiom here is that the Wairua Tapu was "on" her. Tāpae needs to be distinguished from whakanoa: tāpae is to place the power of the past in God's hands, to put it to sleep, while whakanoa is to neutralize the tapu and remove any ritual restrictions. This is a subtle but important difference.
21. If a full rainbow appears, then that is believed to be the god Uenuku. But a half-rainbow is seen as being Tangi Wairua. This rainbow guides them when they are in trouble, or signals that they are on the right course. I have been in cars that have stopped when a half-rainbow appeared directly in front on the road. At this time, the occupants bend their heads in prayer.

22. I came to a similarly incorrect conclusion in my dissertation.
23. David Young (1991: 569) describes the flag quite differently. He writes that it "carries a white crucifix and brown band on a blue background." The original flag was accidentally burned, and has been replaced. I think it likely that there is a flag that is today associated with Matangirei at Parewanui that is different from the one that flies on the marae at Maungārongo. It is also possible that the original flag—since burned and replaced—did indeed look as Young describes. The replaced flag remains extremely important and is flown on all occasions intended to evoke the Māramatanga and its history. For example, it flew at Maungārongo at a *tū wairua* (an instructional period led by Hoana for the younger generation) in 1982, and when the governor-general, Sir Paul Reeves, was welcomed onto the marae in February 1987, and at Matiu Mareikura's tangi in July 1998.
24. Mere Rikiriki apparently asked Mareikura what he wanted and he responded that his desire was to be given the seven o'clock prayer.

Chapter 3: Mareikura, Maungārongo, and the Development of the Māramatanga

1. For example, Princess Te Puea framed solutions to the problems faced by the Waikato tribes in terms that were very specific to local and tribal conditions (King 1977). Binney and Chaplin (1986) and Sissons (1991) make this point for the East Coast. See also Salmond (1991).
2. There are putative kin ties, which isn't surprising given the proximity of Ngāti Apa, Rangitāne, and the Whanganui hapū. However, nobody has ever been specific about the nature of these ties. January 25, the celebration of Rātana's birthday, is a day that continues to attract members of the Māramatanga.
3. I have interviewed his children, grandchildren, daughters-in-law, and other collateral relatives. There is absolute unanimity about the man's character: he was kind, humble, unassuming, and willing to help anybody, no matter how dire the situation, no matter how straitened he personally may have been.
4. Formally, she is referred to as Te Huinga, although her grandchildren refer to her as Kui. (This is the honorific term indicating a woman of the grandparental generation; for those for whom less formality is used, "nanny" usually suffices.) Her name, Hinewaipare, was later given to a child born with spina bifida in the hope that the name would carry with it the power of its original holder. The baby survived but died before adolescence.
5. Merrilyn George, the historian of Ohakune, writes that they "lived between Karioi at Te Rauhāmoa and Ohakune at Maungārongo" (1990: 317).
6. Maungārongo was later moved from its original east–west orientation to face north–south and Tikaraina became the meeting-house. Tikaraina has been rebuilt and added to on several occasions and is now a spacious, carved meeting-house, with many pictures of ancestors on the walls.
7. There is a distinction between Tikaraina tangata, the man, and Tikaraina wairua, the spirit that inheres in the name. That Tikaraina wairua had to be assumed by Mareikura was told to me by several people. However, one of the most knowledgeable thought it unlikely that Mareikura had to assume such responsibility.
8. It is not clear why Aurora was selected to be Tika's wife. She certainly matured into a woman with formidable abilities, composing and receiving songs, interpreting the messages of the wairua. She was beautiful and dignified. Did she show signs of this at fifteen? She

was clearly recognised as somebody special, to be married, therefore, to somebody special. This may be the only marriage that has entered family stories as a taumau marriage; other marriages were facilitated by the proximity of young men and women to one another.

9. While such unions could, in theory, be dissolved, this was not the case here. Both families were clearly determined that Tika and Aurora remain married.

10. Her great-grandson, Koroniria, told me of these children after he had consulted records in the Department of Māori Affairs. It is possible that there were other children.

11. In Māori reckoning, she married her nephew, a term that would include any Māori male of her whānau in the generation below hers. Generation in this case has little to do with age but with the generations that have passed since the original kin tie. Since she is two generations removed from Koroniria, and he is three generations below Te Rewa, she is considered his genealogical senior. (See appendix 1, diagram 4.)

12. According to Mareikura's daughter-in-law, Hine Ataarangi, he told her "this one is for me" and gave her the name. However, he counselled Kataraina to treat the baby normally, not to place him on a pedestal.

13. Tūmanako also means "expect" or "regard any absent object with desire" (Williams 1932).

14. Tūmanako is today a respected elder. He has had five children who in turn have produced, at the most recent count, thirteen offspring. A genealogical line, which had hung by a very slender thread, is now in no danger of disappearing.

15. The difficulty was told to me by Tūmanako's wife in 1987.

16. Indeed, this family has had many deaths before adulthood, and for those who have survived there have been reproductive difficulties.

17. Anarea was transformed. She had experienced nothing like this in the past. She had been a sceptic. Such manifestations would have been suspect and horrifying in her vulnerable state.

18. Of course, Māori constructions differed. One of the paradoxes of writing history derived from oral accounts is the dependence on stories that are formulated and told in post-contact situations. Obviously, understandings of these Māori at that time, despite their strong links with ancestral practice, were thoroughly infected with European categorizations. See Linnekin (1992).

19. Orbell (1991: 1) writes: "Those known as pao were epigrammatic couplets, mostly sung for entertainment, which expressed love, extended greetings and commented upon local events and scandals." In the Māramatanga they are often directives.

20. She is also depicted as somewhat ethereal. Her niece maintains that she was frightened much of the time (Hoana interview, March 1987).

21. Translations of some of her pao during these years are as follows:

> My extended right hand breaks the swirling waters
> So that I may better touch Tangi Wairua.

And:

> May Tumanako, my beloved, be held fast by benevolence,
> The affection that leads to devotion.

Other times, she simply makes her presence known as her relatives are on a trip:

> As the road climbs and descends
> To Kuratahi, return safely my loved one.

At other times, she is specific in her criticism:

It's as well I was found.
I suppose I was noticed by the convoy of visitors.

Hoana suggested that this may mean that the manuhiri have no foundation; they have not noticed her directly. But clearly this pao indicates that her tone is not always positive. In some pao, there is a foretelling of doom. For example, in one she recounts the sadness of hearing bad news on the telephone. Dated a little over a year after her death, this could be recounting the sadness of loss on the telephone. Hoana suggested that the doom these messages seem to foretell is war, World War II. In this case, the bad news by telephone is conscription.

22. The translation owes much to Wīremu Tāwhai.
23. The Comaroffs (1992: 259–60) suggest that it is not clear that the colonized are resisting: "With time and historical experience, the colonized show greater discrimination, greater subtlety in interpreting the European embrace and its implications."
24. Notwithstanding the debate as to whether there was a pre-contact supreme God Io, for the members of Māramatanga there is no doubt, as this pātere shows. Māori always knew of Io and such confusion as exists is a product of a missionary muddle—or arrogance.
25. This second meaning emerges more clearly in the work of Pēpene Ruka. Joan Metge (personal communication 1973) first brought this double meaning to my attention.
26. But see Butterworth (1990: 80).
27. Hoana's life story is told after chapter 5.
28. Of course, twentieth-century prophets are capable of heavy pronouncements, as the pātere above indicates.
29. Aurora, interview, 1972. Moreover, she recognized the spirit as the leader of the Patu-pairehe. Hoana lightly called this being "Big Foot."
30. Interestingly, Aurora told me that the maid appeared in different forms to different observers. To a Pākehā, she could conceivably appear as Pākehā.
31. Her father, Poope, was Kataraina's husband's brother.
32. Linnekin (1991) has made compelling arguments that tradition reveals far more about the present than about the past.
33. On any number of occasions, individuals would thumb through my photocopies of note-books and point out mistakes that had been made in their execution.
34. Anaera was one of the few individuals about whom there was total agreement. Everyone talked about her good nature, her vagueness, and her humility. She was a bit strict with the children when she was supervising the Hui Aranga teams. Just out of curiosity, I asked Hoana to tell me something bad about her auntie. She thought very long and hard. Finally, she said that Auntie Anaera would save all the good lollies for herself. This confirmed my impression that there was not much bad to be said about Anaera.

Narrative: Hine Ataarangi

1. Weuweu's third husband was the brother of the husband of one of her nieces and an uncle of Hine.
2. In 1948, Anaera died. In the 1950s and 1960s, several of Pauro's brothers and sisters and their spouses died. In 1975 Tika died, followed by Aurora in 1982. Pauro died in 1985.

3. In 1972–1973 she and her husband were living in Hastings. But his brother and her cousin, Tika and Aurora, were in Levin, and so Hine and Pauro were frequent visitors, coming for weeks on end. I lived with Weuweu's daughter Ritihira next door on Kawiu marae and I would see them every day. In 1982, I saw them at the rā and then in the days following Aurora's funeral. In 1987, we had long, extensive talks and interviews that were more formal because they were recorded. In 1990 and 1991 I actually stayed in her flat, where we were together most days and did more taping. In 1993, I saw a great deal of her, and our beds were next to one another at the Hui Aranga. While I am relying heavily on the taped interview material, I am also filling in through my personal knowledge of her.

4. In 1987, she told the story of her grandmother's intervention in this manner:

> Well then I cry like a big baby 'cause I knew I wasn't allowed to go. So anyway my grandma, my grandmother said what was wrong with you and I told her. So she came to see my mother. She said to my mother she wanted mum to let me go. Of course at the time I was engaged to a Pakeha boy and she said to mum, "What would you sooner have her to marry a Pakeha or marry one of her own?"

5. This is an anachronism, as their marriage took place in 1930. Pauro said he would have left and joined the army had she not arrived.

6. The tohunga who led the whare wānanga was Tamakehu.

7. She called both her husband and her father-in-law "Dad," but it is probably Mareikura she was referring to.

8. This sort of remark was typical of Hine, who seemed to possess the facility to return to times decades past.

9. Under such circumstances little privacy was possible. This was not terribly difficult for Hine, who found that she could not only adjust to it, but thrived upon public life. By contrast, the closeness of affines, the interpenetration of public and domestic spaces, was more than some (especially women) were able to tolerate.

10. It is of course possible that the child was not that sick, or Pauro would not have jeopardized her well-being. But Hine's perceptions are so often right on the mark that her accounts are hard to doubt.

11. Hine's was my only report of this event and I failed at that time to fix the clear confusions that one finds in this story, for the obvious reason that I did not have this history at my interviewing fingertips. Soon after that, it was too late. King Te Rata was succeeded by King Korokī.

12. According to this version, told to me by Hine in 1987, King Te Rata wanted Mareikura to stay permanently at Waikato. The King movement is clearly important to the Māramatanga. In 1973, the people of the movement welcomed the Māori queen, Dame Te Atairangikaahu, onto Maungārongo marae. In the course of the day's speeches, the links between Mareikura and her ancestors were enunciated.

13. Her musical facility was magical. Within moments of humming to herself, she could recall lyrics and melodies that had not been sung for decades.

14. This has remained a family dynasty. After Pauro's death, their eldest daughter took his place, followed by another of their daughters.

15. Hine had many personal experiences with the connection between food and taonga. Compromising the boundary had caused infant Gabrielle's illness. On another occasion,

244 ~ ENDNOTES TO PAGES 85–93

a *mere* (war club) had fallen behind a seat in a car, near some discarded food, and illness resulted. This was considered a thoroughly reasonable explanation for illness.

16. In addition, neither Iwa nor Pin ever conceived.

17. If you watch the film *Utu*, you will see Hine leading a group waiata. You will see that, although a big woman and in her seventies, she moved with a subtle grace and rhythm; you will hear too the clarity and power of her voice. She must have been really something as a young performer in the concert party. No wonder Pauro was smitten.

Chapter 4: Growth and the Emergence of a New Generation

1. Rangi Walker (1990: 199) points out that this situation was partly the result of Pākehā governmental decisions leading to the inadequate educational preparation of Māori.

2. The people held responsible were Ngāti Rangi, a broadly inclusive tribal designation, rather than Māramatanga alone.

3. Hoana, in 1987, made much of his kindness and generosity. However, she also linked his leadership role to his financial wherewithal, explaining "when you are a family that is indebted in more ways than one, you let these things happen."

4. In those notebooks that I have seen, Ruka's handwriting is startlingly beautiful, clear, and elegant.

5. Mauri translates literally as "life principle." It is believed to have considerable power.

6. Hato Ruka is a transliteration of Saint Luke; the coincidence with Pēpene Ruka's name is accidental.

7. These new foundations emphasised mutuality, shared responsibility, strength, and contemplation.

8. A secondary meaning of huia indicates "something that is much prized."

9. Williams (1990) defines kura as "red" (an indication of potency in the Māori universe as opposed to *maa*, "stripped of power; white"), "precious," "knowledge," and "ceremonial restriction" (tapu), among other definitions.

10. Both Amokura and Pikikura appear in songs of the period. There emerges a hierarchy in the Māramatanga linking God to man. It is somewhat reminiscent of the chain of being that characterized Western thinking. Mortal men are linked to God through several steps: Te Karere, the Virgin Mary, the kura, angels (Michael, Raphael, Gabriel), the Holy Spirit (Wairua Tapu), and God. The most knowledgable members know this hierarchy, and are conscious of where any spirit is located. However, I have never heard the notion of hierarchy explicitly discussed.

11. Bernard Gadd (1966: 454) writes that the raukura stands for "Glory to God on high, peace on earth and good will to all mankind."

12. This was in fact on March 17 but was designated March 18. As a result, the people of Parihaka continue to celebrate the 18th of each month, with March 18 being especially important.

13. Takere means the "main part of the hull of a canoe," or "center," or "chief" or "important part of anything" (Williams 1932: 433). When people explained the meaning of the dining room to me, they would use canoe imagery.

14. Pinenga vividly recalls watching the prayers and thanksgiving (whakamoemiti) that took place in the meeting-house (see Pinenga's narrative).

15. According to Raana (January 1987), these missions last two weeks. During this time, the people join in prayer, say the rosary, and end with a benediction.

16. The second husband of Harimate Mareikura, the father of Rihari. (See appendix 1, diagram 5.)

17. A volume written by the Rev. Francis J. Connell, CSSR, published by Catholic Books, tells a story that is identical in its outline, but varies in rather insignificant ways in its particulars. The foreword written by the Rev. Benedict D'Orazio, CSSR, is dated 1926, while the publication date is 1940. I am assuming that this publication date indicates a later edition.

18. Crete was at the time subject to the Republic of Venice. Father Connell writes that there were several pictures held in great veneration at this time. In the version given by Father Murray, there are Greek inscriptions indicating that this was a picture of the mother of God. In addition, there are Greek words indicating the presence of the archangels Gabriel and Michael (Raana, interview, February 1987).

19. Barney is the brother of Lei. Therefore a sister and brother married a sister and brother. (See appendix 1, diagram 6.)

20. I had heard stories of the first mission from Pauro, Hine (who was not present), and Aurora. Hoana would not tell me about that mission until Pauro's death in 1985.

21. Similarly, Hoana was aware of a change in generations as she related the stories of this mission to me thirty years later.

22. This was probably in November 1962, as the mission took place the following month.

23. Raana confirmed that the wairua had communicated that the first mission had not reached closure; the work begun in 1942 was to be carried on by a future generation.

24. Te Waka o Te Ora (The Canoe of Life) is a navy-blue flag with a white crucifix and a brown boat. This flag, inspired by Pēpene Ruka, was used to open the meeting-house at Levin. Here the imagery evokes the idea of a migration across the Pacific in the seven canoes, but also summons up the Christian ideology of a new order. The different meanings of waka (canoe, vessel, transporter) and ora (life, health, well-being, fulfilment) make for a complex and potent message.

    Te Tohu o Te Rangimārie (The Sign of Peace) was inspired by Peehi. The flag is white with a rainbow. The lettering is in red and white. The rainbow motif exemplifies the movement's concern with communication between the human and spiritual domain, and the rainbow is itself a sign of Tangi Wairua. Rangimārie suggests peace, tranquillity, harmony, and should be distinguished from Maungārongo, discussed below.

    Te Āka o Te Maungārongo (The Ark of Peace) is a light-blue flag with a white picture of a dove and crucifix. Maungārongo suggests truce, cessation from hostilities, everlasting peace. The inspiration for this flag was received by Ritihira, Weuweu's daughter, who sees it as an exhortation from the spiritual realm to "hold the peace." There is also a deliberate connection between the ark of the covenant, Noah's ark, and the notion of a movement of the faithful towards a new life. Ritihira's use of symbolism, and that of many others, tends to emphasize the Christian aspect of the movement's ideology. Because the symbols are multivocal, layered with significance, they are able to encompass multiple meanings and appeal to the range of individuals that comprise the Māramatanga. Several of the movement's flags were burnt in an accidental fire in the late 1960s.

25. Pinenga indicates that the message came through Huinga; although it is recorded in both books, Raana does not indicate the source.

26. Ruapehu, the patriarch, exiled Taranaki because of the latter's behavior. Taranaki made his way across the country to the other coast. Theirs is a painful separation and the mountains look at one another over the distances that separate them.

27. Not surprisingly, a few years later, a mission to Mount Taranaki was designed to effect a reconciliation. See Raana's narrative.
28. Ruapehu is nearly 10,000 feet (2,797 metres) high; Ohakune is below 2,000 feet and the road ends at about 5,000 feet. The remaining climb on this steep, active volcano is difficult.
29. Raana's translation.
30. More likely than not, they were sliding down, but all accounts that I have heard have emphasised skiing.
31. This is a gloss of *kōrero* (talk). It carries connotations of weight and gravity. Even when people are speaking English, they use the word "talk" or "talks" rather than "discussion." I am following the conventions of English usage, but I feel that here it departs in significant ways from that of the Māori.
32. Of course, there were only a few songwriters, and those more knowledgable tended to remember the precise historical context in which the song was revealed.
33. There is a critical exception to this. One woman, who would prefer to remain anonymous, kept long, detailed diaries of her inspirations and thoughts. Unlike other notebooks these have not circulated, and so far as I can tell, their existence is not common knowledge. I was given six of these notebooks, which comprised hundreds of pages. However, I have used them for background and have decided that they are too confidential to quote or cite directly.
34. Jean and John Comaroff (1991: 313) argue that colonizers take over the most mundane aspects of life, to overtake and transform consciousness. I am arguing here that while the same processes were going on in New Zealand, the Māramatanga was staging a conscious attempt to reverse this.

Narrative: Pinenga

1. My interviews with Pinenga, formal and informal, have spanned the thirty years of my fieldwork. In 1982, we did a formal taping of her life story. In 1987, I spent several days at her house and at Aurora's son's house with her. I am never in New Zealand without spending several days at Kuratahi. We have had extensive discussions all the times we have been together, often speaking freely and intimately over coffee, as we prepare dinner, and on one of the most beautiful occasions, under a willow tree, as she prepared flax.
2. Genitals are believed to be unclean (poke), and should be kept separate from food.
3. Pinenga did not learn herbalism from her mother, but she did learn how to set broken bones, albeit indirectly through a brother.
4. Pinenga maintained that her mother knew of and was impressed by Mareikura.
5. This exclusion seems out of character for members of the movement so perhaps it was the young girl's diffidence rather than the members' aloofness that kept them out. Pinenga felt herself to be quite different.
6. Pinenga mentioned in 1982 that Katараina would talk to her about the Māramatanga, but she didn't really listen. Kataraina did, however, teach her daughter-in-law Catholic prayers.
7. Tūmanako thought seriously about leaving with Pinenga. But he maintained that, were he to leave, there would be no coming back. Given the obligations that he felt, he could not take such an irrevocable step.
8. On the tape, Pinenga mentions the difficulty of looking after two children. However, the time and the narrative suggest that she left after losing her second child.

9. The clear exceptions to this are Raana and Hoana who, supporting one another, overcame the isolation of their younger years. Indeed, they were true intimates, looking after one another's welfare. There is very little that they did not share.

10. Pinenga had the opportunity to reciprocate Aurora's kindness. Decades later, after Tika had died and Aurora stayed on in Levin, Pinenga would come often to visit, to chat, to keep the older woman company. In 1982, when Aurora was dying, Pinenga was the one most consistently at her side. Aurora's death coincided with the July rā; yet Pinenga, in the midst of her enormous preparations, quickly left for the hospital as soon as the call came that Aurora was very ill.

11. This is not unique to the Māramatanga. Joan Metge (1995: 62) has pointed out that descent is far more important than marriage.

12. There was another side to this. She was told (I do not know by whom) that were she not to heed the old woman's message, she would find her life more of a struggle than if she simply acquiesced.

13. This is not an uncommon phenomenon. Often there would be priests having what they all cheerfully referred to as "R and R" at Maungārongo or at Kuratahi. Those priests who know members well cannot help being aware of the Māramatanga and the complexity of the relationship between movement and church. What can and cannot be explicitly discussed is lost neither on the members nor on the priesthood.

14. To wrap a coffin in a cloak is to make a statement that the corpse is not naked, but goes dressed into death. This is of course metaphorical, for the coffin not the corpse is adorned with an ancestral garment. If the cloak is to be buried with the deceased, it is tied on the top. Otherwise, it is tied on the bottom, indicating that it will, on some other occasion, be called into use. Women weave the cloaks and are the principal mourners at tangi. This is a distinctive link, furthered elaborated by Annette Weiner (1992), connecting women, cloaks, and death.

15. Her youngest son ran away from school several times. In retrospect, she said that he found it hard to have to explain the importance of his parents, who were on the board of the school, and their apparently special relationship to the priests. Pinenga took this seriously, for it was uncomfortable and unfamiliar for her (as an outsider) to recognize that her son felt he came from a family marked off by the distinctiveness of the school's relationship with his parents. It is an ironic converse of her own position.

16. Pinenga clearly uses "mission" in a broader than usual sense, merging visits at hospitals, more formal marae occasions, and the pilgrimages of the Māramatanga, such as that to the healing waters of Rotokura and to the mountain.

17. My husband, who bakes bread occasionally for as many as ten guests, once took over a day's baking. He loves to tell of the sheer magnitude of the task—yeast by the jarful, sacks of flour, water by the bucket, and kneading a mass of dough sufficient to fill sixty loaf pans!

18. See Metge (1995).

19. Many outside the United States see the difference not as between men and women, but as between America and the rest of the world. It seems to me that what is defined as "feminine" ways of relating can be understood as the mode of the subordinate, while "masculine" means of defining relationships can be seen as typical of dominant populations.

Chapter 5: Expansion and Consolidation

1. The latter appears in the homes of several movement families. While it was of great concern for Father Arbuckle, I noticed no ritual attention paid to the painting, and when queried, members denied that it possessed any special significance.
2. This distinction worked very much to my benefit. My fieldwork began shortly after the erection of the chapel and Hōhepa's conversion. I was living at Kawiu marae, and Hōhepa was an enthusiastic source of information for me. However, Tika, Aurora, Pauro, and Hine would attempt to place Hōhepa's narratives into a wider context for me. Both Tika and Pauro vouched for me and the knowledge I would take away, and were careful to correct any misapprehensions on my part. I did not know about this at the time (Hoana told me this in 1990), but I realise now how unusually fortunate I was, both in their trust and in their tutelage.
3. It is not clear how reluctantly or willingly Maru was given to Ngāti Rangi; however, the terms were made clear. Rank still figured prominently, as it continues to do today, in the Māori world.
4. I was told this story by Rihari, who explained that it was a "routine courtship . . . love at first sight."
5. Their first child was Pou Kaha. Emere's half sister Iwa (see appendix 1, diagram 3) also had fertility problems and ultimately never had any children of her own. Infertility plagued several families, but was not unique. There were also problems with another of the four named boys—Pou Mahara Nui—whose mother, Hinga, had been told never to have sons. Pou Mahara, according to the members of the movement, was doomed from birth. And indeed, he died in his thirties of a brain tumor, leaving his parents with three daughters. Hinga came from the East Coast, so there was nothing that could be done to ameliorate the situation.
6. This lack of commitment in this generation was not at all uncommon among those who carried spiritually significant names. With the exception of Pou Peka Māramatanga, Harimate's son, who grew up in Ohakune, the other three boys turned up for rā and movement events only sporadically and somewhat reluctantly.
7. This kind of sign is quite different from the signs that would be seen by other members of the movement, who were much more likely to receive songs (in Māori) or dream something that would be an indication of Pou Kaha's fate. While I do not doubt Hōhepa, it is important to understand the differences between his universe and that of the more orthodox members of Māramatanga.
8. This rā continued until the early 1980s when Emere and then Maru died. It fell into abeyance for a while and then was resurrected, although not with the entire support of the members. This illustrates the changes that occur in the course of individuals' lifetimes and the variable gravity with which rā are approached.
9. In 1982, shortly after Emere's death, Hoana commented how much Emere was missed by the movement and its members.
10. Pane, Hemi and Roimata, discussed below, are pseudonyms. While the rest of the movement are referred to by their Māori names, with their permission, I never had the opportunity to discuss this issue with these three. I have decided on pseudonyms for that reason, although the individuals themselves are hardly anonymous.
11. An old tohunga, apparently, volunteered to teach ancient arts to Maru. There can be no doubt that these arts would have included mākutu. Since at the time, Maru was firmly

involved with the Māramatanga, there were suspicions that this knowledge could have been given instead to Hemi. One woman voiced the anxiety of others when she said: "That's what's wrong with [Hemi]. He's in the middle and there's no telling which way he'll go." It is possible that this kind of suspicion merely reflected movement attitudes toward outsiders, for Hemi was considered an outsider although he was quite well liked. Quite possibly, this hit on a major paradox of the movement's belief system: power lies in the past. Tapping into that power, for good or ill, reaffirms the importance of that past (see Matiu's narrative for a contemporary response to this dilemma). At the same time, too much of a concern with the past, with ancestral traditions, threatens many members who fear that loyalty has been displaced from the Māramatanga onto other concerns, that traditional knowledge is being emphasized at the expense of that provided by Te Karere.

12. The conjunction of a Catholic image (rosary) with a named wind (paeroa), whose meaning derives from an entirely different domain, is precisely the kind of combination that members of the Māramatanga handle very well. They are content with such a union, seeing neither contradiction nor disparity.

13. By the late 1970s, Hemi and Roimata had ceased to participate. But by the 1990s, they had once again taken their place. Soon after, Hemi died. In the intervening years, there had been domestic crises, they had lived apart for a time, and Hemi had attached himself to another prophet. Throughout much of the 1980s, neither of them came to rā, although occasionally members met them at gatherings devoted to Māori issues. Moreover, both Maru and Emere had died, and the Maketū rā had fallen into abeyance.

   I last saw Hemi in 1993, when he came to the July rā to request formally the return of the Rotorua rā, but now for a different take (purpose). Perhaps by that time he was ill (for he died shortly thereafter): I would not have recognized him, although Roimata looked very much the same. After much discussion, the members agreed that the rā could once again be held in Rotorua.

14. The statue, covered with a white cloth to protect it from dust, was seen by Father Arbuckle as a mystical object of worship.

15. Here the heterodox views of Hōhepa, for he is quite likely (so it seems to me) to be the source of Father Arbuckle's information, proved profoundly embarrassing to the other members of the movement.

16. I remember him very clearly explaining that to seek revenge was to be no better than the individual who had offended against you. In this, according to his wife, he was very much like his father.

17. By contrast, his niece and successor, Hoana, was never entirely at ease—except late at night in the meeting-house, where she loved to participate in discussions that lasted until dawn (see her narrative). But her knowledge was formidable and she commanded the respect (and in some cases fear) of all movement members. She likened herself to her aunt Anaera, who also demonstrated trepidation and nervousness in the face of her considerable abilities.

18. I did not know Anaera, but it was clear that she too was very unassuming. I did know Hoana very well (see her narrative) and she too was modest, unassuming, and unwilling to take credit for work that she honestly believed had been done by the wairua. Many members of the Mareikura family are like this: extraordinary in their capacities and very humble. In a movement such as the Māramatanga, which decrees both equality and leaderlessness, such modesty as well as an aversion to the display of one's virtues, however impressive, is quite likely essential.

19. Pauro almost always included signatures; sometimes this was the Wairua Tapu but more often it was Te Karere. In addition, Pauro included his dreams and thoughts as they came to him when he was travelling. His notebooks are neat and organized, including dates, and the form (dream, pātere, etc.) of the inspiration.
20. Rangimotuhia was the brother of the woman who raised Raana.
21. This is the name members prefer for the location. Patiarero in fact refers to the name of the old marae. It was named Hiruhārama by the Rev. Taylor and is known to Pākehā as Jerusalem; members of the Māramatanga eschew these names—bespeaking their continued resistance to Taylor and his message.
22. The story goes that Rangimotuhia's original intent was to pass down his knowledge to individuals living on the Whanganui River. However, that turned out not to be possible, probably because there were not enough candidates. So he turned to the nearest descendants, those resident in Ohakune and Wanganui, for membership in the whare wānanga. In a similar vein, Matiu was selected after his brother Rihari demurred.
23. Whanganui possesses unique patterns of pronunciation and a specific ettiquette for tangi, not shared by other iwi.
24. Young (1998: 16) also points to Ngāti Rangi as a mid-river sub-tribe. This is the sub-tribe that was originally founded by the sibling group Rangituhia (Kuratahi and Raketapauma), Rangiteauria (Maungārongo), and Uenuku (Raetihi). If this is true, the tribe clearly extends beyond the river.
25. Much of this increased prestige was due to the importance and effectiveness of the Māramatanga's elders and kaimahi: Pauro, Hoana, and Matiu, who became a respected tohunga. Their efficacy clearly led to a re-evaluation of the negative images first held of the Māramatanga (see the narratives of Hine, Hoana, and Matiu for evidence of this). While I have witnessed the deference directed toward the elders from Ohakune and the respect accorded their knowledge, my understanding is strictly inferential.
26. For example, Mareikura forbade carving. Recently carving has made an active comeback. Members of the Māramatanga explain this by saying that Mareikura's prohibition was directed to the people of his time, but now, having learned his principles, it may again be practised safely.
27. The taiaha requires both knowledge and ritual cleansing. It can only be undertaken under the auspices of a tohunga.
28. For example, the legitimacy of learning *te reo* (the Māori language) was (and still is) contested by proponents of the superiority of Western civilization. The importance of European culture and history is the predominant argument of those who oppose the introduction of anything Māori into school curricula or other public institutions.

Narrative: Hoana

1. Rihari and Hoana were raised in Rānana; Riripeti was raised by Anaera and Ruka; one daughter was raised in Patiarero, on the Whanganui River; and a son was raised in Ohakune by family. Rena and Keru raised their two youngest children, but Keru died when the youngest, Matiu, was less than six years old.
2. The Rihari in this chapter is Hoana's husband. Hoana's brother Rihari becomes Raana's husband (see Raana's narrative and appendix 1, diagram 4).

3. These kinds of arrangement were not unusual: Pauro had spent his childhood in Rānana, and Keru and his sister Te Kawau had been raised by Wikitoria and her husband. It was fitting that Hoana should spend part of her childhood in Rānana. In a similar fashion, Pauro and Hine's daughter also spent part of her childhood there, with Te Maa, the third sister of Wikitoria and Te Huinga.
4. Reconciliation of the ancient world and its ways, Catholicism, and the Māramatanga, is accomplished seamlessly for Hoana's generation. However, this had not been the case for Wikitoria, nor for other Ngāti Rangi hapū.
5. Specifically, she mentioned *koromiko* (a plant) for abdominal distress, stinging nettles for high blood-pressure, and flax juice for menstrual problems.
6. Rena's father was a steamboat driver; he died years later in an accident on the river.
7. "Brumbie" is the Australian word for a wild horse, but it carries none of the romantic connotations of, say, "mustang" in the United States. Brumbies are hunted for dog tucker.
8. By that time, Ruka and Anaera had suffered too many losses and were reluctant to raise another child. Hence, Pin was known as a *tonotono*, someone who assisted the Ruka family.
9. Here she bears a striking resemblance to her aunt Anaera: both went into a trance or dreamlike state in which they were contacted by Te Karere, and both had lifetime fears of the dark. Both assumed reluctantly the role of kaimahi.
10. On several occasions I was told, by many different individuals, that Rihari was to be married by arrangement to the present Māori queen, Dame Te Atairangikaahu. This never came about. Had a match been contemplated, it is likely that the main matchmakers were both deceased when each of the principals reached marrigeable age.
11. Te Rongonui died on August 18, 1996 of stomach cancer, survived by his father, his siblings, his wife, three children, two grandchildren, and many cousins, aunts, and uncles.
12. Both Te Rangimārietanga, "Peace," and Maharanui, "Thoughtfulness," were names that were given by the wairua.
13. Women are never taught explicitly but call out when they find they have the words in their hearts. In the early days, Rihari's sister, Mana, would be out in the front because of her wonderful voice.
14. Morgan Kāwana, an official of Rātana marae, was present. In a wonderful presentation— witty and humorous and at the same time self-deprecatory—he captured and held his audience of young people as he explained that all the missionary teachings were already known to the Māori. He also argued eloquently the implausible thesis that the Māori were the lost tribe of Israelites.

Chapter 6: Pilgrimages to Waitangi

1. Belich (1996) and other scholars view the differences as the result of the duplicity of the colonizers.
2. This tradition has been called into question by David Simmons (1976).
3. In 1987, Hoana told me that the first pilgrimage clearly involved the mana mauri that had been recovered by Pin and Pēpene Ruka.
4. The Ngāpuhi people inhabit the north of the North Island and the Waitangi area.
5. This designates Matiu as a successor, even in his early days in the whare wānanga and during his preliminary training with Rangimotuhia. When I met Matiu two years later he was not yet ready to be a leader, at least to my largely uneducated eyes. Yet both

Rangimotuhia and Pauro saw something in the young man so taken with rugby and sports. The sharpness of the elders' judgment when it came to choosing a successor was impressive.

6. There are two messages about preparation for the mission in Pauro's notebook, dated August 25 and November 3, 1970. The first plays on the names given by Mareikura and Pēpene Ruka to a new generation of boys. The names are used to reinforce the suitability of the behavior of the pilgrims as they are about to embark on the missions. There is much mention of mauri and of the time being apt to seek a new understanding. This concern is also seen in Aurora's notebook in a song composed for the second trip, "Written by Kaahi for Waitangi trip 11/8/71." It has four stanzas. The first introduces the speaker, who explains that this is her song for the people of the hunga wairua; the second addresses the four boys; the third explains there is one loving God for all the people; and the fourth reiterates the importance of the Holy Spirit and the fidelity of the people. Thus, this song sets up the boundaries of the mission to Waitangi by invoking information that they have received through revelation and merging it with beliefs about Christianity and the Māori past.

7. Ani had a tendency to employ very overt and obvious symbols, at least to those familiar with the ideology and history of the movement. In many ways this was an asset to me. Although her messages prompted occasional skepticism, Ani's long-time commitment and involvement assured that nobody doubted her sincerity.

8. The church was deserted on a Saturday afternoon. That it was an Anglican church did not detract from its importance. The group had visited it in previous years and everybody felt it was appropriate to stop here at this time.

9. However, those who stayed home took issue with this point of view. They maintained that something like this cannot, by its very nature, be subject to removal; it has roots (thereby making it permanent and immobile) and from these roots all Māori people benefit. Since the other missions, so they maintained, each of them had derived something (one woman, for example, said her health had remained good). In this sense, then, the mission was fulfilled two years ago. They argued, quite self-righteously, that if this was the purpose of the trip, then it was clear that such a pilgrimage was not now necessary. In any event, the idea of removing the mauri was quite unthinkable.

10. While the members of the Māramatanga met tourists at all points on their journey, they kept the reasons for their undertaking entirely to themselves. Thus, for example, they did not discuss their interpretations of unfolding events when they thought they might be heard.

11. Māori are the gourmets of New Zealand. The quality and quantity of the kai (food) are a hazard to any anthropologist.

12. This is my translation of the following Māori. The words of exclamation and emphasis used in the performance of haka have been omitted in the English.

> E te hunga i aroha
> Haere Mai, haere mai
> Whiua te aho
> Haikatia ki roto Waitangi
> Aha ha
> Kia hutia ake
> E Tangi Wairua
> Te Mana, Te Tapu

Te Ihi—Ihi
Te Wehi, wehi
Au—e
Taupiri E.

13. Clifford (1988) makes this point about the Mashpee, a tribe of Native Americans whose position is similar to that of Māori.

Narrative: Raana

1. Modesty and humility are very important virtues for Māori. It is not at all uncommon for powerful, authoritative individuals to demur, to assert that they know nothing. In fact, it was very often precisely this kind of assertion that assured me I had come to the right place.
2. I do not know where her other siblings were raised or where her father was at the time the family was divided. Raana's journey to Kuratahi after her mother's death is not surprising and follows Māori patterns of adoption. Tei was also known as Kiwa Te Kooro.
3. Men, by contrast, do not seem to bear as heavy a responsibility, although I have heard both genders instructed emphatically on the rules governing bodily (especially female) etiquette.
4. Pinenga and Tūmanako's wedding followed four or five years later.
5. In 1987, I was in New Zealand from January to May. I explained that I was planning to write a book and was especially interested in people's notebooks. Every notebook that could be found was given to me and I was permitted to copy them, often on the copying machine located at the marae. Raana, however, brought her notebook out and would read it to me. I have never actually read her notebook.
6. Ruapehu indicated support for the journey and was seconded several hours later as Taranaki loomed into sight. At 7:10 A.M., the following message was received. (It appears in Raana's book only in Māori.)

> Hei konei e koro Ruapehu
> E tautoko i aku haerenga e
>
> Ruapehu, our elder who remains near and
> Who supports my journeys

   This pao indicates both that Ruapehu supports them and that they are travelling away from the mountain. Direction expressed here as "Hei konei" is a critical aspect of Māori oratory and of Māori orientation.
   The second pao, below, also indicates direction, in this case "atu," or away from the speaker.

> Piki ki atu
> Kei te tautoko te hunga wairua
>
> We shall lend support and thereby
> Reinforce [the help of] the spiritual beings.

7. This is not the ubiquitous Pōkarekare ana of the East Coast (see chapter 7).

Chapter 7: Te Umuroa and the Tira Hoe Waka

1. In 1995 I was on the Tira Hoe Waka. There were other Pākehā and people who were not originally from Whanganui. However, when the elders pointedly explained that this was intellectual property and not to be violated, they seemed to be speaking to me, the anthropologist. In respect for this wish for privacy, and since this book is not about Whanganui, I am not going to discuss any particulars of the history that could not be gleaned from newspaper accounts or popular books. The private aspects of the teachings that were so much a part of the Tira Hoe Waka will not be breached. However, the notebooks of Raana and Hoana were given to me by the women themselves for the purpose of my writing and accordingly I do make careful use of them.
2. With each museum opening, a formal Māori ceremony was observed at dawn, and the art itself was welcomed into its new headquarters, with local officialdom usually on the scene.
3. Wall complains about the transformation in Māori culture:

> It seems to me that in my lifetime Maori have gone from being totally uninterested in their own culture; then through a renaissance and out the other side emerging feisty and confident of their place in society, while I'm left wondering what people like me have done to earn their animosity.

4. Another clear example was the "Māori Loans Affair," which surfaced late in 1986 and dominated news coverage for four months. It involved exploration of overseas finance for Māori development, but the details need not concern us here. The press relentlessly kept the issue before the New Zealand public, in the process conjuring up images of Māori inefficiency and immorality. Kernot (1991: 7) demonstrates that the media not only put a bad face on Māori officialdom, but managed, as the scandal continued to dominate the headlines, to identify Māori with "massive benefit abuse and criminal violence . . . The Maori community found itself brought to account before the wider community through an ethnocentric Pakeha media."
5. This section is based on secondary historical accounts, contemporary newspaper reports, letters to the editor, official correspondence among the hapū, the New Zealand and Australian governments, and Hoana's diary of the mission. I was able to question both Hoana and Matiu and was fortunate enough to be present as they each related the story of Te Umuroa's retrieval. I also heard about the mission from members who were not able to go, namely Raana and Rihari. I am especially grateful to Moriana Hancock, who collected much of this material and then photocopied it for me. She also typed Hoana's diary. She hopes to put together a detailed narrative of this journey. This will be a great service to the people of New Zealand, to the Whanganui iwi, and to residents of Maungārongo and their families.
6. Ruth Wilkie (1991: 286–88) in *The Dictionary of New Zealand Biography*, Vol. I; Young (1998: 32) writes that he came from Jerusalem.
7. Wilkie, ibid.
8. Angela Ballara (1991: 245) in *The Dictionary of New Zealand Biography*, Vol. I.
9. There is some discrepancy in the secondary historical sources about many aspects of this story, but none critical for our purposes. Wilkie (1991) lists six others from Whanganui captured with Te Umuroa, while Belich (1986: 73–74) claims Te Umuroa fought not under Te Rangihaeata but under the Wanganui leader Tōpine Te Mamaku.

10. Wards (1968). In some renderings, the Whanganui people clearly were part of a taua, a war party, while in others, they were innocent victims wandering about a strange landscape. Tattersall seems to come down in the middle. Wilkie gives Te Āti Awa as the tribal affiliation of the captors.
11. Wilkie (1991:286–88) writes that the captors shook hands with the men before taking them prisoner. They joined in captivity the renowned Ngāti Raukawa and Ngāti Toa warrior Te Rauparaha.
12. Wards (1968); Tattersall (1973); Wilkie (1991); Young (1998).
13. Wilkie (1991); Tattersall (1973: 9); Young (1998: 32).
14. Grey (quoted in Tattersall [1973: 12]) wrote:

> [A] great advantage would result to this country if these men were from time to time really kept to hard labour, and if they could be allowed to correspond with their friends, their letters passing through the Government of New Zealand. In this manner many of the turbulent chiefs would ascertain that the Government really intended to punish severely all those who connected themselves with murderers and robbers, and would find from the letters of their friends in Van Diemen's Land what the nature of the punishment of transportation really is.

15. For example, a letter in the Wellington *Independent* of October 7, signed "an Englishman," expressed dismay and outrage as events turned against Māori (Tattersall 1973: 9).
16. Grey kept two of them in Auckland. Tattersall (1973: 11) reports that these men were probably released, as no charges were ever lodged against them.
17. According to Tattersall, the New Zealand press was silent on the topic.
18. Wilkie reports that "another portrait of Te Umuroa, thought to be by William Duke, also survives." (Wilkie 1991: 287.)
19. Quoted in Wilkie (1991: 287).
20. Notice that this is a week earlier than Imrie's date, July 19.
21. *New Zealand Sunday Times*, December 28, 1986. Letter from Robin Gray to Koro Wetere, January 21, 1987. Copies of all relevant documents (such as this letter and the memos in notes 22–24) are held by the movement.
22. Māori Affairs Minute Sheet, July 5, 1985.
23. Heald memo, May 27, 1987.
24. August is not a propitious time for sea journeys across choppy waters in the southern-hemisphere winter. The elders had been advised against travelling then (see Department of Māori Affairs memo of June 10, 1987), but they were determined to embark as soon as funds were released.
25. Hoana explained to me that when they heard that there was a crowd in the arrival lounge her heart sank. She was exhausted and wanted only a hot bath and a bed. Instead, she squared her shoulders, told herself she was a Māori, and faced the people. Her assurance as to who she was and what she must do encapsulates the way she conducted herself on this mission and, indeed, in all aspects of her life.
26. Significantly, in Parliament later that week Batt addressed his fellow legislators in the following words:

> Since the arrival of the group on Saturday, I have come to realise how important and how significant it is for the members of Te Atihaunui-a-Paparangi tribe to make this trip to Maria Island. This event will probably be one of the most significant events of

their lives, and I have been moved by their emotion and the importance that this event has to these visitors to our State . . . I would like to conclude however by saying that a representative from the Government was conspicuously absent from the welcome provided to our New Zealand visitors last Saturday. It would be an appropriate gesture if a member of this Government were to welcome these people to our shores. It would be a matter of shame if these important visitors were to leave Tasmania without an official gesture of welcome and goodwill by the Government . . .

27. In her diary, she writes the pōwhiri, which explains to Te Umuroa that his descendants have come to bring him home; the other men in the party also greeted Te Umuroa and they sang an appropriate waiata.

28. These songs were "Aue Te Aroha," which is very upbeat and had been used in early Hui Aranga; "Kote Rite I Ahau" (1943), which is written from the vantage point of a star, who explains to the people the work of the movement; and "Takirikiri" (1944), which discusses the sacredness of the Pacific Ocean and the movement's reliance on circulating messages and ensuring that all are informed. As in so many other songs, the calls of birds signify the ways messages between the sky and the earth are conveyed.

29. Hoana, who travelled frequently both within New Zealand and occasionally internationally, always drew strength from her people and from their ways of doing things. Reading this, I can see her delight as she is recharged when greeted by her relations. It is this that gives meaning to activities such as the returning home of Te Umuroa.

30. The entire story of the tokotoko is extraordinary. According to the members with whom she spoke, Delphina always felt that the stick was both special and the embodiment of an especially kind spirit. She reports bathing and dressing in private, away from the eyes of the stick. After several unsuccessful attempts to mail the tokotoko back to New Zealand, she carried it there herself, something she realized the failures had forced her to do. When she landed in Wanganui, the stick jumped up and almost out of its packaging. She was emphatic that the movement of the tokotoko bore no relationship to the motion of the aircraft. She was met at the airport and escorted up the river. There the stick was given back to Te Umuroa's descendants. But the mysterious events did not stop there. On a perfectly calm day, according to Moriana Hancock, a Pākehā with no especial investment in the beliefs of the Māramatanga or in the putative power of the past, the flax mat, laid out on the marae to receive the stick, folded up. This happened repeatedly, so that the stick had to be brought into the meeting-house. It was then that the mat was quiet.

Are these stories apocryphal? Whatever the case, these incidents have become part of the stories that accompany the repatriation of Te Umuroa.

31. There were certainly Pākehā on the 1995 trip that I was on. However, it was clear that what we were being told was not to be generally distributed. In the context of the Tira Hoe, Pākehā in general were excluded from certain teachings.

32. Jenny McLeod, who had actually told me this story earlier, writes about it from the vantage-point of an accomplished and knowledgeable musician. Writing of the musical sophistication she finds, she discusses her talks with the people about it (1996: 7):

> At Kaiwhaiki (on the lower reaches of the River) I hear something unexpected: strong and sure voices of solo quality singing in extremely sophisticated percussive and refined chromatic harmonies. I'm much surprised, for truly I know of nobody who

could write anything quite like this. When I ask them later who does their arrangements, they don't know what I'm talking about.

The people maintain it all comes naturally, that they have not had special training. They point out that Kaiwhaiki is known for its singing and show the gold record (awarded for selling over 500,000 copies in a population of three million). She is astounded, not at their accomplishment but that she had somehow missed this.

33. Shortly after this Tira Hoe, there was a three-month protest occupation of Pākaitore (Moutoa Gardens) in Wanganui.

Narrative: Matiu

1. However, she died as she entered adolescence, from kidney failure—apparently not uncommon for those with spina bifida. That she survived so long, and was so well most of her life, was miraculous.

2. This shows how people are remembered and how legends grow surrounding specific individuals. Anaera is marked as having special abilities, but with Matiu, the youngest son of the descending generation after the prophet, these abilities could no longer be specified.

3. Spiritual ability therefore exacts a cost: childlessness, a short life, and difficulties in marital relations, although the last seems not to apply to Anaera. Interestingly, these terrible liabilities seem to be markers for women, suggesting that the price of transcending a traditionally assigned role is onerous. Other prophets had children, lived long lives, and enjoyed numerous liaisons with women. It is Mere Rikiriki and other women who suffer in these other domains.

4. Barring the possibility that he was saying this to placate me and to hide any dissension.

5. The reckoning that favours the Rukas relies heavily on blood ties, while the reckoning that suggests equality depends on affinal relationships. Blood is given priority over marriage.

6. While he saw this as a means of trapping him, his friends envied him the taxi ride.

7. This was an indication of the cruelty inflicted on the young boy, for nothing could have been further from the truth. He was and always has been well behaved and exceedingly handsome.

8. Matiu said that although the mountain was wāhi tapu (a sacred place), it was still permissible to use it for recreation. However, there were special places at the top of the mountain and elsewhere where nobody should go; for him the great need was for boundaries with notice to all.

9. This was not the Te Maori exhibition mentioned earlier. Neither this nor the Te Maori exhibition contained works from Whanganui; the people feel their traditional works are too sacred to be removed. Recall the tokotoko of Te Umuroa that demanded return to New Zealand following its original owner; this suggests the reason for this attitude. Similar considerations apply to all Māori art, although not always with the same intensity.

10. Matiu's wish was for Whetu, whom he believed to be gifted, to follow in his footsteps, so he took him along wherever possible as training.

11. My daughter Emily and I were able to meet him there and spend some wonderful time with him, his wife Lei, his brother Dean, and several cast members who had journeyed to North America.

Conclusion

1. They are now documented for us all in the excellent work of Binney (1995); Elsmore (1989, 1998); Gadd (1966); Henderson (1963); Sissons (1991); and Young (1998).
2. Such feeling runs not exclusively against Māori; there is considerable antipathy to New Zealanders of Asian origin, especially recent immigrants.
3. Taussig (1980: 231) has written: "The religion of the oppressed can assuage that oppression and adapt people to it, but it can also provide resistance to that oppression." It is clear that the missionaries had hoped for the former and had found themselves and Māori with the latter.

Appendix 4: Interviews, Research, and Notebooks

1. It is difficult to compose this list, for my time with the people of the Māramatanga was not devoted solely to eliciting specific information at specific times. Instead, important narratives would be recounted as we were having a meal, driving, or playing cards. My tape recorder was often not available. There were, to be sure, some timed, planned interviews, but these, compared with the conveyance of all the informal, yet critical, information were most certainly in the minority. I lived with the people and so heard important information every day.
2. All taped interviews and tapes of rā have been returned to the interviewee or to Maungārongo.

Bibliography

Andersen, Johannes (1941) "Maori Religion." Polynesian Anthropological Studies (Memoir of the Polynesian Society No. 17): 219–61.

Arbuckle, Gerald A. (n.d.) "The Church in a Multi-Cultural Society: Sociological Survey: Pastoral Needs of Maoris and Polynesian Immigrants in New Zealand." Unpublished report. Wellington: Catholic Archdiocesan Archives.

Alexander, R. R. (1951) *The Story of Te Aute College*. Wellington: Reed.

Behar, Ruth (1996) *The Vulnerable Observer: Anthropology That Breaks Your Heart*. Boston: Beacon Press.

Behar, Ruth, and Deborah Gordon (eds) (1995) *Women Writing Culture*. Berkeley: University of California Press.

Ballara, Angela (1986) *Proud To Be White*. Auckland: Heinemann.

Ballara, Angela (1991) "Te Rangihaeata" in *The People of Many Peaks: The Maori Biographies from the Dictionary of New Zealand Biography, Volume 1, 1769–1869*. Wellington: Bridget William Books/Department of Internal Affairs.

Ballara, Angela (1998) *Iwi: The Dynamics of Maori Tribal Organisation from c.1769 to c.1945*. Wellington: Victoria University Press.

Belich, James (1986) *The New Zealand Wars and the Victorian Interpretation of Racial Conflict*. Auckland: Auckland University Press.

Belich, James (1989) *I Shall Not Die: Titokowaru's War, New Zealand, 1868–9*. Wellington: Allen and Unwin.

Belich, James (1996) *Making Peoples: A History of the New Zealanders from Polynesian Settlement to the End of the Nineteenth Century*. Auckland: Penguin.

Belich, James (2001) *Paradise Reforged: A History of the New Zealanders from the 1880s to the Year 2000*. Auckland: Penguin.

Bell, Leonard (1992) *Colonial Constructs: European Images of Maori 1840–1914*. Auckland: Auckland University Press.

Benjamin, Walter (1978) "The Story Teller" in *Illuminations*. New York: Shocken Books.

Bergin, Paul (1986) "Hoani Papita to Paora: The Marist Missions of Hiruharama and Otaki, 1883–1914." MA thesis, University of Auckland.

Binney, Judith (1966) "Papahurihia: Some Thoughts on Interpretation." *Journal of the Polynesian Society* 75: 321–31.

Binney, Judith (1969) "Christianity and the Maoris to 1840: A Comment." *New Zealand Journal of History* 3.2: 143–65.

Binney, Judith (1987) "Maori Oral Narratives, Pakeha Written Texts: Two Forms of Telling History." *New Zealand Journal of History* 21.1: 16–28.

Binney, Judith (1988) "The Ringatu Traditions of Predictive History." *Journal of Pacific History* 23: 167–74.

Binney, Judith (1989) "Some Observations on the Status of Women." *New Zealand Journal of History* 23.1: 22–31.

Binney, Judith (1990) "Ancestral Voices: Maori Prophet Leaders" in Keith Sinclair (ed.), *The Oxford Illustrated History of New Zealand*. Auckland: Oxford University Press.

Binney, Judith (1995) *Redemption Songs: The Biography of Te Kooti Arikirangi Te Turuki*. Auckland: Auckland University Press/Bridget Williams Books.

Binney, Judith, and Gillian Chaplin (1986) *Nga Morehu: The Survivors*. Auckland: Oxford University Press.

Binney, Judith, Gillian Chaplin, and Craig Wallace (1979) *Mihaia: The Prophet Rua Kenana and His Community at Maungapohatu*. Auckland: Oxford University Press.

Brown, Amy, and Jocelyn Carlin (1994) *Mana Wahine: Women Who Show the Way*. Auckland: Reed.

Butterworth, Graham V. (1972) "A Rural Maori Renaissance? Maori Society and Politics 1920 to 1951." *Journal of the Polynesian Society* 81: 160–95.

Butterworth, Graham V. (1974) *The Maori People in the New Zealand Economy*. Palmerston North: Massey University, Department of Social Anthropology and Maori Studies.

Butterworth, Graham V., and H. R. Young (1990) *Maori Affairs: A Department and the People Who Made It*. Wellington: Iwi Transition Agency.

Caselberg, John (ed.) (1975) *Maori Is My Name*. Dunedin: Otago University Press.

Clark, Paul (1975) *Hauhau: The Pai Marire Search for Maori Identity*. Auckland: Auckland University Press.

Clifford, James (1988) *The Predicament of Culture: Twentieth Century Ethnography, Literature, and Art*. Cambridge, Massachusetts: Harvard University Press.

Comaroff, Jean, and John Comaroff (1991) *Of Revelation and Revolution: Christianity, Colonialism, and Consciousness in South Africa*. Chicago: University of Chicago Press.

Comaroff, John, and Jean Comaroff (1992) *Ethnography and the Historical Imagination*. Boulder, Colorado: Westview Press.

Cognet, Father Claude (1893) *Ko Te Katikihama o Te Hahi Katorika*. Lyon.

Connell, Rev. Francis J., CSSR (1940) *Our Lady of Perpetual Help*. n.p.: Catholic Book Publishing.

Dening, Greg (1988) *History's Anthropology: The Death of William Gooch*. Lanham, Maryland: University Press of America.

Downes, T. W. (1915) *Old Whanganui*. Hawera: W. A. Parkinson.

Dreaver, A. J. (1984) *Horowhenua County and its People: A Centennial History*. Dunmore: Palmerston North.

Dreaver, A. J. (1991) "Te Rangihiwinui" in *The People of Many Peaks: The Maori Biographies from the Dictionary of New Zealand Biography, Volume 1, 1769–1869*. Wellington: Bridget William Books/Department of Internal Affairs.

Elsmore, Bronwyn (1985) *Like Them That Dream—The Maori and the Old Testament*. Tauranga: Moana Press.

Elsmore, Bronwyn (1989) *Mana from Heaven*. Tauranga: Moana Press.

Elsmore, Bronwyn (1998) *Te Kotahitangi Marama: New Moon, New World*. Auckland: Reed.

Gadd, Bernard (1966) "The Teachings of Te Whiti O Rongo Mai. 1831–1907." *Journal of the Polynesian Society* 75: 445–47.

George, Merrilyn (1990) *Ohakune: Opening to a New World, A District History*. Ohakune: Kapai Enterprises.

Gilligan, Carol (1982) *In a Different Voice*. Cambridge, Massachusetts: Harvard University Press.

Greenwood, William (1942) "The Upraised Hand." *Journal of the Polynesian Society* 51: 1–80.

Hanson, Allan (1982) "Female Pollution in Polynesia?" *Journal of the Polynesian Society* 91: 335–81.

Hanson, Allan (1989) "The Making of the Maori: Culture Invention and its Logic." *American Anthropologist* 91: 890–902.

Harper, Barbara (1962) *The Story of Mother Aubert and Her Great Work*. Wellington: Home of Compassion.

Heald, Chris (1988) "The Lost Son of Wanganui." *New Zealand Listener*, 10 September 1988: 33–34.

Henderson, J. (1963) *Ratana*. Wellington: The Polynesian Society.

Howe, K. R. (1984) *Where the Waves Fall: A New South Sea Islands History from First Settlement to Colonial Rule*. Sydney: Allen and Unwin.

Ihimaera, Witi (1986) *The Matriarch*. Auckland: Heinemann.

Ihimaera, Witi (1997) *The Dream Swimmer*. Auckland: Penguin.

Kaplan, Martha (1995) *Neither Cargo Nor Cult: Politics and the Colonial Imagination in Fiji*. Durham: Duke University Press.

Keesing, Roger (1982) *Kwaio Religion: The Living and the Dead in a Solomon Island Society*. New York: Columbia University Press.

Kernot, Bernard (1991) "The Press and Ethnic Conflict in New Zealand." Paper presented at the American Ethnological Society Meetings, South Carolina.

King, Michael (1977) *Te Puea: A Biography*. Auckland: Hodder and Stoughton.

King, Michael (1981) "Between Two Worlds" in W. H. Oliver and B. R. Williams (eds), *The Oxford History of New Zealand*. Wellington: Oxford University Press.

King, Michael (1983) *Maori: A Photographic and Social History*. Auckland: Heinemann.

Lindstrom, Lamont (1990) *Knowledge and Power in a South Pacific Society*. Washington, D.C.: Smithsonian Institute Press.

Linnekin, Jocelyn (1992) "On the Theory and Politics of Cultural Construction in the Pacific." *Oceania* 62: 249–63.

McLeod, Jenny (1996) "People, Pathways and Power: Reflections on a Bi-cultural Journey." *Music in the Air* Winter 1996: 2–9.

Metge, Joan (1964) *A New Maori Migration: Rural and Urban Relations in Northern New Zealand*. London: Athlone Press.

Metge, Joan (1995) *New Growth from Old: The Whanau in the Modern World*. Wellington: Victoria University Press.

Moon, Paul (1996) "The History of Moutoa Gardens and Claims of Ownership." *Journal of the Polynesian Society* 105: 347–65.

Munro, Jessie (1996) *The Story of Suzanne Aubert*. Auckland: Auckland University Press/ Bridget Williams Books.

Murray, Janet (1969) "A Missionary in Action" in Peter Munz, (ed.), *The Feel of Truth*. Wellington: Reed.

Orbell, Margaret (1991) *Waiata: Maori Songs in History*. Auckland: Reed.

Owens, J. M. R. (1981) "New Zealand before Annexation" in W. H. Oliver with B. R. Williams (eds), *The Oxford History of New Zealand*. Wellington: Oxford University Press.

Ozick, Cynthia (1994) "Ruth" in Judith A. Kates and Gail Twersky Reimer (eds), *Reading Ruth*. New York: Ballantine Books.

Parsonson, Ann (1981) "In Pursuit of Mana" in W. H. Oliver with B. R. Williams (eds), *The Oxford History of New Zealand*. Wellington: Oxford University Press.

Pomare, E., and G. M. de Boer (1988) *Hauora Maori Standards of Health: A Study of the Years 1970–84*. Special Report Series 78. Wellington: Medical Research Council and Department of Health.

Pool, Ian (1991) *Te Iwi Maori: A New Zealand Population Past Present and Projected*. Auckland: Auckland University Press.

Porter, Thomas William Rose (1914) "Te Kooti Rikirangi: The Real Story of the Rebel Leader with an Account of the Maori Fanatic Religions Pai Marire, Ringatu, and Wairua Tapu" *Auckland Star* Supplement. 28 February to 27 June.

"Rongo Pai" [pseud. of Hector Bolitho] (1921) *Ratana, The Maori Miracle Man: The Story of His Life! The Record of His Miracles!* Auckland: Geddis and Blomfield Printers.

Ross, Hugh W. (1966) *Te Kooti Rikirangi*. Auckland: Collins.

Sahlins, Marshall (1985) *Islands of History*. Chicago: University of Chicago Press.

Salmond, Anne (1975) *Hui: A Study of Maori Ceremonial Gatherings*. Wellington and Auckland: Reed.

Salmond, Anne (1976) *Amira: The Life Story of a Maori Woman*. Wellington: Reed.

Salmond, Anne (1980) *Eruera: The Teachings of a Maori Elder*. Wellington: Oxford University Press.

Salmond, Anne (1991) *Two Worlds: First Meetings Between Maori and Europeans, 1642–1772*. Auckland: Viking.

Salmond, Anne (1997) *Between Worlds: Early Exchanges Between Māori and Europeans, 1773–1815*. Auckland: Viking.

Scott, Dick (1975) *Ask That Mountain: The Story of Parihaka*. Auckland: Heinemann.

Silverblatt, Irene (1987) *Moon, Sun, and Witches*. Princeton: Princeton University Press.

Simmons, David (1976) *The Great New Zealand Myth: A Study of the Discovery and Origin Traditions of the Maori*. Wellington: Reed.

Simon, Judith, (ed.); Linda Tuhiwai Smith et al. (1998) *Nga Kura Maori: The Native Schools System 1867–1969*. Auckland: Auckland University Press.

Simon, Morvin T. (1984) *Taku Whare E: My Home My Heart*. Wanganui: Hanton and Anderson.

Sinclair, Karen (1990) "Tangi: Funeral Rituals and the Construction of Maori Identity" in Jocelyn Linnekin and Lin Poyer (eds), *Cultural Identity and Ethnicity in the Pacific*. Honolulu: University of Hawaii Press.

Sinclair, Karen (1992) "Maori Women at Midlife" in Judith Brown and Virginia Kerns (eds), *In Her Prime: New Views of Middle Aged Women*. Urbana: University of Illinois Press.

Sinclair, Karen (1993) "The Price of Innovation" in Patricia Lyons Johnson (ed.), *Balancing Acts: Women and the Process of Social Change*. Boulder, Colorado: Westview.

Sinclair, Karen (2000) "Knowledge Makes the Man: Matiu Mareikura, a Contemporary Maori Ritual Specialist" in Pamela Stewart and Andrew Strathern (eds.) *Identity Work: Constructing Pacific Lives*. Pittsburgh: University of Pittsburgh Press.

Sinclair, Karen (2000) "Mischief on the Margins: Gender, Primogeniture, and Cognatic Descent among the Maori" in Linda Stone (ed.), *New Directions in Anthropological Kinship*. Boulder, Colorado: Rowman and Littlefield.

Sissons, Jeffrey (1991) *Te Waimana (The Spring of Man): Tuhoe History and the Colonial Encounter*. Dunedin: University of Otago Press.

Smith, Bernard (1960) *European Vision and the South Pacific, 1769–1850: A Study in the History of Art and Ideas.* Oxford: Clarendon Press.

Sorrenson, M. P. K. (1975) "How to 'Civilize' Savages: Some 'Answers' from Nineteenth Century New Zealand," *New Zealand Journal of History* 9.2: 97–110.

Sorrenson, M. P. K. (1981) "Maori and Pakeha" in W. H. Oliver with B. R. Williams (eds), *The Oxford History of New Zealand.* Wellington: Oxford University Press.

Sorrenson, M. P. K. (1990), "Modern Maori: The Young Maori Party to Mana Motuhake" in Keith Sinclair, (ed.), *The Oxford Illustrated History of New Zealand.* Auckland: Oxford University Press.

Stocking, George W. (1987) *Victorian Anthropology.* New York: Free Press.

Tattersall, John (1973) *Maoris on Maria Island.* Napier: Hawke's Bay Gallery and Museum.

Taussig, Michael (1980) *The Devil and Commodity Fetishism in South America.* Chapel Hill: University of North Carolina Press.

Taylor, Richard (1855) *Te Ika a Maui; or, New Zealand and its Inhabitants.* London: William Macintosh; Wanganui: Henry Ireson Jones.

Taylor, Richard (1868) *The Past and Present of New Zealand: with its Prospects for the Future.* London: William Macintosh; Wanganui: Henry Ireson Jones.

Taylor, Richard. (n.d.) "Sermons and Responses." Taylor Papers, Grey Collection: Auckland Public Library.

Te Rangi Hiroa [Sir Peter Buck] (1924) "The Passing of the Maori." *Transactions and Proceedings of the New Zealand Institute* 5: 362–75.

Thomas, Nicholas (1994) *Colonialism's Culture.* Princeton: Princeton University Press.

Thomas, Nicholas (1997) *In Oceania.* Durham: Duke University Press.

Thomson, Jane (1969) "Some Reasons for the Failure of the Roman Catholic Mission to the Maoris, 1838–1860." *New Zealand Journal of History* 3.2: 166–74.

Waitangi Tribunal (1996) *Taranaki Report Kaupapa Tuatahi.* Wellington: GP Publications.

Wakefield, Edward Gibbon (1889) *New Zealand after Fifty Years.* New York, London: Cassell.

Walker, Ranginui (1975) "Marae: A Place to Stand" in Michael King (ed.), *Te Ao Hurihuri: The World Moves On: Aspects of Maoritanga.* Wellington: Hicks Smith.

Walker, Ranginui (1984) *Nga Tumanako: Maori Educational Development Conference.* Auckland: New Zealand Maori Council and CCE, University of Auckland.

Walker, Ranginui (1987) *Nga Tau Tohetohe: Years of Anger.* Auckland: Penguin.

Walker, Ranginui (1990) *Ka Whawhai Tonu Matou: Struggle Without End.* Auckland: Penguin.

Ward, Alan (1973) *A Show of Justice: Racial 'Amalgamation' in Nineteenth Century New Zealand.* Auckland: Auckland University Press.

Wards, Ian (1968) *The Shadow of the Land.* Wellington: Department of Internal Affairs, 1968.

Weiner, Annette (1992) *Inalienable Possessions: The Paradox of Keeping-While-Giving.* Berkeley: University of California Press.

White, Geoffrey (1992) *Identity through History.* Cambridge: Cambridge University Press.

Williams, Herbert W. (1971) *A Dictionary of the Maori Language.* 7th edn. Wellington: Government Printer.

Williams, John A. (1969) *Politics of the New Zealand Maori: Protest and Cooperation, 1891–1909.* Auckland: Auckland University Press.

Wilkie, Ruth (1991) "Te Umuroa" in *The People of Many Peaks: The Maori Biographies from the Dictionary of New Zealand Biography, Volume 1, 1769–1869.* Wellington: Bridget William Books/Department of Internal Affairs.

Wright, Harrison (1959) *New Zealand 1769–1840*. Cambridge, Massachusetts: Harvard University Press.

Young, David (1991) "Mere Rikiriki" in Charlotte Macdonald, Merimeri Penfold and Bridget Williams (eds), *The Book of New Zealand Women*. Wellington: Bridget Williams Books.

Young, David (1998) *Woven By Water: Histories from the Whanganui River*. Wellington: Huia.

Index

Featherston, Isaac, 2
Fuouy, Father Dan, 205
Fuouy, Father Tom, 205–7

Gabrielle, 79
Gray, Robin, 184
Grey, Governor George, 19–20, 183

Hancock, Moriana, 176
Harimate, 50, 95, 97, 98, 100, 104, 139, 157, 159
Hawke, Prime Minister Bob, 184
Hawke's Bay culture club, 83, 86
Heald, Christopher, 185, 188–90, 192
Heke, Hone, 155, 165
Hemi (Hoana's son), 143
Hemi (Mareikura's whāngai), 68–9, 82
Hemi (Matiu's son), 203
Hemi (Roimata's husband), 124
Hine Ataarangi
    ability as singer, 129
    as elder, 117, 123
    friendship with Anaera, 52–3
    friendship with Aurora, 52–3
    in Hastings, 86
    at Levin, 8, 55, 121
    life story, **74–85**
    at Maungārongo, 139, 141
    name changed, 55–6, 65
    notebooks, 104
    one of KS's teachers, 9, 12, 39
    on pilgrimages to Waitangi, 146, 162
    trained for responsibility, 67
Hinewaipare (Matiu's granddaughter), 210
Hinewaipare Te Huinga Mākere Pauro Marino. See Te Huinga
Hinga, 95, 97, 98, 100, 155
Hiria, 95, 158, 160
Hiruhārama, 28, 31–2, 34
Hoana (Rihari's wife)
    afraid of the dark, 216
    on Anaera, 58, 70
    close to Raana, 170, 171–2, 175, 177
    community service, 181
    death, 12, 168, 178, 195–6

on journey to Maria Island, 185–91, 193
as kaimahi, 48, 68, 72, 87–8, 115, 216, 217, 218
life story, **135–52**
on Māramatanga teachings, 68
marriage, 170–1
Matiu defers to, 159, 200
member of Maungārongo culture club, 83, 88, 106, 170
on Mere Rikiriki, 40, 42, 43, 45, 47
on mission to Ruapehu, 97, 98, 100, 102
native speaker of Māori, 88, 201, 207
never misses a rā, 119
not a genealogical senior, 131
in Ohakune, 89
one of KS's teachers, 8–9, 10, 39
at Patiarero whare wānanga, 130, 164
on pilgrimages to Waitangi, 155, 159, 162, 163–4
on Riripeti's tangi, 70
starts kohanga reo, 167, 175
on threat of utu in Whanganui, 87
on Tira Hoe Waka, 195, 196
at Waiuru, 119
Hoana (Te Huinga's mother), 50
Hoani Te Oriki, 50
Hoani Wiremu Hīpango, 30
Hōhepa (of Kawiu marae), 8, 119–21, 122
Hōhepa (of Kuratahi), 168
Hohourongo, 51
Hori Enoka. See Mareikura, Hori Enoka
Hui Aranga, 71, 83, 86, 87, **92–3**, 102, 107, 115, 119, 123, 127–8, 132, 133, 146, 147, 149, 170, 217
Huia Raukura, 91, 120
Huinga, 95, 97, 99, 114, 170
Hurinui, Emily Frances Broughton. See Weuweu

"I Te Rangi Tuatahi," 60–4
Imrie, J. J., 184
Iwa, 58, 83, 87, 104, 117, 123, 159
Iwi Transition Agency, 181

Joe, 185, 189